European Integration After Amsterdam

Institutional Dynamics and Prospects for Democracy

Edited by

KARLHEINZ NEUNREITHER

and

ANTJE WIENER

UNIVERSITY PRESS

OXFORD
UNIVERSITY PRESS

Great Clarendon Street, Oxford OX2 6DP

Oxford University Press is a department of the University of Oxford.
It furthers the University's objective of excellence in research, scholarship,
and education by publishing worldwide in

Oxford New York

Athens Auckland Bangkok Bogotá Buenos Aires Calcutta
Cape Town Chennai Dar es Salaam Delhi Florence Hong Kong Istanbul
Karachi Kuala Lumpur Madrid Melbourne Mexico City Mumbai
Nairobi Paris São Paulo Shanghai Singapore Taipei Tokyo Toronto Warsaw
with associated companies in Berlin Ibadan

Oxford is a registered trade mark of Oxford University Press
in the UK and in certain other countries

Published in the United States
by Oxford University Press Inc., New York

British Library Cataloguing in Publication Data

Data available

Library of Congress Cataloging in Publication Data

European integration : institutional dynamics and prospects for democracy after
Amsterdam / edited by Karlheinz Neunreither and Antje Wiener.
Includes bibliographical references and index.
1. European Union. 2. Democracy. I. Neunreither, Karlheinz. II. Wiener, Antje.
JN30. E85 1999 341.242'2—dc21 99-051896
ISBN 0-19-829641-X (hbk.) ISBN 0-19-829640-1 (pbk.)

10 9 8 7 6 5 4 3 2

Typeset by Best-set Typesetter Ltd., Hong Kong
Printed in Great Britain
on acid-free paper by
Biddles Ltd
Guildford and King's Lynn

Preface

This book is the product of a number of meetings held in Brussels, where most of the participants had the opportunity to discuss their work not only with academic colleagues but also with practitioners from the institutions of the European Union. These meetings were organized by the Research Committee on European Unification of the International Political Science Association (IPSA). The editors gratefully acknowledge the financial and logistical support provided by the European Parliament and the European Commission.

Antje Wiener worked on the book while on a European Commission Human Capital and Mobility Fellowship at the Sussex European Institute, University of Sussex, and then on a Jean Monnet Fellowship at the Robert Schuman Centre of the European University Institute in Florence. She would like to thank both institutions for generously funding work in beautiful surroundings, and for colleagues and staff who provided stimulating discussions and wonderful support.

Karlheinz Neunreither, as Chair of the aforementioned Committee, is happy that, with the present volume, it has resumed its tradition of academic publication. While working on this project he, too, has benefited particularly from exchanges of views with colleagues and practitioners, but also with his students at the University of Heidelberg, where such subjects as the Amsterdam revision of the Treaties, institutional dynamics, and democratic theory and the European Union were discussed extensively in graduate seminars.

Last, but by no means least, we would like to express deep respect and many thanks to Fiona Hayes-Renshaw for providing outstandingly precise, professional and efficient advice while editing this volume. Further thanks are due to Dominic Byatt of Oxford University Press for ongoing encouragement throughout the production process.

K.N.
A.W.

Contents

List of Figures

List of Tables

List of Abbreviations

ACP	African, Caribbean and Pacific
ARNE	Antiracist Network for Equality in Europe
BSE	bovine spongiform encephalopathy
BvG	*Bundesverfassungsgericht*
CAP	Common Agricultural Policy
CDU	German Christian Democratic Union
CEECs	Central and Eastern European countries
CEN	European Committee for Standardization
CENELEC	European Committee for Electrotechnical Standardization
CFSP	common foreign and security policy
COM	Commission document
CONF	IGC document
Coreper	Committee of Permanent Representatives
COSAC	conference of european affairs committees of the national parliaments
DGs	directorates general
EA	Europe Agreement
EC	European Community
ECB	European Central Bank
Echo	European Community's Humanitarian Office
ECJ	European Court of Justice
ECR	European Commission Report
EMU	Economic and Monetary Union
EP	European Parliament
EPP	European People's Party
FEPU	foreign economic policy union
IGC	Intergovernmental Conference
JHA	justice and home affairs
LI	liberal intergovernmentalism
LMU	labour market union
MEP	Member of the European Parliament
MFU	monetary and fiscal union
NAFTA	North American Free Trade Agreement
NATO	North Atlantic Treaty Organization
NGOs	non-governmental organizations
NTB	non-tariff barrier (to trade)
OJ	Official Journal of the European Communities
PES	Party of European Socialists

PPA	public policy analysis
PSOE	Spanish Socialist Party
qmv	qualified majority voting
SEA	Single European Act
SDU	structural/developmental union
SOU	Statens Offentlige Utredningar (Official Investigations by the Swedish State)
TEC	Treaty establishing the European Community
TENs	trans-European networks
TEU	Treaty on European Union
TIU	trade and investment union
UNICE	European Union of Employers' Confederations
VRA	voluntary restraint agreement
WEU	Western European Union
WP	White Paper
WTO	World Trade Organization

List of Contributors

Giuseppe Ciavarini Azzi	Secretariat General, European Commission
Gerda Falkner	Max Planck Institute for the Study of Societies, Cologne
Simon Hix	London School of Economics and Political Science
Beate Kohler-Koch	University of Mannheim
Christian Lequesne	Centre d'Etudes et de Recherches Internationales (CERI), Paris
Peter Leslie	Queen's University, Kingston, Ontario
Michael Nentwich	Austrian Academy of Sciences, Vienna
Karlheinz Neunreither	University of Heidelberg
Jürgen Neyer	University of Bremen
Mark A. Pollack	University of Wisconsin-Madison
Ulrich Sedelmeier	Central European University, Budapest
Jo Shaw	University of Leeds
Alexander C.-G. Stubb	Permanent Representation of Finland to the European Union
Ulf Sverdrup	ARENA The Research Council of Norway at the University of Oslo
Helen Wallace	Sussex European Institute
Antje Wiener	Queen's University, Belfast

1

Introduction: Amsterdam and Beyond

ANTJE WIENER and KARLHEINZ NEUNREITHER

As we enter the third millennium, European integration is at a turning point, a fact that affects the research agenda on the subject. Whereas in the past, students of European integration focused on the development and institutional accommodation of major projects, the new challenge lies in grappling with the implications of an ongoing step-by-step process of constitution-making. The major (economic) projects, such as the common market and Economic and Monetary Union (EMU), having been launched in previous decades and now under way, other often less spectacular, albeit far-reaching (political) promises, such as the constitutionally entrenched offer of membership to other democratic European states, or the creation of closer links with the citizens, remain to be fully addressed.

This book demonstrates that although the 1996–7 intergovernmental conference (IGC), which culminated in the signing of the Treaty of Amsterdam on 2 October 1997, was clearly not an example of radical institutional change akin to previous IGCs, it nonetheless sustained the notion of a turning point. The change we see in the research agenda evolving from Amsterdam stems from the paradox of a high degree of continuity of step-by-step constitutional politics, despite a new pluralism, and a return of intergovernmental politics. Our observation is grounded in the context in which the IGC was convened, and in the issues negotiated there. In so doing, we stress that the importance of major economic projects for the process of European integration cannot be overestimated. Yet, rather than launching a new project, Amsterdam raises questions about the problems posed by the continuity brought to the fore by the transferral of these economic projects into day-to-day politics and policy-making in a non-state.[1]

First, the Amsterdam IGC was not convened with the intention of launching a major economic project, but was planned as a follow-up conference, with

We are particularly grateful to Ulf Sverdrup, Andrew Moravcsik, Helen Wallace, and an anonymous reviewer for comments on earlier versions of this chapter. The final responsibility for this version lies with the authors.

[1] It is therefore correct to observe that: 'Amsterdam represents the beginning of a new phase of flexible, pragmatic constitution-building in order to accommodate the diversity of a continent-wide polity' (Moravcsik and Nicolaidis 1998: 36).

a mandate to amend provisions in the Maastricht Treaty. As such, it was the first IGC to be routinely included in the European Union's often unpredictable and invisible process of institutional change. In contrast to the previous five conferences,[2] Amsterdam was the first IGC not to be convened on an *ad hoc* basis, but was planned in advance as part of the Maastricht Treaty. According to Article N(2) TEU, it was to

> examine those provisions of this Treaty for which revision is provided . . . considering to what extent the policies and forms of co-operation intro-duced by this Treaty may need to be revised with the aim of ensuring the effectiveness of the mechanisms and the institutions of the Community.

Whereas the previous three IGCs had the common purpose of preparing for enlargement, in contrast to the Amsterdam mandate, these conferences had been convened to sustain major economic projects. In particular, the Single European Act (SEA) was adopted in 1985 and the 1990–1 Maastricht IGC was convened with the purpose of establishing the Single Market and EMU respec-tively. They had been carefully and extensively prepared by special working groups. The Dooge Report, the Commission's White Paper on the Single Market, and the Delors Report were key documents in this process. The working groups were set up specifically to discuss institutional adaptation in order to accommodate the requirements of the new projects.

Despite the pre-planned date, and the cautious mandate for Amsterdam, a number of quite outspoken reactions by officials, participants, and Euro-enthusiastic academics suggest that the outcome of the negotiations was rather modest. Nonetheless, changes have been initiated, albeit entailing no bold pro-jects, but rather many less spectacular, yet more complex negotiations over pro-cedures, principles, and institutions. The Solomon-like judgement offered by Falkner and Nentwich in Chapter 2 is that, according to the expectations of the Euro-enthusiasts, the IGC was 'both a success and a failure'. Among the suc-cessful outcomes were the extended co-decision procedure, which conferred new powers on the European Parliament (EP); the addition of a chapter on employment; the reinsertion of the Social Policy Agreement into the treaty; and last but by no means least, the communitarization of parts of the third pillar (internal and external frontiers, policies on visas, asylum and immigration, and judicial cooperation in civil matters) and, perhaps more importantly, the incorporation into the treaty of the Schengen *acquis*, with further implica-tions for immigration and asylum policies. The latter was actually deemed a 'massive transfer of powers to the Community' according to some observers

---

[2] The previous conferences were: the 1950–1 conference, which resulted in the establishment of the European Coal and Steel Community (ECSC); the 1955–7 conference, which led to the establishment of the European Economic Community (EEC) and the European Atomic Energy Community (Euratom); the 1985 IGC, which led to the Single European Act (SEA); and the two 1990–1 Maastricht IGCs on EMU and Political Union. (See: European Commission, Representa-tion of the United Kingdom, Background Report–BR/09/95: September 1995.)

(Petite 1998: 3/I; see also den Boer 1997a). As regards future institutional politics, it is important to note the lack of agreement about institutional changes to accommodate new member states (see Sedelmeier, Chapter 12), and the subsequent decision to convene yet another IGC before enlarging to more than twenty member states. With fifteen current member states and six candidates (Poland, the Czech Republic, Estonia, Hungary, Slovenia, and Cyprus) currently in accession negotiations, this IGC will be a condition for enlargement.

Some of the main areas to be tackled by the 1996–7 IGC were identified at the Corfu European Summit in June 1995. They included: the scope of the co-decision procedure; security and defence; a hierarchy of Community acts; and energy, tourism, and civil protection. The Council also established a 'Reflection Group' headed by the Spanish Secretary of State, Carlos Westendorp, in charge of an intergovernmental group of senior diplomats who were to prepare the IGC.[3] In addition to the treaty's mandate, the group was asked to address institutional questions linked to the prospect of future enlargement, including qualified majority voting in the Council and the number of Commissioners. Under the heading 'Adapting the European Union for the Benefit of its Peoples and Preparing it for the Future', the Conference of Representatives of the Governments of the Member States established five themes for the 1996 treaty revision process:

(1) an area of freedom, security and justice;
(2) the Union and the citizen;
(3) an effective and coherent foreign policy;
(4) the Union's institutions; and
(5) enhanced cooperation or 'flexibility'.[4]

At first sight, the emerging political style after Amsterdam appears to be a politics of 'muddling through' as an addition to the *ad hoc* politics of 'last-minute power-brokering' during the Maastricht negotiations (Curtin 1993: 19). Indeed, a path-dependent view suggests that the shift bears the imprint of past contextual changes. After all, German unification had led the then German Chancellor, Helmut Kohl, and the late French President, François Mitterrand, to call for a second IGC in 1990.[5] As a result, what is now commonly known as the Maastricht IGC was the outcome of two parallel IGCs, one on EMU, the other on Political Union. While the first was carefully prepared by a Commission report, the second conference could not draw on any 'specially prepared

---

[3] The group included representatives of the Ministers of Foreign Affairs of the 15 member states, as well as representatives of the EP and of the Commission.

[4] See: CONF 2500/96, Brussels, 5 December 1996.

[5] In 1990, a now famous letter, signed by Chancellor Kohl and President Mitterrand, and addressed to the Irish Presidency of the Council, suggested that an IGC on political union be convened. The goals it suggested for the IGC were: 'to strengthen the democratic legitimation of the union, to render its institutions more efficient, to ensure unity and coherence of the union's economic, monetary and political action, and to define and implement a common foreign and security policy'. See *Agence Europe*, No. 5238, 20 April 1990: 6.

blueprint for reform' (Curtin 1993: 17). The short notice at which the political conference at Maastricht was convened left almost no time for the drafting of special reports. As a result, a number of long-standing policy proposals, such as the 1986 Commission proposal for voting rights for 'foreigners' in local elections,[6] were dusted off and placed on the agenda without much bargaining over details at the time (Ross 1995a). The post-Cold War context thus contributed to establishing a new *ad hoc* approach to treaty reform. Consequently, the Amsterdam IGC was not convened to bring about dramatic changes, but to accommodate the loose ends left by the Maastricht Treaty, and to prepare the institutions for enlargement. Amsterdam, then, to no small degree, was a result of the last-minute power-brokering at Maastricht.

In sum, with no major new economic projects launched, with the single market and EMU well under way and, in contrast, with Political Union remaining a rather vague notion, Amsterdam casts light on day-to-day politics which, it can be argued, pose a new challenge for the project of governance in a non-state. This project often borders on the constitutional, and subsequently brings to the fore the question of what the principles which govern this polity are. This question has, so far, often remained hidden in the background. Meanwhile, the spotlight has been on market-making which, in the 1980s in particular, spurred a strong interest in institutional design, and kept such constitutional issues as questions of principled organization, membership, norms, and values in the background. This book demonstrates that Amsterdam has brought these questions back onto the agenda. While the general shift in the type of IGC has not gone unnoticed (see, for example, Moravscik and Nicolaidis 1998: 17), it remains to be explained and explored further. Does Amsterdam mark the shift towards a new style of constitution-making? And if so, why did it occur and, perhaps more importantly, how can this shift be explained?

The contributions to this volume do two things: they offer a view on the emergence of the Amsterdam agenda; and they elaborate on the implications of this agenda for the future of European integration. In so doing, they offer normative, conceptual, and comparative answers to these questions, with a view to developing a new research agenda on constitutional politics in a future non-state. We argue that the shift towards constitutional issues is rooted not only in the political agenda of the European Union (EU), but also in shifting models of political and economic organization in the member states (see Pollack's Chapter 14). For the first time, the political agenda entails accession negotiations with Central and Eastern European countries (CEECs). Furthermore, the abolition of internal border controls, one of the remaining unresolved tasks of the common market project, is to be completed through the communitarization of the Schengen Convention and parts of the third

---

[6] See: *Bulletin of the EC*, Suppl. 7, 1986, 'Voting rights in local elections for Community nationals'. The term 'foreigners' refers to nationals of a Community member state who live in a member state other than their home country.

pillar.[7] Both developments contribute to the process of polity formation, both deepening and widening the Euro-polity. Paradoxically, however, this push towards integration is accompanied by a number of institutional changes and political decisions which challenge the picture of ongoing integration, and indicate a shift towards a new pluralism in the Euro-polity. This critical stance towards supranationalism is expressed most clearly on the one hand, by the institutionalization of the Luxembourg Compromise as regards the application of flexibility and, on the other, by the allowance in the enhanced cooperation procedure of greater opting-out regarding the communitarization of Schengen. Both add to the 'damage' done to the *acquis communautaire* at the Maastricht IGC (Curtin 1993: 18). The Amsterdam negotiations and outcome hence suggest that European integration has not remained untouched by debates and changes of government in the member states.

At the heart of the book lies the challenge of coming to terms with an ongoing story of institution-building and constitution-making in a polity which is still what Jacques Delors once called an 'unidentified political object' (a UPO). The questions discussed by the contributors are:

- What exactly has Amsterdam changed in comparison with Maastricht?
- How do these changes affect the institutional balance within the Euro-polity?
- What are the implications for the lingering quest for more democracy?
- Are the institutions, once designed for a much smaller and more homogeneous group of member states, equipped to deal with these projects and promises?
- How did the Amsterdam IGC contribute to tackling these challenges?

The contributors to this volume approach these questions from different perspectives. Part I addresses the issue of changing institutions (see the chapters by Falkner and Nentwich, Lequesne, Ciavarini Azzi, and Kohler-Koch); Part II elaborates on prospects for democracy (see the chapters by Hix, Neyer, and Neunreither); Part III discusses the constitutional entrenchment of the concept of flexibility, and the challenge of enlargement (see the chapters by Stubb, Wallace, Leslie, and Sedelmeier); and Part IV (the chapters by Sverdrup, Pollack, Shaw, and Wiener) offers theoretical perspectives on constitutional change.

This design was chosen to offer not only a timely treatment of the Amsterdam IGC and its implications for the future, but also to provide a framework for elaborating on theoretical perspectives on European integration. The perspectives presented in this book include policy studies, interdisciplinary approaches which see the EU as a *sui generis* but not incomparable case, as well

---

[7] The Amsterdam Treaty includes a new Protocol with a view to incorporating the Schengen Agreement on the Abolition of Border Controls into the EU's legal order. Once identified, the Schengen *acquis* will be transferred into the first (Community) and third (Justice and Home Affairs) pillars, with movement matters belonging to the first pillar and police matters to the third.

as comparative politics. By including different arguments, this volume seeks to encourage further discussions with a view to refining the research agenda in European integration studies. It also offers detailed descriptions of the processes of negotiation, bargaining, and communication which led to the final agreement at Amsterdam, that is, to the 'Consolidated Treaties'. All contributions share the assumption that the resulting institutional changes will determine the path beyond Amsterdam to a great extent.

In Part I, four chapters highlight the impact on institutional change from the narrow perspective of the detailed discussion of treaty changes throughout the IGC (Falkner and Nentwich), to the role of the Commission and the impact of interest groups (Lequesne and Ciavarini Azzi), and to addressing institutional change as embedded in the concept of regional integration (Kohler-Koch). In Chapter 2, Gerda Falkner and Michael Nentwich begin this assessment with the provocative question as to whether or not the Amsterdam Treaty offers a blueprint for institutional balance. They take on the Herculean task of trawling through the entire treaty in order to discuss changes with a view to the institutional balance established by the new treaty. Christian Lequesne and Guiseppe Ciavarini Azzi (Chapters 3 and 4, respectively) then proceed to discuss the role of the European Commission (Lequesne), and to assess critically the novel form of legislative procedure established by the process of the implementation of directives (Ciavarini Azzi). They highlight the complexity of the Commission as a governing institution and a major player in EU governance, and provide an insight into the often tedious and time-consuming procedure of legislating at the European level. This fresh view on the Commission's role is particularly important at this point, as governance beyond Amsterdam is likely, in Ciavarini Azzi's words, to be more concerned with 'implementing existing policies than creating new ones'. The discussion of possible access points for interest groups in this process is another factor of crucial importance for the period of constitutional politics and policy-making which lies ahead. In Chapter 5, Beate Kohler-Koch explores this perspective even further, arguing that regional integration is, indeed, 'a social process'. She subsequently endorses a bottom-up perspective, which allows the observer to focus on the impact of social forces on institutional change. This perspective is sustained by her elaboration of a new methodological approach for future research on regional integration, which is centred on the observation that institutional change is not an issue reducible to intergovernmental bargaining, noting that 'even the best institutional design can only offer opportunities to those actors who bring about regional integration'.

In line with the specific and complex procedural and institutional challenges which are part of an increasingly constitutional debate in European integration, Part II offers a detailed discussion of the prospects for democracy in the EU. The contributions focus on such central elements of liberal democratic theory as accountability, legitimacy, party politics, and institutional design. The chapters stress the importance of traditional forms of representation, including the elements of party politics and, subsequently, the impact of a left–right axis (Hix), normative concepts of legitimate governance (Neyer), and political representation (Neunreither), and proceed to explore their implications for post-Amsterdam democratic governance in the EU. Arguing that both the Maastricht and Amsterdam Treaties have increased democratic accountability, Simon Hix sets out in Chapter 6 to pursue the question of whether or not the 'quasi-parliamentary model of EU executive selection really allowed Europe's voters to chose the EU executive?'. To do so, he turns to party politics as a crucial element in the electoral process.

In contrast to Hix's suggestion that the Euro-polity is an entity best studied with the tools of traditional comparative politics, in Chapter 7 Jürgen Neyer, in discussing prospects of democracy, stresses the importance of the EU's *sui generis* character. He elaborates on the possibilities for democratic governance by focusing on novel forms of deliberation in the area of comitology as a new space for supranational deliberation. This research is based on the argument that 'convincing normative justifications (of supranational governance) must not be developed in the absence of general reflections about the procedural and substantive requirements of a democracy but need to take account of the very nature of the European polity'. This approach leads him to focus on processes of deliberation specific to the institutional framework provided by, and developed within, the Euro-polity. In Chapter 8, Karlheinz Neunreither sheds light on the European Parliament's representative options after Amsterdam, particularly given the integration of the new principle of flexibility into the treaty. Neunreither's three scenarios concern the options of representing either the whole or parts of the EU, or alternatively (and on a more sombre note), an increase in the democratic deficit which might be faced by both the EU and the now closely interlinked member states in the absence of an evolution of models of democratic representation.

Part III takes up the discussion of flexibility, future perspectives on integration, and the challenge of enlargement. In Chapter 9, Alexander C.-G. Stubb provides a fascinating insight into the three stages of integrating flexibility as a 'basic principle' into the treaty. This close-up study of the practitioners' day-to-day bargaining and negotiation, which follows the conceptual discussion of three basic forms of flexibility (enabling clauses, case-by-case flexibility, and pre-defined flexibility), allows for an understanding of how and why rather revolutionary treaty changes occur when they do. Building on flexibility as a concept which 'emerged as one of the keywords in the practitioners' discourse during the IGC', Helen Wallace in Chapter 10 elaborates on the implications of flexibility for European integration. Taking a historical perspective, she argues that, like the principle of subsidiarity, flexibility functions as 'both a rationale and an operating tool for rearranging the division of labour between the European and national policy arenas'. This perspective on flexibility highlights the important and timely question of asymmetry with a view towards further enlargement.

In Chapter 11, along with a thorough conceptual debate about the possible abuses of asymmetry, Peter Leslie takes up the normative questions of membership in a political community interrelated with the establishment of basic principles. Placing the discussion on flexibility within the larger context of political transformation with relevance beyond the EU, he argues that the EU is a form of asymmetrical political organization, that is, 'a political structure in which some of the member states participate more fully than others'. The dilemmas posed by this sort of political organization, Leslie argues, are here to stay and therefore need to be carefully explored. In Chapter 12 on Eastern enlargement after Amsterdam, Ulrich Sedelmeier demonstrates that, beyond normative questions of membership and the respective institutional arrangements at stake, the EU's collective identity towards the CEECs plays a decisive role in the process of enlargement. He argues that although the IGC failed to meet the high expectations of institutional change for 'fair' representation within an enlarged EU, this 'need not mean that enlargement will not happen'. The analysis offered by Sedelmeier is grounded, first, in the historical experience of the integration process in previous decades, and second, in the constructivist argument that a 'pure rationalist understanding of the EU as a club . . . fails to capture important factors which underlie EU policy towards the Central and Eastern European countries'.

In Part IV, the last four chapters seek to place European integration in general, and the Amsterdam IGC in particular, within the broader framework of a theoretical agenda on European constitution-making which remains to be developed. In Chapter 13, Ulf Sverdrup argues that, in contrast to a liberal intergovernmentalist perspective on European integration (Moravcsik 1993, 1995), a historical institutionalist account of the dynamics of institutional reform can 'reveal important aspects of political reform which have previously been neglected'. Shifting towards domestic changes in the EU member states, Mark Pollack in Chapter 14 sets out to develop an equally historical, yet quite different theoretical perspective on European treaty-making. Within the framework of new institutionalist analysis, Pollack stresses the impact of domestic politics on treaty-making. To that end, he discusses, on the one hand, models of organizing the European political space according to a left–right axis (see Hix, Chapter 6) and, on the other, domestic debates over economic models such as neo-liberalism versus regulated capitalism (Hooghe and Marks 1997). This approach leads Pollack to the provocative suggestion that Amsterdam can most appropriately be dubbed a 'Blairite Treaty', reflecting, in fact, the 'third way' model of politics, which has been promoted by New Labour as a model which is neither neo-liberal nor regulated capitalism, but firmly occupies the middle ground between the two.

In Chapter 15, Jo Shaw brings the question of constitutional settlement in the EU to the fore of the post-Amsterdam research agenda. She focuses on the 'construction of the citizen as a constitutional figure' in the EU, and addresses the challenge posed by the introduction of a factual 'post-national citizenship' for the normative concept of citizenship as 'full membership' in a community. Shaw notes that the actors participating in the practice of constructing this new citizenship are not only individual citizens, but also institutional actors such as the Commission and the European Court of Justice (ECJ). In her account of constitution-making, she emphasizes the ongoing tension between the 'hard legal core and its soft political contours' in the Euro-polity. To address this tension, she endorses a constructive interdisciplinary perspective, including the methodological tools of legal studies and political science. In Chapter 16, Antje Wiener builds on this perspective from a political scientist's position, acknowledging the crucial impact of legal changes on EU constitution-making. Her analysis is centred on the changing *acquis communautaire*, demonstrated by the case of citizenship policy. She argues that the *acquis communautaire* is, in fact, socially embedded in debates which are fed by ideas, shared values, and norms. As such, it reflects institutional change as policy outcome, and at the same time facilitates an institutional context for future policy-making. Understood as the 'embedded *acquis communautaire*', the concept offers an interdiscplinary access point for the study of the 'institutionalization of governance beyond the state and despite states'.

The challenge of methodological scrutiny is of particular importance, as the supranational model of governance is currently undergoing a process of deep-rooted transformation. Internally, the EU has launched two ambitious projects: the single market and monetary union. Externally, it is more and more challenged as an economic and political global player, and has embarked on the difficult task of integrating the candidate countries from Central and Eastern Europe. Will it be able to do so? Will its institutions, designed for a much smaller and more homogeneous number of members, be strong enough? And can the still rather weak democratic basis of the EU be strengthened? These are core questions of this book.

The Amsterdam IGC is the third major treaty revision to occur in about a decade, quite an acceleration compared to the fact that during the preceding thirty years (between 1957 and 1986), no comparable revision took place. Looking ahead, it seems safe to predict that this process will continue. Indeed, the next IGC is expected to be convened around the year 2000 or soon after, in any event before enlargement becomes effective. That IGC will have to address the questions left unresolved in Amsterdam, including the rebalancing of the votes in the Council and the composition of the Commission. Consequently, after many years of institutional (and constitutional) stability, the EU is now entering a phase of relatively dynamic successive constitutional adaptations. An analysis of this process should not be restricted to the limited view of major treaty revisions, but requires a closer look at the institutional dynamics of multi-level governance, which is embedded in the daily practices of the actors involved. The 1996–7 IGC demonstrated that the heads of the EU member states and governments were in no mood for radical changes, neither 'forward' towards a state-like European centre of decision-making, nor indeed in any other distinguishable direction. On the contrary, the overall approach was rather incremental; it resembled a repair shop more than a design centre. Accordingly, this book does not concentrate on the Amsterdam Treaty revisions alone, but takes the treaty as a point of departure in order to look ahead.

The theme of this volume originated in discussions and seminars held in Brussels during the Amsterdam IGC, where the majority of the contributors met with senior EU practitioners. The seminars were organized by the Research Committee on European Unification of the International Political Science Association (IPSA), and generously funded by the European Commission. To address this bold academic enterprise, the editors chose a methodologically cooperative approach in the preparatory period of the volume, which differs from the majority of edited volumes in the field. Two criteria were central to the choice of theme, and for the final selection of contributions. First, by creating the opportunity to discuss their papers with well-informed practitioners, the researchers' assumptions were submitted to a scrutiny not otherwise readily available to researchers. This conference format sustained the editors' interest in extending the research agenda from the necessary and invaluable analysis of the specific treaty changes, to focusing on the problems, mechanisms, and hidden interests which brought about these changes. Second, during the workshop which followed the conferences, the contributions were discussed by the group of contributors on the basis of a specific format which required the participants to be able to present and comment on at least four other chapters.[8] As a result, the hypotheses, methodological approaches, structure, style, and facts of each chapter were subjected to a special scrutiny, aiming to combine the richness of diversity with the necessary coherence.

As the reader will observe, this is not a book where each contributor was given a standard list of questions to answer, as is often the case. On the contrary, each one retains his or her own tools of analysis, some taking an overall, more distant view, while others zoom very closely onto specific questions.

In general, the volume expresses an interest in the role of institutional questions, arguing that one of the major lessons of the EU's history during the past forty years has been that these questions tend to evolve slowly and often without much noise, yet once put into practice, their constitutional implications can be enormous. However, extraordinary occurrences can also prove the opposite to be the case. The events that led to the collective resignation of the Commission in the Spring of 1999 add to the topicality of our approach: they

---

[8] We are grateful to Beate Kohler-Koch for suggesting this format.

demonstrate that institutional evolution is not linked to treaty reforms alone, but that important factors which are discussed in several of our chapters also play an important role. The contributions in this volume suggest that two aspects were crucial to the outcome of Amsterdam. First, despite the IGC's official agenda and mandate, it is important to realize that the IGC meetings overlapped with preparations for EMU on the one hand, and major elections in a number of member states on the other. Both contributed to an invisible agenda in the negotiators' minds, which had a considerable impact on the proceedings. Second, the broadly defined issues discussed at Amsterdam were not only a product of the interests involved at the time, but were also shaped by a degree of institutionalization unprecedented in the history of European integration. This book seeks to link questions of institutional dynamics and prospects for democracy within the context of the changing parameters of European integration, and changing paradigms in world politics.

PART I

Changing Institutions

2

The Amsterdam Treaty: The Blueprint for the Future Institutional Balance?

GERDA FALKNER and MICHAEL NENTWICH

The 1990–1 intergovernmental conference (IGC) was convened only twenty-nine months after the last treaty reform had come into force.[1] In the institutional field, which is our concern here, the 1991–2 IGC had by no means resolved all the pressing problems. In particular, some crucial questions relating to prospective further enlargements of the European Union (EU) had not been tackled.[2] That those items which were explicitly postponed by the pre-Maastricht IGC were but the 'tip of the iceberg' became obvious during the final phase of the negotiations leading to the 1995 enlargement, when the so-called 'Ioannina Compromise' showed that the institutional structure had been stretched to its limits. In particular, the perspective of a further enlargement of the Union to the East and South made it clear that the institutional mechanisms (designed for a Community of only six members) which had so far only been adapted mechanically without changing the original principles, would not match up to the needs of a Union of some twenty-eight member states. At various meetings held after the Maastricht Treaty was signed, in particular at its meetings in Cannes (June 1995), Madrid (December 1995), and Turin (March 1996), the European Council therefore put additional items on the agenda of the (then) forthcoming IGC.

In this chapter, we will first contrast the most important of those official tasks with the eventual Amsterdam Treaty. We will then outline in some detail the four most significant reforms in the institutional and procedural fields contained in the treaty:

---

[1] This could have come as a surprise only to the uninitiated, as Art. N para. 2 of the Treaty on European Union (TEU) called for a conference of representatives of the governments of the member states to be convened in 1996, with a view to examining those provisions of the Maastricht Treaty for which revision was envisaged from the outset. In addition to the effectiveness of the EC's mechanisms and institutions, the revision was thus planned to review notably the Common Foreign and Security Policy (the second pillar) and Justice and Home Affairs (the third pillar). See Arts. [B 5th indent; J.4 para. 6 and J.10 TEU and Art. 189b para. 8 EC] and Common Declarations No. 1 and 16 annexed to the Final Act of the Maastricht Treaty.

[2] For an overview of the reform debates see, for example, the contributions to Edwards and Pijpers (1997) and Falkner and Nentwich (1995).

(1) 'appropriate representation' in the European Parliament (EP);
(2) the appointment of the Commission President;
(3) the latter's powers concerning the internal organization of the Commission; and
(4) the new powers and competences of the EP.

In the conclusions, we will ask whether the Amsterdam Treaty outlines a new balance between the EU's institutions.

An Overall Assessment of the Amsterdam Treaty

Article 2, 5th indent of the Treaty on European Union (TEU)[3] concerns 'to what extent *the policies and forms of cooperation introduced by this Treaty may need to be revised* with the aim of ensuring the effectiveness of the mechanisms and the institutions of the Community' (emphasis added). In that respect, the IGC did precisely what it had been asked to do. With regard to some of the new policies dating from 1991, the Amsterdam Treaty brings about procedural innovation (public health, vocational training, environmental policy, and trans-European networks—TENs). No changes will take place concerning youth training, cultural, consumer, and cohesion policies. With regard to co-operation in the field of justice and home affairs (JHA), the IGC came to the conclusion that only a few issues were currently suitable for transfer to the first pillar (asylum, visas, and immigration). However, the new Title IV of the Treaty of the European Community (TEC) includes a series of deviations from the standard procedures of the first pillar; after five years, and particularly if a specific Council decision to this effect is taken, some of these peculiarities will disappear.

Another explicit task of the IGC, agreed in Maastricht, was to potentially widen the scope of the co-decision procedure 'on the basis of a report to be submitted to the Council by the Commission by 1996 at the latest' (Article [189b] EC). In fact, the scope of the co-decision procedure was significantly widened in Amsterdam, not least by the near abolition of the cooperation procedure. Furthermore, the procedure was simplified and improved, on the basis of experience gained since it had come into operation (see below). In this respect, too, the conference carried out its mandate.

The Brussels European Council (10–11 December 1993) had also asked the IGC to consider '. . . any measures deemed necessary to facilitate the work of the institutions and guarantee their effective operation'. Only partial progress was made in this area (see below): the upgrading of the

---

[3] In this text, we refer to the new numbers of all EU and EC Articles as agreed in Amsterdam. The numbers of Arts. in force before this reform which no longer exist are included in square brackets.

directly elected EP through the reform and extension of the co-decision procedure, the legal upgrading of the transparency rules in the treaty, and the new organizational structure for the common foreign and security policy (CFSP) may be seen as the main achievements of the 1996–7 IGC. On the other hand, the variety of available decision-making procedures is still confusing, and there has been only a limited move from unanimity to majority voting.

Some of the IGC's tasks were clearly not fulfilled. For instance, the budgetary procedure is not mentioned in a single line of the new treaty, despite the fact that the Inter-institutional Agreement of 29 October 1993 had requested the IGC to propose improvements to this procedure. When adopting the institutional provisions of the Accession Treaties admitting Austria, Finland, and Sweden, the member states and the applicant countries had furthermore agreed, in the *communiqué* of the December 1993 Brussels European Council that 'the IGC to be convened in 1996 will consider the questions relating to the number of members of the Commission'. Although relevant also in the wider context of efficiency, the issue of the size of the Commission was postponed at Amsterdam.[4] That the reweighting of the votes in the Council was also rescheduled must be seen in the context of the decreasing likelihood of the forthcoming enlargements happening as soon as initially envisaged by some. Given the clear differences between the smaller and larger states during the IGC, it was a pragmatic choice to postpone taking any decisions on those issues which will probably not prove to be of crucial importance before the next enlargement.

In general, such reforms as had been envisaged with a view to a further widening of the Union are still basically missing.[5] The conference did not succeed in putting in place the necessary institutional changes which would allow the enlargement negotiations to concentrate on policy issues. Neither the distribution of the seats in the EP, nor the future size of the Commission, nor the future weighting of votes in the Council were tackled in a precise manner. Although Protocol 11 on the institutions indicates possible solutions, these remain rather vague and open to further discussion. In other words, the preparation for enlargement was postponed.

In short, looking at the institutional and procedural results of Amsterdam, the conclusion must be drawn that the IGC was both a success and a failure: it

[4] Art. 1 of Protocol No. 11 'on the institutions with the prospect of enlargement of the European Union' annexed to the Treaty of Amsterdam envisages that, at the date of entry into force of the first enlargement of the Union, the Commission will comprise only one national per member state. This new distribution of seats in the Commission is, however, conditional: the five larger states will give up their second Commissioner only if the issue of the weighting of votes in the Council of Ministers has been settled by the same date.

[5] The European Council, meeting in Corfu on 24–25 June 1994, had asked the IGC to consider '. . . any other measure deemed necessary to facilitate the work of the institutions and guarantee their effective operation in the perspective of enlargement'.

successfully managed to agree on at least some important reforms, but it failed to prepare for the next enlargements.

The Most Significant Aspects of the Reforms

The 1997 treaty will not be remembered for particularly eye-catching or, in the short term, far-reaching institutional and procedural reforms. It does not represent a qualitative leap towards a more democratic system of EU governance. If the latter is understood as a regime in which the rulers are held accountable for their political actions by the citizens,[6] the 1997 treaty continues along the path of incremental reform which, for a long time, has been the trademark of European integration. Once again, the EP is strengthened to some extent, and the electorate is thus somewhat better able to sanction the exercise of Euro-politics in European elections (the frequently national character of EP elections remaining a crucial problem to be tackled). As regards transparency—another important aspect of democratic control—only marginal reforms were introduced. No improvements (or at least no direct ones) can be reported concerning further (possible) features of democratic governance, such as direct citizen participation[7] or a collective citizens' identity.[8]

Although much clearly remains to be done to 'democratize' the EU,[9] a number of remarkable innovations were agreed whose implications for the Union's institutional balance should not be underestimated. (Laffan 1997a: 302; Dinan 1997: 199)[10].

The European Parliament and 'Appropriate Representation'

As a former President of the EP has said, there is no other parliament like it (Dankert 1997: 212). One of its many special characteristics is that the citizens represented in it are not equal political subjects, in that the weight of a vote differs considerably between member states: whilst a German Member of the European Parliament (MEP) represents more than 800,000 citizens, a Belgian

[6] For similar recent definitions, see e.g. Schmitter 1997: 15; Jachtenfuchs 1997: 47; van Parijs 1997: 287. On the closely related topic of citizenship, see Ch. 15.

[7] For specific recent contributions on this topic, see notably Abromeit (1998) and Nentwich (1998). Grande (1997) and Zürn (1996) also discuss these aspects in addition to others related to democracy at European level.

[8] In the case of the EU, much writing has stressed the lack of a collective identity as a problem of Euro-level democratization; see e.g. Jachtenfuchs (1997:48) and Zürn (1996).

[9] On the multifaceted discussion of Euro-level democracy and constitutional choice, see notably the recent volumes edited by Føllesdal and Koslowski (1997) and Weale and Nentwich (1998).

[10] Due to limitations of space, we can only highlight a few aspects of the Amsterdam reforms. For a much more detailed account, including many tables and detailed references, see Griller et al. (1999).

MEP represents only about 400,000 people, and a Luxembourg MEP represents just 66,000 citizens.

From an institutional perspective, the EP's main goal has always been to become one of two 'legislative chambers' in the EU. Within this model, the EP would be the representative of the people of Europe, whereas the Council would represent the states. In its May 1995 report for the IGC, the EP made this perfectly clear when discussing the issue of reweighting votes in the Council: '. . . it is in the Parliament that population is represented. Council represents States' (EP Resolution 17 May 1995b, PE 190.441, pt. 22.iii).[11] In other words, proportionality should not be the goal of the Council, but it should be improved in the EP. The Amsterdam Treaty deals explicitly with the issue of proportionality: Article 189 [137] EC has been amended by a new second paragraph fixing the maximum number of MEPs at 700. Article 190 para. 2 [138a] EC, which now includes a table of the number of MEPs per member state, is complemented by a new subparagraph, as follows: 'In the event of amendments to this paragraph, the number of representatives elected in each Member State must ensure *appropriate representation* of the peoples of the States brought together in the Community' (emphasis added).

It should be noted that this rule was not intended to apply immediately, but only in the event of the amendment of Article 190 para. 2 EC (in other words, probably not before the next enlargement). The setting of a ceiling on the maximum number of MEPs, combined with the need to secure appropriate representation, ensured a tricky agenda for the IGC on enlargement: applying the current system, Poland's MEPs alone (representing some 38 million citizens) would occupy almost all of the remaining available seats. Since it is most likely that Poland will be among the next wave of EU members, and that it would not be the only new member, the enlargement negotiations, which began in March 1998 (Presidency conclusions of the Luxembourg Summit, 12–13 December 1997), will have to tackle the issue.[12]

While the stipulation on the maximum number of seats is clear and precise, the appropriate representation formula in Article 190 para. 2 EC is open to interpretation. Obviously, the negotiators of the founding Treaties thought that the terms agreed were appropriate, otherwise they would neither have signed the Treaties nor proposed that their respective parliaments should ratify them. The new provisions should not be regarded as simply superfluous, however. Rather, they may be interpreted as containing first, the acknowledgement of the basic idea that the representation of the population in the EP should also be appropriate in the future (i.e. when the rather rigid adaptation rule applied in all previous enlargement negotiations no longer applies, because

---

[11] On the EP's demands with a view to the 1996–7 IGC, see Dankert (1997).

[12] As regards the legal value of this clause, the new wording does not bind future negotiators when trying to find a compromise formula on which all will be able to agree.

the maximum size of the EP has been reached);[13] and second, it gives some sort of guidance for future negotiations on this issue, since the term may be analysed and interpreted. It is significant that Article 190 para. 2 EC does not read 'equal representation' or 'proportionate representation', but 'appropriate representation'.[14] This allows room for further (normative) considerations.

Two principles might be taken into account in order to achieve the goal of representativity. First, the vote of each EU citizen could be of approximately equal weight. However, this rule cannot be applied systematically if only 700 seats are available, because of the great differences in size between the member states: the ratio between the populations of Luxembourg and Germany is approximately 1 : 205. Given that there are other large member states in the Union, a total of 205 MEPs for Germany is out of the question, because the maximum of 700 MEPs would quickly be exceeded. Consequently, the number for Germany has to be lower than 205, which would mean that Luxembourg would not get a single MEP (and there are several other equally small states among the applicants, in particular Cyprus). Thus, the larger the Union gets, the more states would share the 'Luxembourg destiny' of not getting a single representative in the EP.

Second, since the building of new transnational electoral districts for the purpose of European elections is out of the question for the foreseeable future, the only alternative solution in order to attain at least 'conditional proportionality' is a minimum threshold rule: in order to ensure representation of all the (still separate[15] and some quite small) peoples of the Union, at least one MEP would have to be attributed to each state. This rule, however, does not seem to ensure *appropriate* representation, since a single MEP cannot represent the political spectrum of his or her country of origin in accordance with the outcome of the (European) elections.[16] At least three seats per country would

[13] The rule may be summarized as follows: A new member state should be given a number of MEPs which is smaller than or equal to the number of the next largest member state (in terms of size of population) and larger than or equal to the number of the next smallest member state; the details are open to negotiation. This rule obviously leads to a constant increase in the total number of MEPs.

[14] Bieber (1997: 239) argues in this respect that the term 'appropriate' is so vague as to be unhelpful in deciding the question of whether it means 'proportionate' or 'minimum' representation. He therefore concludes that the Amsterdam Treaty in fact adds nothing to the present situation. As we have argued, we look on the new wording as a point of departure for further consideration and negotiations.

[15] The term 'separate' refers to the widely shared perception that there is (as yet) no single 'people' of Europe, but rather a series of peoples of the different European states.

[16] As Duff (1997: 150) puts it: 'While a reduction for all is inevitable, the importance of the small states having enough MEPs to allow for a fair representation of the major strands of political opinion must not be overlooked'. For a different system to 'reconcile the principles of "one man one vote" with the need to proect small state representation' (Laffan 1997a: 303), see the EP's De Gucht Report, summarized in Laffan (1997a).

therefore be needed to ensure fair representation of a country's political forces.[17]

However, the application of these two principles (strict proportionality and a minimum of three MEPs per state) would mean that the five largest member states would gain from the changes, whereas all other countries would lose seats.[18] In short, the proposed reform might be interpreted as corresponding to the EP's preferred option. However, Protocol 11 'on the institutions with a view to further enlargement' annexed to the new treaty indicates that no corresponding reform (i.e. in the direction of 'one country, one vote') will be introduced in the Council in the foreseeable future; the system of weighted votes is still beyond question and will probably be further adapted towards greater proportionality. While improving proportionality in the EP in the manner foreseen by the Amsterdam Treaty will bring the EP closer to the principle of equal representation as outlined in democratic theory and as usually practised in national parliaments, it should be noted that only the largest countries (and Germany in particular) will be winners in practice. Reweighting the votes in the Council as indicated by the Treaty of Amsterdam would again be in the interests of the large countries only. Even when taking into account the 'special case theorem' (i.e. the EU as a *sui generis* system), it will be difficult to put the suggested reforms into practice, that is, to modify the traditional federal pattern of representing the population and the states in two separate chambers in a way which unilaterally strengthens the larger states. At least empirically, Joseph Weiler's (1988) assumption is still valid: so long as there is no redefined, integrated European polity, the social legitimacy of the European system remains precarious, and it is thus difficult to convince the members of the separate polities of Europe to give up power (in this case, seats in the EP) even for the sake of such widely acknowledged democratic principles as equal (or at least more 'appropriate') representation. Fundamental controversies over the institutional set-up of the EU may be expected to come to the fore once the governments begin to tackle the details of the tricky issues that were postponed in Amsterdam.

---

[17] The three MEPs would not necessarily come from the centre, the right, and the left political movements of a country; if one particular party were very strong, it might send all three MEPs to Strasbourg. In our view, this would still be an 'appropriate' representation of this country's political spectrum, even though a minority might not be represented. Given that three representatives for a state is clearly a lower limit, the rule proposed in our text is intended to avoid the extreme case where, if only one seat were available, three almost equally large parties in a country would be 'represented' by the party which is the largest of the three (if only by a few per cent of the vote).

[18] Most striking would be Germany's enormous gain in seats: an additional 32 or 38 (depending on the method of calculation, and taking account of a minimum number of seats for the smallest member states).

Choosing a Commission President

As far as the Commission is concerned, two institutional innovations should be noted: a change in the procedure to nominate its President, and changes to the internal balance of the Commission.

The Maastricht Treaty reforms gave the EP the dual right to be consulted when the Commission President is chosen by the member governments, and to give its assent to the investiture of the college as a whole. Under the Amsterdam Treaty, the assent of the EP is needed for the appointment of the Commission President,[19] and its approval is required for the new team of Commissioners. However, it is still the member governments who nominate the candidates. The nominee for President will be given a greater say in the choice of the members of the college. In the past, the nominee was only 'consulted' by the appointing member states, whereas the Amsterdam Treaty gives him or her a right of assent.[20] This acknowledges the enhanced status of the President-to-be, who, by that point, will already have been the subject of a vote of confidence in the directly elected EP.

Given this new investiture procedure on the one hand and, on the other, the enhanced role of the President *vis-à-vis* his or her colleagues in the college of Commissioners (see below), we conclude that the character of the 'appointing-the-Commission game' might change in the medium term (see Hix, Chapter 6). Most likely, the presidential candidate will be invited to a hearing at the EP before the formal appointment takes place, and his or her political programme will in future be subject to parliamentary scrutiny. Due to this partial[21] shift from secret diplomatic negotiations to a more open and public procedure, the terms of the debate on European policy-making could be reshaped along party political lines, even though Delors' suggestion[22] that each political party should nominate a candidate before the 1999 European elections was not followed in the short term. This might, in turn, prompt the development and public marketing of alternative ideological designs for the European agenda.

---

[19] Art. 214 para. 2 sub-para. 1 EC: 'The nomination shall be approved by the European Parliament.'

[20] Art. 214 para. 2 sub-para. 2 EC: 'The governments of the Member States shall, by common accord with the nominee for President, nominate ...'. In practice, one can imagine the nominee being present at the decisive negotiations in the Council (meeting as the representatives of the governments of the member states) and giving his or her final and formal approval to the decision.

[21] The shift is partial, in so far as it is still the member states which, by common accord, choose the nominee for Commission President; in the earlier phases of the investiture procedure, the EP is thus involved at best indirectly, as the member states will anticipate the EP's stance to some extent.

[22] See e.g. *Der Standard*, 26 June 1998.

Internal Organization of the Commission

As already mentioned, the decision on the future size of the Commission was postponed at Amsterdam. In the eyes of many, however, the key question has less to do with the actual number of Commissioners and much more to do with the internal organization of the Commission. In this respect, several changes were agreed upon.

First, the role of the Commission President was strengthened. The new first sub-paragraph of Article 219 [163] EC reads: 'The Commission shall work under the political guidance of its President'. It should be noted that 'political guidance' is less than a right to determine decisions or even to set compulsory (framework) guidelines (Bieber 1997: 240). Article 213 para. 2 [157] EC on the independence of the Commissioners and Article 219 para. 2 [163] EC on majority voting in the Commission remain unchanged. In the second sub-paragraph of Declaration No. 32 attached to the Final Act 'on the organization and functioning of the Commission', the President's leading role is further qualified: '. . . the President of the Commission must enjoy *broad discretion* in the allocation of tasks within the College, as well as in any reshuffling of those tasks *during* a Commission's term of office' (emphasis added). This enhanced competence with respect to the allocation of tasks during the Commission's term in office, and not merely when the candidates are appointed, may lead to 'a considerable power to discipline the otherwise undismissible members of the Commission' (Wessels 1997: 127; our translation).

Quite apart from its probably undisputed effects with respect to the institution's efficiency and the coherence of its policies, both strengthening the Commission President by giving him or her organizational prerogatives and reorganizing the Commission's structure with a view to possibly centralizing specific policy areas in the hands of a few higher-order Commissioners (see below) might lead to a more person-oriented public perception of the Commission. Just as the heads and senior ministers of national governments are paid more attention than other members of a government, this might, in the medium term, result in more public awareness for some Commissioners, and thus for the entire Commission as a central political actor in the Union. In this context, it is noteworthy that the Commission's right of initiative is now expanded to the areas in the third pillar[23] and the new Title IV on the free movement of persons—areas which are of particular interest to the EU's citizens as a whole.

In addition to dealing with the role of the Commission President, the IGC acknowledged and supported the Commission's intention to prepare a 'reorganization of tasks within the College . . . in order to ensure an optimum division between conventional portfolios and specific tasks' (Declaration No. 31 on

---

[23] It should be noted that, in contrast to the policy areas dealt with in the first pillar, the Commission shares the right of initiative with the member states in the third pillar.

the Commission, sub-para. 1). This reorganization was scheduled to be effective before the year 2000, that is, when the next Commission was due to come into office.

The reorganization will include a corresponding restructuring of the Commission's subdivisions (Declaration No. 31 on the Commission, sub-para. 3). The only explicit target set by the IGC in this respect was that there should be a vice-president responsible for all external affairs matters (in the 1995–9 Commission, responsibility for foreign policy and external commercial relations was divided between six Commissioners[24]). This must be seen in the context of the proposed new type of CFSP 'troika'[25] consisting of the Council Presidency, the new High Representative for the CFSP, and the external affairs Commissioner. According to Article 18 para. 4 [J.8] TEU and Article 27 [J.17] TEU, the Commission will be 'fully associated' with the work carried out in the CFSP field.[26]

The EP as Co-legislator

Reducing the EU's democratic deficit has often been equated with increasing the EP's legislative role, as is still the case even in recent writing, which also stresses other aspects of the EU's democratic deficit (see Grande 1997 for further references). In this respect, the Amsterdam Treaty introduces two changes: first, the reform of the co-decision procedure and second, the upgrading of the involvement of the EP in many cases.

The *reform of the co-decision procedure* (Article 251 [189b] EC) must be considered as one of the major achievements of the IGC. The following changes were agreed:

• If the Council accepts the EP's amendments at its first reading, it may adopt the act at this very early stage. Given the fact that carrying the procedure on to the (cumbersome and time-consuming) conciliation procedure stage is rather unpopular among MEPs as well as ministers, this can be considered a major change in so far as the MEPs will be inclined to draft their amendments carefully, trying to anticipate the Council's views on the issue in order to get the approval of the governments already at this early stage.[27]

[24] Responsibility for foreign policy and external commercial relations is divided up as follows between the Commissioners: Santer—CFSP; van den Broek—CFSP; Pinheiro—Lomé, ACP; Marin—Mediterranean states, Near and Middle East, Latin America, parts of Asia; Brittain—Commonwealth, foreign commercial relations; and Bonino—humanitarian aid.

[25] Note that the old *troika* between the former, the current, and the next presidency has been replaced by a new leading group which might be called a '*duika*' (a two-headed horse), consisting of the current and the next presidency only.

[26] This means that the Commission will be informed of, and consulted about, all activities in the CFSP field, but will have no right of initiative, as it does in the first pillar.

[27] We are grateful to Michael Shackleton of the EP for this argument. On the other hand, there are also good reasons for doubting that the EP will indeed react like a rational actor (we are grateful to Karlheinz Neunreither for this point).

• If, in turn, the EP approves the Council's common position during its second reading, the act is deemed to be adopted without being referred back to the Council.

• If, in its second reading, the EP fails to take a position within three months, the act is deemed to be adopted in the version of the Council's common position; this seems to be the last remaining imbalance between the two 'chambers', since the decision finally taken would not, in this case, necessarily reflect a jointly agreed text.

• The EP can reject the common position directly during its second reading; that is, it no longer has to notify the Council in advance of its intention to reject. Consequently, the Council's ability to convene the Conciliation Committee at this stage was dropped.

• If, in its second reading, the Council accepts the EP's amendments, the act is deemed to be adopted without any further formal decision.

• A third reading still exists, but it was changed in such a way that the Council may no longer resume its original common position after a failure of the Conciliation Committee; this had been one of the main criticisms of the original co-decision procedure.

• Various new time limits were introduced to ensure that the period between the EP's second reading and the outcome of the whole procedure does not take longer than nine and a half months; only the first reading will still be without time limits. In any case, experience shows that, due to the existing time limits, co-decision is already the fastest procedure available, despite the possibility of three readings in both chambers.[28]

These changes show that, on the issue of the reform of the co-decision procedure, the EP came very close to obtaining what it had asked for in the IGC. In fact, the changes to a very large extent eliminate the procedural imbalances between the two major players, the Council and Parliament. Any remaining differences can be perceived as a functionally useful distribution of roles between two legislative chambers, while the overall political weight of the two institutions within the co-decision procedure may now be considered equal. Moreover, it can be argued that the last significant formal inequality—the requirement for the EP to make a pronouncement on the Council's common position within a reasonable period—mainly represents a strong incentive for effective internal organization. Furthermore, it seems plausible that cases of parliamentary non-decision in the second reading will, in fact, indicate an overall positive rather than a hostile reaction by the EP to the common position: those MEPs who are definitely against the measure as shaped by the Council are more likely to ask for far-reaching amendments than to block EP decision-taking, since a blockade leads directly to the adoption of the unwanted

---

[28] Information given by Andrea Pierucci, European Commission.

act. The only realistic scenario in which no decision might be taken by the EP would seem to be when both immediate approval and also the making of amendments enjoy considerable support among MEPs. In such a case, it is possible that neither the absolute majority of votes cast (for approval) nor the absolute majority of MEPs (for the amendments) might be reached, because those who want to approve know that their preferred outcome is the default solution, and they may therefore not be ready to compromise. In addition, it is quite likely that there will be a majority for at least some (minor) amendments and thus a decision. The EP's performance in recent years shows that it has almost always been successful in producing opinions on time. The pressure on the EP is obviously great, since its very reputation is at stake; the MEPs can hardly press for greater participation in the legislative process if they fail to fulfil their allotted tasks.

It should be noted, however, that the new wording of Article 251 [189b] EC does not contain a parallel provision to cover the Council not acting within the time limit of three months in its second reading: if the Council fails to reach a decision on the EP's amendments in time, the procedure simply comes to a halt,[29] but the legislative act is not deemed to be adopted according to the EP's version as it is in the opposite case. At this stage of the legislative procedure, however, the Commission's opinion has an important role to play, and it would therefore not be clear which version of the text was the latest: the EP's or the version amended by the Commission. From this perspective, strict equality between the two legislative chambers would not offer an adequate solution to the peculiarity of the triangular institutional set-up.

Against this background, we conclude that the reform of the co-decision procedure finally puts the EP on an essentially equal footing with the Council (at least as far as this procedure is concerned; see also Wessels 1997: 128). Given that this procedure will be applied in many more cases than before (see below), the 1996–7 IGC is indeed a major step towards a bicameral legislative model (with two strong players) at the EC level. It is interesting to note that the wording of the treaty did not take this gradual shift from a strongly Council-centred to a more balanced bicameral system into account: while in the Single European Act (SEA) the formula 'the Council shall . . . in cooperation with the European Parliament adopt . . .' was used, the Maastricht Treaty does not mention the EP in most cases: 'The Council shall, acting in accordance with the procedure referred to in Article 189b . . . , adopt . . .'.[30] The Amsterdam Treaty will not change the remaining imbalance in the wording of the treaty,

[29] Such an outcome might eventually be challenged before the European Court of Justice (ECJ), either via the Art. 230 [173] EC procedure (by challenging the final result for procedural shortcomings), or via Art. 232 [175] EC (failure to act, in infringement of the treaty).

[30] There are a few exceptions to this rule (see Arts. 229, 230, 241, 251 para.1 and 253 EC). All of these cases, however, are general provisions, and contain no specific power to act.

although the titles of the legislative acts based on Article 251 EC already include the EP (e.g. 'Directive . . . of the European Parliament and the Council of Ministers on . . .').

Having started out as a purely consultative body composed of representatives delegated from each of the national parliaments, the past few decades have seen an extension of the EP's competences with each major treaty reform. In the aftermath of the first direct elections in 1979, the EP itself gave an important impetus to the 1986 SEA which introduced both the cooperation and the assent procedures, although its 'Draft Treaty on European Union'[31] was not accepted as such by the governments. Nevertheless, pure consultation was retained as an alternative mode of EP involvement for many areas of European policy-making. The Maastricht Treaty continued along these lines by adding yet another procedure; 'co-decision' under Article 251 [189b] EC gave more far-reaching (although not yet equal) powers to the EC's parliamentary chamber, but it was far from representing the one and only standard procedure. The result of this incremental reform process was a patchwork-style landscape of EC decision-making: in each case, one of approximately twenty variants[32] of the four main procedures applied. None of them, however, put the EP on an equal footing with the governments represented in the Council. Therefore, the EP's demands for the 1996–7 IGC focused not only on improving co-decision, but also on making it the only standard procedure in all EC law-making.

Yet again, no uniform decision-making procedure was established by the Amsterdam Treaty. However, many specific changes were introduced, among which we would like to highlight the following points.

In the TEU, Article 7 [F.1] gives the EP an additional right of assent when the Council determines a breach of the Union's principles by a member state. By contrast, there is still almost no involvement, or at least only consultation, in the second and third pillars of the Union: with regard to some areas of the third pillar (Article 39 para. 1 [K.11] in connection with Article 34 para. 2 [K.6] TEU), a special consultation procedure will apply, which already exists under one provision in the first pillar, namely in connection with the conclusion of international agreements (Article 300 para. 3 [228] EC). The Council may lay down a time limit (which shall be no less than three months) for the delivery of the EP's opinion; in contrast to the ordinary consultation procedure, the Council may act without this opinion if it is not delivered in time (see Article 39 para. 1 TEU). In those areas which will be

---

[31] This draft for a Treaty on European Union with innovative decision-making procedures and institutional provisions, adopted on 14 February 1984 (OJ 84/C 77/33), is also known as the Spinelli Draft Treaty, because it was initiated by the so-called Crocodile Group, led by the Italian MEP, Altiero Spinelli.

[32] The exact number depends on the way in which one counts; the subcategories mainly account for variations in the majority applicable in the Council and the various bodies consulted.

'communitarized', that is, transferred from the third to the first pillar,[33] the EP will not be involved at all, or will at most be involved on a consultative basis during the five years after the entry into force of the new treaty. After five years, the competence to harmonize the rules and procedures concerning visas will automatically be subject to the co-decision procedure, whereas for the rest of the decisions taken under the new Title on free movement of persons, this transfer has to be decided unanimously by the Council after consulting the EP (see Article 67 para. 2 EC).

In those areas already covered by the EC, the reform did not bring about a single legislative procedure. The state of affairs after Amsterdam can be summarized by the following five points. *First*, with regard to certain central issues where the Amsterdam Treaty introduces new provisions or amends existing ones, the EP is still only consulted (e.g. authorizing the establishment of closer cooperation among some member states) (Article 11 para. 2 EC), measures outlawing discrimination (Article 13 EC), most decisions on asylum and immigration (Articles 64 and 67 of the new Title on the free movement of persons), and parts of the social and research and development (R&D) policies.

As far as those articles which remained unchanged by the Amsterdam Treaty are concerned, three provisions should be pointed out:

1. The new main legal basis for action in the field of agricultural policy (Article 37 [43] EC), will also provide for consultation only in the future. However the provision on public health (Article 152 para. 4 [129] EC) was changed to include areas previously governed by Article [43] EC, that is, veterinary medicine and phytosanitary measures. Since decisions in the area of public health are already being taken under the co-decision procedure, we may conclude that the EP now has at least 'a foot in the door' on the way to becoming a decisive co-legislator in the agricultural field. However, in the important area of the common agricultural market organizations, the Council acts after having merely consulted the Parliament.[34] This is particularly deplorable since, in this area, neither the EP nor the national parliaments[35] have a say with regard to the content or the budget of the policy.

[33] See the new Title IV EC on visas, asylum, immigration and other policies related to free movement of persons, which includes the Community's competence, for example, to take limited emergency measures against immigration, or to decide on uniform visa rules; see Arts. 64 and 67 of the new Title.

[34] The EP's position during the IGC as formulated by its two representatives, Elisabeth Guigou and Elmar Brok, seems to have been that decisions of principle at least, but not necessarily decisions on the day-to-day business of agricultural legislation, should be taken according to the co-decision procedure.

[35] This is because the Community has an exclusive competence for the agricultural policy, which is financed entirely by the EC budget. Furthermore, Council decisions in this field are taken by qualified majority, which means that national parliaments wishing to influence the decisions taken at Community level by binding their Minister for Agriculture may be unsuccessful, because he or she can be outvoted in the Council.

2. Another important area in which the EP is still involved on a consultative basis only is the harmonization of legislation concerning indirect taxes, such as turnover taxes and excise duties (Article 93 [99] EC).

3. Finally, Article 308 [235] EC remains unchanged. It allows the Council to adopt legislation which cannot be based on more specific competences but which is nevertheless considered 'necessary to attain, in the course of the operation of the common market, [if] one of the objectives of the Community and this Treaty has not provided the necessary powers'. This is the so-called 'subsidiary competence' provision, which has provided the legal basis for many important legislative acts.[36]

Second, the cooperation procedure has been replaced by co-decision in most cases, but not in relation to Economic and Monetary Union (EMU) (Articles 99 para. 5; 102 para. 2; 103 para. 2; and 106 para. 2 EC). It should be remembered here that 'cooperation' gives the EP no power of veto.

Third, although co-decision applies to only eight of the 36 new competences attributed to the EC/EU by the Amsterdam Treaty, there are 14 (15)[37] issues where the procedure has been changed to co-decision. These are in addition to the 15 set out in the Maastricht Treaty (see the list in Annex V.b of the 1995 Council report, footnote 33). In future, the EP will thus be a co-legislator under 37 (38) provisions altogether; included among these are central legislative powers of the Union, such as most common market-related provisions, and at least some types of decision in most of the other policy areas (with some exceptions and qualifications however, as outlined in the two preceding and subsequent points).

Fourth, there are also some new cases of non-involvement of the EP, however: for example, when decisions are taken on further member states joining an existing form of 'closer cooperation' (Article 11 para. 3 EC), on emergency measures relating to immigration (Article 64 EC in the new Title IV on the free movement of persons), on recommendations on employment policy (Article 128 para. 4 EC in the new Title IV on the free movement of persons), on the implementation of social partner agreements in social affairs (Article 139 [118b] para. 2 EC), on adapting or supplementing R&D programmes (Article 166 para. 2 [130i] EC), and on the suspension of rights deriving from the EC Treaty for a member state which is in breach of fundamental principles of the Union (Article 309 EC). In the field of economic policy too, the EP is

---

[36] In Annex VIII to its Report on the Operation of the Treaty on European Union of 6 April 1995, the Council counted 86 cases in the period from 1992 to spring 1995 where Art. 308 EC had been invoked, in areas such as the establishment of a number of bodies, in financial issues and in other areas as varied as the consolidation of existing Community legislation, the Community trade mark, and budgetary discipline.

[37] If one includes Art. 67 para. 3 of the new Title IV EC on the free movement of persons, which will apply after five years, another case must be added; hence the numbers 15 and later 38 in brackets.

often only informed of decisions taken by the Council (e.g. Articles 99, 100, 104, and 114 EC).

Fifth, it is worth noting that no changes were agreed on the EP's participation in the budgetary procedure, although this issue had been put explicitly on the IGC agenda by the Interinstitutional Agreement of 1993 (OJ 93/C 331/1 of 7 December 1993; see also EP Resolution PE 190.441, pt. 34 of 17 May 1995b). Furthermore, the EP will still be involved in CAP reform and tax harmonization on a consultative basis only (see above). Even under the Amsterdam Treaty, therefore, the EP is still far from being a co-equal player in financial matters. On the other hand, the EP's involvement in budgetary matters has been extended to some degree. Third pillar operational expenditure will now fall under the EU budget, unless the Council decides otherwise (Article 41 paras. 2 and 3 [K.13] TEU); the same applies to second pillar operations except military actions (Article 28 paras. 2 and 3 [J.18] TEU); and finally, the EP will have more influence under co-decision with respect to the fight against fraud (Article 280 [209a] EC).

In attempting an overall assessment of the extension of EP competences under the Amsterdam Treaty, it should be remembered that few had expected the IGC to result in a 'landslide' regarding EP competences in EC/EU decision-making. Nevertheless, significant improvements from the EP's point of view were agreed. We consider it likely that co-decision will henceforth be perceived as the future standard procedure, with consultation or cooperation soon being considered as the exception to the rule. In future, this might not only change the public perception of the EP's powers *vis-à-vis* the Council, but might also make it easier to switch to co-decision as the single legislative procedure at a later IGC.

For the moment, however, under the Amsterdam Treaty, the list of areas where the Council is authorized to act without being dependent on the EP's approval is still considerably longer than the co-decision list (Duff 1997: 146ff.). Of course, a proper assessment should not only consider numbers, but must also take into account the importance of the respective competences. In this respect, it should be noted that a large proportion of the 'traditional' competences of the old European Economic Community, in particular those related to the establishment of the common market (the 'four freedoms'), have been shifted to co-decision, including the prominent Article 95 [100a] EC. Turning to the newer competences, the picture is quite different. Like many national parliaments, the EP is involved to a lesser extent in foreign policy (international agreements and the CFSP in general), monetary policy (e.g. defining the statute of the European Central Bank—ECB), classic governmental activities (such as emergency measures and amending programmes during their execution), and where corporatist patterns prevail (in social policy). However, it is easy to overlook the fact that there is also a long list of matters in which the Council acts as a genuine legislator without Parliament acting as a co-legislator: for example, the EP is merely consulted in the field of agricultural policy; in the area of the third pillar, whether 'communitarized' or not; with regard to some decisions in the field of social policy and also tax law; and even in the classic common market-related areas of competition law, state aids and transport policy. One of the major wishes of the EP, namely that the co-decision procedure (Article 251 [189b] EC) should apply when the Community institutions act as legislators (see EP Resolution PE 190.441, pt. 29 of 17 May 1995b), was thus only fulfilled to a quite limited extent.

In even sharper contrast to national parliaments, however, the MEPs have only a limited say in quasi-constitutional matters, such as decisions regarding flexible cooperation and the suspension of rights deriving from the treaties. Most strikingly, the EP is not involved at all in amendments to the EC/EU's 'constitution' (i.e. treaty reform conferences).[38] On the one hand, the two chamber set-up of the EC/EU (i.e. the collaboration of the Council and the EP in the legislative process—the Commission's role is a completely extraordinary one) resembles national systems in many instances, while on the other hand, some very specific features still prevail. Might there be a coherent hypothesis to explain this dichotomy? First, it seems plausible to argue that each IGC brings the EC/EU decision-making structure a little closer to a federal state model, with a parliamentary and a state chamber. However, this statement needs to be qualified by saying that the European case is a unique type of federal decision-making structure, at least so far. Furthermore, this step-by-step approach always lags behind the parallel increase of competences of the Union. In most cases where a new competence is introduced, the default solution is still that the EP is outside the decision-making core, and that the Council decides alone. With a few exceptions,[39] it seems to take at least one[40] if not more[41] IGCs in order to get the EP involved on an equal footing

[38] It should be mentioned, however, that the EP has to give its assent to the admission of a new member, and therefore indirectly to those treaty changes which are necessary in order to incorporate the new member into the treaty framework (see Art. 49 [O] TEU).

[39] For example, cultural, consumer protection and public health policies, as well as the Trans-European Networks (TENs) were introduced by the Maastricht Treaty, and immediately made subject to the co-decision procedure. It is, however, arguable that these cases are not important exceptions: the competences are rather limited, and were already partly covered by other provisions, as was the case with consumer protection.

[40] For example, development cooperation was introduced by the Maastricht Treaty subject to the cooperation procedure, and upgraded to the co-decision procedure by the Amsterdam Treaty. Furthermore, environmental policy was introduced by the Single European Act subject to the consultation procedure, and upgraded by the Maastricht Treaty to co-decision.

[41] For example, the provisions on the European Social Fund were inserted into the Single Act subject to the cooperation procedure, and only upgraded to co-decision by the Amsterdam

with the Council. Again, the Amsterdam Treaty followed this trend, for example with respect to the (partial) communitarization of the third pillar, most 'competences' in the new area of employment policy, and many other changes. This suggests that the EP might only be involved to a greater degree after the bulk of decisions in the area have already been taken. Most common market-related issues have already been decided; what remains is (to a certain extent) 'peanuts' in comparison to what was decided pre-1992. By contrast, current issues, such as those falling under the third pillar, will be settled over the next few years, and the EP might again only be involved once the new policy has by and large been implemented. The same might be true for EMU, employment policy and tax harmonization.

To sum up: in the political context of the IGC, most commentators agree that the EP's role was upgraded by the new treaty, and many see it as the winner in the Amsterdam process (Dehousse 1998; Brok 1997: 211; Nickel 1997: 220; Wessels 1997: 130; Schönfelder and Silberberg 1997: 209). Viewing the changes in the light of the many remaining imbalances which still favour the Council, however, it is impossible to come to an enthusiastic overall assessment of the Amsterdam changes, when these are compared to the EP's original demands: in most areas of its activities, the Union is still a long way from being a balanced bi-cameral legislature.

Another key issue in the pre-IGC discussions was the plea for a reduction in the number of different decision-making procedures. The most radical call came from the EP, which asked for an almost uniform decision-making procedure in legislative matters, reducing the number of procedures to three: co-decision as the norm, assent for constitutional matters and consultation for the CFSP (European Parliament, Resolution PE 190.441, no. 29, 17 May 1995b).

The Amsterdam Treaty did not meet these expectations. Whilst replacing the cooperation procedure (Article 252 [189c] EC) with co-decision (Article 251 [189b] EC) in most cases, it left the provisions on EMU untouched. Furthermore, the new Treaty added some new variants, such as the new procedure for adopting the statute of the MEPs,[42] or a (limited) right of initiative of the member states, which has now been introduced into the first pillar (Article 67 para. 1 EC). Moreover, the consultation and assent procedures, as well as many other variants, still persist.

Treaty. This might also be the case with monetary policy and industrial policy, both of which were introduced by the Maastricht Treaty, but left untouched by the Amsterdam Treaty.

[42]   This procedure entails an Opinion from the Commission, the approval of the Council acting unanimously, and decision by the EP.

Towards a New Institutional Balance?

It is easy to overlook the overall significance of the institutional arrangements decided at Amsterdam, because they appear rather unspectacular when viewed separately. Viewed from a distance, however, the Amsterdam Treaty constituted a major step forward in a process begun by the SEA and continued by the Maastricht Treaty: that of making the EP a co-legislator with powers equal to those of the Council. Until the Amsterdam Treaty, co-decision was biased in favour of the Council, and it was the exception rather than the rule in EC policy-making. Our analysis has shown that the new co-decision procedure puts both 'legislative chambers' on an equal footing. Due to the continued co-existence of other decision-making procedures (not only in the second and third pillars, but even in the first), in many areas of activity the Union is still far from being a two-chamber system, as demanded by the EP. But although there is still a long way to go quantitatively, it is plausible to argue that, in a qualitative sense, co-decision will in future be perceived as the paradigm of EC decision-making.

In that sense, the incremental changes to the EC's institutional balance from 1979 (the date of the first direct elections to the EP) to 1999 (the date of the entry into force of the Amsterdam Treaty) amounted as a whole to a fundamental reform whose basic principles are by now clearly outlined. This does not imply that incremental reform will no longer take place. On the contrary; further adaptations, such as the extension of co-decision to those legislative areas not yet covered, seem to be useful (with a view to improving democratic accountability, at least to some extent[43]) and likely further steps.

Starting from the neo-institutionalist assumption[44] that, once in place, institutions (in the wider sense) shape not only the strategies but even the preferences of political actors, and thus usually represent trajectories for further developments, the new pattern of institutional balance under co-decision as established by the Amsterdam Treaty may be expected to basically remain the same: first, a much more politicized Commission, drawing legitimacy from the way in which it came into office; second, an EP which basically plays an amending role, but nevertheless has a decisive say regarding the life and death of legislative acts; and third, a Council of Ministers which is no longer in a position to *de facto* impose its views on the other institutions in EC decision-making, most notably the EP.

---

[43] Without doubt, however, a democratic, political EU system in the wide sense of the recent debate on the 'democratic deficit' would demand many more changes. For a number of innovative proposals on how to democratize the Union, see e.g. Zürn (1996), Grande (1997), Føllesdal and Koslowski (1997), Weale and Nentwich (1998).

[44] On new institutionalism and path dependency with a view to the 1996–7 IGC, see Ch. 13.

There are as yet no signs that, even in the medium term, a new compromise formula between the EU governments might lead to a fundamentally different relationship between the main institutions. This statement may be substantiated by the following considerations. First, it seems unlikely that the EP will acquire predominance over the Council in the foreseeable future. No relevant political actor (not even the EP) actively promotes a model such as the Austrian system of a directly elected *Nationalrat* (Parliament) and a second chamber, the *Bundesrat* (representing the *Länder*) with a veto right restricted to only a few cases. Bearing in mind that all further treaty changes will have to be negotiated by the governments sitting in the EU Council, politically it is naïve to expect anything beyond an extension to further areas of EU policy-making of the current equal position of the EP and the Council under co-decision.

Second, the EP has dropped its demand to gain a genuine right of initiative, which would have ended the Commission's monopoly in this area.[45] Evidently, an EP right of initiative would alter the institutional balance considerably, since the Commission would be almost 'out of the game' whenever the EP took the initiative. However, in order to make it more than just a formal right, the EP would have to change its working structure fundamentally, with a view to creating detailed draft legislation. At the moment, no such political will exists, not even among the MEPs; nor is there sufficient working capacity. The present division of labour between an agenda-setting Commission and two decision-making bodies seems to be widely accepted, and thus unlikely to be changed in the near future.

Third, the problem of how to reweight the votes in the Council is still on the agenda. Whatever the outcome of future negotiations, it seems plausible to expect that it will not fundamentally change the Council's position within the institutional triangle, nor will it alter the character of that institution to such an extent that it affects the Union's decision-making system as a whole. The debate has two opposite poles, demanding that the Council be made either a fully representative body, or else a US Senate-like body with equal weight for all states. It is probable that neither of these extremes will be put in place, since the former is strictly opposed by the smaller member states, and the latter by the larger ones. Therefore, only minor changes in the middle ground are to be expected, without fundamental consequences for the status and functioning of the Council.

These arguments underpin our hypothesis that the new treaty (particularly its reform of the co-decision procedure) outlines an interinstitutional balance

---

[45] Compare the EP's report of 17 May 1995 on the functioning of the Union with a view to the 1996 IGC (PE 190.441, pt. 21.I) with the Herman Report of 9 February 1994 (PE 203.601/endg. 2, Art. 32 of proposed Constitution).

for the EU's legislative process which is likely to be refined rather than fundamentally challenged in the foreseeable future.

3

The European Commission: A Balancing Act between Autonomy and Dependence

CHRISTIAN LEQUESNE

Since the 1980s, the growing interest of political scientists in the transfer of policy-making from the national to the European Union (EU) level has been an occasion for revisiting research on the EU's institutions in general, and on the Commission in particular (Muller 1994; Mény, Muller, and Quermonne 1995; Wallace and Wallace 1996). This has taken place in Europe and to a lesser extent in the United States within a broader evolution of political science research on the EU from international relations theory to comparative politics (Sbragia 1991; Hix 1994; Lequesne and Smith 1997).

A rich set of case studies now exists on the formulation and implementation processes of Community policies. A wealth of material can be found on competition policy (Dumez and Jeunemêtre 1991; Cini 1994), social policy (Majone 1993a; Wendon 1998), energy policy (Haaland Matlary 1993; Schmidt 1998), telecommunications policy (Schneider, Dang-Nguyen, and Werle 1994; Schmidt 1998), economic and social cohesion (Smith 1996; Hooghe and Keating 1994) and the environment (Liefferink and Skou Andersen 1998). A journal was even established in Britain in 1994 (*The Journal of European Public Policy*) to publish articles on policy-oriented research on the EU. Most of these studies have two characteristics. First, they are monographic and empirical, and second, they go beyond a state-centric approach to European integration, taking into consideration multilevel and network forms of governance in which Community, national and subnational (public and private) actors interact to formulate and implement EU public policies (Peterson 1995). Among the new research tracks opened up by these studies, there has been a revisiting of the

This chapter is a revisited version of an article published in the *Revue Française de Science Politique* (*RFSP*), 46 (3), June 1996. I am grateful to Jean-Lue Parodi, editor-in-chief of the *RFSP*, for permitting the translation and reutilization of certain parts of the article, and Guiseppe Ciavarini Azzi, Karlheinz Neunreither, Paolo Ponzano, Ulf Sverdrup, and Antje Wiener for their comments on this new version.

European Commission, which is no longer viewed as an institutional monolith, but rather as a complex multi-organization (Cram 1994).

In more precise terms, public policy analysis (PPA) now has the following characteristics:

• It regards the Commission as a set of diverse agents (Commissioners, cabinet members, officials in the Directorates General (DGs), experts and consultants) with different ideas, interests, and social representations depending on the policy sector, and who are able to mobilize resources differently from one policy field to another in order to influence and control the EU's political agenda (Nugent 1995; Sedelmeier, Chapter 12).

• It shows that different organizational and administrative cultures exist among the Commission DGs, and that these cultures induce different styles of public action (Cini 1997).

• It offers an opportunity to revisit the assumptions put forward by the neo-functionalists in the 1960s about a European space of interest representation in which the Commission is supposed to play the pivotal role (Mazey and Richardson 1993).

• In looking at processes of implementation in detail, PPA allows a more careful study of the reception and translation by national and local actors of such norms and principles as partnership, additionality, and evaluation, which are promoted by the Commission DGs in their proposals (Smith 1996).

• Finally, the fact that many EU public policies are oriented towards market regulation rather than the distribution or redistribution of revenue has opened up a debate about the emergence of a European regulatory state, from which the Commission, as the regulatory agency, could draw bureaucratic influence (Cram 1993; Majone 1996).

Taking these different works into account, this chapter adopts an institutional approach, and looks at the Commission from the inside without developing any particular case study. I will first show how EU Commission agents can mobilize specific resources in order to behave as 'policy entrepreneurs' in the EU polity with a certain degree of autonomy from the national governments. I will then defend the autonomy argument, by arguing that this policy entrepeneurship is also constrained by endogeneous and exogeneous factors which make the Commission dependent on the national governments in the EU polity.

This balancing act between autonomy and dependence is considered to be the main characteristic of the European Commission. It is also an invitation to look at supranational institutions by linking two analytical perspectives. On the one hand, supranational institutions are the creation of national governments in order to facilitate their interests and bargaining. During the Amsterdam intergovernmental conference (IGC), each of the fifteen governments was (or was not, as the case may be) concerned with a constitutional reform of the Commission (as regards the number of Commissioners, or the procedure for the nomination of the Commission President and of the college) in order to keep their respective power in the EU polity. On the other hand, supranational institutions are also the products of their organizational dynamics.

I choose to concentrate more specifically on this second dimension, not because I find the first one irrelevant, but simply because I consider that opening up the Commission's 'black box' through PPA provides a good opportunity for demonstrating that supranational institutions assume different roles in the EU depending on the policy sector in question. This element of differentiation is, of course, important for an understanding of the Commission *per se*. More importantly, it is also an invitation to think about the EU as a polity mix between a co-ordination of social subsystems (governance), and a political order run by a single authority and general rules (government).

How does the Policy Entrepreneurship Emerge?

The Commission is a multi-organization rather than a monolith (Cram 1994). It is composed of a variety of agents (Commissioners, cabinet members, officials in the DGs, consultants, and so on), who have a range of organizational resources at their disposal with which to influence the formulation of EU policies with a certain degree of autonomy from the national governments as well as from interest groups. I would like to stress four of these organizational resources: first, the 'constitutional power' to initiate public action; second, the capacity to instrumentalize the loose notion of 'Community interest'; third, the ability to mobilize ideas and expertise against the tide of general opinion; and finally, the specific use of regulation as an instrument for public action.

Constitutional Power does Matter

EU policy-making is far less unidimensional than most neo-realist or intergovernmentalist theorists' analyses would lead us to believe, but nor is it a political market in which various policy networks coexist in parallel with only the rules set up by their members to stabilize interactions. Inspired by such neo-institutionalist analysts as Hall or March and Olsen, Simon Bulmer has convincingly demonstrated that the study of EU policy-making needs to link subsystems of agents with institutional variables which mediate (and do not determine) actors' choices, exchanges and outputs (Bulmer 1994, 1995). Institutions are thus considered in a broad sense to mean formal institutions, informal institutions and the conventions, norms and symbols embedded in them, and policy instruments and procedures (Bulmer 1995: 8).

From this institutional perspective, the EU treaties and their reform—like the most recent one in Amsterdam—may be considered as a set of rules which represents the political capability of the different actors, as well as that of the other actors in EU policy-making. It would of course be very naïve to consider that, according to these treaties, the Commission is 'the' autonomous actor which sets the EU's policy agenda. Data show, for instance, that of 507 proposals adopted by the Commission in 1996, only 3 per cent were the result of spontaneous initiatives from the DGs. In comparison, obligatory proposals relating to the conclusion of international agreements by the member states represented 24 per cent of the total, and the outcome of member states' demands 5.8 per cent (Commission 1997c; see also Ponzano 1996). Nevertheless, the fact that the Commission has the formal right to aggregate policy demands and to put them on the EU's agenda influences the attitude of its officials, and has shaped their identity (Douglas 1986).

Given that this formal right is a unique element of their task as compared to that of the officials of most secretariats of international organizations, Commission agents are often better at packaging policy demands than at managing them afterwards (Ludlow 1991; Laffan 1997c). The obligatory drafting of the texts gives them a certain power to influence the norms for the negotiation of EU policies (Wallace 1990). National ministers and officials discovering the Brussels arena for the first time are often struck by the fact that being the drafter of texts with the possibility of choosing the wording is a decisive resource in the hands of the Commission's agents when trying to influence negotiations in the Council. This is emphasized by the fact that, according to the Treaty of the European Community (TEC), any development of an EC policy for which a legal competence has not been established in a specific treaty article is only possible on the basis of a Commission proposal (Article 308 [235] TEC). The Commissioners must thus convince the national governments that an initiative is necessary. However, since the Treaties of Maastricht and now Amsterdam, this has become more difficult for the Commission because both texts emphasize the necessary application of the principle of subsidiarity (see below). This also explains why, when an institutional review is being discussed, Commission officials automatically establish a linkage between any possible sharing of their right of initiative (as is the case in the field of the common foreign and security policy—CFSP, unchanged under the Amsterdam Treaty) and the weakening of their policy entrepeneurship (Vibert 1995).

Defending the Community Interest

Research undertaken by anthropologists has shown that a form of Community ideology, defined as a system of ideas and values, exists within the Commission.[1] This ideology is based on the identification of its officials with the defence

[1] Mostly published in French, the works of Marc Abélès and Irène Bellier (see References) are not much quoted by EU specialists. A glance at the footnotes of most articles on the EU published in English-language journals by the younger generation of academics shows a striking lack of references in languages other than English. It confirms the notion that one possible effect of globalization is an increase in parochialism!

of a so-called 'Community' or 'European interest' (Abélès 1994). It would be misleading to seek an objective definition of such a loose notion. Community interest is a discursive element, referring to the existence of a European common good projected into an inbuilt future. My argument is that the discursive defence of the Community interest constitutes a resource for Commission officials, because it is very difficult for other actors in the EU polity to contest its positive value. Laura Cram (1994) has shown, for instance, how national administrations opposed to a proposal put forward by DG XIII (tele-comunications, information technology, and research) to elaborate an information technology (IT) policy were unable to contest the Commission's argument that this policy would improve the competitiveness of EU firms *vis-à-vis* those from Japan and the United States. In another policy sector, Andy Smith (1996) has observed that the term 'economic and social cohesion', coined within DG XVI (regional policy and cohesion) during the 1988 reform of the structural funds, refers to the positive image of a European interest or a European common good which is difficult to contest, even for a British neo-liberal. A discursive element like the Community interest must therefore be taken into account, because it is frequently utilized by Commission agents in interinstitutional negotiations, and also *vis-à-vis* the national governments and social actors. It is a resource which shapes the policy process, but its weight differs from one policy negotiation to another.

Mobilizing Ideas against the Tide

Public policy analysis regularly stresses the ability of Commission agents to mobilize ideas and expertise against the tide of general opinion. They refer to a capacity for inventiveness (Metcalfe 1994) which is an important component of policy entrepreneurship (Zysman and Sandholtz 1989). From what does this policy inventiveness stem?

First, Commissioners and Commission officials draw influence from a policy cycle which is longer at EU than at national level (Smith 1996). Appointed for five years by common accord of the national governments after a vote of approval by the European Parliament (EP), Commissioners do not have to cope with the same uncertainty as members of governments in most West European democracies. On the one hand, their mandates are not subordinated to the trust of a *primus inter pares* President. The fact that the Amsterdam Treaty will give the latter a formal say over the nomination of the other Commissioners will probably not greatly increase the President's hierarchical power. On the other hand, the parliamentary censorship provided by the Treaty of Rome has always been very theoretical, because it is a collective process addressing the college of Commissioners as a whole, it is difficult to implement in an EU political system which is, by definition, non-majoritarian. Moreover, up to the time of the Treaties of Maastricht and Amsterdam, the EP had no influence on the renomination of the Commission. Of the eight motions of censure adressed by the EP to the Commission between 1972 and 1998, six were put to the vote and two were withdrawn just after their registration. None of the eight succeeded.

Martin Donnelly and Ella Ritchie have observed (1994: 34) that a further element of stability derives from the distribution of portfolios, which may be expected to remain in the same hands for the length of the Commission's term. The only exception to this is when enlargement of EU membership has required new members to be admitted to the Commission, which necessitates some redistribution of portfolios. Pressures from the EP can also lead to a limited reorganization of portfolios. In 1997, for example, the Commission President, Jacques Santer, was forced to take the BSE (bovine spongiform encephalopathy) file away from the Commissioner in charge of agriculture, Frans Fischler, and to give it to Emma Bonino, the Commissioner charged with consumer protection. Although this was not a full redistribution of portfolios, it shows that the EP also has an emerging influence on the internal organization of the Commission.[2]

The relationship between the policy inventiveness of a Commissioner and the policy cycle should nevertheless be nuanced. Inventiveness also depends to a large degree on the hierarchical position occupied by a particular policy at a given moment on the EU's political agenda, an agenda which is by no means set solely by the Commission. It also depends a great deal on the effectiveness of the cabinet, the private office of advisers (drawn from the French model of public administration) recruited from within the Commission DGs or the national administrations, to assist the Commissioner in his or her job.[3] It depends finally on the working relationship (sometimes cooperative, but at other times conflictual) established by the Commissioner with the directors general and the directors of the DGs for which he or she is responsible. Some detailed empirical studies on these issues would be most useful. Even if some new research seems to be in progress,[4] there is still, with the exception of George Ross' 1995 book on the Delors' cabinet (Ross 1995a), a dearth of scientific knowledge on the college of Commissioners and on the cabinet system.

As regards the DGs, Andy Smith (1996) has observed that one consequence of the weak intra-organizational mobility within the Commission (which is more acute in some DGs than in others) is that officials can become specialists in their policy sectors, and can then invent policies which emphasize the

[2] I am grateful to Karlheinz Neunreither for this point.

[3] One of the seven cabinet advisers is frequently (by convention rather than obligation) of a different nationality to that of the Commissioner. He or she is symbolically called the 'foreign member'.

[4] I refer here to the current work of Liesbet Hooghe of the University of Toronto, and of Andy Smith of the Institut d'Études Politiques, Bordeaux.

role of the Commission. However, a strong degree of specialization together with a low level of mobility can generate the reverse of inventiveness—routine, and an inability to innovate. As in all bureaucratic organizations, such tendencies exist within the EU Commission. This problem of inertia was underlined in the 1998 issues paper on staff management, prepared by the Commission official, Tony Caston, for the EU Commissioner for budget and personnel, Erkii Liikanen. Caston recommended that part of the performance assessment in staff reports should be oriented around the training needs of the individual, including the need for mobility.[5] On the other hand, the criterion of nationality, which clearly influences careers from the level of head of division (A3) to that of director general (A1), is an idiosyncrasic factor which can strengthen the motivation of the *fonctionnaires,* who need to attract the attention of their national cabinets to further their careers. In an interview with the author in April 1996, an official from a founding member state did not hesitate to say that, although the support of 'his' national cabinet helped him to be appointed to an A3 position, he had also been chosen because he had done a good job in the task force charged with Spanish and Portuguese enlargement. This argument should, however, be nuanced because, while some governments have a systematic policy of pushing their nationals within the Commission through the permanent representations and the cabinets, others do it in a much looser manner. France, Spain, and Britain belong to the first group,[6] while Germany and Belgium appear more in the second group.

Apart from the policy cycle, the mobilization of ideas against the tide of general opinion and inventiveness in the Commission also stem from the diversity of national and professional backgrounds among the officials (which is higher within the Commission than in most national administrations), and from their capacity to draw in outside expertise. Such expertise is available through the regular consultation by the DGs of about 500 advisory committees, composed of independent experts, representatives of national administrations (officially in their personal capacity), and of interest groups. The latter are drawn both from the Euro-groups based in Brussels, but also directly from the national professional organizations, as in the case, for example, of the Advisory Committee for Fisheries, which advises DG XIV (fisheries policy). The contribution of these committees to expertise should not be overestimated, however, because a lot of Euro-groups have weak organizational

---

[5] This paper, entitled 'Personnel Policy in the European Institutions: Towards the future' is but one element of Liikanen's reformist staff policy. Liikanen's plan is to reform career paths and training, but also (under pressure from national governments, who no longer want to pay for such privileges) to abolish some allowances and benefits which Commission officials currently receive (such as household, dependent, child and educational allowances, or the expatriation allowance, which corresponds to 16% of an official's salary). Reactions to the Caston report have been so negative among Commission staff that a one-day protest strike was organized on 30 April 1998 at the request of the six staff unions.

[6] In both the French and British permanent representations to the EU, an official is charged with following the careers of that member state's nationals within the Union's institutions.

resources and, more importantly, have a weak degree of legitimacy *vis-à-vis* their national members. The real resource for efficiency lies rather in the flexibility accorded the officials to establish informal and case-by-case consultations with national interest groups and experts. Two implications follow from this. First, Commission officials are able to cast their net as widely as possible in the fifteen EU member states, thereby gaining a diversity of ideas; and second, they are able to recruit outside experts into the DGs by means of temporary contracts (employing them as temporary agents, consultants, and so on). There is a total lack of transparency as regards the recruitment and the statute of the various consultants working in the DGs, and for the operational programmes based in third countries (e.g. the countries of Central and Eastern Europe—CEECs, and the former Yugoslavia and the Mediterranean countries). According to a well-informed press agency (*Agence Europe*, 8 May 1997), the Commission employs between 1,000 and 2,000 such consultants. The relevant point for our analysis is that the programme for administrative reform (MAP 2000)[7] has provided each DG with a system of budgetary envelopes, and the responsibility for managing some organizational aspects of general training. One consequence of this reform is that the recruitment of consultants no longer requires the green light from DG IX (personnel). The existence of too many consultants in a DG can therefore generate a situation which is absolutely the reverse of inventiveness: a dissipation of ideas, and a loss of coherence in the resulting policy plans.

Policies through Regulation

Two main variables have been proposed by Giandomenico Majone (1996) to show that regulatory policies (i.e. those which enable a political organization to exert a continuous and specific control on activities generally considered beneficial for the society as a whole) are well-adapted to the structure of EU policy-making. First, there is a permanent need for the economic agents to limit the obstacles to the completion of a single market. Second, the Community budget provides a weak margin of manoeuvre to develop new distributive or redistributive policies, given that a budget of about 85bn Ecus in 1998 represented only 1.25 per cent of the member states' GNP, and that 82 per cent of expenditure was devoted to agricultural market support (45 per cent), and to the structural funds (37 per cent). Among the various EU institutions, the Commission probably gets more bureaucratic influence than any of the others from the large degree of confinement of the Community's policies in the field of regulation. Because they have the formal right to initiate policies, the cabinets and DGs are tempted to propose regulation supplies. They are also tempted to

[7] Approved by the college of Commissioners in April 1997, 'MAP 2000' is an extension of the 'SEM 2000' programme, introduced in 1995 by Commissioner Liikanen to improve the management of the Commission's internal budget (which represented 2.8bn Ecus in 1998, i.e. 3.07% of the total Community budget).

aggregate regulation demands from national administrations and interest groups who want to limit the negative effects of divergent national regulations on their activities. In the face of demands from interest groups, Commission officials experience an increase in their influence in the policy-making process, because they represent a solution to very concrete problems on issues such as technical standards, pollution, and competitiveness.

Nevertheless, the other side of the coin is that regulatory policies external-ize most of the implementation costs onto economic and social actors at national level. Laura Cram (1993) has described this phenomenon as 'calling the tune without paying the piper'. For example, when it is decided at EU level that the installation of a catalytic converter should be obligatory on new cars in order to reduce toxic emissions, such a decision externalizes not only the implementation procedures but also the effective costs onto firms and con-sumers (Mény 1995). Interest groups which consider themselves to be losers in this process are then strongly tempted to look first to the Commission (which is perceived as 'the' EU permanent bureaucratic agency), and to make it accountable for the negative effects of policies which have in fact been accepted by national governments (even if majority voting in the Council means that not all the governments always agree with a decision), and by the EP. It was in order to limit this scapegoat effect that the former Commission President, Jacques Delors, insisted on the introduction of the principle of subsidiarity into the Maastricht Treaty (Article 3B). Drawn from the federalist experience (Millon Delsol 1993), subsidiarity is a principle of policy self-restraint which states that, in areas which do not fall within its exclusive competence, the Com-munity shall take action '. . . only if and in so far as the objectives of the pro-posed action cannot be sufficiently achieved by the member states'. Although the Commission adopted a new policy in 1993 (characterized chiefly by a decrease in the number of new proposals—down from 61 in 1990 to 19 in 1996—and an increasing use of Green Papers) to allay the fears of 'centralism' voiced by central as well as regional governments, subsidiarity remains difficult to implement.[8] The main reason is that the primacy of the market, which has dominated the evolution of the European polity since the origins of the EU, induces an increasing process not only of deregulation but also of re-regulation, from which follows the necessity to adopt more and more decisions at the centre (Scharpf 1992).

The Limits to Policy Entrepreneurship

The policy entrepreneurship of the Commission in the EU polity is limited by a number of endogenous and exogenous factors, three of which will be high-

---

[8] Details concerning the implementation of the principle of subsidiarity were reaffirmed in a Protocol annexed to the Treaty of Amsterdam.

lighted here: the strong degree of bureaucratic segmentation; the interference of national governments in the appointment of agents; and weak citizen perception of Commission accountability.

Bureaucratic Segmentation

As with most bureaucratic organizations, the Commission is highly segmented in terms of the distribution of responsibilities and authority. This segmentation is a source of diversity and of inventiveness, but it also gives rise to conflict, which affects policy entrepreneurship. Empirical studies have shown that each DG is characterized by its own organizational identity (Abélès and Bellier 1996) or administrative culture (Cini 1997), which is linked to its historical background and to the substance of the policy it administers. The anthropologist, Irène Bellier, observes for instance that the regulatory efficiency and the parochialism of DG VI (agriculture) is in stark contrast to the openness to the world which prevails in the DGs in charge of external relations, whether they are dealing with diplomacy or technical assistance (Bellier 1995). Yet the close identification of each official with 'his' or 'her' DG is nothing special when compared to the identification of a national civil servant with his or her ministry or his or her administrative corps. Moreover, the identification of *fonctionnaires* with a particular DG does not mean that exchanges of ideas and information with colleagues from other DGs are totally out of the question. For instance, the small team of *fonctionnaires* from DG I which was in charge of hurriedly devising the Phare economic programme towards Eastern Europe in 1989 had close contacts with colleagues from DG VIII who had been working on financial aid towards the African, Caribbean, and Pacific (ACP) countries for some thirty years (Deloche and Lequesne 1996). For special events, such as the Amsterdam Treaty or the enlargement negotiations with the CEECs and Cyprus, *ad hoc* structures called task forces are set up, composed of officials recruited from the various DGs. The Santer Commission has seen the creation of interservice groups, interservice structures (like the one for the implementation of assistance to third and developing countries, involving DGs I, IA, IB, VIII, and the European Community's Humanitarian Office—Echo), networks of directors general, and even groups of Commissioners (e.g. on external relations and trans-European networks—TENs). They are very similar to the interministerial structures and procedures which national governments and administrations set up to reach bureaucratic compromises at home. In a certain sense, conflicts of interest between DGs are not very original, when compared to what can be observed through a bureaucratic politics paradigm in national administrations.

More original and interesting are the methods of conflict resolution within the Commission. In Brussels, final decisions never follow an 'imposed style', that is, an intervention by the President to decide which conflictual position should prevail. Instead, decision-taking in the Commission is an incremental process of compromises which are worked out successively and in parallel at different levels: among the desk officers in the DGs, then among the staff of the cabinets, then among the heads of the chefs des cabinets', and so on, until the college of Commissioners puts the file on its formal agenda (Lamy 1991). This consensus-oriented policy style is linked to the weak leadership role of the President of the Commission compared to most West European heads of government, even when an influential politician like Jacques Delors holds the post (Ross 1995a). The formal statement entered into the Amsterdam Treaty that: 'The Commission shall work under the guidance of its President' will probably not change anything about this situation. It should not be forgotten that the President of the Commission has only one vote like all the other Commissioners, when decisions are taken by simple majority in the weekly college meeting where, according to the principle of collegiality, each member can intervene on all Commission files.[9] The President has no real possibility to ask for individual sanctions against a Commissioner who is not doing his or her job properly. Because the territorial (or national) dimension remains the essential component for the composition of the college, the autonomy of each appointee is the condition for the equilibrium of the system as a whole. This autonomy is clearly increased when the Commissioner is in charge of a portfolio like competition or foreign trade which appears prestigious in the policy agenda, and/or when they are former ministers from a large member state with a certain reputation on the world scene, a good example being Leon Brittan.

The need for consensus at every level of the Commission is a direct result of this lack of leadership at the level of the college, which also gives rise to a policy style characterized by slowness and *lourdeur*, which can reduce the motivation of officials in the DGs, as well as their outside interlocutors. On the other hand, this very slowness can benefit the Commission's interlocutors, particularly officials from the national administrations, by allowing them time to adjust and refine their negotiating strategies.

Nationality Influences Careers

Intergovernmentalist theorists have always overestimated the structural dependence of supranational institutions on national governments (Moravcsik 1993; for a critique of this view, see Lequesne 1998a). It is nevertheless true that supranational institutions act partly within the constraints of member state prefer-

---

[9] Derogations from the principle of collegiality do exist. The main one is the procedure of *réhabilitation*: the college delegates to a specific Commissioner the right to take management or administrative decisions in a specific field, e.g. agricultural or competition policy, without any obligation to consult the whole college (Commission Internal Rules of Procedure, Art. 11).

ences (Pollack 1998). The recruitment of agents into the Commission is a good illustration of these constraints.

Although the Maastricht Treaty required that the formal approval of the EP be requested (a procedure reinforced in the Amsterdam Treaty), the heads of state and government of the member states still appoint the President of the Commission and the nineteen Commissioners according to purely domestic criteria (Darnoux 1995). The appointment of the President is an interstate bargain which can be highly conflictual. For example, the British Prime Minister, John Major, vetoed the application by the Belgian Prime Minister, Jean-Luc Dehaene, to replace Jacques Delors as Commission President in January 1995, because he mistrusted the Christian Democrat leader, whose entire political career had been spent in coalition politics at home, and who had also supported the constitutional evolution of his country towards federalism. After this very controversial episode, the Luxembourg Prime Minister, Jacques Santer, was chosen to chair the college, even though he was at least as federalist as Dehaene. Major was out-manoeuvred, because it was correctly assumed that he could not say 'no' a second time.

The distribution of portfolios among Commissioners is subject to interstate bargains of similar intensity. In the 1995–9 Santer Commission, the coveted dossier of external relations was the subject of such dispute among the governments that it was split into five different portfolios. This fragmentation of tasks does not enhance policy coherence on EC external affairs. Consequently, President Santer proposed annexing a Commission declaration to the Amsterdam Treaty stating the desirability of bringing external relations under the responsibility of a Vice-President in the new college taking up office in 2000. But it is not at all certain that the governments will follow this reasonable recommendation.

To state that a Commissioner only represents his or her government would be as simplistic as to consider that he or she is exclusively defending the 'Community interest'. The relationship between individual Commissioners and their national governments reveals in a much more complex way the autonomy/dependence dialectic which characterizes the whole institution. On the one hand, the Commisioners' legitimacy, not only inside the Commission but also *vis-à-vis* the other EU institutions (e.g. the EP) and non-governmental actors (e.g. interest groups and consumers) depends on their ability to defend the EU's norms apart from and against their own governments. This happens regularly. During the Maastricht negotiations, for example, Jacques Delors totally disagreed with the position of the French government on a pillared structure for the treaty (Lequesne 1998*b*). The Belgian Commissioner, Karel Van Miert, in charge of competition in the Santer Commission, threatened the Belgian government with legal proceedings in February 1996 if it did not stop illegal subsidies on exports to national companies. On the other hand, Commissioners regularly plead the interests of their state within the college, giving a clear priority to their national loyalty. This explains why, during the negotiation of the Amsterdam Treaty, most of the governments (especially those from the smaller countries) categorically refused to countenance the idea put forward by the French Minister for European Affairs, Michel Barnier, of having a 'narrow' college based on the rotation of Commissioners. Exemplifying the 'nationalization' of the college, Keith Middlemas (1995: 234) has noted that Padraig Flynn, the Irish Commissioner, spoke out against Bruce Millan, the Commissioner responsible for regions, in favour of his (Flynn's) government's refusal to settle for a lesser allocation than had allegedly been promised from the budget of the structural funds. There are many such examples. Every Commissioner is prepared to support his or her country *vis-à-vis* the college when it deals with competition rules affecting a national entreprise, for example, or a transfer of funds from the EU budget. Trying to determine whether a Commissioner gives more weight to national or to Community loyalty is neither very interesting nor very rewarding. Empirical evidence highlights both attitudes, depending on specific negotiations and policies. This very duality is the relevant point, illustrating the inherent tensions between territorial and functional interests which occur at all times in the EU polity.

The appointment of high-ranking officials—from head of division (A3) to director general (A1) level—is also subject to intensive interstate bargains between the cabinets and the permanent representations of the member states (Lequesne 1993). The unofficial principle of geographical balance represents the basis for negotiation among cabinet members and government officials. Behind it lurks the reality that governments try to influence a diffuse policy-making system which they are no longer fully able to control. While the interference of national criteria in the appointment of high-ranking staff (a minority, let it not be forgotten, of the 17,000 *fonctionnaires*) may push some of them to be creative, it can also be highly frustrating for others. The preference sometimes accorded by the cabinets to outside candidates (known inside the Commission as 'parachuting') in order to maintain the geographic balance can leave some inside officials, recruited on their own merits by open competition (*concours*), with the impression that they belong to a bureaucracy in which the Weberian principle of competence is not respected. Some Commission officials have even contested the appointment of outside candidates in the Court of First Instance, which has competence for the settlement of disputes between the EU institutions and their agents. One such example is the case brought by two Commission officials, Messrs Boos and Fisher, who believed they were qualified to apply for the position of director (A2) in DG XIV (fisheries policy),[10] to which the college had appointed two outsiders in order to guarantee the geo-

---

[10]   Court of First Instance, Case 58/91.

graphical balance. However, the Court of First Instance did not require that the recruitment procedure be cancelled.

Second, national ministers and officials are very influential in the interinstitutional negotiations which follow the formal sending of a Commission proposal to the member states, as well as to the other EU institutions and organs, although this is not the place to go into the details of the EU's decision-making process. The budget is a key issue. Together with the members of the EP (the MEPs), ministers decide annually how much money the EU will spend on public policies within the limits of an existing pluri-annual scheme. This programming exercise, which starts again in 1999 for the period 2000–6, is of paramount importance. It reflects the global compromises governments are prepared to accept collectively, having individually balanced their contributions to the budget (the EU's 'own resources') with the outcomes they expect from the various policies, and more specifically from those (the Common Agricultural Policy—CAP—and regional policies) which have a distributive impact on their national territories. Although the MEPs' legislative powers were increased significantly by the Single European Act (SEA) and the Maastricht and Amsterdam Treaties, national ministers and officials have retained most of the decision-taking power in the Council of Ministers and its administrative substructures (the Committee of Permanent Representatives (Coreper) and the working groups).

A representative of the Commission (either a Commissioner or an official, depending on the level) is always present in Council negotiations to defend the proposal (including the budgetary proposal) on the table before the governments (Rometsch and Wessels 1994). Although some Commission representatives are very skillful at acting in collusion with the presidency ministers or officials, their influence fluctuates greatly from one dossier to another. Once the decision has been formally adopted, Commission agents are also frequently constrained (to a greater or lesser degree) by the committees of national civil servants which are set up by the governments to control their capacity to adopt executive measures.[11] More importantly, Commission officials suffer from poor positioning in the networks of actors responsible for the implementation of EU policies at the national and local levels (McAleavey 1994; Smith 1996).

The Accountability Gap

Since the Maastricht Treaty, the notion of the 'democratic deficit' has been a recurrent argument in the national political debates on the EU. During the

---

[11] On this aspect of EU decision-making, known in EU jargon as 'comitology', see the Decision of the Council, 13 July 1987. In 1998, about 200 such committees were in existence. See also Ch. 7.

national processes of ratification of the Amsterdam Treaty, the opponents of the EU institutions in the member states frequently focused on the Commission and its perceived lack of accountability, because the Commissioners are not elected by direct universal suffrage and because parliamentary scrutiny of their actions is still weak. What answer can be given to these critics, whose argument is mostly founded on a state-centric approach to democracy, and perceived by the Commission officials as an obvious limit to their policy entrepeneurship?

Empirical evidence does not support the argument that the policies prepared by the Commissioners and the officials within the DGs are immune from political control. However, it must be admitted that control in the EU is exerted through a series of monitoring procedures which are diffuse and weakly transparent. Examples include amendments from national ministers and officials; amendments from MEPs (especially in the context of the co-decision procedure extended by the Amsterdam Treaty); jurisprudence from the European Court of Justice; yearly and *ad hoc* reports from the Court of Auditors; and policy statements from interest groups. Although the same system of checks and balances is applied more and more to the policy activities of national governments, most citizens do not understand how it works at EU level. The main reason for this is that, in the member states, these specialized forms of control coexist with the instruments of representative democracy (i.e. elections, political parties, majority versus opposition debates, and so on). Although such instruments exist at EU level, they are still very weak. Apart from a minority who are actively involved in the policy networks, most citizens are not aware of the controls which are applied on a daily basis to Commission activities, through a combination of bureaucratic and judiciary procedures rather than the single scrutiny power of one elected body, such as the EP or the national parliaments. This question, which implies an inevitable diffusion of politics in the EU, is the most important limit to the legitimacy of the Commission.

Conclusion

The EU polity is a good illustration of what Alberta Sbragia (1993) has called a 'balancing act' between actors, interests, and public policies, which are sometimes deterritorialized (or functional) and sometimes remain strongly embedded in territories (national as well as subnational). Different levels of aggregation may be considered in order to analyse the political dynamics induced by this permanent balancing act. More than thirty years ago, neo-functionalists emphasized the shift of interests and loyalties of national elites from their national governments to the new EC institutions. More recently, institutionalist works have studied functional interactions and fusion between

EU and national institutions (Wessels 1992). In this chapter, devoted to the Commission, I have tried to show that the internal functioning, resources, and actions of the various agents of a supranational institution (but also of national or local ones), is another level of analysis which should not be neglected when examining the EU polity as a whole.

4

The Slow March of European Legislation: The Implementation of Directives

GIUSEPPE CIAVARINI AZZI

The EC (European Community) Treaty provides for the directive, a form of legislative cooperation between the central level and the member states, which is more or less unknown in other systems. In federal systems, for example, a clear distinction is drawn between federal legislation and state legislation. A Community directive is binding on the member states as to the result to be achieved, but leaves them free to decide the means to achieve it. Directives are specifically designed for the approximation and harmonization of legislation connected with the common market. In other areas, such as agriculture, transport, and the free movement of workers, the Community can choose between directly applicable legislation (regulations) and directives. In these areas, the directive will be used if the aim is not to impose standardization but progressively to adapt and harmonize national regulations. For example, almost all the legislative instruments used to complete the internal market (to meet the 1992 target) were directives.

A directive is, in a sense, neither supranational nor national, but lies somewhere between the two. For the purpose of implementing directives, the member states could almost be regarded as an extension of the Community institutions. However, the practice has sometimes diverged from the theory expounded in the Treaty, and in the past directives have been adopted containing not only general guidelines but also specific provisions, leaving only a very small margin of discretion for the member states. The detailed nature of these directives, and the delay in implementing them on the part of the member states, have led the European Court of Justice (ECJ), acting to protect the citizen, to declare certain directives or some of their provisions to be directly applicable.

The number of directives in force or, more precisely, which have 'reached the deadline for implementation', has increased steadily. Figure 4.1 shows that

The opinions expressed in this chapter are purely personal.

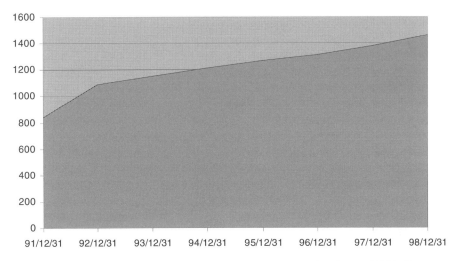

Fig. 4.1. The number of directives applicable at the end of each year (1991–8).

the drive to complete the single market in 1992 led to a significant increase in their number.

Responsibility for the practical implementation of Community policies thus rests largely with the member states. How effective is the cooperation between the two levels? This question will become increasingly important in the future for two reasons. First, the function of the European Union (EU) in the years ahead is likely to consist more of implementing existing policies than of creating new ones. Second, the future enlargement of the EU will inevitably entail problems of implementation for the new member states. In this context, we need to ask two crucial questions. How effectively are Community directives being implemented? How effective is the control exercised by the Community institutions? Political science has rarely considered these questions from a horizontal point of view. However, a number of multidisciplinary studies have been carried out on these subjects, most of them at the instigation of the Maastricht European Institute of Public Administration (EIPA) (see in particular Ciavarini Azzi 1985; Mény 1985; Pappas 1994; Siedentopf and Ziller 1988). Some of their conclusions remain valid today, while others need to be qualified, as we shall see below.

Are Directives Ultimately Transposed and Applied?

The Facts

The member state must first take the necessary measures to transpose the directive, and these must then be notified to the European Commission. In

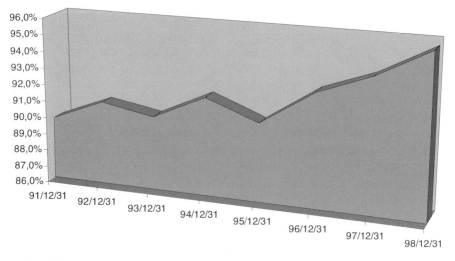

Fig. 4.2. The average rate of transposition of directives at the end of each year (1991–8).

practice, the member states are usually careful to do so, in order to avoid infringement proceedings. The Commission thus has very precise information on the national implementing measures adopted. The statistics which it distributes can provide a basis for answering the questions under consideration here, although statistics are of limited value in this area because directives vary in importance.

According to the latest published figures (31 December 1998),[1] the member states have on average taken measures to transpose 95.7 per cent of the directives in force. This is a relatively high rate, as can be seen from Fig. 4.2, which shows the trend since 1991. The average rate has generally been increasing since 1991. The decline in legislative output resulting from the completion of the internal market has undoubtedly helped to push up the rate. It is also clear that the average includes some highs (e.g. in 1992, thanks to the exceptional efforts of the member states to meet the 1 January 1993 deadline for the completion of the internal market), and occasional lows (e.g. in 1995, the result of various 'teething problems' experienced by the three new member states who joined the EU that year, and quickly resolved since).

There are, however, disparities between the member states' performances. As Fig. 4.3 shows, on 31 December 1998 these varied from a minimum of 93.62 per cent (Italy) to a maximum of 98.21 per cent (Denmark). The same trend is

---

[1] COM(1999) 301 final, p. 8.

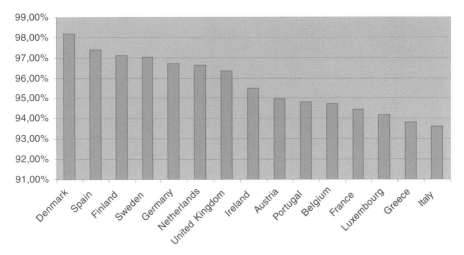

Fig. 4.3. Breakdown by member state of the rate of transposition of directives as of 31 December 1998.

confirmed overall by Fig. 4.4, which shows the number of infringement proceedings pending on 1 August 1999 for each member state for failure to notify the Commission of national implementing measures.

Differences in performance between the member states used to be more marked. Today they are much less pronounced: the difference between Italy and Denmark highlighted in Fig. 4.3 relates to only sixty-three directives. They are, however, important; in an economic area that is now largely integrated, the slightest delay in implementing Community rules in one member state can have important consequences for the other members.

But it is not enough for a member state simply to have taken measures to transpose the directives. These measures must conform with the directives to be transposed, if the intended aim is to be achieved. What is the degree of conformity? How can we measure it statistically? Figures on infringement proceedings initiated by the Commission for non-conformity give some indication of the degree of conformity. Figure 4.5 shows the number of infringement proceedings for non-conformity pending on 1 August 1999 by member state.

The ranking of the member states is roughly the same as for failure to notify measures transposing directives. The differences are slightly greater if we look at the specific application of implementing measures, as shown in Fig. 4.6.

What are the reasons behind the delays in transposing directives? What is the explanation for the differences in performance between the member states?

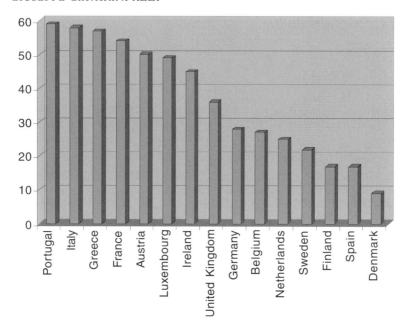

Fig. 4.4. The number of pending infringement proceedings for failure to notify the Commission of national implementing measures (situation as of 1 August 1999, by member state).

Reasons for Success or Failure

Before considering the reasons attributable to the member states, we should consider factors inherent in the directives themselves. These fall into two categories. First, there are problems arising from the highly detailed and complex nature of certain directives, which cause difficulties for most member states. Take, for example, the habitat directive on the conservation of wild flora and fauna, which should have been transposed by 30 December 1997. Infringement proceedings were started by the Commission against twelve member states, and in seven cases this led to referral to the ECJ for failure to act.

The Community is aware that improving the quality of the drafting of legislation, including directives, will make implementation easier.[2] It has also spoken out formally in favour of less detailed directives in the interest of more effective application of the principles of subsidiarity and proportionality.[3] However, these principles are not always put into practice. The need to find a

---

[2] Declaration No. 39 annexed to the Final Act of the Treaty of Amsterdam, which called on the institutions to draw up common guidelines on the quality of drafting, and to follow them in the various stages of the decision-making process.

[3] Protocol on the application of the principles of subsidiarity and proportionality, annexed to the Final Act of the Treaty of Amsterdam. See also COM(1998)345 final, 1–2.

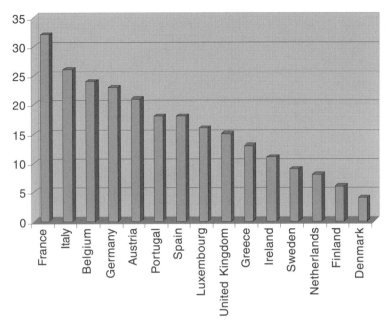

Fig. 4.5. The number of pending infringement proceedings for non-conformity (situation as of 1 August 1999, by member state).

compromise in the Council and Parliament can sometimes lead to Commission proposals being made more complex, for example.[4]

A second source of difficulties for member states is when a directive does not simply require the transposition of rules (e.g. the recognition of qualifications) but calls for active (and expensive) steps to be taken, such as the construction of a water treatment plant. Clearly, the implementation of these directives entails extra effort on the part of certain member states which may not have the necessary infrastructure, and must undertake major investment to secure it. However, these are measures that are essential for 'active' integration, going beyond the idea of the simple 'common market' to include protection of the citizens, the environment, and public health.

Then there are the factors inherent in the member states themselves. The first concerns the way governments (and administrations) are organized for implementing Community law. Governments and administrations have an essential role both in preparing legislative, regulatory, and administrative acts, and in implementing the measures taken in practice. Most member states, particularly when confronted with an increase in the number of directives to be transposed in the early 1990s, had to devote extra attention to co-ordination in this area. In many cases they used the co-ordination instruments for EU affairs

[4] See the examples given in COM(1998)345 final, 8 and 9.

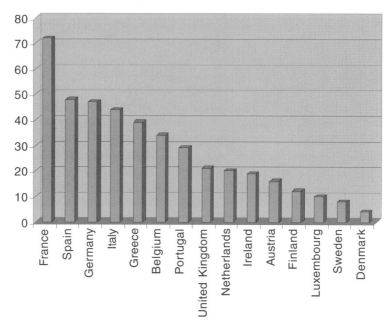

Fig. 4.6. Infringement proceedings pending for incorrect application of national measures implementing directives (situation as of 1 August 1999, by member state).

which were already in operation for preparing Community decisions, making the necessary adjustments (Pappas 1994). The co-ordination formulae differ from one member state to the next, but this is not the place to analyse them in detail. There are numerous examples of co-ordination under the direction of the prime minister or the foreign ministry, joint co-ordination by the ministries of foreign and economic affairs, a hybrid formula, or one which assigns a major role to committees. Experience shows that there is no miracle solution. A formula that works in one country may not work in another, because numerous other factors come into play, most notably the administrative culture, which is also decisive when it comes to execution. Research published by Siedentopf and Ziller for the EIPA in 1988 showed that, once transposed, Community law is applied no better or worse than domestic law.[5]

A second factor is whether the state is centralized or not. Clearly, states with a federal or regional system *a priori* have more problems with transposition than centralized states because, where power rests with *Länder* (Germany and Austria), regions (Belgium and Italy), or autonomous communities

[5] See Vol. 1, Section VI by Ciavarini Azzi.

(Spain), it is these entities which are, at least to some extent, in charge of transposition, while the central state remains legally answerable to the Community institutions. It is no coincidence that states with federal or regional systems are among those experiencing the most problems in the areas covered by Figs 4.3–4.6.

A third factor is the role of the national parliament in the legislative process, which varies from one member state to another. Although the national parliament is almost always involved in implementing acts which touch on the core of parliamentary responsibilities (e.g. taxation), this is not the case for the transposition of technical directives. In many cases, a directive may be transposed in one member state by means of legislation and in another by administrative act or regulation. In a third member state, it might be the subject of a vote on a framework act, followed by statutory instruments. There are significant differences between the member states in this respect. But there are other differences too. The way in which parliament operates differs from one country to another, as does the time taken to approve implementing measures.

Is the role of the national parliament in the implementation of directives automatically a cause of delays? By no means. On the whole, and despite the delays and unforeseen contingencies inherent in the parliamentary process, parliaments do 'play the game' in the implementation of legislation when they are called upon to act. As studies carried out into this question show (Siedentopf and Ziller 1988), parliamentary procedures are not the main cause of delays in the implementation of Community law in most countries. Contrary to what is sometimes thought, the delays most often arise from the failure of governments to present bills to amend domestic legislation in time. There are, of course, exceptions. In Italy, for example, the complexity and length of parliamentary procedures, coupled with the extent of parliament's legislative powers, has been a source of problems in the past, for which a solution had to be, and was, found—the system of the annual Community Act created by the 'La Pergola Act'. This solution in turn now needs to be perfected (see Guizzi 1995: 491ff.).

There is a fourth factor, which should not be overlooked—the role sometimes played by interest groups in the implementation of directives. Their involvement takes on a more or less institutionalized form, depending on the member state.

One other finding of the research conducted to date deserves a mention. There is an important link between the negotiation of a directive (upstream phase) and its implementation (downstream phase). The member states which are the toughest in negotiations are not necessarily those which will have problems during implementation (Ciavarini Azzi 1985: 354–7; and Ciavarini Azzi in Siedentopf and Ziller 1988).

If they have been involved in its preparation, ministerial departments, decentralized entities, and parliaments will have a more positive attitude towards the implementation of Community law in general, and the transposition of directives in particular. The same applies, *mutatis mutandis*, to interest groups: if important groups have not been consulted in the upstream phase, they may constitute a serious obstacle in the downstream phase, whereas in different circumstances they can play a leading role.

Is there Effective Monitoring?

How does Monitoring Work?

As the 'guardian of the treaties', the Commission is at the centre of the monitoring system. It is responsible for ensuring that treaty provisions and the decisions of the institutions are properly applied, whether they are directly applicable (like regulations) or require transposition into national law (like directives). Whenever the Commission identifies an infringement in either case, it invites the member state in question to submit its observations or justifications within a given period (this is known as the 'letter of formal notice'). The given period is usually two months, but will be less in the case of serious infringements directly affecting the working of the internal market. If the member state persists in its infringement, and its observations do not persuade the Commission to alter its view, the Commission will issue a reasoned opinion with which the member state is required to comply within the time limit prescribed by the Commission, failing which the Commission may refer the case to the ECJ. The Court's judgment is binding on the member state and the Community institutions alike. All the aspects of these provisions, which give considerable powers to the Commission and the Court, are applied in practice. In 1998, for example, the Commission commenced infringement proceedings in 1,101 cases, issued 675 reasoned opinions, and referred 123 cases to the ECJ. Following referral by the Commission, the Court gave judgment in 64 cases in 1998, in 63 of which it found against the member state. Table 4.1 gives the figures for letters of formal notice, reasoned opinions, and referrals to the ECJ by member state for the period 1994–8. These figures show that only a very small number of cases are referred to the ECJ. Many cases (1,961 in 1998) are dropped in the course of proceedings, because the member state has regularized its position.

What proportion of these cases involve directives? Figure 4.7 shows that the majority of letters of formal notice, reasoned opinions, and Court referrals issued by the Commission in 1998 relate to directives. It also shows that infringements relating to directly applicable law (the treaties and regulations) are less likely to be put right before reaching the Court than those relating to directives. The prominent role of directives is also apparent from Table 4.2,

TABLE 4.1. The European Commission's infringement proceedings (1994–8)

Member State	Letters of formal notice					Reasoned opinions					Referrals to Court				
	'94	'95	'96	'97	'98	'94	'95	'96	'97	'98	'94	'95	'96	'97	'98
B	77	80	72	93	88	41	19	62	33	78	10	6	20	18	20
DK	57	42	22	64	40	14	1	0	1	10	0	0	0	0	1
D	90	92	62	116	88	66	25	37	35	46	5	10	8	19	5
EL	96	113	58	109	95	85	26	51	23	51	17	12	17	10	16
E	86	81	59	104	78	53	15	30	23	36	9	6	9	7	6
F	90	97	88	157	121	49	17	46	49	94	8	6	11	15	23
IRL	70	67	43	86	63	47	3	36	14	46	12	6	4	6	10
IT	102	114	75	123	110	60	36	71	36	91	12	17	9	20	16
Lux	64	71	39	74	62	36	9	28	14	39	6	3	4	8	11
NL	73	59	32	65	28	20	4	9	11	23	4	0	2	3	3
AU	0	4	132	109	76	0	0	2	38	38	0	0	1	0	4
PO	96	115	54	116	80	54	22	49	35	57	5	4	6	14	5
FIN	0	2	290	78	52	0	0	0	8	16	0	0	0	0	1
S	0	2	69	75	54	0	0	0	6	15	0	0	0	0	1
UK	73	77	47	92	66	21	15	14	8	35	1	2	1	1	1
Total	974	1016	1142	1461	1101	546	192	435	334	675	89	72	92	121	123

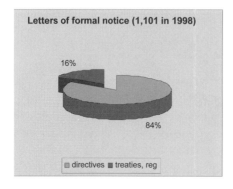

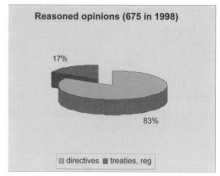

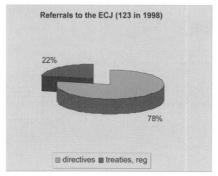

Fig. 4.7. Directives as a percentage of letters of formal notice, reasoned opinions, and referrals to the European Court of Justice (ECJ) in 1998.

which gives an overview of ongoing infringement proceedings by member state.

Monitoring and Raising Awareness

On the whole, we may conclude that monitoring the implementation of directives does produce results, as demonstrated by the average rate of transposition (see Fig. 4.2). But these results are not the outcome of infringement proceedings alone. The role of the Commission in raising awareness and liaising with the member states should not be forgotten. Scarcely a day goes by without some contact between the administration in Brussels and the national administrations, or other interested parties, on the subject of the implementation of Community law. Mention should be made in particular of the annual meetings between Commission departments and their national counterparts in the various capitals to review progress on the transposition of directives. In the internal market field, the approaches to the relevant ministers in the specialist

TABLE 4.2. Infringement proceedings pending (1 August 1999)

	Directives				Directly applicable law	Total
	Failure to notify	Non-conformity	Incorrect implementation	Total Infringements on directives	Treaty, regulations, . . .	
Austria	50	21	16	87	21	108
Belgium	27	24	34	85	41	126
Denmark	9	4	4	17	12	29
Finland	17	6	12	35	9	44
France	54	32	72	158	77	235
Germany	28	23	47	98	32	130
Greece	57	13	39	109	33	142
Ireland	45	11	19	75	11	86
Italy	58	26	44	128	43	171
Luxbg	49	16	10	75	7	82
NL	25	8	20	53	19	72
Portugal	59	18	29	106	21	127
Spain	17	18	48	83	38	118
Sweden	22	9	8	39	8	47
UK	36	15	21	72	19	91
Total	553	244	423	1220	388	1608

Council meetings, the European Council's measures to raise awareness, and the close cooperation between administrations have all undoubtedly contributed to progress on many fronts. The European Parliament (EP) also plays a role, by encouraging the Commission and working with national parliaments. Finally, the role of the national courts should not be forgotten, even if it remains limited. European case law has established that private individuals who have suffered losses as a result of failure to transpose a directive granting them rights are entitled to compensation from the member state, and may sue for damages.

How Might the System Evolve in the Future?

Despite the progress achieved to date, delays continue to occur in the implementation of directives, albeit on a lesser scale, and are increasingly less acceptable in an integrated economy. Monitoring and raising awareness remain topical issues. In this context, the Commission is trying to make its efforts more effective. Faced with a steadily growing number of complaints about alleged infringements of all kinds by the member states (1,128 in 1998, compared with 957 in 1997), the Commission has become increasingly convinced in recent years of the need to set priorities in the cases it deals with; cases involving the transposition of directives are regarded as a priority. It also recently took steps in this area to accelerate the decision-making process, and to dialogue with the member states involved.

Another option open to the Commission, introduced in the Maastricht Treaty, is to impose penalties on member states which fail to comply with Court judgments on infringements. There have been numerous instances in the past (and the problem still exists today) of delays in complying with Court judgments, mainly relating to the transposition of directives. In such cases, the Commission can now take the case to the ECJ, and ask it to impose a specified penalty. The Commission first used this option in January 1997, and since then it has requested this sanction a total of sixteen times. The threat of penalty has proved an effective deterrent: Eleven of these cases were settled—nine of them even before the Commission formally submitted its application. At the time of writing, there were only four applications for penalties before the Court.

Transparency is another instrument that can have a positive impact on solving infringement cases. Since 1996, it has been standard practice to publicize decisions on reasoned opinions and referrals to the Court by issuing press releases. The same applies to letters of formal notice concerning failure to notify national measures implementing directives, and failure to comply with Court judgments; these are, by their nature, public infringements. Conversely, in the case of other letters of formal notice, the principle of confidentiality is respected, because at this preliminary stage it is more conducive to regularizing the infringement.

The Forward View

The Future of Community Legislation

For the past few years, the number of Commission proposals for legislation[6] has been declining, as can be seen from Fig. 4.8; there were 790 such proposals in 1990, but only 571 in 1998. The drop in the number of proposals for new legislation is particularly striking (from sixty-one in 1990 to only thirty-five in 1998). There are undoubtedly several reasons for the declining number of proposals. First, the legislative programme for the single market and economic and monetary union has been completed, and the requisite legislation is substantially in place. In addition, the Commission, through better application of the subsidiarity principle, has in many cases decided to do without a legislative proposal, and in many cases it has followed the proportionality prin-

---

[6] Commission proposals include proposals not only for new legislation, but also for implementing and follow-up measures, for amendment of existing legislation and for instruments concerning international relations.

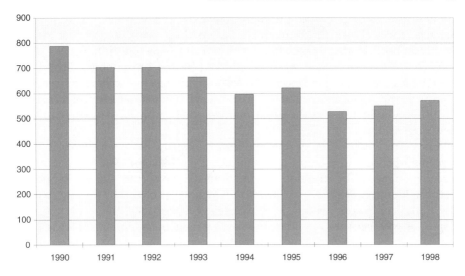

Fig. 4.8. Total Commission proposals (1990–8).

ciple, preferring some alternative to legislation: agreements with industry, self-regulation, and so on (agreements with the social partners are an example of this trend).

There is every sign that this trend will continue. Of course, there are new areas of activity, such as foreign and security policy, judicial cooperation, and cooperation on domestic security or employment, where the general public has high expectations, but where national governments are jealously guarding their prerogatives. The EU will have to find new ways of acting effectively through new modes of operation, not necessarily involving legislation as such.

What is clearly to be expected is that, in the next few years, the accent will be placed more heavily on monitoring the application of legislation. The member states and the Commission must be ready for this.

The Prospect of Enlargement

Giving effect to forty years' accumulated experience of Community integration will be one of the greatest challenges of the forthcoming enlargement. Agenda 2000, presented by the Commission in July 1997, offered a first survey of the situation. It acknowledged the efforts made under the existing 'Europe Agreements' with the countries of Central and Eastern Europe. It added that, if these efforts were pursued, the Czech Republic, Hungary, and Poland should, in the medium term, be able to incorporate the bulk of Community legislation and establish the administrative machinery needed to apply it. But Estonia, Latvia, Lithuania, Slovakia, and Slovenia would have to increase their efforts for some time before they would reach that stage. Bulgaria and Romania, meanwhile, were not in the picture in July 1997. The Agenda 2000 pre-accession strategy, adopted by the Luxembourg European Council at Luxembourg in December 1997, accordingly highlights the strengthening of the applicant countries' institutional and administrative capacity (institution-building), and the adjustment of their business structures to the new dimension.

Since April 1998, each of the applicant countries has been involved in a screening process in relation to the *acquis communautaire*. For the countries already engaged in accession negotiations (Cyprus, the Czech Republic, Estonia, Hungary, Poland, and Slovenia), which will probably be the first to join the European Union, the aim is to ascertain whether they can accept the full *acquis*, or whether they require transitional arrangements in certain areas. But it is also to ascertain when, apart from these areas, they will have legislation which is fully in compliance with Community law, and when they will have the administrative and institutional capacity which Community law requires. The object of the screening exercise with countries not yet negotiating and for which the date of accession is more remote (Bulgaria, Latvia, Lithuania, Romania, and Slovakia) is to measure their ability to absorb the *acquis* and the difficulties they will encounter in giving effect to it. The obvious purpose here is to prepare them for future accession negotiations.

The transposition of directives is inevitably at the heart of these talks, which have clearly manifested the applicant countries' willingness and desire to transpose directives. But let there be no mistake about it: the real problem does not lie in the applicant countries or in the existing member states. What really matters is the ability to devote adequate budgetary and human resources to managing the legislation which is adopted. The Central and Eastern European countries often simply do not have these resources, hence the importance of the Union's assistance with institution-building and business adjustment.

Conclusions

By and large, the novel experience of the directive has turned out well. But there is still room for improvement, especially in the run-up to enlargement, when the difficulties encountered by fifteen member states will be exacerbated. The structures in the member states to accommodate directives will call for careful attention, and the enforcement stage will have to shift gradually from the Community to the national courts. They are the ones who ultimately have to deal with the effects of national transposition. But this will be a slow evolution.

The EU itself will also have a role to play, in ensuring that both new and existing directives are easier to apply. Here, I am referring to legislative simplification, to improving the quality of the drafting of Community legislation, to consolidation, and to recasting (see COM(1998)345 final). Above all, the original concept of the directive must be resurrected, which requires the member states to achieve a specified result but leaves them free to determine how to do so; this means that directives should be less detailed. The national legislative and other bodies responsible for transposition would then have their true role restored to them. But this will depend not only on the Commission, but also on the member states themselves, as they often tend to add detail to a directive when it is being examined by the Council, in order to meet their specific concerns. The slow march of European legislation could then be accelerated somewhat.

5

Beyond Amsterdam: Regional Integration as Social Process

BEATE KOHLER-KOCH

Conventional wisdom teaches us that regional integration is shaped by constitutional politics. Both politicians and political scientists have followed the Amsterdam process closely because they share the opinion that upgrading the power of the common decision-making bodies and enlarging the scope of Community policies will make all the difference. We have witnessed three intergovernmental conferences (IGCs) in the past ten years. Each was aimed at restructuring the architecture of the European polity to make European common action more likely and more efficient, and each was supposed to strengthen both negative (i.e. market) and positive (i.e. policy) integration. Decisive steps have been taken. As regards market integration, the decision to set up a monetary union with a single currency is, without doubt, the most important move towards deepening European economic interdependence. In addition, the competences for regulatory policies in policy fields such as the environment, consumer protection, and research and technology have been enlarged, and the scope of common action has been further extended, both in the field of the common foreign and security policy (CFSP), and in justice and home affairs (JHA). The Treaty revisions agreed at Amsterdam may not have satisfied the more ambitious expectations, but they have increased the scope and range of European integration. There are good reasons, therefore, for scrutinizing the outcome of recent Treaty negotiations.

In this chapter, however, I will not deal with any of these IGCs. I do not question the assumption that the Treaty revisions have had an impact on the institutional set-up of the European polity, nor that Community responsibilities have been enlarged. A different approach is adopted here, because I take issue with the argument that regional integration is mainly an affair of intergovernmental treaty-making. Both economic and political integration may be promoted by setting up a favourable legal framework, but even the best institutional design can only offer opportunities to those actors who bring about regional integration. Markets thrive on exchange relations between autonomous actors, and the living constitution of any polity is a matter of daily political practice. Intergovernmental agreements may establish the framework for economic and social actors, but it is they who, by uncoordinated and decentralized action, turn the territory of the European Community (EC) member states into a common market and a political union.

My main argument is that regional integration is a social process, and that political scientists should take a bottom-up view, concentrating their research on the development of the social forces and attitudes which support the construction of a new socio-economic and political space. By so doing, we will gain a deeper understanding of the development of the European Union (EU), and a better assessment of the state of transnational integration. In the first part of this chapter, I will present my argument in more detail, starting with some conceptual clarifications concerning regional integration and institution-building. In the second part, I will present some findings from my own empirical research. These findings may be read in one of two ways: either as an illustration of the kind of methodological approach I am suggesting for future research on regional integration, or as evidence of the ambivalent state of the EU today.

What are we Looking for?

Regional Integration: Pinning Down an Elusive Concept

For some years now, regional integration has been on the international agenda again. Today's buzzwords in international relations discourse are 'globalization' and 'regionalization'. Institutionalized cooperation between neighbouring countries has emerged in different areas of the world, with a great variety in terms of form and substance. Talking about international regionalism often entails little more than putting a uniform label on very distinct ways and means of joining forces.[1] Despite all these variations, two properties may be considered as the core characteristics of any type of region, namely 'territoriality' and 'cohesion'. A region has more or less clearly outlined geographical limits; it is a space which is distinct from others, due to its higher degree of cohesiveness which introduces an element of unity in diversity. Regional integration, then, is a process of system-building, because it shifts boundaries and redefines core actors. A region has evolved whenever a geographical area has become affected by 'territoriality', that is, '. . . an historically sensitive use of space', which is 'socially constructed and depends on who is controlling whom and why' (Sack 1986: 3).[2] Only when it has become an implicit point of reference in daily practice has a particular space acquired the quality of a 'territory'.

---

[1] In view of the multifaceted reality, it is no surprise that 'region' and 'regionalism' are ambiguous terms in international relations literature: 'The terrain is contested and the debate on definitions has produced little consensus' (Hurrell 1995: 333).

[2] To my mind, Sack, in his definition of territoriality, puts too much emphasis on the aspect of 'control' and too little on social interaction in space and the meaning given to that space.

A region may be, above all, an economic territory or a social and legal territory. A market may evolve from an open space of economic activities, or where distinct rules concerning market entry, rules of behaviour, terms of exchange and so on are prevalent. They contribute to the evolution of a particular economic structure and a self-perpetuating division of labour. Such an evolution, however, will only occur when an effective and durable economic policy regime is in place, around which actors' expectations converge.

In political terms, a region emerges when it becomes the privileged arena for consultation, co-operation, and peaceful conflict resolution, and when its members share a propensity to give preference to internal commitments instead of responding to competing international arrangements. Such attitudes may be supported by formal institutional arrangements, but parallel action may very well come about without institutional support. Negotiating positions and voting behaviour in international arenas show patterns of permanent coalitions that are not always supported by any formal organization. Regionalism in political terms, therefore, is first of all a social construct. Like nations, regions are imagined communities (Anderson 1991) which may or may not be supported by institutions.

It is important to note that, in terms of creating a political space, regional integration has several dimensions. One is the formation of a community of will. Citizens may consider themselves as members of a local, regional, national, or European political entity. They will not necessarily shift their loyalty from one level to another, but they may extend it beyond the borders of an already established political space. Quite another dimension is the formation of a regional political system. In the neo-functionalist approach, regional integration has been equated with '. . . the evolution over time of a collective decisionmaking system among nations' (Lindberg 1970: 650). In their understanding, political institutions to which governments delegate authority and through which they take joint decisions are at the heart of political integration. And the neo-functionalists have emphasized '. . . that a political system can persist without the existence of a matching cultural or social system' (Anderson 1991: 653).

Little research has been done on the interdependence between the emergence of a regional political system and the evolution of a political community. All we know is that, whenever it has been a declared policy to create a political region, institution-building has been considered to be central to the process. Institutions lend stability to concurrent behaviour because they provide the procedural framework for taking collective decisions, and they give those decisions direction by defining the common cause and by laying down corresponding principles and norms of appropriate behaviour. In so doing, institutions support the cohesiveness of a region. Formal organizations for joint decision-making are indispensable when regional political integration aims to transform an association of member states into a corporate actor. Whenever members accept binding commitments with regard to their exercise of political power, they cease to be fully sovereign, thereby invoking a system transformation from regional association to supranationalism.

Variations in types of regional political systems are quite pronounced. They may vary in scope and range of joint decision-making, and in terms of their international or supranational character. Quite apart from these institutional properties, regional political systems may have very different shapes. Integration may turn an area into a multilevel system of government, in which member state representatives are still the gatekeepers in the policy process. Irrespective of the international or supranational nature of the organization, agreements will be negotiated between governments and the essence of these negotiations will be two-level games. But integration may also push the confederation type of polity[3] towards more transnational interpenetration. Patterns of interstate bargaining will then be replaced by a system of 'penetrated governance' (Kohler-Koch 1998e: 6), and the Union itself will become the relevant unit of policy-making. In such a system, interest aggregation and representation is not organized in a two-step process, but stretches immediately beyond national borders.

The European Union (EU) is a good case to use in order to investigate whether political organization is the most important and perhaps the only necessary factor required to promote regional integration. From the very beginning, the European Communities aimed at creating a 'distinctive model of internationalization' (Laffan 1997b). The founding Treaties provided a deliberate political programme to establish a distinct regional entity, and also set up an organization to give it momentum. European regional integration has always been an exercise in shifting boundaries and in creating a common economic, legal, and political space. The merging of national economies into a common market, where capital, goods, services, and people are free to move, of necessity created an economic area distinct from the world market. Economic regionalism was at the top of the West European agenda.

The same holds true for the European Community (EC) as a legal space; after all, European integration is integration through law. The supremacy of EC law has long been accepted, and compliance with EC regulations is well established. The Community has built a multitude of regional regimes and produced a high level of legal harmonization and standardization. Furthermore, political organization and regime-building have been an important stimulus for increased regional interaction. But did these strategies provide sufficient ground to build a distinct regional system? When analysing economic regionalism in Europe, the answer is ambiguous. In terms of economic

---

[3] In the language of the German Constitutional Court's ruling on the Maastricht Treaty: *Staatenverbund*.

interconnectedness and interdependence, the boundaries of economic regions in Europe have never quite matched the borders of the European Economic Community (EEC). Patterns of exchange relations cross Community borders, and also form clusters within the territory of the Community. Even before Austria joined the EU, the Austrian economy was part of a distinct economic region embracing Germany and Switzerland. This economic regional cluster, like other economic regions, survived the construction of a customs union (the EEC) and the European Free Trade Area (EFTA), and even persisted when its members joined competing economic associations.[4] There is strong historic evidence that the trends in economic regionalization are '. . . primarily the result of comparatively durable geographic, cultural and economic determinants and only to a lesser extent the result of more recent, regionally confined measures of integration policy'.[5] In recent years, the strength of economic determinants have been well documented in studies of the patterns of global trade and investment relations. Although Europe is still an area with a high density of economic exchange, it is quite obvious that an Atlantic and—even more pronounced—a Pacific region are about to emerge (Plümper 1997), neither of which is supported by a political organization.

When it comes to links between the organization of politics and the emergence of a regional political community, the evidence is not clear-cut either. The EU (or, to be more precise, the EC) is an established political system. Whether it is also an emergent political community is still in question. There is a shared understanding all over Europe that joining forces to solve common problems is of mutual advantage, and only a small number of people question whether Europe should be the relevant space to unite. Nevertheless, the boundaries of this political community are blurred. Identification with Europe stretches beyond the limits of the EU, and within the EU itself, varying patterns coexist. With respect to those attitudes on which political communities are founded, overlapping patterns exist and dividing lines cut across the EU. This holds true for both mutual trust (Niedermayer 1995) and matching societal norms (Hofstede 1996).

It is only as a political system that the EU has clear-cut boundaries. Although the Union is still open to future enlargements, its present geographical limits are unequivocal. Being a political system, the EU has ways and means of contributing to internal cohesiveness, a subject which brings us back to the importance of institutions and of intentional political design.

---

[4] A cluster analysis of trade relations among countries in Western Europe provides strong evidence that, even before the 1995 enlargement of the EU, the member countries of the EC and those of EFTA did not form separate groups. On the contrary, there were strong clusters overlapping the borderlines between both organizations, or forming strongholds within those areas, as in the case of the Benelux countries, and Spain and Portugal (Borrmann *et al.* 1995: 22).

[5] Sautter 1983, quoted in Lorenz 1991: 4.

Institution-Building: Intentional Design or Social Process?

Whether or not building political institutions will bring about a transformation of political space is, in the first place, an empirical question. It is closely linked, however, to theoretical and methodological reasoning. There are different ways of conceptualizing political institutions, and of relating particular properties of institutions to the solidity of regional political integration. The focus will be different depending on which approach is adopted, and more or less attention will be paid to IGCs.

The mainstream approach adheres to a narrow understanding of political institutions and institution-building. Given their interest in the future of political integration, political scientists have paid a good deal of attention to the output of intergovernmental negotiations. In so doing, they have followed the political discourse. Since the mid-1980s, any discussion about deepening the process of European integration has been related to the question of how best to reform the institutional set-up of the Community. Institutional reforms were also at the core of the Treaty revision at Amsterdam. Both member governments and the media attributed great importance to them, and many political scientists shared this view.

The main reason why political scientists have concentrated on intergovernmental conferences (IGCs) is epistemological rather than political. Integration theory is still dominated by an international relations approach. Explaining the *relance européenne* has revived the debate about the nature of community-building, and the consequences for the autonomy of the state in Europe. In the United States especially, it is still a debate between 'intergovernmentalists' and 'neo-functionalists'. Both camps have concentrated all their energies on the three-way argument as to whether integration has challenged the autonomy of the state, weakened its authoritative control over national citizens, and established a supranational authority acting in its own right (Sandholtz and Zysman 1989; Burley and Mattli 1993; Wincott 1995a), or whether the member states continue to control the integration process and dominate EU policies (Moravcsik 1991a, 1993, 1994, 1995; Milward 1992; Garrett and Lange 1995).

Because of this very particular focus,[6] both sides have looked at institution-building as the deliberate choice of a selected group of actors, be it governments acting alone or Community agents supported by influential economic actors who are jointly pressurizing reluctant governments to go along with them. This approach is based on a narrow understanding of political institutions, which views them as merely fulfilling the task of formal organization. Institution-building, then, is about appointing political agents, attributing

---

[6] Different views are taken by Marks *et al.* (1995), who argue that the state-centric view should be replaced by a multi-level governance approach, and by Caporaso (1996), who uses Cox's concept of 'forms of state'.

power and responsibilities to those agents, and establishing rules and procedures for the taking of authoritative decisions.

I suggest that a different view of institutions and institution-building should be taken.[7] Viewing the issue more broadly, institutions may be seen as a set of governing principles, rules, and practices that are accepted as legitimate, and are incorporated into daily routines. Seen in this light, institution-building is not merely a matter of intentional design and constitutional agreements, but rather a social process which will come about by decentralized action. Treaty agreements on the transfer of competences to Union bodies and on decision-making procedures and rules concerning policy implementation are only part of the picture. The EU, like any political system, is shaped by practices and concepts of governing which may be quite deviant from the formal organization of politics written into the Treaties. The principles, norms, and rules of co-operation around which actors' perceptions converge are of the utmost importance for the life of a political institution. Therefore, I would argue that a sociological understanding of institutions is a better approach for assessing the development of a political region. To put it in a nutshell: whether or not a sturdy political system evolves will depend on the informal parts of institutions, that is, the emergence of shared concepts, the reorientation of actors towards a new framework of action, and the incorporation of common norms and rules into their daily practice.

This kind of institution cannot be set up by an IGC. A compatible view of institution-building is to view it as a social process of institutionalization. This raises questions of origin, maintenance, and change of institutions, which may be answered in quite different ways. One views the emergence of institutions as the coming about of a 'spontaneous order' (Hayek 1967). I agree with this line of argument to the extent that it starts from the assumption that institutions are the intended and unintended consequence of individual decentralized action, and a process of social selection. However, I reject the assumption that the selection process follows the logic of the market, and may best be explained by a transaction cost approach.[8] I prefer to follow North (1995: 23), who has pointed out that political markets are prone to inefficiency, and that the selection process does not function in the way conceptualized by rational choice models.

I suggest we look at those processes that make institutions socially accepted,

---

[7] For a more elaborate presentation of this concept, see Kohler-Koch (1998a), which summarizes the theoretical framework of a comparative research project on the role of regions in European governance.

[8] The essence of the argument is that institutions are about ordering the exchanges of individual actors in an efficient way, and minimizing transaction costs. In order for the private orderings to become institutionalized, there must be some means of generalizing them. 'Here, the competitive pressure of the market comes into play, selecting those orderings that are best at minimizing costs' (Knight and Sened 1995: 4).

and that contribute to the social construction of what constitutes an 'exemplary' and 'appropriate' political order. This is the process by which particular principles and norms of action and the ensuing criteria of rational behaviour (Lepsius 1995) become embedded in institutions. This kind of institution-building is contingent on existing institutions, be they at international or national level. European integration may be cited as an illustration of this type of institution-building. Guiding concepts (*Leitbilder*) and matching rationality criteria have had a considerable impact on the construction of European institutions (Schneider 1977, 1986). From the outset, the founding members were determined to build a Community 'with limited authority, but real powers' (Robert Schuman), and to establish a 'working peace system' (David Mitrany) based on economic and social welfare, which would be brought about by a common market. Integration was to take place by opening up markets and ensuring the free movement of goods, services, capital, and labour. Because guiding principles and the rationale of appropriate behaviour are 'context-specific', a changing context will put their validity into question. Therefore, with the completion of the customs union and later, with the expansion of the integration objective from a common market to economic and monetary union (EMU) and the CFSP, the guiding principles and criteria of rational behaviour shifted, and these shifts became part of the living constitution before they were codified in treaty revisions.

Given the imminent developments in the EU, it is important to assess the sort of social interaction which contributes to institution-building from below. The question most central to such an investigation is whether the EU has become a boundary-spanning organization of politics, populated by numerous actors incorporating common principles into their own daily practice. Taking a bottom-up view will reveal the social development of institutions, and will help us to understand '. . . patterns unfolding over time' (Skocpol 1992: 58).

Empirical Evidence to Consider

This chapter can only give some examples of the kind of research needed to find out more about the social construction of a political space which stretches beyond the nation state. Scattered evidence is presented which will shed some light on the different dimensions of Europe as a political region. The first two subsections deal with the EU as a perceived political community. Public opinion surveys give some clue as to how the general public evaluate regional integration over time, and what political unit they feel they belong to.[9] The survey

[9] Apart from the publication edited by Niedermayer and Sinnott in 1995, which was part of the European Science Foundation Project 'Beliefs in Government' (Kaase and Newton 1995), I will refer to a Ph.D. project under my supervision, which is also based on the Eurobarometer databank installed at Mannheim University (Schmidberger 1997).

data will be disaggregated, so that the relevance of the subnational, national, and European spaces may be studied. The underlying hypothesis is that European integration will expand the political space beyond the nation state, while at the same time raising new borders within or across national systems. Will perceptions of relevant and accepted political communities change in response to the way in which a social space is affected by the EU?

The final two subsections deal with transnational institution-building and the transformation of the multi-level system of authoritative decision-making into an interpenetrated system of interest intermediation. Emphasis will be placed on shared concepts which make the EU appear to be the appropriate unit of policy-making, and which favour the redefinition of political boundaries.[10] In addition to attitudes, patterns of interaction will be scrutinized. Different kinds of interest groups have built a dense web of boundary-spanning policy communities and established a European-wide system of interest representation.[11] The boundaries of these networks and the territorial reach of intermediary organizations in general need to be delineated empirically.

Identity and Support for Europe

A long series of public opinion surveys, published as the Eurobarometer, has produced a wealth of data on public opinion over the years. These surveys demonstrate how the general public has assessed European integration over time, and what unit they feel they belong to.[12] Although the long-forgotten debate over what brings about and sustains political community beyond the nation state has been revisited in recent years, neither its theoretical underpinnings[13] nor our empirical knowledge has improved markedly.[14]

If we discard the assumption that 'tangible homogeneity' in terms of common language, culture, and history is the necessary prerequisite for a democratic community,[15] then empirical attitudes reflecting overlapping identities and loyalties will be decisive. The suggestion is that: (a) the boundaries of the political community may stretch beyond the nation state when people share

[10] The data are taken from a survey covering subnational entities in five EU member states, which was part of an international research project on 'Regions as Political Actors in European Integration' (REGE) (Kohler-Koch 1998b).

[11] The data used are from an ongoing Mannheim research project on European interest intermediation (Kohler-Koch 1998c).

[12] The wording has changed over time; the public was first asked about which geographical unit it belonged to, later if the correspondent thought of him or herself more as a member of a particular nation or as a European. For an in-depth analysis of the data, see Niedermayer and Sinnott (1995).

[13] Deutsch (1966) is still the main reference work on this point.

[14] For a recent controversy, see Howe (1995) and Obradovic (1996).

[15] This was the argument of the German Constitutional Court in its ruling on the Maastricht Treaty. See Winkelmann (1994).

the belief that others are part of the same community and can be trusted; and that (b) people will support a polity which—for different reasons—they consider to be 'a good thing' and which they identify as an entity to which they belong.[16]

For the general public, a 'united' Europe as well as membership of the EC/EU is 'a good thing'. At the aggregate level, attitudes are durable despite oscillations over time. This makes it plausible to argue that public opinion is shaped not so much by experience as by general attitudes and expectations. In the original six member states, the attitude of the public was very positive; the same holds true for the southern countries which joined in the 1980s. The first northern enlargement in the early 1970s admitted two countries (Britain and Denmark) where the public continued to be rather sceptical about the benefits of unification for more than a decade. 'Societal learning' obviously does not function according to the simple equation that the length of exposure to regional integration will determine the level of support. Even tangible benefits like net per capita payments from EC funds do not necessarily produce a positive response. There is no unequivocally positive correlation between funds received and a feeling of having benefited from the EC/EU or with the assessment of membership as being 'a good thing' (Bosch and Newton 1995: 81). (See Fig. 5.1.)

When it comes to the feeling of 'belonging', of being 'a European citizen' or 'a European', the empirical findings do not support the often quoted hypothesis (Duchesne and Frognier 1995: 201) that the sense of European identity depends on the length of EC membership. What may be even more surprising is that there is no direct relationship between national pride and European identity (Duchesne and Frognier: 202). A sense of belonging, evidently, may embrace several political units, and the development of an attachment to Europe will not weaken a national identity. Apart from obvious variations between countries, there is a striking difference between the North and the South in Europe. A sense of belonging is strongest and most lasting in Greece, Spain, France, Italy, and Portugal. When, however, people are asked how much they trust people from other countries, those who consider themselves more European than others do not rate highly. The people most trusted by the average respondent are those from the smaller countries in the centre of Europe. Among the least trusted are the Italians, the Portuguese, and the

---

[16] I will not go into the debate about whether the attitudes measured in the Eurobarometer surveys merely indicate a 'permissive consensus' (Lindberg 1970), or whether they can be interpreted as political 'support' (Niedermayer and Westle 1995). Niedermayer (1995) aggregated four questions relating to 'unifying Europe', 'membership', and 'scrapping' the EC being a 'good/bad' thing into one indicator for 'diffuse support'. A question relating to the 'benefit' of being a member of the EC was taken as an indicator of 'specific support'. Schmidberger (1997) suggests three dimensions of European 'orientation', namely 'instrumental', 'reflective', and 'affective'.

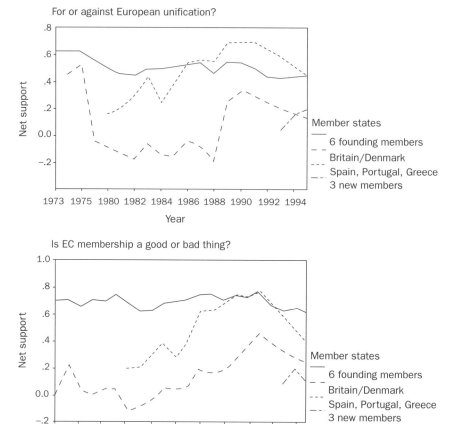

Fig. 5.1. Overall support for European integration (1973–94). This ranges from very much in favour (+1) to very much against (−1). In 1992 the wording of the question changed (indicated by the dash and dot line), and focused on the benefits of membership.

Source: Schmidberger (1996).

Greeks, but also the British (Niedermayer 1995; Hofrichter and Niedermayer 1991). Nevertheless, trust is slowly increasing all over Europe, and being a member of the EU makes a difference in the extent to which countries are trusted.

When looking for trends, it is difficult to find general patterns of all-embracing 'evolutionary tendencies'. There is striking evidence that support for 'unifying Europe' or considering EU membership an advantage does not require any initial experience. 'Learning processes' may strengthen but can also weaken this support, and very little is known about the reasons why this should be so. There are ups and downs which can be related to strong political initiatives like the *relance européenne* in the mid-1980s. Rising expectations related to the Single Market project were followed by a more sober level of public support.

Nevertheless, in most EU countries there is still a good deal of positive or at least permissive support for 'Europe'. On deeper analysis, however, it is clear that a large gap exists between the general public and top decision-makers. Support for European integration has always been stronger among the well-educated and higher income groups. What is striking is the high level of support for EU membership among top decision-makers (Commission 1996c). An overwhelming majority responded in the affirmative to a question in a Eurobarometer survey in 1996 as to whether membership of the EU was a 'good' or a 'bad' thing (EU average 94 per cent). The support ranged from 91 per cent of the media group to 96 per cent among civil servants (Commission 1996a: 4). Top decision-makers also broadly agreed that their country benefited from EU membership. Both responses were in sharp contrast to attitudes held at the same time by the general public, only 48 per cent of which felt that the EU was a 'good' thing, and only 45 per cent of which considered that their country had benefited from EU membership, compared to 91 per cent among top decision-makers.[17] In addition, functional elites in the EU member states strongly supported such core policies as the introduction of a single European currency, a majority being 'very much' in favour compared to only 20 per cent of the general public.[18]

It is not only the level of support that differentiates top decision-makers from the ordinary European citizen. The most striking difference is the range of response between countries. Compared to the general public, there is a strong convergence of elitist attitudes. General support among elites ranges from 98 per cent in Germany to 84 per cent in Sweden. This is a small variation (14 percentage points) when compared to a variation of 48 percentage points in the assessment of the general public.[19]

We still lack systematic data, but there is sufficient evidence to show that the

[17] In the general Eurobarometer survey, 34% responded that their country did not benefit, and 21% were unable or unwilling to give an opinion, which again is in sharp contrast to top decision-makers, among whom only 8% claimed no benefit (Commission 1996a).

[18] In 1996, 51% of top decision-makers said that they were 'very much for' the introduction of a single currency, 34% 'somewhat for', 7% 'somewhat against', and 6% 'very much against'. Comparable figures for the general public were: 20% 'very much for', 33% 'somewhat for', 15% 'somewhat against', and 18% 'very much against' (Commission 1996a: 10).

[19] The highest score for EU membership being 'a good thing' was 75% in Ireland, Italy, and the Netherlands, and the lowest scores were recorded in Austria (27%) and Sweden (29%) (Commission 1996a: 4).

gap is widening, and a two-tier Community is emerging: the EU is a political space for a 'Europeanized' elite, but this is not an attractive option for the ordinary citizen. Elections to the European Parliament (EP) provide a good case study in this regard. The political parties' election campaigns are supported by increased public relations activities by both the EP and the European Commission, which jointly manage to raise public awareness at election time. However, the effects in terms of increased knowledge, let alone public support, are limited. There is no mass mobilization, and more importantly, the small increase in public awareness is neither permanent nor cumulative (Wessels 1995). To claim that the elite has neglected its teaching function is not the point. The low turnout in the European Parliamentary elections of 1999 proved once again that there is little evidence of a steady growth of a strong sense of European political community.

'De-nationalization' and an Emerging Europe of the Regions?

Given that there is so little evidence for system-building beyond the nation state, how can the alleged process of 'de-nationalization' be explained (Zürn 1995). The assertion is that there is a dialectic process of supranational integration and subnational disintegration. Regionalist movements, it is claimed, have not lost but have rather gained political attention and support in the process of European integration (Lange 1998). A large amount of literature has been produced in recent years claiming that a 'Europe of the regions' is about to develop.[20] It seems plausible to argue that people's attitudes are shaped by their regional environment. The economic, social, and political context they live in is affected in a very particular way by being a member of the European Community. Rural areas and regions with declining industries generally find it harder to meet the competitive challenge of the single market. Economically deprived regions in the European periphery have similar problems, but they benefit from a large amount of financial aid from EC funds. The transfer of resources is a tangible benefit of Community membership, but for those living in a border region at the centre of Europe, the economic benefits may be less tangible. The Community's 'Interreg' Programmes provide only a small amount of money when compared to the capital flows going to the least developed regions. Nevertheless, the historical experience of border regions with national borders distorting economic exchanges and dividing historic neighbourhoods makes them more receptive to the intangible benefits of supranational integration. Are these different settings mirrored in public attitudes?

When conceptualizing orientation towards Europe in three different dimensions, we should be able to trace the above situations in public

---

[20] At Mannheim, we have several hundred entries on this topic in our data bank.

attitudes.[21] Starting from the assumption that we have a rather well-informed and rationally calculating public, any transfer of Community resources that is likely to increase the economic welfare of a region should have a positive impact on the 'instrumental orientation' of its citizens. A European orientation may be called 'reflective' (Schmidberger 1997: 64–5) when the attitude is not shaped by calculable benefits, but rather by a general assessment that, in an era of international interdependence, it makes more sense to aim at effective problem-solving through international cooperation. In this case, supporting European integration is not a matter of the amount of money received; it arises rather from the conviction that the EU is the appropriate level to deal with problems which are no longer confined within national borders. It is a generalized form of support compared to 'instrumental orientation'. It is, however, still based on some rational reasoning about what is appropriate and beneficial. 'Identitive support' is a different matter; it implies 'affective orientation' (Schmidberger 1997: 65–6). A readiness to identify oneself with 'Europe', to develop a European allegiance parallel to a national, regional, or local one may be sustained by experience and insight. The long shadow of the past (i.e. Europe's history, which is a tale of wars and cut-throat competition), and the shadow of the future (i.e. trends towards globalization that cannot easily be controlled by small nations), make turning to Europe a plausible option. Nevertheless, identitive support has a strong emotional component and is a diffuse rather than a rationally calculated orientation.

Political support is based on these three orientations. The term 'de-nationalization' could usefully be applied to a situation where the different kinds of support vary across regions in Europe. The citizens of depressed regions which gain only small amounts of transfer payments would have little cause to develop a positive instrumental orientation towards the EU. Border regions at the centre of the EU, supported by Community programmes to develop transnational ties, might adopt a more positive attitude, based on a reflective approach. National capitals, on the other hand, situated in a wealthy regional environment, would be unlikely to have a positive pro-European orientation.

A systematic testing of these hypotheses shows, first of all, that there are hardly any traces of 'de-nationalization' in Europe today. Variations between different types of regions within nations are small, compared to variations between nation states. (See Fig. 5.2.)

Quite obviously, 'de-nationalization' has not happened. The individual properties of the regional environment and the way in which they are affected by European integration have only a limited impact on public attitudes. Membership of a national community makes all the difference. When trying to explain variations in attitude, the most important factor is nationality. The subnational environment is not negligible, but it is a minor factor, with

[21] See Schmidberger 1997: 63–70; 96–8.

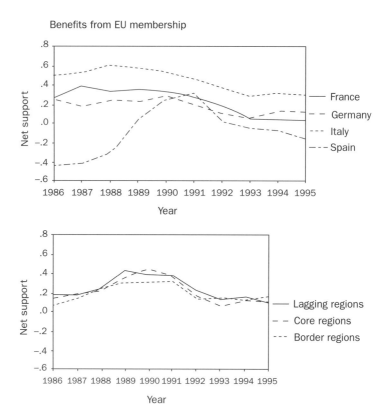

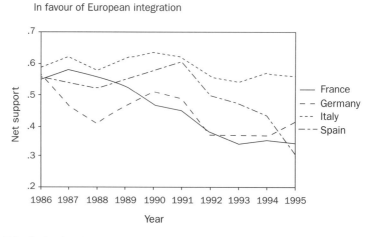

Fig. 5.2. National and regional variations in support of European integration (1986–95).
Source: Schmidberger (1997: 112, 113, 135, 158).

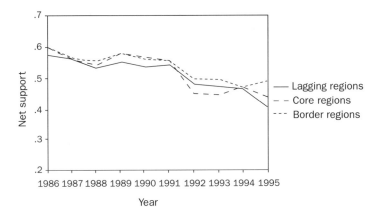

European identity

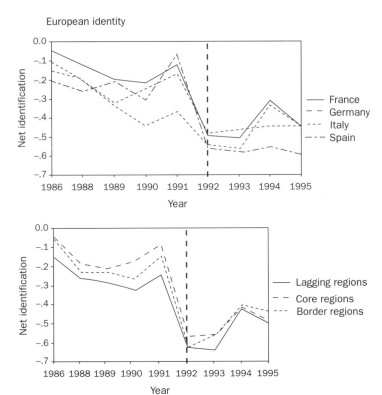

Fig. 5.2. (cont.)

one exception: people in border regions are more inclined to claim superiority for supranational policy-making. The high esteem in which they hold European integration is, however, well in line with a concurrent strong loyalty to the nation state. And although there is a more pronounced 'reflective orientation' towards Europe, it is not supported by a strong degree of 'identitive support'. This is no higher in border regions than in any other type of region in Europe.

Shared Concepts about Managing the European Region

From the data already presented, it is clear that there is widespread support among the European elite for transnational co-operation. The EU is considered to be the appropriate level of policy-making for an increasing number of policy issues. A necessary, but not sufficient, condition for accepting the EU as the relevant 'political space' would be to assess core policies as a matter of common concern. A readiness to transfer decision-making competence to the Union must be supported by a firm belief that political action is taken on the basis of a 'logic of appropriateness' (March and Olsen 1994: 5). This logic is incorporated in the EU's institutions, and reproduced and transformed in the interactions which accompany European policy-making. It embraces 'leading concepts' which give direction to European politics. Conceptual orientation has always been highly relevant in the supranational context, because joint decisions are not legitimized by a government supported by a democratic vote and equipped with powers of enforcement. European politics is an ongoing negotiation marathon among autonomous actors. Concurrent views on what European co-operation is basically about will help to balance difficult trade-offs between heterogeneous interests.

From the very beginning, the European Communities were based on a particular 'logic of integration'. The treaties gave rise to an action programme committing the contracting parties to specific objectives, to principles, norms, and rules of proper conduct and adequate procedures. In particular, representatives of Community organs feel dedicated to *'une certaine idée de l'Europe'* (Pescatore 1983). This, however, is not a diligently worked-out master plan of action, an all-encompassing and coherent philosophy, but rather a 'floating signifier', changing over time and according to context. It is a process of conceptual 'framing' with many participants. The European Commission, as the privileged agenda-setter in Community affairs, plays an important role in this regard. Increasingly, the EP too calls the tune. Although individual actors may initiate ideas, shared concepts only emerge when actors' expectations converge. Dense patterns of communication and regular interaction are not sufficient to give precedence to a particular concept and turn it into a point of general reference. If it is to succeed, it has to be in line with established and accepted 'regimes', that is, with principles, norms and rules around which actors' expectations converge (Krasner 1983). Concepts are not disseminated as abstract ideas, but are embedded in substantial policies. Involvement in Community programmes, therefore, entails being exposed to particular rules of the game and ideological packaging.

The questions of whether functional elites across national borders share concepts which call the appropriateness of these very borders into question, and whether direct involvement in Community activities will make them more acceptable, are empirical ones. The data on which I base my argument are taken from an elite survey,[22] testing the concurrent evolution of a new policy space at both supranational and subnational level. A 'Europe of the regions' has been forcefully promulgated both by the EP and by the Assembly of European Regions. The guiding principles attached to the concept are 'market orientation', 'subsidiarity', and 'partnership'. The concept slowly emerged in the second half of the 1980s, and gained its full momentum with the reforms of the EC's regional policy and structural funds in 1988 and 1993. From the outset, it carried connotations of economic and political modernization: The key notions in the debate were those of mobilizing indigenous resources by local strategies of flexible production, strengthening political autonomy through economic competitiveness, and bringing politics closer to the people. The different elements of that conceptual compound have been analysed individually as follows:

(1) the role (elite) actors attribute to regions in European affairs;
(2) the preferred economic strategy; and
(3) ideas about effective and legitimate governance.

At first sight, the data provide striking evidence that there is a dominant, European-wide concept: first, regions are and should be a relevant political space; second, market orientation should be predominant in the European political space; third, polities will be best governed by strategies of partnership and co-operative governance.

The survey and personal interviews gave clear evidence of a surprisingly high degree of support for strengthening the regions in European affairs. Variations are rather territorial (i.e. between nations rather than between types of actors). The overall high level of support is surprising because, at the time of the survey, popular regionalism was not at its peak. Institutional self-interest does not have explanatory force either, as there is little variation between the

---

[22] The survey 'Regions as Political Actors in European Integration' (REGE) covered different actor categories (business, trade unions, industrial and professional associations, politics, administration and science) from relevant organizations at regional level. In each of the five big member states, an economically less developed and a more affluent region was selected; the data set is based on 1250 questionnaires returned.

attitudes of public and private actors.[23] These findings do not, however, imply a trend towards a 'Europe of the regions'; rather a 'Europe with regions' can be said to be emerging. The notion of 'strengthening the regions' receives a high degree of support, particularly in those countries where political power is concentrated at national level. These, however, are the very same countries that attribute high importance to any kind of state agency, be it at regional, national or European level. It is a distinct 'Southern' pattern (embracing Spain, Italy, and France), and there is no evidence that the upgrading of the regions would be to the detriment of the state. In other words, despite being strongly in favour of strengthening a subnational political space, there is no push for a 'Europe of regions' which would resemble the oft-cited 'sandwich model' (i.e. the nation state squeezed between strong regions and an even stronger EU).

The picture becomes even more differentiated when analysing what it is that respondents associate with the concept of European regionalism. There is a clear North–South divide as regards what regionalism is about, and the kind of strategy for regional development to be pursued. In the South, a 'Europe of the regions' is equated with preserving more cultural pluralism, and paying closer attention to the needs and desires of citizens. In the North, respondents expect that it will strengthen areas which are already competitive, and counterbalance centralizing tendencies.

A similar North–South cleavage is evident when evaluating the governing principles of the European polity. There is broad agreement that it makes sense to adhere to market regulation. The concept of regional competitiveness is strongly supported in different parts of the Union,[24] although respondents in the South are afraid that EC rules regulating competition may produce harmful effects on their own region. In general, 'Northerners' were more in favour of strengthening market forces, whereas in the South more emphasis was put on social cohesion and sustainable growth. Most pronounced was the strong backing for measures aimed at 'safeguarding trade', the euphemistic formula used for protectionist measures.[25]

Extending the relevant unit of policy-making to the subnational and supranational levels results in changed attitudes regarding appropriate modes of governing. According to our data, the concept of 'co-operative government' has gained ground all over Europe. A close public–private partnership is considered to be best suited to effective problem-solving (85 per cent). Good governance is no longer equated with authoritative decisions taken at the top of the hierarchy; rather, state agencies should take the role of intermediaries, being in close

---

[23] On average in Europe, 75% of private and 79% of public actors are in favour of strengthening the regions in European affairs.

[24] Overall, 85% of respondents were in favour of regional competitiveness.

[25] The questions were phrased according to the terminology used by the Commission in its White Paper on Growth, Competition and Employment (Commission 1993*b*).

contact with economic and social actors (75 per cent). There are hardly any discernible differences according to actor categories or nationality. The widely promulgated and shared philosophy of public–private co-operation in joint problem-solving and of a new mode of 'discursive government' is reflected in daily practice in the way that many consultative bodies, steering committees, and other types of regional networks have been established.

The Transnational Organization of Politics

Designing a new conceptual space for politics and incorporating new understandings about guiding principles is one aspect of institution-building; the other concerns organizing the processes of politics and establishing networks of interaction. To whom do people turn with their demands? What networks are established for coalitions of influence or joint problem-solving? What is the reach of intermediary organization? From our empirical research on interest intermediation, it is clear that the organization of politics has been restructured, although it does not pass the threshold of constitutional change. In many policy areas, the Union is now definitely the relevant unit of the policy process. Its most characteristic features are: boundary-spanning networks, transnational advocacy, coalitions and penetrated systems of governance.

Nowadays, Brussels is a crowded arena, with a multitude of transnational actors. The number and scope of European federations of interest associations has increased steadily as integration has deepened. The launching of the single market programme promoted a further expansion of Euro-level interest organizations, and drew additional actors into the game.[26] The sheer number of actors eager to serve as transmission belts between all kinds of different 'local' interests and Community bodies is impressive. To attempt to assess their importance merely by counting numbers would be misleading. First of all, their numbers and resources must be compared to the size of the interest group sector at national level. Such a comparison makes European-level interest groups look like a *quantité négligeable*. Second, it makes little sense to compare individual interest groups without examining the type of interest representation in which they are involved. Numbers may count in a pluralistic system of competitive lobbying, but in a neo-corporatist system of institutionalized interest intermediation, influence can best be exerted when only a few actors participate. Add to this the fact that presence cannot be equated with access, and that access does not imply influence, and it is clear that little insight is to be gained by merely describing interest groups and their activities at the European level.

[26] The Commission's directory lists more than 600 organizations, but this gives only a partial picture, because only Euro-level federations are included. The number of interest groups, 'public affairs' consultants, and liaison offices maintained by public actors and private companies in Brussels is estimated at several thousands.

Analysing transnational networking in a comparative perspective will give a more accurate account of the importance of the European political space. We asked representatives of different types of organizations to tell us:

(1) what regular contacts they have with other organizations at regional, national, and European level;
(2) the importance they attributed to those organizations; and
(3) their experience with their contacts (i.e. whether the organizations they had addressed proved to be helpful or not).

Notwithstanding national and regional variations, the data gave rise to a rather uniform picture: the nation state is still the most important political arena. With regard to European affairs, however, national governments and interest associations are neither the gatekeepers nor the transmission belts for transnational interest representation. All the actors questioned have established close direct links at European level. Among the European organizations, the European Commission ranked highest in terms of contact and importance.[27] Above all, the Commission proved to be most helpful when actors wanted to have their interests heard. It is noteworthy, too, that regional public actors are an important, and often even the main, transmission belt for 'local' interests onto the European level. The active participation of subnational actors in EC affairs does not, however, imply any crowding-out of national actors or sectoral interest organizations. There is no zero sum game, either between levels of government, or between private and public actors. Here again, the evidence is quite clear. It is not a 'Europe of the regions' which is developing, but a 'Europe with regions'. Regional actors look for support from other regional actors; no region is turning into a unitary actor. Regional governments do not speak on behalf of a particular interest group within the region; they merely provide some additional support.

Further proof that the EU has developed into a distinct political space lies in the existence of transnational advocacy coalitions. The EU is by no means a 'layer cake' system, such as might be associated with the multi-level governance model. Detailed case studies reveal an intricate web of transnational relations between interested parties.[28] Advocacy coalitions are organized around policy issues in networks which loosely couple actors in three dimensions, namely transnational, horizontal, and vertical. They evolve around core groups living in close and durable contact with representatives from both the Commission and the EP. Euro-level associations often take the lead, but only a few

---

[27] In a large number of cases, regional liaison offices also ranked highly. The EP, the member states' permanent representations, chambers of industry and commerce, interest associations, and consultants received low scores (Kohler-Koch 1998d).

[28] Evidence is taken from an ongoing research project: 'Pressures on the European Parliament/PEP' (Kohler-Koch 1998c).

of them have the capacity to act on their own behalf. They are not unitary actors; rather, they play the role of a forum for their members. In many cases, they are even used by a minority of actors who may command superior resources, such as the big players in business associations (Green Cowles 1994), or for whom the stakes are high; making them eager to push a point which is less relevant for other members. Examples of such interventions are those in favour of animal welfare and consumer protection, on which the British member organizations are usually the driving force. Their activities are backed up by an attentive public, supported by dedicated activists, experience, and superior resources.

Advocacy coalitions focus mostly on narrow policy issues. Compared to the nation state, the EU is not yet the relevant political space in which to fight for fundamental issues of *Ordnungspolitik* (i.e. basic philosophical orientations to be written into the Treaties). Amsterdam was the first IGC which gave rise to a public debate on the nature of the enterprise. Mazey and Richardson (1996) have identified three broad coalitions within this public debate: business interests rallying behind 'competitiveness' and 'efficient decision-making'; the environmental lobby, as the most prominent rival advocacy coalition advocating 'greening the Treaty'; and, in a weaker position, the European trade unions demanding a genuine Social Union. Coalitions include national governments (or rather individual ministries of member state governments), individual directorates in the Commission, and EP intergroups.[29] The weakness of the trade unions demonstrates that all actors do not have equal opportunities to press their point. Success depends not only on lobbying skills and resources, but also on the compatibility of the organization's philosophy with the dominant rationale of European integration (Kohler-Koch 1997). After all, the integration process is not 'innocent' (Caporaso 1996: 7).

A good illustration that, in some policy fields at least, member states have become merged into one political space, is the increase in transnational activities on a horizontal level. Transnational interest groups join forces to put pressure not just on the European Commission and the European Parliament, but also on individual national governments.[30] Furthermore, they become engaged in private interest governance, ranging from codes of conduct like the one agreed upon by European public affairs agencies, to the regulation of business practices promoted by sectoral associations like the chemical industry. Interest intermediation is no longer a multi-level game; it now views the EU as a single stage for action.

The European Commission has been very active in recent years in

---

[29] Intergroups comprise Members of the European Parliament (MEPs) and representatives of interest groups; they play an important role in soliciting support from members of different party groups in favour of a particular issue.

[30] The most prominent case is the pharmaceutical industry.

'networking'. With little money and skillfully designed 'action programmes', it has managed to breed new boundary-spanning networks. European subsidies for economic restructuring or for research and technology are often linked to transborder co-operation. The Commission encourages the creation of transnational self-regulating organizations among recipients, providing them with resources, granting them privileged access to information and consultation, or even entitling them to be the only legitimate interlocutor in a particular policy area.

Particularly in those domains where Community competences are still weak, as in culture, education, or welfare and health care, the Commission has established consultative committees, and financed and organized the creation of transnational networks. It has helped to produce clientelistic pressure groups which have then demanded an additional transfer of competences and resources to the Community. Often, those newly built transnational networks are in competition with established national organizations. Whether they will have to live in the shadow of national institutions, or will become dominant policy communities in their own right, is a matter of organizational strength and conceptual framing. As long as national organizations are not confronted with supranational policies that directly affect their interests, they will experience difficulties in getting organized beyond the nation state. The lead may even be taken by weak transnational networks, less rooted in the domestic environment, but well-adapted to international relations and oriented towards Community-level concepts.

The different agencies set up or supported by the Community constitute a more solid cornerstone of such a penetrated system. The Europe-wide committees for standardization—CEN (the European Committee for Standardization) and CENELEC (the European Committee for Electrotechnical Standardization)—are the best known, though not the only, self-regulating institutions. There is strong support for a 'fourth branch' of Europe-wide governance. The newly established agency for pharmaceuticals is definitely a part of this move, and a similar agency has been proposed for dealing with the certification of medical devices (Altenstetter 1996).

These regulatory agencies are a complement to the unique structure of the EC. Their most outstanding characteristic, when compared to other international bodies, is that they are governed by supranational law. The supremacy of EC law and the active, pro-integrationist rulings of the European Court of Justice (ECJ) is one part of this; the other is that national courts are part of a decentralized system of enforcement of EC law, which is independent of any governmental interference. The EC is a community of law, both in terms of being governed by legal agreements, and in terms of the independent third branch of government enacting legal control and ensuring the compliance of actor behaviour. The robustness of Community integration, therefore, depends on the incorporation of the principle of the supremacy of European law and of the ensuing norms, rules, and procedures into the daily practice of national courts. At what point practices and expectations will converge is heavily influenced by the legal discourse in which the courts are embedded.

Conclusions

The message of this chapter is that the future of regional political integration will not be decided by intergovernmental conferences. It is a social process, which can best be analysed by taking a bottom-up approach. We must look at societal interests that work in favour of strengthening a European political space. Business interests support economic integration, but are hardly ever in favour of a stronger state. Trade unions, consumer, and environmental groups call for more regulatory powers, and strong rather than weak Community institutions are in their interest. The evolution of a political space, however, is not so much the result of intentional design, as of social actors pursuing partisan interests, and accepting the upgrading of European institutions whenever the substantial policy outcome is to their liking. There will be a general propensity to support political integration when governing principles and norms, which are considered to be appropriate, prevail in the new political space. By taking part in the common policy process, all kinds of actors help to shape the living constitution of the Union. This may make it easier to reconcile with national and subnational political systems, and might even contribute to some kind of convergence. Above all, it will produce a high degree of familiarity, and will make it easier for actors to move freely in the new political space.

From the limited empirical evidence available, we can conclude that there are widely shared belief systems spanning national boundaries. Policy networks have been extended to include both the supranational and the transnational dimensions. Transnational advocacy coalitions have evolved which derive their strength and importance from the organizational infrastructure of the European polity, and they gain stability from the general belief that the EU is a relevant and legitimate policy-making unit.

The EU has turned into a political region, in the strict sense of our definition of a political region as a privileged arena for the organization of politics and shared concepts of governance. Nevertheless, the organization of politics and the particular profile of belief systems manifestly have strong national characteristics. It is clear that the EU is not about to become a substitute for nation states, but it is and will remain a 'Europe with states'. In internal as well as in international affairs it is a corporate actor, in terms both of being able to unite in common action, and of being a Community of law. It is a collective actor, in terms of being an institutionalized negotiating system which helps autonomous actors to decide jointly and to pursue their interests, interests which may be parallel to, or in competition with, those of the Union. It is a penetrated system of governance, because the dense web of boundary-spanning policy networks gives access to decision-making in each of the political spaces. With the support of these transnational networks, interested parties exert influence at all the different levels of policy-making. It is not only Brussels which is subject to a Europeanized system of interest inter-mediation; the national systems, too, have become part of a Europeanized political space.

PART II

Prospects for Democracy

6

Executive Selection in the European Union: Does the Commission President Investiture Procedure Reduce the Democratic Deficit?

SIMON HIX

The holders of political power in the European Union (EU) institutions must be made more accountable. This issue was forced onto the European agenda in the wake of the Maastricht Treaty, following the Danish rejection of the Treaty in a referendum, the narrow votes on the treaty in both the French referendum and the British parliament, and the German Constitutional Court ruling that the EU cannot be integrated further unless the institutions are made more democratic (Weiler *et al.* 1995*b*). The so-called 'permissive consensus', where Europe's leaders can build a European polity without requiring *a priori* consent from their voters, no longer exists. The EU heads of government consequently declared that a central goal of the intergovernmental conference (IGC) preparing the reform of the Maastricht Treaty, which produced the Draft Amsterdam Treaty, was to make 'the institutions more democratic' (European Council 1996*a*: 2).

The challenge for the EU institutions, however, is that a central element of the practice of democracy in all political systems is the ability of citizens to 'throw out' the holders of executive office, through the process of competitive elections (see in particular Weber 1918; Schumpeter 1943; Schattschneider 1960; King 1981). In a parliamentary system, this operates through an 'indirect' mechanism: where the executive must command a parliamentary majority, immediately following parliamentary elections. In a presidential system, in contrast, the mechanism is 'direct': where voters make a direct choice between rival candidates (Lijphart 1992; Shugart and Carey 1992; Sartori 1994).[1]

The author would especially like to thank Brian Barry, Richard Corbett MEP, Keith Dowding, Patrick Dunleavy, Karlheinz Neunreither, Mark Pollack, and Antje Wiener for their comments on earlier drafts of this chapter.

[1] There are also several hybrid systems: e.g. where the head of the executive is directly elected, but the cabinet requires parliamentary approval (e.g. the semi-presidential or directly elected premier models); or where the executive is approved by parliament, but is not required to command a permanent majority (e.g. the Swiss collegial executive model).

But the EU has a 'dual executive' (Lenaerts 1991). On the one hand, national governments (in the Council and European Council) possess long-term executive power:

(1) they set the overall political and legislative agenda (such as who qualifies for Economic and Monetary Union—EMU);
(2) they delegate short-term executive and regulatory power to the Commission;
(3) they have the sole right of policy initiation in the intergovernmental provisions on the common foreign and security policy (CFSP) and justice and home affairs (JHA);
(4) and they maintain a monopoly over the forces of coercion (i.e. the police and the armed forces).

On the other hand, in the everyday making of EU social and economic policies, the EU Commission exercises considerable executive power:

(1) it has an influential leadership role (as in the Delors Plan for EMU);
(2) it has the sole right of legislative initiative;
(3) it is the 'guardian of the Treaties';
(4) it has powerful rule-making powers in the regulation of the EU single market (as in EU competition policy); and
(5) it is responsible for the execution and administration of legislation (in co-operation with the member states) and the budget.

In the exercise of these powers, moreover, whereas the Council is a true 'collegial executive' with a rotating presidency, the Commission is more like a national cabinet, where the Commission President is the *primus inter pares*, the 'first among equals'.

Prior to the Maastricht and Amsterdam Treaties, neither of these branches of the dual EU executive was accountable via the classic indirect or direct methods. When exercising executive power, the Council operates as a 'consociational' institution (Taylor 1991; Chryssochoou 1994): decisions are made by unanimity, which allows each member of the executive a 'mutual veto' to protect a vital interest of its constituents or its 'pillar' (Lijphart 1969). Qualified majority voting (qmv) in the Council only takes place under certain legislative procedures, and especially where legislative power is shared between the Council and the European Parliament (EP) under the cooperation and co-decision procedures. Furthermore, the Amsterdam Treaty mandated the Council to make a clearer distinction between when it is exercising legislative power and when it is exercising executive power, as a prerequisite for making the EU legislative process more transparent.[2] As a result, when acting as the EU

---

[2] Art. 207 [151] of the Amsterdam Treaty states that: 'The Council shall define the cases in which it is to be regarded as acting in its legislative capacity, with a view to allowing greater access to documents in those cases' (Council of the European Union 1997).

executive, the Council is not collectively accountable to Europe's voters, either directly, or indirectly via the EP. Nevertheless, each individual member of the Council is accountable via the national channels of executive selection (i.e. through national general elections). Therefore, as long as Council decisions are taken by unanimity when exercising executive power, every European citizen has an indirect say in the process, through the election of the national government. In other words, the legitimacy of the Council in this regard is identical to that of other collegial executives in consociational systems, where each 'societal pillar' is an equal participant in executive power, as in the fixed system of representation of the linguistic groups and *familles spirituelles* in the Swiss Federal Government.

However, the accountability of the Commission is even more problematic. Prior to the Maastricht Treaty, the Commission President was chosen unanimously by the national governments. This was more akin to choosing the head of an international organization than selecting a chief executive. As a result, the EP argued in its 1984 Draft Treaty on European Union, and in the subsequent reports to the IGCs which produced the Single European Act (SEA) and the Treaty on European Union (TEU—the Maastricht Treaty), that it should have a role in the selection process. The EP used the argument that Europe's voters are not interested in EP elections because they have no impact on the make-up of the executive. Hence, by giving the EP a say in choosing the Commission President, European elections would really start to matter (see for example Lodge 1995). Backed by a large majority of the member states and the European Commission, this proposal was introduced in the Maastricht Treaty, and reinforced in the Amsterdam Treaty. The result of these reforms is a quasi-parliamentary system (i.e. the classic 'indirect' mechanism) for selecting this second branch of the EU executive, whereby the Commission President is nominated by the member states and ratified by the EP immediately following the EP elections.

According to this reading, therefore, the Maastricht and Amsterdam Treaties *have* increased the democratic accountability of at least one part of the EU executive. But has this quasi-parliamentary model of EU executive selection really allowed Europe's voters to chose the EU executive?[3] Can European citizens expel the Commission President? Or is more fundamental institutional reform needed? These questions remain unanswered without further theoretical and empirical investigation. First, however, the operation of the new Commission President investiture procedure and academic consensus regarding its impact is discussed in more detail.

---

[3] Strictly speaking, the reforms established a particular form of parliamentary model, whereby the executive requires the support of a parliamentary majority only on investiture, but not through its whole term in office. This is therefore more similar to the Swiss collegial executive system than the classic parliamentary models which exist in most national settings in the EU.

Choosing the Commission President: Towards a Parliamentary Model?

The New Commission President Investiture Procedure

As a result of the 1991 Maastricht Treaty, Article 214 para. 2 [158] of the EC Treaty states that

> The governments of the Member States shall nominate by common accord, after consulting with the European Parliament, the person they intend to appoint as President of the Commission.

Furthermore, the rest of the article (paras. 1 and 3) specifies that the term of office of the Commission is five years, with the first Commission subject to these rules beginning its term on 6 January 1995. In other words, the terms of the Commission and the Parliament are concurrent. This enables the issue of the Commission President to be debated at the first plenary session following each set of EP elections.

When the EP drafted its new Rules of Procedure, however, the Members of the European Parliament (MEPs) deliberately took Article 214 [158] to imply that they would be entitled to take a vote by a simple majority on the governments' nominee, and that if the vote were negative the nominee would be withdrawn. This was a very specific reading, as the word 'consultation' could imply that the Parliament would simply be required to issue a statement on the nominee, which the governments could subsequently disregard. Nevertheless, the EP's interpretation of the new investiture procedure was confirmed in a written response by the then president-in-office of the EU Council, Klaus Kinkel (the German Foreign Minister), to a question by the EP President, Klaus Hänsch. In this letter, Kinkel accepted that if the EP votes against the governments' nominee, the Council will find a new candidate.

Furthermore, the Amsterdam Treaty institutionalizes the EP's 'interpretation'. On the recommendation of the Bourlanges and Martin Reports, Article 214 (para. 2) [Article 158] states that

> The governments of the Member States shall nominate by common accord the person they intend to appoint as President of the Commission; the nomination shall be approved by the European Parliament.

In effect, 'after consulting with the European Parliament' has been replaced by 'the nomination shall be approved by the European Parliament'. The Parliament's right to vote by a simple majority on who should be the Commission President is thus confirmed.

The Academic Consensus: A Major Reduction of the Democratic Deficit

The 'consensus view' among scholars of the EU is that these changes significantly reduce the EU's democratic deficit. As three of the EP's own institutional experts argue

> These changes will not in themselves make the relationship between the Community's executive and its elected parliamentary body akin to that which exists between the government and the lower chamber of a parliament in member states, but it is certainly a step in that direction. The fact that European elections will be followed by the formation of a new executive potentially adds to the significance of the elections.   (Corbett *et al.* 1995: 249)

Or, as a former Secretary-General of the Commission remarked:

> Very soon the preliminary approval of [the Commission President] by the Parliament will be the decisive factor; the final appointment by the governments will retain only a formal character.   (Noël 1992)

And, concerning the Amsterdam Treaty, two other leading EU scholars have argued

> . . .this might in the medium run change the character of the game of how the President is selected. His or her programme will be under parliamentary scrutiny. Due to this shift, the terms of the debate might be reshaped on party-political lines. This might, in turn, prompt the design and marketing of alternative ideological designs of the European agenda. (Falkner and Nentwich 1997: 4)

In other words, the academic consensus is that the new Commission President investiture procedure establishes a new source of indirect legitimacy for executive authority in the EU via the European elections and channelled through the EP. If this were in fact the case, it would eliminate a major element of the democratic deficit.

However, this reading of the new procedure rests on two rather spurious assumptions: first, that in EP elections, voters are able to choose between rival candidates for the Commission President, or at least rival platforms for European-level action; and second, that the investiture of the Commission President will be determined by a majority in the EP—which reflects an electoral majority—and not by (or at least, in addition to) the unanimity of national governments in the European Council. Before these assumptions can be accepted, however, they must be subjected to theoretical analysis and empirical testing.

Theoretical Analysis: Party Leaders, MEPs, and the Commission Presidency

The key political actors in the Commission President investiture procedure are the (national) party leaders (the main protagonists in European elections and the participants in the European Council), and the MEPs. These actors have certain political goals (e.g. re-election). However, the ability to pursue these goals is mitigated by two factors: first, the strategic behaviour of competing actors (e.g. parties in the case of national party leaders); and second, by the structure of institutional constraints, which can determine, for example, which actors are more capable of achieving their goals (Shepsle 1989). In other words, the issue for theoretical investigation is: how does the structure of European elections and the Commission President investiture procedure shape the strategic behaviour of parties and MEPs?

Party Leaders: In Pursuit of National Government Office

Most theories of party behaviour assume an interaction between two primary goals: 'political office' and 'public policy' (see for example Downs 1956; Riker 1962; Strom 1990). The structure of the EU system ensures that these goals are rewarded more at national level than at European level. The EU has an increasingly central role in setting social and environmental standards in the EU single market. However, the major areas of public policy and public expenditure, such as health, education, and housing, are still controlled by national governments. Moreover, the focus of media attention is on the holders of national executive office rather than European executive office (such as the Commission President), and national executive office-holders have a central (executive and legislative) role at European level, in the EU Council and the European Council. In other words, the key political office for party leaders in the EU is still national government, the pinnacle of which is the national Prime Minister (or President in the case of France and Finland). The office of Commission President is of secondary importance, and is only important to national party leaders if it can help or hinder their chances of (re-)capturing national governmental office.

So what does this mean for the process of selecting the Commission President?

First, in EP elections, an implication of this national party preference structure is that, regardless of whether or not the EP has a say in the selection of the Commission President, national parties will fight EP elections as a rerun of a national general election. Because national parties primarily seek national government office, the opportunity to use European elections (like regional and local elections) as a chance to vote 'for' or 'against' the party or parties which hold national executive office will be simply too great to waste. National party leaders, particularly in opposition, will use European elections as a chance to voice a protest against governing parties.

This theoretical analysis was first proposed around the time of the first direct elections to the EP, in Reif and Schmitt's (1980) famous 'second-order national election' model of EP elections. The expectation of the model is that there will be a lower turn-out in EP elections than in national ones (because they do not influence the make-up of national governments), and there will be more votes for opposition, minor, and protest parties than in the previous general election (Reif and Schmitt 1980; Reif 1984; Eijk and Franklin 1996). In addition, although the question is not addressed by Reif *et al.,* the assumption that national governmental office is more important than the Commission presidency implies that the second-order election model will still hold even if the EP has the power to choose the Commission President.

Second, in the actual Commission President investiture procedure, an implication of this national party preference structure is that national parties will be more concerned about (re-)capturing national governmental office than about the party affiliation of the Commission President. Because parties also seek public policy, and the policy agenda of the EU can constrain the choices of national governments, national parties would like to have a Commission President with a similar policy agenda—in other words, from the same political family (e.g. Socialist, Christian Democrat, Liberal, Conservative, and so on). However, because the impact on policy of the Commission President is weaker than that of national governmental office, national parties are not prepared to jeopardize their chances of winning national governmental office simply to secure a Commission President with the same policy platform.

However, given the structure of the new Commission President investiture procedure, this trade-off between office and policy goals has particular implications. As the procedure is currently designed, parties in national government (represented in the European Council) collectively choose a nominee for Commission President. These parties consequently have a 'vested interest' to ensure that this candidate is approved by the EP in the subsequent EP investiture vote. It would be embarrassing for the parties in national government if the MEPs from these parties were to vote against the European Council candidate. Opposition parties and the national media would point out that the governing party was divided, that the European policy of the party was unclear, and that the leader of the governing party was incompetent. Hence, parties in the European Council will do everything they can to ensure that their MEPs do not jeopardize their chances of holding on to their precious office goal. Meanwhile, the incentive structure for parties in opposition in the domestic arena is much weaker, since they have no *a priori* commitment to any particular candidate for the post of Commission President.

MEPs: Enforcing National Party Loyalty

The other key actors in the Commission President investiture procedure are the individual MEPs. Like other parliamentarians (and national party leaders), MEPs make trade-offs between office and policy goals: between re-election and their 'sincere' ideological position (Mayhew 1974; Cox and McCubbins 1993). All MEPs are dependent on their national parties for securing re-election. In most member states (Austria, Denmark, Finland, France, Greece, Luxembourg, Netherlands, Portugal, Spain, and Sweden), candidate lists are drawn up and controlled by the national party leaderships. In the others, MEPs are elected on regional lists (Belgium, Germany, and Italy), in multi-member constituencies (Ireland) or in single-member constituencies (Britain before 1999). However, even in these latter systems, MEPs acknowledge that the elections are party-centred rather than candidate-centred, and hence that their re-election is more dependent on national party (leaders') fortunes than their individual popularity or performance in the EP (Bowler and Farrell 1993). In other words, the MEPs' ability to secure their office goals depends on national party support for their behaviour in the EP.

However, the MEPs' ability to secure their policy goals depends on the EP party groups, which control the key committee appointments, the appointment of the President and Vice-Presidents of the EP, the choice of *rapporteurs*, and the legislative agenda of the plenary sessions (Hix and Lord 1997, ch. 5). If individual MEPs deviate from EP party group positions, their chances of securing these goals are consequently reduced. Although the EP party groups have a limited ability to suspend the group membership of an individual MEP, the prospect of promotion to an important committee position or *rapporteur*-ship can be withdrawn, and entire national delegations can be expelled by a simple majority in a party group meeting. As a result, whereas the second-order structure of EP elections facilitates EP party group fragmentation, the structure of internal EP rules and incentives facilitates the coalescence of individual MEPs and national party delegations into fewer EP party groups (Bardi 1996). Moreover, as this incentive structure has evolved, the cohesion of the EP party groups in roll-call votes has increased dramatically, as data on the 1984–9 and 1989–94 sessions demonstrates (Attinà 1990; Quanjel and Wolters 1993; Brzinski 1996; Raunio 1996).

The fundamental issue, therefore, is: what happens when the office and policy goals of individual MEPs' conflict? If national parties have no vested interest in MEPs' behaviour, MEPs can keep both their national party leaders and their EP party group leaders happy at the same time. However, when national party leaders have a vested interest in MEPs' behaviour, a trade-off must be made. For example, if a national party wants an MEP to vote in favour of a proposal, and the majority position of his or her EP party group is against the proposal, the MEP is torn: either to vote against the national party and with the EP party group, thereby risking de-selection in the next EP election; or to vote with the national party and against the EP party group, risking removal of important privileges and policy influence in the EP. Because of the structure of MEP candidate selection, however, the rational strategy in this situation is to side with the national party. The (national party) threat of de-selection far outweighs the (EP party group) threat of expulsion from the group: de-selection not only means removal of an MEP's main office goal, but also the removal of the ability to achieve policy aims through a seat in the EP, whereas expulsion from an EP party group only reduces the chances of achieving an MEP's policy goals.

There may be few occasions when national parties have a vested interest in EP votes, and MEPs are obliged to make this trade-off. However, as is clear from the previous discussion about national party leaders, MEPs clearly face this trade-off in the Commission President investiture procedure, because parties in national government make an *a priori* commitment to a particular candidate in the first round of the procedure in the European Council. Because of the threat of de-selection, MEPs from these parties are unlikely to deviate from this support for the European Council candidate, regardless of the position of their EP party group. The remaining MEPs, from parties not holding prime ministerial or presidential office in the national arena, can be expected to vote 'for' or 'against' the Commission President candidate on the basis of the candidate's policy position. In this case, MEPs from the same party family (or on the same side of the left–right division in the EP) as the European Council candidate are likely to vote 'for', whereas the rest are likely to vote 'against'.

The result, however, is that the coalition in the EP of 'parties represented in the European Council' plus 'EP party groups with similar policy preferences to the European Council candidate' is almost always going to beat the coalition of 'parties not represented in the European Council who also do not share the same policy preferences as the European Council candidate'. In other words, because of the structure of the investiture procedure (where parties in national government have a vested interest in the EP vote), and the structure of MEP candidate selection (by national parties rather than by EP party groups), the European Council candidate for Commission President is unlikely ever to be rejected by the EP under the new investiture procedure. This theoretical analysis consequently suggests that there is little practical difference between the original Commission President selection process, where the EP did not have a say, and the procedure established by the Maastricht and Amsterdam Treaties.

This theoretical investigation produces two hypotheses. First, regardless of whether or not the EP has a say in the Commission President investiture procedure, EP elections will still be fought as second-order national contests; and second, even under the new Commission President investiture procedure, the

European Council will be able to impose its wishes in the EP vote. These propositions are directly contradictory to the consensus view about the new Commission President investiture procedure. Before the consensus view can be rejected convincingly, however, these theoretical arguments need to be tested empirically.

Empirical Test: The Consensus View Refuted

EP Elections: 'Second-order National Contests'

The second-order national election model of EP elections was clearly true for the first two direct elections to the EP, in 1979 and 1984 respectively. In the 1989 and 1994 EP elections, however, it has been argued that certain 'European' characteristics did emerge: a transnational concern for the environment and a consequent breakthrough for a number of Green parties in 1989 (Curtice 1989), and a widespread anti-European vote in 1994 (Smith 1996). Nevertheless, as Table 6.1 shows, the general principles of the second-order model still held in these contests.

Turnout continued to fall (from 68 per cent in 1979 and 65 per cent in 1984 to 63.4 per cent in 1989 and 58.6 per cent in 1994), and a large proportion of voters in most member states continued to vote for parties they would not nor-

TABLE 6.1. Second-order European election results (1989 and 1994)

Member state	1989		1994	
	Turnout (%)	Voted differently in national elections (%)	Turnout (%)	Voted differently in national elections (%)
Belgium	90.3	12.6	90.2	18.5
Denmark	47.4	35.4	52.9	42.9
France	48.8	27.2	52.7	40.8
Germany	62.3	11.8	60.0	14.2
Greece	93.1	8.1	84.2	12.4
Ireland	65.9	28.7	44.0	23.8
Italy	81.4	19.7	74.8	20.7
Luxembourg	96.2	15.0	88.5	14.3
Netherlands	48.8	12.4	35.6	19.6
Portugal	51.1	9.7	35.5	12.7
Spain	54.7	22.2	59.6	12.5
Britain	57.0	13.0	56.6	16.0
EU12	63.4	17.6	58.6	20.2

Source: Calculated from data in van der Eijk and Franklin (1996).

mally choose. In Denmark in 1989 and 1994, and in France in 1994, the high proportion of voters choosing other parties indicated the emergence of a different party system for European elections. In these member states, therefore, European elections began to take on their own dynamic, with voters and parties beginning to be aligned on the pro-European and anti-European, as well as on the traditional left–right dimensions (Hix and Lord 1996b). In all the other member states, however, European elections continued to be fought by national parties about national executive power.

All three European party federations—the Party of European Socialists (PES), the European People's Party/Christian Democrats (EPP), and the European Liberal, Democratic and Reform Party (ELDR)—mentioned the connection between the EP elections and the selection of the Commission President in their 1994 European election manifestos. These manifestos were signed by the national party leaders of the member parties of the federations, at special party leaders' meetings. At a meeting in Brussels in December 1993, the Socialist party leaders even discussed whether they should propose a candidate for the Commission presidency prior to the European elections (Hix and Lord 1996b). However, Europe's voters and domestic parties took no notice. As in all the other European elections, the European parties' manifestos were ignored, and European issues were conspicuous by their absence.

In other words, the theoretical hypothesis that EP elections would still be fought as second-order contests regardless of the role of the EP in the Commission President investiture process is confirmed. EP elections are not about who holds executive power at European level, or even about rival agendas for European action. This may change with a uniform electoral procedure, where some candidates are nominated by the European party federations, and where the transnational election manifestos are used more widely. However, national parties would still have a strong incentive to fight the campaigns as mid-term 'beauty contests' for national government. National executive office (the post of Prime Minister) is still a more prestigious prize than the Commission presidency. Consequently, genuine 'European' elections could only exist if national electoral competition could be prevented from interfering in the EP election process. But it is difficult to imagine how this could ever happen in more than a few member states, regardless of the electoral rules. This is a real blow to the consensus view about the new investiture procedure.

The Commission President Investiture Vote: A Coalition of Governments, Not Voters

Turning to the second theoretical hypothesis, the first (and, at the time of writing, the only) time the Article 158 Commission President investiture procedure was used was in July 1994, following the June 1994 EP elections. On 24–25 June, at the Corfu Summit, the European Council was unable to agree on a nominee, due to John Major's refusal to back Helmut Kohl and François Mitterrand's choice (the Belgian Christian Democrat Prime Minister, Jean-Luc Dehaene) because the British government perceived him to be too 'federalist'. Klaus Kinkel, the President-in-office of the Council, hastily organized an emergency European Council for 15 July, and Kohl persuaded Jacques Santer, the Luxembourg Christian Democrat Prime Minister, to allow his name to be put forward. He was subsequently supported unanimously by the heads of state and government of the member states.

On 21 July, at the first plenary session of the new Parliament, the MEPs voted on whether they would accept or reject the European Council's nominee. The day before the vote, Jacques Santer attended the meetings of the Party of European Socialists (PES) and European People's Party (EPP) groups, to urge them to vote in his favour. Following these meetings, however, the PES group voted overwhelmingly to oppose him, for a number of reasons: first, because they objected to the secretive nature of the nomination process in the European Council; second, because they feared that he was the 'lowest common denominator' candidate of the British Prime Minister; and third, because they argued that Europe's voters had supported a centre–left majority in the 1994 EP elections. The EPP, in contrast, voted to back him as a fellow Christian Democrat and a former president of the EPP party federation. The other groups followed the lead of either the PES or the EPP, or else simply opposed Santer as a vote against the EU in general. As a result, the day before the vote, the line-up was as shown in Table 6.2.

TABLE 6.2. The European Parliament group line-up for or against Jacques Santer (20 July 1994)

Line-up		Seats
For Santer	European People's Party (EPP)	157
(Right)	European Democratic Alliance (EDA)	26
	Forza Europe (FE)	27
	Europe of Nations Group (EN)	19
	Non-attached members	14
Total		243
Against Santer	Party of European Socialists (PES)	198
(Centre, Left, and Anti-EU)	European Liberal, Democrat and Reform Party (ELDR)	43
	European Unified Group (GUE)	28
	Group of the Greens (V)	23
	European Radical Alliance (ERA)	19
	Other non-attached members	13
Total		324
Total MEPs		567

Source: Corbett *et al.* (1995).

Would this be translated into a real vote on 21 July? If the consensus view of the new procedure were right (i.e. that the EP's electoral choices could be translated into action by the EP party groups), then Jacques Santer should have lost the EP investiture vote. However, on 21 July, 262 MEPs voted in favour of Santer's nomination, with 244 against, 22 abstentions and 39 absentees. In one of the highest roll-call turnouts in the EP's history, Santer was elected Commission President by only 18 votes. Of those who voted, the line-up of the EP party groups on the previous day explained 88.9 per cent of MEP behaviour; in other words, 56 MEPs (11.1 per cent) voted against their party group positions. Had these MEPs voted with their party groups, Santer would have lost. So, what explains this breakdown of the 'natural' EP electoral/party group majority against Santer?

As our theory suggests, most of these MEPs who broke from their party group line did so under the instructions of their national parties. These MEPs were members of parties in government at the national level, who had already supported Santer in the European Council. For example, after the majority vote in the PES group meeting the day before the vote, the leader of the Spanish Socialist party (PSOE) delegation informed the PES meeting that his party would not stand by the PES group position. Madrid had instructed the PSOE delegation to support Santer, regardless of the PES group line. We can reasonably assume that this was the case for all parties which had been represented in the European Council (i.e. parties which held prime ministerial office at national level). The winning coalition in the investiture vote was therefore composed of parties in the European Council plus parties on the right in the EP, and not a simple left–right majority from the EP elections. And, as Table 6.3 shows, this coalition structure explains 96 per cent of MEPs' behaviour in the investiture vote, and 7.1 per cent more than a simple left–right explanation.[4]

This confirms the theoretical hypothesis that, because the European Council went first in the investiture process, national parties in government had an incentive to impose their wishes on their MEPs in the EP vote. National parties were able to do this because they control the selection of candidates in EP elections. For the MEPs torn between a national party position (for Santer) and an EP party group position (against Santer), the national parties could threaten to prevent the MEPs from standing in the next EP election.

Therefore, the only time the Article 158 investiture procedure has been used

---

[4] A large proportion of the other 4% is explained by the nine Portuguese Socialists who voted for Santer, despite the fact that their party was in opposition in Lisbon. An interview with one of these members suggested that they were concerned that a negative vote would postpone EU enlargment to admit Austria, Sweden and Finland (scheduled for 1 January 1995), and that such a postponement would jeopardize the agreement by the potential new members to make a significant contribution to the EU Cohesion Fund, of which Portugal is a large net beneficiary.

TABLE 6.3. The winning coalition: 'European Council plus European Parliament right'

	For Santer	Against Santer	Total
European Council plus EP Right	245 48.4%	3 0.6%	248 49.0%
Non-European Council plus EP Left	17 3.4%	241 47.6%	258 51.0%
Total	262 51.8%	244 48.2%	506 100.0%

Amount of explained MEP behaviour (shaded areas): 96% (significant at the 0.001 level).
Source: Gabel and Hix (1997).

so far suggests that the second assumption of the consensus view is also weak. Despite previously high levels of party group cohesion, the EP party groups were unable to translate the 1994 electoral majority into a positive vote either for or against a Commission President. Instead, the national governments were able to impose their choice on the Parliament, through the creation of an unholy alliance in the EP, made up of parties whose leaders had backed Santer in the European Council plus 'natural allies' (from the same party family as Santer), who would have voted for him anyway. Consequently, the Commission President was still the choice of Europe's governments, and not of Europe's voters.

Normative Implications: Limits of the Parliamentary Model at EU Level

Contrary to most academic commentators, therefore, these theoretical and empirical results suggest that the Maastricht and Amsterdam reforms do not in fact allow Europe's voters to choose who holds executive office in the EU, and hence expel them next time round. At face value, the new procedure for selecting the Commission President pushes the EU towards a parliamentary model of executive selection, by attempting to connect executive selection to a majority in EP elections. However, at a theoretical level, there are no incentives for parties to compete for the office of the Commission President, and there is every incentive for individual MEPs to side with the wishes of their national party leaders (to preserve their re-election) rather than the majority opinion of their EP party group.

These theoretical arguments are also confirmed at an empirical level. First, the 1994 and 1999 EP elections were still fought by national parties on the performance of national executives, and not over rival candidates for the

office of Commission President. Second, the winning majority in the EP investiture vote in 1994 was a 'prime ministerial coalition', made up of parties holding
prime ministerial office at national level, plus minority (centre–right) partisan
allies of their nominee in the EP, and not a 'European party coalition' of the
(centre–left) European parties / EP party groups which had 'won' the June 1994
EP elections.

Presented with this evidence, Nentwich and Falkner (1997: 8) contest this
view, claiming that it 'might underestimate the dynamics of European-level
politics because of the gradual increase of powers of the EP'. Moreover, Nentwich and Falkner remain 'convinced that the system set in place by the Amsterdam Treaty will give forceful impetus with a view to politicising and
Europeanising the selection of the European executive'. But the theoretical and
empirical results suggest that this developmental argument only holds if there
is a substantive shift from national to European politics: where national party
leaders see the office of the Commission President as a partisan appointment,
and are willing to jeopardize their capture of national government office to
secure the Commission presidency for their own 'party family'. In practice, this
means that Prime Ministers would be willing to allow their MEPs to oppose a
candidate whom they had already supported in the European Council, and face
the wrath of the national media and opposition parties as a consequence of this
volte face. Without this incentive, and this practical consequence, the 'prime
ministerial coalition' in the European Council will always prevail on the 'European party coalition' in the EP.

Until this transformation from national to European-level party goals occurs
(which I believe to be a long way off), the Commission President investiture
procedure as set out in the Maastricht and Amsterdam Treaties will do little to
increase the accountability of the holders of EU executive power. Nevertheless,
if one accepts that this outcome is a function of the institutional rules—that
the outcome is a 'structure-induced-equilibrium' (Shepsle 1989)—then further
institutional reform may rectify this situation.

In terms of the institutional design of executive selection, the EU has two
basic options. The first would be to stick with a parliamentary model of
executive selection, but to allow EP party groups to exercise a genuine choice
over the candidate for Commission President. This would require breaking the
bond between domestic parties and EP party groups, by preventing national
parties from controlling the selection of MEPs. For example, the EP party
groups, the national delegations of MEPs from each party, the transnational
party federations, or local and regional party organizations would be responsible for selecting candidates in EP elections, and national party head offices
would be actively prevented from influencing the candidate selection process.
This could, perhaps, be imposed through a legally enforceable clause in a
uniform electoral procedure for EP elections.

Alternatively, the bond between national parties and EP party groups could be maintained, but the vested interest of national parties in the EP vote could be removed. For example, the EP could be allowed to choose the Commission President from a list of candidates which had been approved by the European Council, and the European Council could subsequently vote on the EP's choice. Either of these reforms would restrict the ability of the parties in government in the European Council to impose their wishes on their MEPs in an EP investiture vote. Without this interference, the EP party groups could act cohesively to transform the majority in EP elections into a majority vote for or against a Commission President. In other words, the procedure would operate as a genuine parliamentary model of executive selection, as the academic consensus envisages.

A fundamental problem, however, is that even if these reforms were introduced, EP elections would still be fought as 'national contests'. Regardless of whether or not the EP party groups are cohesive, voters would still make their choices in EP elections based on competition for national executive office, even with a uniform electoral procedure. Despite the development of some 'first-order' characteristics in EP elections in Denmark and France, the probability of a transformation of EP elections in all member states into a contest about rival candidates for the post of Commission President is close to zero.

A second basic option, therefore, would be to abandon the parliamentary model and to transform the EU into a (partial) presidential system, by introducing some form of direct election of the Commission President, such as a two-ballot contest (along the lines of the French model), or via an electoral college (along the lines of the American model).[5] In such an election, it would be much harder for political parties to fight a campaign on the performance of the national governments, because the electoral choices on offer would be very different from the national and EP contests. Each national party or parliamentary group would be forced by the national media to 'come out' in favour of one or other candidate. Moreover, this non second-order dynamic could be enhanced through specially designed rules for nominating candidates for the Commission presidency. For example, each candidate could be required to be supported by one party (or group of MPs and MEPs) in every member state. This would guarantee that one section of the elite in every member state would be responsible to their electorates for the actions of the winning candidate (Laver *et al.* 1995). In practice, this would probably mean that each European party family would put forward a separate candidate. For example, if this were the case in 1994, the Socialists, with the approval of the PES party leaders' summit, would probably have backed Felipé González, whereas the Christian

---

[5] I use the word 'partial' to reiterate that executive power would still be shared with the national governments (that the EU would have a 'dual executive'), and hence that the consociational (non-majoritarian) part of the EU executive would remain intact, to counterbalance the natural majoritarian tendency of a direct election of the Commission President.

Democrats, with the approval of the EPP party leaders' summit, would have backed Jean-Luc Dehaene or Ruud Lubbers. Of course, the result of such an election would be a significant politicization of the post of Commission President, which the national governments probably do not want. Nevertheless, a politicization of executive power, whether via a parliamentary or presidential model of executive selection, is a necessary prerequisite for establishing political accountability.

Overall, the exercise of political power at European level is increasingly questioned by Europe's citizens. Part of the problem is that the current institutional framework, including the reforms of the Maastricht and Amsterdam Treaties, does not allow voters to decide who holds (or does not hold) executive office in the EU. This can only be rectified by further institutional changes, either to give the parliamentary model a real chance of working, or to introduce an element of presidentialism into the system. Either way, partisan competition (between EP party groups or the transnational party federations) rather than national competition (between the governments in the European Council) is the only way Europe's citizens will be able to choose 'who governs' at European level.

7

Justifying Comitology: The Promise of Deliberation

JÜRGEN NEYER

The Amsterdam Treaty underlines that the European Union (EU) neither is, nor will in the foreseeable future become, anything comparable to a nation state. Institutional reforms provided for in the Treaty are not part of a process of reinventing majoritarian governance on a supranational level, but follow a logic of 'bits and pieces', of minor changes, and incremental reform. After Amsterdam, the European project remains what it has always been: an effort to develop institutions and decision-making procedures which enable the European Community (EC)[1] to cope with transnational economic interdependence. Because the European project has to do so without any master plan to follow, it is a journey with a non-identifiable goal, driven largely by institutional experimentation and restrained only at the margins by the imperative not to sacrifice member states' democracies.

The rise of comitology[2] is certainly not the most important expression of this process; it is, however, indicative of this very aspect of the European project. In functional terms, its origin resulted from the need to relieve the Council of some of its legislative burdens by delegating decision-making powers to the Commission. The member states, however, were not willing to empower the Commission to legislate independently, but sought a way of avoiding the adverse consequences of delegation. The different procedures foreseen by the Comitology Decision[3] are therefore aimed at providing a set of options for different degrees of delegation and control, which can be applied by the Council—and, since the adoption of the Single European Act (SEA),

---

[1] This chapter, in both its analytical scope and its normative reasoning, is only concerned with the first 'pillar' of the EU. I therefore use the term 'EC' and not 'EU'.

[2] For an early account of the comitology phenomenon, see Bertram (1967). Recent descriptions of the history of comitology are provided by Vos (1997) and Demmke *et al.* (1996). For a legal typology of committees, see Knapp (1996). A quantitative assessment is provided by Falke (1996). The most important case law concerning comitology is collected in Türk (1996) and Bradley (1997).

[3] Council Decision 87/373/EEC of 13 July 1987, laying down the procedures for the exercise of implementing powers conferred on the Commission, OJ 1987 L 197/33. Replaced on 28 June 1999 by Council Decision 99/468/EC, OJ 1999 L 184/23.

increasingly by the European Parliament (EP)—as seems appropriate for the purposes of putting Community policies into practice. Although comitology was not foreseen by the Treaties, it has today become a most important institutional forum for the everyday conduct of European legislative discourse. It is therefore not only witness to the growing importance of issues of implementation, but also underlines the significance of 'unconstitutional' elements of European governance, such as the relevance of policy networks consisting of non-governmental organizations, member state administrations, and the Commission and its supposedly independent scientists. Comitology combines legal and administrative tasks in one institution, thereby resembling a kind of 'political administration', underlining the fact that state-oriented analytical categories are inadequate for describing, understanding, and justifying the European polity.[4]

The purpose of this chapter is twofold. First, it provides some basic data on comitology and introduces the normative concerns voiced by the EP. Then, responding to the interinstitutional debate and the recent reform of comitology, the chapter proceeds by asking for adequate normative justifications of supranational governance and their implications for the new Comitology Decision. It is argued that convincing normative justifications must not be developed in the absence of general reflections about the procedural and substantive requirements of a democracy, but need to take account of the distinctive nature of the European polity. One way of formulating such a justification is provided by the concept of deliberative supranationalism.[5] This concept corresponds to theoretical interpretations emphasizing the *sui generis* nature of the EC (see Jachtenfuchs 1995; Jachtenfuchs and Kohler-Koch 1996a; Neyer and Wolf 1996). It assumes that the legitimation of governance within constitutional nation states remains inevitably one-sided and parochial. Since democracies presuppose and represent collective identities, they have few mechanisms for ensuring that 'foreign' identities and their interests are taken into account within their decision-making processes. Deliberative supranationalism, in this regard, respects the member states' constitutional legitimacy, while at the same time clarifying and sanctioning the commitments arising from its interdependence with equally democratically legitimized states, and with the supranational prerogatives which the institutionalization of this interdependence requires. It therefore rejects the idea of establishing a political hierarchy above

[4] This article draws on the research project 'The Europeanization of risk regulation of technical goods and foodstuffs ("Comitology")' conducted at the Centre for European Law and Politics, University of Bremen, financed by the Volkswagen-Stiftung and chaired by Christian Joerges. The author is grateful for critical comments and intellectual assistance provided by Hervé Dupuy, Christian Joerges, Beate Kohler-Koch, Oliver Gerstenberg, Harm Schepel, and both editors of this volume.

[5] The general outline of the concept of deliberative supranationalism has been elaborated in Joerges and Neyer (1997a). For a more recent elaboration, see Neyer (1999).

the nation state, and emphasizes the need for transnational discourse and deliberation.

The analytical scope of deliberative supranationalism is confined neither to issues of procedural rules nor to effective governance. By simultaneously underlining the functional need to harmonize diverse regulatory traditions without sacrificing the achievements of national regulatory standards, and emphasizing the requirement that (inter)governmental legislation be conducted within a framework of entrenched procedural rules, the concept rejects any contradiction between the two. Rather, they are viewed as being two coexisting sides of one coin, which may only provide an adequate source of legitimacy if they occur in tandem. An essential challenge for facilitating deliberative interaction, therefore, is to identify the conditions under which both can simultaneously be expected and be put into practice. Three necessary conditions are outlined in this chapter:

(1) the definition of the substance and boundaries of legislative discourses;
(2) an understanding of governmental preferences as claims rather than as reflections of intrinsically legitimate national interests; and
(3) the existence of a competent third party which reflects shared normative concerns.

In the concluding remarks of this chapter, it is argued that comitology is a normatively attractive decision-making procedure to the extent that it can facilitate intergovernmental discourse and promote transnational social integration. In order to make it compatible with the requirements of responsible and responsive governance, however, its future reform must enhance the discursive capabilities of governmental delegates, provide more accountability by increasing transparency, and clarify the role of the EP in the political administration of the EC.

Comitology and its Critics

Comitology has significantly altered the way in which the EC copes with economic interdependence and conducts decision-making relevant for the administration of the internal market. It is no longer only in the legislative procedure in the Council (including cooperation with the EP) in which member states meet and discuss their differing approaches to market-building; delegation and comitology provide the opportunity to restrict the legislative procedure to laying down the essential requirements of harmonization, leaving the interpretation of those provisions to the Commission and member state experts. In accounting for the rise of comitology, it is necessary to understand that market-building in the EC, as elsewhere, is not simply a technical question. It very often touches on politically and culturally sensitive issues, such as determining acceptable levels of risk involved with different standards for products and methods of production. Market-building therefore needs to be understood as a complex endeavour to make not only markets, but also whole societies, compatible with one another.

In the EC, this complex undertaking was, from its inception, concerned with the question of adequate institutions and decision-making procedures. Until the introduction of the third indent of Article 202 [145] in 1987, almost all legal acts were agreed upon according to Article 205 [148] and/or Article 249 [189]. Bargaining in the Council was not restricted to basic legislative activity, such as defining the general aims of secondary legislation, but also very often involved defining the means for implementing them, adapting legislation to technical progress, and specifying the technical details with which products were expected to comply. Even agreement on administrative and technical details, such as the definition of recipes for foodstuffs, was sought by means of intergovernmental bargaining and generally needed unanimity to be concluded (Gray 1993: 2–3). Little wonder, then, that market-making was characterized by inefficiency, slow progress, and over-detailed legislation!

Backed by the famous *Cassis de Dijon* decision of the European Court of Justice (ECJ), the Commission announced a new legislative strategy in 1979, based on an interpretation of the ECJ ruling as being supportive of a principle of mutual recognition. This interpretation maintains that all products which are legally marketed in one member state may not be restricted in any other member state. In its Communication of 8 November 1985, the Commission explained the implications it would draw from its understanding of the Court's decision. The Commission stated that the legislative approach followed in the past needed to be revised by drawing a distinction between '. . . on the one hand matters which, by their very nature, must continue to be the subject of legislation and, on the other hand, those whose characteristics are such that they do not need to be regulated' (point 7). All actions proposed by the member states falling outside these 'essential topics' would, when notified through Directive 83/189, be subjected to the principles outlined in Article 28 [30].

Furthermore, in pursuit of the policy laid down in this Communication, the Commission proposed a new legislative strategy to the Council, which relied on the instrument of so-called 'framework directives'. Such directives, it maintained, should be restricted to laying down only the essential requirements which products need to comply with, and should refrain from dealing with technical specifications. At the same time, the Commission requested a wide delegation of powers for the enactment of implementing legislation, which was finally granted by the amendment of Article 202 [145]. In its third indent, Article 202 states that the Council shall 'confer on the Commission in the acts which the Council adopts, powers for the implementation of the rules which the Council lays down'. It soon became clear, however, that the Council was not prepared to invest the Commission with the exclusive power to implement programmes which so often touch on economically important interests and politically sensitive issues. Instead, in the so-called 'Comitology Decision' of 13 July 1987,[6] the Council made it clear that member states were not willing to loosen their intergovernmental grip on the implementation process. More constructively, the Comitology Decision rejects the idea of a supranational central implementation machine headed by the Commission, and thus indirectly forces national governments into a cooperative venture.

In the Comitology Decision, the Council distinguishes between several different procedures under which the Commission is to execute its implementing powers, overseen by the member states. These so-called comitology procedures represent different specific combinations of autonomy on the part of the Commission and control by the member states. The advisory committee procedure emphasizes efficiency and collective interests by merely requiring the Commission to consult the member states. In the case of the management committee procedure, more extensive consultation is necessary in order to avoid a negative qualified majority in the committee. If the Commission fails to do so, the Council may take a different position, acting by qualified majority. The regulatory committee procedure, finally, forces the Commission to seek a qualified majority to support its proposal; it therefore may not only result in significant delays, but also gives great weight to the particular interests of the member states. If the measures envisaged by the Commission are not in accordance with the opinion of the committee (or if no opinion is delivered), the Commission shall deliver the proposal to the Council. Acting by qualified majority, and taking into account the position of the Parliament, the Council may submit an amended proposal, resubmit its proposal or present a new legislative proposal. As opposed to its predecessor, the new Comitology Decision also provides for non-binding criteria relating to the choice of committee procedure, increased public access to documents and a right of the Parliament to receive *inter alia* information about committee agendas and the results of their votes.

The importance of comitology for the everyday conduct of Community affairs can be illustrated by the fact that only 11 per cent of all Union legislation enacted by the Council and EP since 1993 has been directly implemented by the member states. The overwhelming majority of Union legislation is administered by the Commission (Dogan 1997: 38). In 1994, the Commission adopted a total of 7,034 legal acts (mainly as part of its implementing powers), of which 3,064 were regulations, 3,635 were decisions, 33 were directives, 26 were recommendations, and 263 were opinions (Falke 1996: 117). Furthermore, the range of implementing measures undertaken by the Commission in

---

[6] See fn. 3.

collaboration with comitology committees is not restricted to executive activities on a concrete, individual level (such as imposing market restrictions on certain products) and general advisory work in a broad range of topics, but also includes legislation of an abstract and/or general type, such as the adoption of directives intended to harmonize technical or economic developments. Although comitology committees are primarily set up to control the Commission's power, empirical evidence shows that the working style in most comitology committees is rather cooperative, aimed at facilitating mutual understanding and centred around the exchange of experiences with colleagues from other member states and Commission officials (Eichener 1997: 222–60; Joerges and Neyer 1997a: 280).[7]

Broad quantitative data are useful for drawing an overall picture of comitology, but any more detailed description is confronted with the problem that comitology refers not to a particular institution but to a huge number of committees, with a very particular legal status and a catalogue of decision-making procedures in common. They differ not only in terms of the applicable decision-making procedure, their working styles and problem-solving philosophies, but also in the range of tasks they are expected to perform.[8] According to the EC budget, a total of 409 committees existed in 1996, of which 339 had to be consulted by the Commission in the course of EC rule-making.

The Parliament's Lament

The expansion of bureaucratic competence in the administration of the internal market and the fusion of legislative and administrative activities in comitology have led to fierce criticisms from the EP as regards the latter's compatibility with the established institutional balance.[9] While the EP had been unhappy about the entire procedure for a long time[10] and had characterized the Comitology Decision already in July 1987 as an 'alarm bell demonstrating the

[7] Falke (1996: 142) reports that in nearly 12,000 meetings of agricultural management and regulatory committees between 1971 and 1995, only eight out of approximately 50,000 decisions were unfavourable. In its Opinion 'Reinforcing Political Union and Preparing for Enlargement' of 28 February 1996, the Commission lists a total of only six cases which were referred back to the Council in the period 1992–5.

[8] For a recent collection of case studies on committees in the EU, see Joerges and Vos (1999) and van Schendelen (1998).

[9] For a critical account of that argument, see Vos (1998).

[10] For an excellent and detailed account of the EP's struggle with the Council and the Commission to become involved in comitology, see Bradley (1997). He characterizes the overall attitude of the EP towards comitology as one of 'deep distrust, boiling over on occasion into barely disguised hostility' (at 231).

manifest lack of political will on the part of the member states to give practical effect to the objectives of the SEA',[11] its criticism gained momentum with
the adoption of the Treaty on European Union (TEU). The EP now argues that
the third indent of Article 202 [145] only refers to acts which the Council has
adopted, and therefore cannot be applied to acts adopted under the co-decision
procedure, which implies 'full equality of Parliament and Council'.[12] The
Council, on the other hand, argues that the execution of legal acts of the EC
is, according to Article 10 [5], the sole competence of the member states. It is
only by autonomous decision that they delegate parts of their sovereign powers
to the Commission, and then only in so far as it seems necessary to them
(Jacqué 1996). The EP's efforts to enlarge its competencies by participating in
the implementation of European legal acts are therefore not covered by the
provisions of the European treaties, but should be viewed as an intrusion into
the competencies of the member states and a violation of treaty provisions.
The Council furthermore argues that it is the member states, not any
European institution, which command the expertise to decide on how best to
integrate European legal acts into their respective national legal systems.
Finally, the Council argues, comitology deals only with the technical implementation of secondary law, and therefore does not need to be under the
general supervision of the EP, which should restrict itself to cooperating in the
elaboration of basic legal acts, leaving the implementation of these acts to the
administrative machinery and the deliberations of technical experts.

Following the EP's refusal to accept implementing procedures under which
the decision-making power could revert to the Council alone (types II and III),
and the first failure of a co-decision procedure, both institutions agreed on a
so-called *modus vivendi*.[13] It was claimed that this provisional agreement was
without prejudice to the positions of principle of the institutions concerned,
and pending any revision to be discussed at the 1996 intergovernmental conference (IGC). It provided that the EP should be informed about all draft
general implementing acts and any negative opinion delivered by supervisory
committees. Furthermore, the Council should adopt measures being referred
to it only after giving the EP a reasonable time in which to deliver an opinion,
and by taking due account of the EP's point of view. The *modus vivendi*,
however, has not brought the interinstitutional debate to an end. Not only did
it fail to put the Council and the EP on an equal footing, but it has also failed
on its own limited terms. The Commission has not provided an adequate flow
of information to the EP, nor has it always allowed the EP sufficient time to
adopt a position. Although the IGC was expected to solve the interinstitutional
problem (probably by changing the third indent of Article 202 [145]), it failed
to do so, and only required the Commission to prepare a proposal for the
reform of comitology before the end of 1998.

[11] OJ 1987 C 246/42.   [12] OJ 1994 C 20/176.   [13] OJ 1996 C 102/1.

The Normative Foundations of Supranational Governance

What are the appropriate guidelines for reform? Is the EP right to claim that comitology is part of a process of intergovernmental fusion which bypasses the Parliament's right of co-legislation, and must therefore be condemned for distorting the institutional balance? Or is it an expression of the need to establish efficient structures of governance which are technically able to cope with complex interdependence as it exists in the EC? Obviously, answering these questions is no easy task. Which normative criteria should be applied to comitology? If they are the criteria of majoritarian democracy, defenders of the comitology procedure are in a difficult position: comitology is under the control neither of the European nor of the national parliaments; it is neither transparent in terms of openness to the media nor accessible to the general public; it is a process conducted behind closed doors by means of confidential deliberations among appointed experts.

Justifying Supranational Governance

Any justification of comitology needs to confront these issues. Such a justification, however, must start by identifying basic normative criteria, from which it is possible to deduce implications. These criteria cannot be developed in the absence of general reflections about the procedural and substantive requirements of a democracy, but need to take account of the distinctive nature of the European polity. But what is the nature of the beast? Few issues in European integration studies have attracted more attention and provided less acceptable conclusions. This chapter has no wish to join the chorus of those trying to capture the whole thing analytically,[14] but approaches the problem in a less ambitious way, by focusing on some basic normative underpinnings of the EC. It therefore starts by adopting Weiler's (1995a: 249) understanding of the idea of a community which 'is not meant to eliminate the national State but to create a regime which seeks to tame the national interest with a new discipline'. The primary object of the EC in this perspective is to provide the member states with an institutional framework which accepts the normative limitations of state-based constitutional democracies (i.e. disregarding external effects), and focuses on harmonizing structurally inward-looking polities. The indisputably correct claim that, were the EC to apply for membership of the EU, 'it would not qualify because of the inadequate democratic content of its constitution' (Offe 1996: 145, own translation) is therefore of only limited relevance for assessing the normative status of the EC. The fact that, with the exception of Article 177 [130u] of the new Treaty establishing the European Community (TEC) (which deals with the identification of normative criteria for develop-

---

[14] For recent attempts, see Caporaso (1996) and Risse-Kappen (1996).

ment aid), the word 'democracy' is not mentioned at all is neither mere accident nor an expression of some 'New Reason of State' aimed at bypassing subnational constituencies by means of inter-executive politics.[15] It merely bears witness to the deliberate intention that EC decision-making should not be about organizing the self-governance of a European collective of individuals, but rather about coping with transnational economic interdependence in a limited number of issue areas.

The fact that majoritarian procedures are of the utmost importance when justifying democratic governance in the member states does not automatically mean that the EC must also be democratized by means of majoritarian procedures. This must be borne in mind when assessing the legitimacy of the EC. Whereas the concept of democracy can be understood as referring to a set of political institutions backed by accepted (or even constitutionalized) norms which are aimed at enabling a collective of individuals to rule itself, the EC's normative rationale is its existence as a non-majoritarian institution, achieving consent and legitimacy by means of argumentation and legal integration (Majone 1998). Rather than simply measuring the difference between an ideal typical democracy and the practice of the Community, a more accurate starting point is to argue that the EC's normative claim only holds to make the member states' economies compatible with one another. Rather than conceptualizing the EC as a more or less democratic polity, therefore, it seems more convincing to follow Majone (1998) and conceptualize the EC as a non-majoritarian regulatory apparatus, which is not a substitute for member state polities but adds decision-making procedures to their political systems and reforms existing ones. To argue that supranational governance neither is nor should be conducted in institutions which claim democratic legitimacy does not imply, however, that their adequate normative yardstick is simply efficiency (but see Majone 1994b: 31). The intrusion of supranational governance into national legal systems and therefore its relevance for influencing public order in the member states is far too intense not to have to comply with additional requirements, such as ensuring transparency, accountability, subsidiarity, parliamentary scrutiny, and substantive rationality. What is needed to guide normative reflection about decision-making procedures in the EC, therefore, is a justification of supranational governance which takes into account not only the fact that the concept of democracy cannot be easily translated into the EC, but also rejects the claim that a sufficient degree of legitimacy for the European decision-making system can be provided by efficiency alone. Finally, it should also be mentioned that a growing number of European citizens seem to put increasing emphasis on a decentralized Community which situates legitimacy

---

[15] 'The strategy of the New Reason of State consists in the reorganization of statehood . . . with the aim of entering into inter-governmental commitments which can be removed as far as possible from the sphere of domestic political debate and thus rendered immune to revision' (Wolf 1997: 74). See also Moravcsik (1994).

and political power at the lowest level possible. Demands for the centralization of the sources of legitimacy and political power therefore carry some inevitable flavour of obsolescence. In contrast, arguing for an understanding of the EC as a collection of decision-making procedures which need to be justified in terms of their contribution to making interdependent democracies compatible with one another avoids the trap of demanding centralization in the name of democracy, and is open to alternative forms of legitimate governance.

Compared to democracy, legitimacy is a much broader concept; analytically, it is not restricted to indicating the degree of self-determination which a collection of individuals realizes in a polity, but it can be understood as referring to the degree to which a decision-making procedure can convincingly be justified by reasonable arguments,[16] and is therefore accepted by its addressees. It should be noted that reasonable arguments will very often (but not always) be those which apply principles of self-determination. Affirmative arguments are normally used to explain the reasons for the existence of parliaments, the organization of referendums or the application of the principle of subsidiarity. On the other hand, however, reasonable arguments can also be in sharp contradiction to notions of self-determination: in arguing for the independence of institutions such as courts or central banks, most people today emphasize the requirement that neither the general public nor the legislature should be able to interfere with their deliberations. Their legitimacy does not derive from being part of a process of organizing self-determination but, on the contrary, is based on an assumed isolation from interference by parliaments or the general public. Assessing the legitimacy of an institution or decision-making procedure, therefore, does not simply involve the extent to which they are in conformity with principles of self-determination; it also entails relating the claim for self-determination to the equally necessary condition of respecting functional imperatives concerning the problem-solving capacity of decision-making systems.

A further necessary requirement of a legitimate supranational decision-making procedure is its promotion of what Dworkin calls 'integrity' (1991: 164–7). Integrity as a concept of legitimate decision-making builds on the assumption that any legislative body needs to treat like cases alike. It therefore requires that past legislative decisions have a restraining impact on the range of options available to legislation. As Dworkin argues, integrity in legislative activity is as much a necessary political ideal as a precondition for a legal act to be recognized as expressing a certain view of fairness, justice or decency. This requirement, however, is far from being problem-free: it cannot imply that past decisions should be viewed as something sacrosanct, removed

---

[16] This understanding is in accordance with Habermas' definition of legitimacy as the *Anerkennungswürdigkeit einer politischen Ordnung* (cited in Guggenberger 1986: 271).

from the possibility of even major changes and therefore tying legislation to old-fashioned values and/or scientific errors. It merely emphasizes the need for a coherent legal framework, within which society conducts its daily affairs, and in which major changes (if considered necessary) need to be backed not only by a majority of opinions but also by convincing arguments. Any assessment of the legitimacy of a decision-making procedure therefore needs to take into account at least three elements: (1) respect for the principle of self-determination; (2) its problem-solving capacity; and (3) the integrity of law.

Facilitating Deliberative Discourses

This triple requirement can be satisfied by neither an orthodox supranational nor an intergovernmental decision-making procedure alone: both fall short with respect to either the principle of self-determination or a high degree of problem-solving capacity, and neither of them has procedural guarantees that decisions taken are in principle in accordance with past decisions. An ideal typical orthodox supranationalist perspective starts from the assumption that one of the basic problems of European decision-making derives from the fact that member states still insist on their national sovereignty. Because they are reluctant to accept that interdependence requires a re-establishment of hierarchical political relationships at the European level, thereby giving supranational majoritarian principles clear precedence over intergovernmental consensus principles, the problem-solving capacity of European decision-making systems remains insufficient. Without major reform and the establishment of European statehood, so the argument goes, member states cannot cope efficiently with problems of market failure, and will have to face ineffective and therefore undemocratic supranational institutions (Mancini 1998). What is needed, the argument continues, is either a broad extension of majoritarian principles or the establishment of a supranational European executive, probably by means of empowering independent agencies (Majone 1998). The problem with this perspective is rather obvious: the overwhelming majority of the member states regard both majoritarian rule and authoritarian imposition at European level as being simply unacceptable politically (i.e. illegitimate), because it does not take account of the fact that democracy—and therefore supreme political legitimacy—is rooted in their national political systems and not at the European level. Empowering the Community to make collectively binding decisions by means of simple majority voting, hierarchical imposition, and authoritarian enforcement would be highly problematic. As a general norm of European governance, it would imply a major shift of emphasis away from democratic self-determination and towards European statehood. Only under very limited circumstances, therefore, can simple majority voting, independent agencies, and expanded supranational administrative competencies be viewed as being in accordance with the normative imperatives of a decentralized democratic polity.

Intergovernmental co-ordination is equally insufficient for satisfying the triple requirement of self-determination, problem-solving capacity, and integrity. Co-ordination denotes an ideal type of decision-making, which assumes member state preferences as being intrinsically legitimate reflections of democratic procedures, which therefore may be outvoted only under very restricted conditions (Moravcsik 1997; Beitz 1991). Under the conditions of bargaining, each and every member state has the right to veto decisions, which implies that agreements need to be unanimous. While any outcome of a co-ordinative procedure is, at least from a formalistic point of view, normatively problem-free (because all parties have agreed), it carries the risk of 'lowest common denominator politics', can easily be utilized by single parties for strategies of obstruction, and provides no procedural mechanisms to ensure that decisions respect the integrity of law. Legal provisions deriving from intergovernmental co-ordination are moulded by substantive compromises, package-dealing, and the logic of two-level games (Putnam 1988). Respect for the law's integrity is rather detrimental to intergovernmental co-ordination, and difficult to accommodate. The extension of qualified majority voting (qmv) by the SEA and the Treaties of Maastricht and Amsterdam has changed a lot with regard to the risk of 'lowest common denominator politics' and the danger of obstruction (Lewis 1998a). As regards safeguarding integrity, however, qmv changed nothing.

As opposed to both an orthodox supranationalist normative perspective (extension of majoritarian and hierarchical elements) and an intergovernmentalist perspective (strategic bargaining, eventually modified by qmv), a deliberationist type of decision-making has the potential to perform according to the triple criteria mentioned above. Its capacity to do so, however, depends on at least three necessary conditions. These can be summarized as procedural requirements which any deliberative decision-making system needs to incorporate.

The most important procedural requirement of a deliberative legislative discourse among member state delegations is to agree on as concrete as possible a *definition of the discourse*, including: first, the collective aim of the participants in the group (e.g. the balancing of Articles 28 [30] and 30 [36]); and second, the substantial boundaries of the discourse. As Stephen Holmes rightly argues, 'a conversation is invariably shaped by what its participants decide *not* (emphasis added) to say' (1988: 19). In order to avoid destructive conflicts and cognitive overload, controversial themes are very often suppressed by means of 'strategic self-censorship' or, as Rawls (1985) has put it, 'the method of avoidance'. Examples of this are ubiquitous in European politics: at the most basic level, they can be found in the principle of enumerated competencies, and more concretely in the Commission's 1997 Green Paper on foodstuffs,[17] which states that the only relevant topics for legislative discourses are those dealing with issues of public health and safety. Accordingly, in the deliberations of the Standing Committee for Foodstuffs, the members of the Committee do not mention explicitly the distributive implications of measures adopted, but only assess their contribution to health and safety aspects.[18] In discriminating between legitimate and illegitimate arguments, and providing criteria for assessing the validity of an argument (scientific evidence), cooperation among delegates is conducted according to agreed principles, and any agreement reached must be legitimized by reference to the underlying principle of promoting health and safety. The integrity of law demands not only that compromise be reached, but also that a convincing reason for the policy outcome can be supplied.

The second most important procedural requirement of any deliberative discourse may be described as *arguing, not bargaining*. It must be agreed that the act of casting votes plays only a minor role in decision-making, and is less important than argumentative interaction. In effect, this means that the preferences of delegates are not viewed as intrinsically legitimate reflections of the individuality and democratic nature of any single member state's preferences, but only as governmental claims which attain their normative status by being convincing to the other delegates. The act of convincing, however, is far from common to traditional notions of intergovernmental interaction. Delegates are normally assumed to be hierarchically subordinated to national ministries, to represent national interests and to try to persuade others of their point of view—but not to be convinced by the arguments of others. Deliberation therefore presupposes a disposition to accept not only other points of view as equally legitimate concerns, but also that governmental delegates have the necessary room for manoeuvre to change their opinion—even if that contradicts what their ministers assume to be in the national interest. Deliberation therefore also demands an increase in the discursive capabilities of delegates by means of either more efficient intermediary structures between them and their ministries or, if that is not possible, a significant increase in their discretionary competencies. What at first sight seems to be a basic practical problem in terms of internal ministerial hierarchies, and an equally crucial normative problem in terms of the responsiveness of delegates to domestic constituencies, is ultimately a necessary precondition for reaching multilateral agreements beyond simple aggregation. If all delegates insisted on their status as representatives of an intrinsically legitimate domestic interest, all solutions apart from identifying common denominators would be ruled out and systematically excluded. The main decision-making method of a deliberative discourse, therefore, is to

[17] COM(97)176 final.
[18] For empirical work on deliberative interaction in the Standing Committee on Foodstuffs, see Joerges and Neyer (1997a,b).

argue, which means backing up claims with evidence. As opposed to the situation in a voting procedure, where slight unhappiness with a provision counts as much as strong support for it, different intensities of preferences in deliberative discourses need not be ignored, but can become an essential issue in a process of pooling individual judgements (Miller 1993: 75–7). The mode in which discourses are conducted in a deliberative procedure can be understood with the help of Dworkin's conceptualization of legal reasoning (1991: chapter 2): each of the actors in a given legal dispute interprets a given norm relevant for the decision to be taken (in our terms: a substantive definition of the discourse) according to his or her subjective understanding of its meaning, and by openly describing his or her way of deducing implications from an agreed norm. In so doing, a sample of different interpretations emerges, which may only rarely converge towards a commonly shared opinion of what kind of concrete measure or behaviour a given norm requires. By openly describing subjective ways of deducing implications from a norm, however, legal reasoning helps to clarify differences of understanding, and is accessible for critical evaluation by third parties.

The *existence of a third party* which reflects shared normative concerns (substance and boundaries of discourse) is another necessary procedural requirement for a deliberative system of decision-making. It serves the double function of giving an opinion in cases which cannot be solved by means of discourse among the parties themselves, and of providing incentives to actors to behave in accordance with the requirements of deliberation. Analytically, this third party could, for example, be a court (assessing the legal status of arguments), a scientific body (assessing the scientific soundness of arguments), or even the general public (assessing to what extent arguments are in accordance with a given political will). From a normative point of view, there can be little doubt that, in an ideal world, it is always the general public which acts as the third party. In so doing, the public can control whether political agents comply with substantive and procedural requirements of a given definition of discourse, thereby enabling itself to impose political costs on non-compliant governmental actors. Under conditions of enlarged discretionary competencies of governmental delegates, this control would obviously be of the utmost importance. However, in the real world of scarce informational resources and often highly technical matters on the legislative agenda, it may often be the case that neither an interested general public nor interested media actually exist. In these cases, the general public needs to be supported by functionally equivalent third parties which act in its interest. Which of the three possibilities mentioned above would be the relevant one in a given decision-making system would depend directly on the nature of the definitions of a given discourse. If these definitions include, for example, the provision that arguments are only to be viewed as legitimate if they refer to scientific evidence, the relevant third party might be a scientific committee. If the definitions are more broad and only provided by secondary or even primary legislation, the relevant third party might more correctly be the ECJ. In all European discourses above treaty law (e.g. IGCs), however, the third party needs to be equally broad, and must be the general public and/or the national legislatures. In all three instances, the function of the third party is not to give authoritative decisions which lay the ground for executive enforcement, but to provide a disciplinary function to the actors involved in the discourse, to induce them to refrain from openly selfish arguments, and to legitimize their preferences by referring to the normative criteria laid down in the definitions of a given discourse.

Conclusion: Comitology as a Means of Facilitating Deliberation

What is the relevance of the above reflections for suggesting a new normative perspective of comitology? The argument presented so far holds that neither hierarchical-majoritarian nor strategic intergovernmental decision-making can, by themselves, provide the legitimacy needed for European decision-making. Both need to be at least supplemented by elements of a deliberative discourse. Delegation, in this perspective, is not simply to be understood as a means of out-sourcing those tasks which are of minor importance, referring only to technical implementation. Rather, it needs to be understood as structuring the legislative process itself, introducing elements of procedural rationality and substantial integrity into intergovernmental bargaining. Its most important justification is the double acknowledgement of the need for, and the difficulty of facilitating, deliberative decision-making, as well as its potential for restricting the bargaining process in the Council to formulating basic standards and criteria for framing the way in which disputed issues are dealt with. It is the essential elements of the problem-solving process itself, therefore, which are being delegated. Delegation needs to be viewed as an expression of the intention to change the logic of the decision-making process from one dominated by strategic bargaining and preference aggregation to one conducted by means of deliberative interaction. Accordingly, comitology refers to a set of decision-making procedures which are neither simply characterized by different intensities of member state control, nor ones which can be understood as merely technical devices for propelling efficiency. Rather, comitology refers to a redefinition of the terms under which problem-solving is conducted, and resembles a kind of intrinsically political administration rather than an apolitical and technical procedure.

It is important to emphasize that intergovernmental deliberation is neither *per se* legitimate nor separate from democratic governance. In the perspective outlined above, it is viewed as a necessary supranational supplement to state-based majoritarian democracy and international cooperation. It focuses not on substituting state-based majoritarian democracy, but on enabling the EC to harmonize equally legitimate but highly divergent member state preferences, and to cope systematically with the external effects of state-based democratic decisions. Comitology is not to be misunderstood as any real world expression of the normative ideals being proposed above, but as a procedure to be legitimized and criticized against the yardstick of its ability to realize the promise of a deliberative decision-making procedure. The appraisal of comitology and its criticism, therefore, are two sides of the same coin: the need for deliberation in propelling the efficiency of decision-making, as opposed to the degree to which the promise of deliberation remains unfulfilled.

The political price for comitology so far has largely been paid by the EP. Article 202 [145(3)] can easily be interpreted as a partial negation of the legislative rights given to the EP by the introduction of Article 189b EEC. In agreeing to the comitology procedure, the EP in effect gave up some of its legislative rights, while making it clear that it strongly disapproves of the whole procedure. At least in the long run, comitology implies the danger of either a hollowing-out of the co-decision procedure (because important legislative activities are delegated to the Commission), or else of falling victim to a chagrined Parliament which rejects any legislative act which does not specify every technical detail. These dangers should have been taken more seriously by the Commission and the Council when they agreed on the recent reform of comitology. This would be much more promising if it had as its basic element a compromise between the Council and the EP regarding the conditions under which both can accept delegation. Such a compromise does not need to give Parliament the right to participate generally in executive legislation (for which it is not an adequate institution). One possible way of dealing with the EP's political demands without involving a legislative body in mainly executive implementation might be to introduce a right of revocation for both institutions for all implementing acts referring to basic legislation conducted under the co-decision procedure. Such a right would mean that both institutions could, under certain specified conditions, require the Commission not to implement its decisions, but to refer them back to the legislative procedure. Agreeing to such a proposal would imply that both the Council and the EP could be rather relaxed about increasing the discretionary competencies of delegates; they could step back from the demands of overseeing the day-to-day practice of comitology, while remaining in a position to enter the decision-making discourse whenever particular topics become of crucial importance to them.

Finally, any reform which is oriented towards realizing deliberative ideals needs to incorporate a huge leap towards increased transparency. To date, comitology committees have generally conducted their affairs behind closed doors, and have denied access to the media and interested parties. This practice is neither necessary nor useful; it is detrimental to the promise of deliberation. Except for deliberations concerning highly sensitive issues, such as the fixing of prices of agricultural products or the allocation of grants under Union expenditure programmes, comitology committees should generally convene publicly, and should grant access to all those actors who claim a legitimate interest in the matters on the agenda. Increased transparency would both encourage delegates to behave according to the definitions of given legislative discourses, and would also provide the public and member state legislatures with a more accurate account of what governmental delegates in committees are actually doing. Realizing deliberative ideals ultimately carries the promise of a new logic of intergovernmental cooperation; secret diplomacy, the practices of illegitimate scapegoating and credit-claiming, and the factual non-accountability of 'faceless bureaucrats' would all become features of the past. The normative ideal of intergovernmental cooperation would escape from the realm of secretly aggregating domestically constituted preferences, and would become something closer to sector-specific 'little parliaments' (even if composed of governmental delegates) with clearly identifiable personal accountabilities. Such a proposal might seem rather radical when compared to our common understanding of the practice of intergovernmental politics. It is, however, no more radical than the existing incompatibility between intergovernmental bargaining and the need to justify the practice of the political administration of European politics.

8

Political Representation in the European Union: A Common Whole, Various Wholes, or Just a Hole?

KARLHEINZ NEUNREITHER

Who represents whom in the European Union (EU)? And what is actually represented? In the Treaty, the component parts of the EU are well provided for: the member states are represented via their governments in the Council, the peoples of the same member states are represented in the directly elected European Parliament (EP), the regions are represented in the Committee of the Regions, and finally various economic and social groups are represented in the Economic and Social Committee (ESC).

But is there political representation of the EU as a whole? This would be a purely theoretical and perhaps, given some research paradigms, a slightly out-of-date question, were it not for such things as the notion of flexibility or differentiated integration, which was introduced by the Amsterdam Treaty. How will flexibility affect political representation in the EU, especially in the EP? I argue in this chapter that, despite its dynamic evolution, the EP might have major difficulties in remaining indivisible in acting as a single body on all EU policies, even if in the future these policies are endorsed by only a limited number of member states.

In such a situation, several scenarios are possible. One EP strategy, which would be close to a federal option, would consist in defending its right to represent the whole of the EU, and not just its constituent parts. Other scenarios include a strengthening of national parliaments, or an increase in the so-called democratic deficit, which might result in a thinning-out of political representation, both in the member states and in the EU.

In this chapter, I do not intend to present an exhaustive analysis of political representation in the EU; this would require a different, much more detailed and methodological approach. My objective here is rather to highlight some of the basic problems which the EU will have to face in the coming years, against the background of the institutional discussions which have taken and are taking place in connection with the Amsterdam Treaty reforms.

The Limited Constitutional Agenda of the Amsterdam Treaty Revision

For more than two years, the EU was engaged in a process of Treaty revision which contained important institutional elements.[1] Many suggestions were tabled, both by the formal participants (above all the member states and the EU institutions), and by indirectly involved groups, including political parties, non-governmental organizations (NGOs), and others. But the longer the inter-governmental conference (IGC) proceeded, the more it became evident that the EU's constitutional agenda was rather limited, and that it was not address-ing fundamental questions, even those with which it will inevitably be con-fronted shortly, above all with the introduction of a common currency and its possible economic and political impact. The reason for this is rather simple: the governments wanted at all costs to avoid reopening the debate on the major achievement of Maastricht—the monetary union. Consequently, not only were many questions concerning this union (including the so-called stability pact) treated at a subconstitutional level, but the entire process of treaty revision was presented as a pragmatic approach, a lean process involving minimal adapta-tion. In other words, questions about the political end goal of the EU were not even asked, and far-reaching alternative constitutional designs were not advanced.

On the other hand, it had become clear that the Community method had to be adapted to the realities of the present situation, and that a serious evalua-tion could no longer be avoided. Future enlargements are obviously an in-centive in this respect, but even with the present fifteen members, the EU is not well prepared to handle the forthcoming internal and external challenges successfully. New concepts, such as differentiated integration or flexibility,[2] were discussed and cautiously introduced in the Amsterdam Treaty. However, in the absence of an overall scheme, it is not very clear how, if applied on a larger scale, they would be linked to the existing fundamental notions, such as political representation, democratic accountability, or the role of the citizen.

From the outset, the French presidency tried to limit the conference agenda, but the Cannes European Council of June 1995[3] gave the Westendorp prepara-

---

[1] A narrow interpretation of Art. N of the Treaty on European Union (TEU) would have limited the IGC to examining only the present pillar structure, and the question of whether to include additional EC policies. More political commentators felt there was a greater need for an overall review of the EU before enlargement. On this second approach, see e.g. the *Working doc-ument on the realization of the Union*, by the French MEP Jean-Louis Bourlanges, PE 212.45O/fin., part I.3.

[2] In this chapter, I use the notions of 'differentiated integration' and 'flexibility' interchange-ably. The more recent 'politically correct' notion of 'closer' or 'enhanced cooperation', which was finally favoured by the IGC, adds to the existing confusion. See also Stubb (1996) and his Ch. 9 in this book.

[3] For a critical analysis of the French position, see Ross (1995b).

tory group a rather wide mandate. Those who expected this to result in a fundamental discussion not only of the present functioning, but also of the future of the EU, including its economic, social, political, and societal impact at the end of this century, were destined to be disappointed. The preparation of the IGC did not address the most important questions arising from the Maastricht ratification process (itself perhaps the first challenging and widespread public debate on European integration in most EU countries): why Europe at all, how much of it, and how should it be organized?

The main reason for the auto-limitation of the Westendorp group was not the restrictions of its mandate but its composition. It was not a group of independent 'wise men', but was mainly composed of direct and personal representatives of the Foreign Ministers of the member states. The addition of two Members of the European Parliament (MEPs)—the German Christian Democrat, Elmar Brok, and the French Socialist, Elizabeth Guigou—was useful, certainly, but they could not change the overall orientation of the group. The Commission, too, had chosen, a somewhat low profile, being less prophetic in its preparatory report than during the launching of the Single Market under Jacques Delors. Obviously, the aggressive noises made against the 'Brussels bureaucracy' during the ratification debates in some member states, which had left the Commission out in the cold, had had an effect.

The EP, on the other hand, which had much to gain and little to lose in widening the constitutional debate, chose a more pragmatic approach than many might have expected. As a matter of fact, since its Spinelli report of 1984, the EP had become the main institutional defender of a federal option for the EU over the years. The first signs that the underlying consensus in the Socialist and Christian Democratic groups was breaking up came to light only when the Herman report was not put to the vote in the plenary in January 1994, but was only considered as a basis for further discussions. The reports on the results of Maastricht and the preparation of the IGC which followed[4] clearly marked a departure from the former institutional choice: the EP now considered itself less as a challenger of the basic options for the EU, and more as a pragmatic co-player in the mainstream of a slow but acceptable evolution.

As far as our immediate subject, political representation, is concerned, this situation does not contribute very much to a clarification of the issues involved. The discussions in the IGC, it must be said, contained a number of important institutional elements: for example, the Council presidency, the weighting of

---

[4] For the fate of the Herman report, see EP Resolution on the Constitution of the European Union, 10 February 1994, in EC OJ No. C 61/155. The first direct example of the new pragmatic approach is found in the Resolution on the Functioning of the Treaty on European Union with a View to the 1996 intergovernmental conference (Bourlanges/ Martin report) of 17 May 1995 in EC OJ C 151. This approach was confirmed by the Dury/Maij–Weggen report in March 1996 (EC OJ C 96), and more recently by a resolution on the present state of the IGC of 17 March 1997, doc. PE 257.133.

the votes of the member states in the Council, the composition of the Commission, and the limited extension of the powers of the EP. These may all be considered as incremental adaptations, except for the introduction of the principle of flexibility. This innovation indicates most clearly the need for clarification of the notion of political representation in the EU. Maastricht, it should be remembered, had only introduced limited adjustments in this respect. The two basic lines of representation were fundamentally unchanged: (1) the representation of member states in the Council; and (2) the representation of the peoples (plural) of these same member states in the EP. The Committee of the Regions added a new, but rather weak dimension.

Parliamentary Representation in the EU

The EP consists of 'representatives of the peoples of the States brought together in the Community' (Article 189 [137] of the Treaty of the European Community—TEC). The treaty does not assume a single basis of representation, a whole, a nation, a common European people, but an aggregation of the peoples of the member states. The treaty does not recognize a single EU *demos*, but rather fifteen *demoi*, even given direct universal suffrage and a common electoral procedure or common principles[5] in all member states (Article 190 [138] TEC). The representatives of these peoples can, it is true, also be nationals of other EU states, as EU residents may participate in EP (and local, but not regional or national) elections (Article 19 [8b] TEC), thus somewhat blurring the original formula of clearly separated national 'constituencies'. To some extent, where you live becomes just as important as which national passport you hold, somewhat of an extension of *jus terrae* or *jus loci*.

Thus, the EP, the only EU institution endowed with a direct basis of legitimacy by universal elections independent of the political order of the member states, does not derive its credentials from a single base, but rather from fifteen

---

[5] The Amsterdam Treaty facilitates a possible agreement on the procedures for EP elections by no longer insisting on a 'uniform procedure', and providing that it would be sufficient if elections were held 'in accordance with principles common to all Member states' (TEC 190 para. 4). The EP seized on this invitation and voted a text in July 1998 (the Anastassopoulos report), which is based on the principle of proportional representation. Further elements concern a preference for regional lists (in larger states), an optional threshold not exceeding 5 per cent, and the possibility of preferential voting. The question of whether a certain percentage of seats should be set aside in a national list for candidates from other EU countries was not finally decided. This proposal (EP minutes of sitting of 15 July 1998, Part II, PE 271.049, 10–11) was forwarded in the form of a Draft Electoral Act to the Council, which has to approve it unanimously. It will then be presented to the member states for adoption according to their own constitutional requirements. It goes without saying that this progress was largely due to the Blair government lifting the veto concerning a modification of the British procedures for EP elections by giving up the first-past-the-post system.

separate ones. This might remain a purely theoretical question (i.e. whether the whole is greater than its component parts), were it not for the fact that it directly affects the position of the MEPs, the parliamentary representatives. If they are elected on a national basis, does not their loyalty belong to that entity, to their member country, or to their national political party? And, more crucially, if the country in which they are elected does not participate in a specific EU policy or given action, will the respective MEPs exercise their mandates, participating in discussions, voting by majority, allowing credits, designating high-ranking political personalities?

Indeed, what is striking, is the absence of any reference to the nature of the parliamentary mandate in the Amsterdam Treaty. What is even more striking is that the EP did not ask for a clarification of this important question in its submissions to the Amsterdam IGC. It might have been useful to have had something about the freedom of the mandate, the general interest of the EU, or some other high-sounding principle included. The 1976 Council act concerning the elections mentioned a few guidelines, and the EP's internal rules of procedure contain some short remarks on this subject: The MEPs 'shall exercise their mandate independently'. They shall not be bound by instructions and 'shall not receive a binding mandate' (Rule 2). This is a rather low legal level for such a basic issue. Astonishingly, the EP has never taken up this matter as an issue for a possible treaty revision. Nevertheless, the Amsterdam Treaty provides a possibility to fill this gap. Article 138 para. 4 TEC asks the EP, with the approval of the Council, to lay down regulations and general conditions governing 'the performance of the duties' of its members. If this new article is used not just to clarify a number of current issues, such as a possible declaration of personal interests, but also to launch a fundamental debate on the parliamentary mandate itself, this would be most useful.

It could be argued that, the European Community (EC) Treaty provisions aside, the reality of the EP's political role has evolved substantially, and that this fact should be taken into account. This argument is certainly valuable for many aspects of the EP's activities. As a number of studies show, the EP has, indeed, shown proof of a remarkable institutional evolution (Corbett *et al.* 1995; Westlake 1994; Neunreither 1999). It now bears little resemblance to the original assembly of national delegated MPs, who had little time to spend outside the obligations of their national mandate. In Jean Monnet's vision, it was, together with the European Court of Justice (ECJ), an institution of control and scrutiny, not of decision-making. The 'Common Assembly', as it was first called, boldly left these conceptual limitations behind.

The question here concerns the extent to which the extraordinary institutional evolution of the EP has resulted in a readiness on the part of its members to fulfill a role which would require a very strong identification with the EU as a whole, comparable to the identification which still, despite all differentiations and nuances, exists in nation states. Here, the answer is less reassuring (Norris

and Franklin 1997; Ionescu 1996). It could be argued that this individual consciousness is not required, and indeed that it exists only very partially in national
systems. It would then be left to the EP as an institution to represent the whole,
and not to its component members, who might have other loyalties. This would
be a situation close to the day-to-day reality of many parliaments. The difference is that, in a national system, identification with the overall construct is
usually strong, despite partisan and other divisions. Separatists and others are
the exception. In the EU, a comparable identity does not exist, not through language, through common history, or any other important factors contributing
to a 'we' feeling.

But why insist on the old-fashioned notion of a whole at all? Are we not told
that the EU still contains strong, if not predominant, elements of an international organization, that we should coin new terms for it like consociation, that
it is *sui generis*, that its corporate or neo-corporate character gives more importance to the constituent parts than to a somewhat artificial whole? If the EU is
a negotiating system, a sort of permanent bazaar, are not the participants, the
traders, more important than the roof of the tent (in the case of the EU, a legal
system) in which they are trading?

As far as the EP is concerned, we have noted that it has achieved much in
overcoming its original fragmentation (Hix and Lord 1997). Nevertheless, there
are limits to this. The selection of candidates is still almost exclusively dominated by national political parties. The election campaigns are also fought
largely on national and not European matters. Furthermore, there has been no
attempt to put into practice one of the main functions of elections, that of
enabling the voters to identify themselves with leading personalities. The most
striking example was the nomination procedure for the President of the Commission in 1994, which coincided with the elections to the EP. The chance to
present some of the outstanding European personalities to the public at large,
and thus to strengthen the image of the Commission as a possible forerunner
of a parliamentary responsible government, was lost.

The situation was rather different in the lead-up to the subsequent
election, which occurred in June 1999: The Santer Commission had resigned
in March 1999, confronted with charges of maladministration and nepotism.
Although the EP was a driving force in this process, it was not prepared to play
a significant role in the selection of the new presidential candidate. Consequently, the member governments were once again free to make their own
choice, and they nominated Romano Prodi at their Berlin summit, just a few
weeks before the date of the European elections. Another opportunity to per-
sonalize this event was thereby lost. Faced with dramatically decreasing voter
participation figures, the EP must re-examine its strategy, and come up with
non-incremental solutions. Otherwise, it risks marginalization—not through
the deliberate actions of its main counterpart, the national governments, but

by a more insidious withering away of its basis of legitimacy because of voter disinterest.

As a result, there is still room for improvement on the long road towards a real 'European' Parliament, always supposing that we want to embark on that journey. Our immediate question is slightly different. Will the EP be strong enough to face the challenge inherent in differentiated integration? Will its internal coherence be sufficient, and will it be in a position to stave off external attacks from some national parliaments and the media on its basis of legitimacy? The image of a half-built house has often been used in connection with the EU. Will the EP be intimidated into retracing its steps on a difficult path, or will it be challenged to look ahead as it always has done? In the latter case, it might be well advised to analyse more precisely where it stands, and to elaborate a strategy for the future.

The Theoretical Dimension: Who Represents Whom?

Political representation is closely linked to the emergence of the nation state.[6] While Thomas Hobbes (1651) argued within a framework of absolutism, Edmund Burke (1774) formulated interesting ideas about the nature of the parliamentary mandate from an elitist, conservative position, and on the American side, the Federalist Papers took up the subject (The Federalist 1777). About a century later, John Stuart Mill (1861) elaborated a detailed catalogue of principles of representative government, and Walter Bagehot (1867), only a few years later, put aside all niceties and told us bluntly that Parliament was just an addition of functions, the most important of which was the division into majority and opposition.

In this century, a great variety of research paradigms has emerged. On the one hand, the functioning of political elites became a core theme (Weber 1921; Schumpeter 1942; Downs 1957; Sartori 1987), in which the delegation of power from the many to the few through the act of elections became pivotal, and the citizens were sometimes seen mainly as subjects of propaganda and manipulation. On the other hand, and especially in the United States, the liberal tradition remained very strong, slowly evolving towards a pluralist approach, which maintained the image of a rational individual, the Common

---

[6] One of the best critical introductions to the concept of representation remains Hanna Pitkin's both scholarly and readable study (1967). It is balanced in its approach, and as far as our immediate subject is concerned, calls for close links between the representative and his constituents, combined with elements of leadership and independence (162–6). This analysis is somewhat closer to the American system. Europe's party democracies with the strong loyalties of the electorate and the members of parliament to their party, especially in those systems with national or regional lists, seem to be less at the centre of her analysis.

Man, but also included the agglomerated structure of society and the resulting interplay of interests (Friedrich 1950, 1963; Truman 1953; Easton 1965). Parliamentary representation in these approaches was understood to be participation in bargaining and the levelling-out of interests. It would then be sufficient if certain criteria for the composition of the society and for the access of various interests were guaranteed, leaving the rest to the free market of competition.

Other schools of thought are more critical, and insist on the need for structural improvements via enhanced chances of participation of the citizens (Barber 1984; Habermas 1992a,b). Others feel that the output side of the democratic process has not been given adequate attention, and they want to correct this within a more comprehensive analysis (Scharpf 1994). While these approaches differ greatly among themselves, they have one thing in common: they analyse the relationship between those who are represented and those who represent them in terms of a segmented or highly differentiated society. One of the main questions posed is: To whom is the loyalty of an elected member of parliament directed?—To his or her national political party? To his or her regional or local party? To his or her constituency? To private interest groups?

Nobody would deny that these are very salient questions. In fact, they are paramount for the exercise of the mandate of a deputy or congressman. Even more, his chances of re-election, or rather of being reselected for office, largely depend on them. The question is whether his mandate implies more than the representation of this or that group, whether he also has a direct obligation towards the polity as a whole. Some constitutions hint at this dimension: The German constitution stipulates that the members of the national parliament (the *Bundestag*) represent the German people as a whole (*Grundgesetz*, Article 38). The Belgian (Article 32) and Italian (Article 67) constitutions even proclaim that the members of their second chambers, who are elected on a regional basis, also have a national mandate and nothing less.

Political science and public philosophy have neglected this aspect to a large extent, and it is necessary to go back quite a distance in order to find arguments along these lines, usually from conservative authors complaining about the deficiencies of party democracy (Leibholz 1929). Alternatively, we can look in more contemporary approaches for elements in such distinct schools as postmodernism (Derrida 1984; Lyotard 1985; Seitz 1995) or communitarianism (Walzer 1983; Taylor 1989; Etzioni 1996). In fact, with a few exceptions, political theory has come a long way from the days of Edmund Burke, who claimed that parliament was not a representation of different and hostile interests, but 'a deliberative assembly of *one* nation, with *one* interest, that of the whole' (Burke 1774: vol. II, 12ff). Burke emphasized the independent role of a member of parliament in the exercise of his mandate, during which he should certainly remain in close contact with his constituency, but should mainly be guided by his own judgement. His is the role of a 'trustee' who is given full confidence for a given time, as compared to that of an 'agent' who has to follow instructions from his 'principal'. These two notions still constitute the extreme poles between which the parliamentary mandate is situated.

Burke's ideas had a mixed reception. Carl J. Friedrich (1950: 266) considered them to be a romantic configuration which never existed, while other classical authors like Harold Laski (1925) thought they were still valuable, even in a party democracy. What is more striking is that they still serve as a reference point in quite state-of-the-art analyses of political representation (Esaiasson and Holmberg 1996: 49–51, 62, 116, 312). On the other hand, studies following the lead of postmodernist philosophers like Foucault take up the subject from another angle, which will not be discussed here: the whole does not exist in an objective way, it is only created in the process of representation (Seitz 1995: 25–6). Here, we find a striking similarity to authors like Dolf Sternberger who, writing in the completely different context of constitution-building, suggest that the people, the *demos*, only comes into existence in the act of democratic elections and does not exist outside of it (Sternberger 1986).

Where does the European parliamentarian fit into this theoretical discussion? Obviously, his or her political role is likely to be analysed by using existing concepts which have been elaborated for analyses of national political systems. Exceptions to this general rule are quite rare (Schmitter 1996). This observation is confirmed by studies of political representation. Michael Marsh and Pippa Norris have recently brought together a number of scholars and analysed the various aspects of parliamentary representation in the EP, including territorial and social representation, voter participation, and representational roles (Marsh and Norris 1997). This study adds substantially to our knowledge of the subject. Nevertheless, the concepts are those elaborated in national systems, with one difference: in a nation state, one option for representation would be to give priority to the whole polity. This option is not even suggested in the EU (Katz 1997), where the member state is the largest territorial unit. So the question must be asked: where is the unity in the European community, where is the union in the European Union polity?

Another point concerns the integrationist position of the EP as compared to the population at large. This 'mismatch' is confirmed and dubbed 'poor quality of representation' (Marsh and Wessels 1997: 238, 239). The need for 'better representation' becomes paramount 'if the EP is to perform adequately on behalf of the European citizens' (Marsh and Wessels 1997: 240). For the authors, the ideal type of representation seems to be a 'double mirror' model, where not only are the various social and other groups represented, but their opinions and beliefs are also mirrored as closely as possible. The problem of a necessary distance between the general views of the electorate and the representative body (Haarscher 1996) is not addressed.

One could argue—with caution, trying to avoid the pitfalls of elitism—that in a forward-moving polity like the EU, this distance plays a more important role than in comparatively static national states, and that the question would be not so much how to eliminate it by changing the composition of the EP, but rather how to make it instrumental in representative/voter relations. In other words, the elements of a process between MEPs and their electorate (including the structures necessary for their own re-election, above all the national parties) would have to be introduced.

The MEPs should not try to forget about their 'advanced' insights into EU affairs and go back to a 'pre-informed' stage in order to get better marks in academic studies. What is needed is a much more effective dialogue, a public forum for the discussion of EU issues which keeps this distance at an acceptable level, but where the permanent efforts to reduce it (from 'above' and 'below') lead to an overall evolution of the understanding of EU governance. What is also needed is a dynamic rather than a static approach to the complex problems of the interplay between the representatives and the represented, which could be an important element in a future theory of democratic governance beyond the nation state.

This is, of course, a broad subject. As far as representation is concerned, many issues will remain of the 'representation from above' type (Esaiasson and Holmberg 1996). Agenda-setting by elites (on such issues as monetary union and border controls) is likely to continue to be more important than in the member states, although in the Danish and other cases we can see the first signs of a 'representation from below'. The absence of a clear majority/minority cleavage of the government/opposition type at EU level is a major deficiency in this context, and results in the dislocation of discourses from the EU into national arenas (Neunreither 1998a). In the EU, the dynamic dimension of representation is still more important than in national systems. The dialectics of this process (Kluth 1995), applied to a transnational negotiating system, need to be explored further.

Another dimension opens up if we include non-state actors like NGOs, citizen movements, or other representations of diffuse interests. The access of these groups and the dialogue with them may become a constituent element for the future governance of the EU (Koslowski and Wiener, forthcoming).

Flexibility: The End of the Federal Dream?

The Amsterdam IGC to some extent formalized a debate which, up to then, had been more political and academic: the debate on flexibility or differentiated integration. The idea behind it is quite simple—the original Community was conceived as a unitarian system. Decisions should be taken by all and according to Community rules, and they should apply to all. Exceptions were foreseen, it is true, but they were also granted according to EC rules, and mostly concerned temporary measures enabling a country to catch up with EC standards. The Maastricht Treaty introduced a major deviation from this principle by allowing member states not to agree on common objectives, to opt-in or opt-out of newly formulated policies. Was this the moment of expulsion from the federal paradise? Perhaps it is too early to come to a final conclusion on this question. The damage done in Maastricht was in any case limited in two respects: (1) the following enlargement negotiations with Austria, Finland, and Sweden made it clear that no future members could expect to get the same exceptions; and (2) the institutional set-up of the EC remained intact.

The question put forward in the Amsterdam revision was whether and in how far clauses of general differentiated policies should be introduced. What interests us in this context is the impact of this flexibility on the institutions, and beyond that on the EU political system, its transparency, its legitimacy, and—as seen from the outside—its credibility as an actor in international affairs. One gets the impression that these implications were not fully examined. During the last months of the IGC, the delegations were obviously too busy to define areas which might be suitable for flexibility, with the result that the consequences for the institutions remained of secondary interest. Finally, a distinction was drawn between two groups of institutions: those which are basically of a collegial nature (e.g. the Commission and the European Court of Justice); and those which are not, the latter being those composed of the member states (e.g. the Council and the European Central Bank). In this unofficial listing, the EP was also classified as a collegial body.

The immediate consequences of this are far-reaching: the collegiate bodies will continue to act as a whole, even in cases of 'closer cooperation', while the others will have to split up. The Council, the most important 'non-collegial' institution, will deliberate and, more importantly, vote with only those members present who will actually participate in a given 'advance' project. Incidentally, this principle will only apply at the political level; the Council Secretariat will continue to function as a unit.

The Commission, in contrast, will not split up. It will stay together as a unit, at both the political and the administrative levels. In other words, a Commissioner will continue to be responsible for environmental, research, or educational programmes, even if his or her government has declined to participate, his or her national parliament has voted against it, and the financial contributions for the programme have come from other member countries' taxpayers. The beginning of institutional strains can be imagined. Will the Commission be the same as it is today? Will its collegiality not begin to suffer?

But our subject is not the Commission, it is political representation. Here lies the heart of the matter. If the EP is indivisible, if it will always stay and act together as a unit, then a major battle has been won for a certain vision of the EU, that of a territorial entity provided with strong central political institutions, at least the beginning of a whole which Edmund Burke would recognize. In fact, the EP has chosen exactly this position. In its first Resolution on the IGC in May 1995, it stated that: 'The European Parliament as a whole will be responsible for exercising control over Union policies which are pursued by a limited number of Member states on a temporary basis'.[7] This position was maintained throughout the negotiating process and in March 1997, confirmed in a formal vote. In this Resolution, the EP 'condemns' the suggestion of the Dutch presidency, in cases of 'close cooperation', to limit participation in parliamentary debates and votes to those members who are elected in the respective states.[8]

The Amsterdam Treaty provides clauses for closer cooperation, and includes rules on how to adapt voting in the Council. The general approach is that only those states which have signed up to an additional integrationist or cooperative initiative will participate in actual decision-making. Certainly, the EP has always demanded to be part not only of the advisory and scrutinizing group of EU institutions, but of the decision-making one as well. First in budgetary matters, then in general legislation through the introduction of the cooperation and co-decision procedures, these demands have been at least partially satisfied. The EP's role in legislation, it must be emphasized (and even its own resolutions are often confusing on this important point), is not one of 'exercising control over Union policies', as cited above. It is participation in the core of EU decision-making.[9]

The present situation is curious. The revised Treaty does not foresee specific rules of procedure for the EP in the event of flexibility decisions. Consequently, a substantial institutional dilemma seems to be in the making. An example will illustrate the issue at stake. Let us assume that eight or nine of the present fifteen member states agree, following consultation of the EP, a positive proposal from the Commission, and a qualified majority vote in the Council, to embark on an activity involving closer cooperation. It is likely that, at least in

---

[7] See EP resolution of 17 May 1995, EC OJ C 151.   [8] *Idem.*

[9] It is quite surprising that a number of major EP documents do not distinguish between parliamentary control and participation in legislation (see e.g. the Neyts–Uyttebroeck report on relations between the EP and national parliaments, Doc. PE 221.698/fin., 22 May 1997). In fact, we are dealing here with two quite different parliamentary functions. Participation in legislation, as in the co-decision procedure, is never control. One legislative chamber never 'controls' the other one, they share a given power. Accordingly, we do not speak of the 'control' of the US Senate over the House of Representatives in legislative matters, nor is the term used in other bi-cameral systems. In the EU, the Council cannot be controlled by the EP in legislative matters either. That is why the EP's (rather successful) line of argument—that co-decision should be introduced in all cases where the Council votes by majority and where the national parliaments have lost control over their own minister—is not logically correct. In addition, the function of national control cannot be easily transferred to the EU: if the Danish or Finnish parliament loses control over the voting behaviour of their respective ministers, it is no help to them if the EP has been given the right of co-decision for these questions. Participation in legislation is a genuine right of any parliament, and the EP should claim it as such.

the first pillar, this activity will include legislative decisions, whether directives addressed to the participating member states to be transformed into national legislation, or directly applicable regulations. The EP will then be required to give its opinion on the respective drafts, or to participate more directly through the co-decision, or possibly in some cases, the cooperation procedure. Even in its simplest form (an opinion), the outcome will by definition be influenced by members from non-participating states. Whether this influence would be decisive is of secondary importance. The basic question concerns the nature of parliamentary participation in EU legislation. If its nature implies that the representatives of those who are the object of such an act should have a say in shaping and deciding on it, then there is no reason why representatives from other countries should participate in this activity.

It goes without saying that the original EC Treaty is not designed to handle such questions. It was based on the concept of the unity of the system without defining the consequences of this unity and indicating at least some general principles. What a relief it would be to read in the Treaty that the parliamentary mandate should be exercised in the general interest of the Union, and that each MEP, while being elected in a given member state, is also a representative of the Union as a whole. But there is nothing of the sort to be found in the Treaty, and not even the EP itself asked that the parliamentary mandate be highlighted in the Amsterdam IGC by means of such provisions, which are traditional in continental constitutions.

The crucial question to be faced by the EP is whether to go ahead and act as a representation of the whole of the EU, which would then have to be defined more closely, or else to be condemned to take a backwards step, and face up to the hard fact that it is in the end not much more than an assembly of representatives from the various member states, a view which was dear to General de Gaulle. Differentiated integration presents a major challenge to this institution, which it must face in one way or the other. Of course, the EP could apply a 'wait and see' strategy. The Amsterdam Treaty limits possible areas of application considerably, and it will take time before concrete proposals are discussed and enacted. After all, no major debate has taken place on the fact that British MEPs participated fully in the EP's activities concerning the Social Chapter, despite their country's opt-out on the subject until May 1997.

On the other hand, there are at least four pressing reasons for a thorough reconsideration of the issue. First, if the principle that the EP represents the whole of the EU population needs to be confirmed (either at a lower legal level, by EP resolution, interinstitutional agreement, and so on, or at a higher, constitutional level, in application of Article 190 [138] para. 4 TEC), then it might be rather late to get a substantial majority for such an initiative within the EP itself. In fact, the EP has given up its mainstream option of a quasi-federal evolution of the EU, and has joined the ranks of those who prefer not to mention final goals (Neunreither 1995b: 16–20; 1999). Certainly, this has short- and medium-term advantages, but it prevents the EP from taking action on this matter of substance.

Second, the national parliaments are still awaiting fulfillment of the promise of closer participation in the EU. Most of them, for the time being at least, reject the idea of an additional parliamentary chamber composed of national MPs at EU level; nor are they even in favour of a radical change of the present role of the conference of European affairs committees of the national parliaments (COSAC) to the same end.[10] But this position could change if a major debate were to be launched on the legitimacy of the EP acting with all its members on matters where only a few of them participate. If the EP has major difficulties over splitting up, the national parliaments do not; they are 'variable geometry' by definition. Adequate representation of the various wholes by those who are elected to that end might become the subject of an argument.

Third, and closely related to this, anti-EU political forces are likely to take up this matter, as soon as a concrete and popular case arises. Would it help the identification of the citizens with the EU if they were told that the MEPs of those member states which refused to participate in certain policies were to have a possibly decisive say in their handling, including normative rules or individual decisions which might be directly applicable? How would the Court rule on such a case? The classical principle: 'No taxation without representation' might be reversed in policies with budgetary consequences to become: 'No representation without taxation'.

Fourth, time does not stand still, and the EU is rapidly moving towards enlargement. Six months after the end of the IGC, talks started with a number of applicant countries. This increases the pressure for more flexibility within the Treaty, in all three pillars, but makes the adaptation of the principles of political representation more difficult. Should the EU tell these

---

[10] The Maastricht Treaty contained two Declarations on the subject of closer cooperation between the EP and national parliaments. The first, Declaration No. 13 (annexed to the EC Treaty), mentioned the goal of encouraging 'greater involvement' of national parliaments in EU activities. The instruments provided for that end were rather modest: more information and more contacts with MEPs interested in the same issues (in practice, at committee level). In contrast, Declaration No. 14 was, and still is, 'full of dynamite'. It invites the EP and the national parliaments to meet 'as necessary' as a Conference of the Parliaments (or 'Assizes'). This declaration was never enacted. The Amsterdam Treaty changed the content of Declaration No. 13, and 'upgraded' it into a Protocol on the role of national parliaments in the EU. There are two new elements in this text: The first concerns procedures for better and more timely information for the national parliaments on EU draft legislation, including pre-legislative consultation documents. The second element consists of an increase in the role of COSAC (the Conference of European Affairs Committees), which can now submit contributions to the EU institutions. However, the aspect of cooperation with the EP has disappeared. Declaration No. 14 attached to the Maastricht Treaty is no longer mentioned. In general, it must be said that relations between the EP and the national parliaments are frequently characterized by misunderstandings, jealousy, and other irritating factors (Neunreither 1994b).

countries that the representatives of the present fifteen member countries are indivisible, but that the five or more newcomers could not count on the same privileges?

We are not arguing here that flexibility or closer cooperation should be avoided at all costs. On the contrary, flexibility may be necessary on a much wider scale for the further evolution of the EU. The point is that it is likely to create major difficulties for some institutions, and above all for the EP. The minimum to be expected in such a situation is a thorough discussion of these problems.

Possible Scenarios, Likely Challenges

The title of this chapter indicates three possible fundamental choices for the further evolution of political representation in the EU:

(1) the strengthening of the *common whole*, perhaps but not necessarily a federal solution;
(2) a return to the still functioning national basis, the *component wholes*; and
(3) the possible collapse of the representational system, resulting in a *hole* in our democratic web of government.

Let us start with the last scenario.

The Hole Scenario

This scenario may sound somewhat exaggerated. But we also talk about the hole in the ozone layer, when in fact what it is is a thinning-out of this layer. In the same way, we might talk about a thinning-out of existing structures and processes of political representation, which may at first pass unobserved, then be merely the object of scientific observation, and only then of possible public debate. The main question is whether a decrease in political representation in functional terms has taken and is still taking place. These functional terms include full acting capacities for parliaments, transparency of policy processes and accountability, as well as an acceptable output for the citizens, maintaining or even strengthening their trust and belief in the political system.

This decrease has been analysed in the context of the debate on the democratic deficit. We will not go into the details of this debate here, but will only insist on its composite nature (for more detail, see Neunreither 1994a). It is argued that, due to the transfer of powers from the national to the EU level, substantial functions have been lost by the national parliaments, which are being exercised not by the EP, but by the Council, resulting in an imbalance between parliaments and executives. The decrease in political representation is also obvious in the weakness of the intermediate structures (above all, the political parties and the media), and of the relations with the citizens.

If the evolution of the EU has weakened the effectiveness of political representation, this is only partially linked to the insufficient transfer of powers to the EP. If full parliamentary powers were transferred to it, the EP would become not only the main EU legislator, but also the body which decides on a European government (or, in its absence, the composition of the Commission, but as a political choice). The majority and the opposition would have to be formed on an EU basis, and the European discourse would finally include clear options and preferences for the voter. The question is whether the EP, the political parties, indeed the whole EU construct, is prepared for such a radical change (Hix and Lord 1997; Hix, Chapter 6; Neunreither 1998a).

In the absence of an EU discourse, the national political discourses will continue to predominate, along with the EU-bashing in which they habitually engage. This uneasiness is increased by complex, opaque procedures and a multitude of bureaucratic committees with enormous powers of decision (as illustrated by the BSE case). The introduction of the Euro and its far-reaching implications will add to this situation; for the first time, a small committee of experts will be given a free hand in deciding on basic data for the economies of the participating countries, but also *de facto* for the non-participating neighbouring countries. Yet, while their competences will be similar to those of the *Bundesbank*, they will not be integrated into a legitimate political system. As a result, there are reasons for not excluding *a priori* a further deterioration in political representation, both in the member states and in the EU.

The Component Wholes Scenario

If the EU institutions have such difficulties in making a qualitative leap forward, why not strengthen the existing national bases of legitimacy? National parliaments, once much better informed than they are now on EU affairs (a process which requires such a relatively small input that the present deficiencies are difficult to understand), could closely follow the handling of European questions by their governments. They could discuss EU questions more frequently, both along lines of national interests and political cleavages. In this scenario, if majority voting in the Council could not be avoided, ministers could at least report to a national parliamentary body before decisions are taken. In addition, a permanent parliamentary institution composed of national MPs could be set up as a watchdog in Brussels. Instead of complaining that at least half of their legislative work derives from EU decisions, the national parliaments could try to regain control over it.

Furthermore, this scenario is capable of responding to all kinds of flexibility initiatives. The composition of any institution in this context could vary

according to the subjects treated. So why not make better use of the component wholes? This question is not easy to answer. If the creation of additional
institutions for this purpose is envisaged, the main obstacle would be the foreseeable increase in the complexity of decision-making. If more scrutinizing
bodies are created, more blockages are likely to be produced; for example, if
additional institutions composed of national MPs could go to the ECJ at any
stage of the legislative procedure to institute a legal check on subsidiarity, many
proposals would risk facing substantial delays.

As a result, efficiency advocates an equilibrium between central institutions
and national ones. The EU has lived with this equilibrium so far, and has
undertaken several incremental readjustments. Where it has failed is in the
domain of political representation, where no comparable efforts have been
made. At present, the national parliaments play their part mainly on the
executive side of representation, by providing a democratic base for their governments to act within the Council. If we put to one side their partial involvement in the transformation of EU directives into national legislation, they do
not have a direct role to play on the parliamentary side of political representation. While avoiding the creation of new institutions at EU level, there may be
substantial possibilities for evolution in the member states. It is possible that
the introduction of the Euro and the difficulties the EU institutional system
will have legitimizing the decisions resulting from it will serve as an incentive
in that respect.

The EU as a Single Whole Scenario

I suggested, when discussing flexibility, that it might be difficult for the EP to
act as an indivisible institution on matters in which only some member states
participate. A national parliament, even in a federal state, would not encounter
the same problems. Its members would be considered as representatives of the
whole people, and could therefore not be excluded from decision-making at
the federal level. Where is the difference? In national systems, even in federal
ones, the basis of legitimacy is firmly established as a unitary one. This is even
the case with elected senates, where the senators are formally elected by the
people of their respective state or region, but exercise their mandate within a
national political system. Even if a national or federal programme only applies
to some constituent parts, it nevertheless remains within the national sphere of
government. The same can be said of the EU's structural programmes: they
are common initiatives which only affect a number of regions. Nobody would
require a division within any EU institution on this.

The category to be introduced by flexibility is of a completely different
nature. There is, to my knowledge, no precedent in national federal systems
whereby some of the constituent parts are authorized to enact a policy in a
field where the federal government is competent either exclusively or jointly

with these parts. This new category implies that the centre—the Commission, the majority of the member states in the Council and the EP—would be interested in such an initiative, but unable to act. This interest would be demonstrated by agreeing that the initiative contributes to the further uniting of the whole.

Flexibility is not an authorization for member states to enact agreements among themselves in policy areas where they have exclusive competence. These kinds of international agreements already exist. In federal systems, the possibility often exists for a few or all of the constituent parts to conclude agreements among themselves in fields where they are competent. In Germany, for example, the *Länder* have competence for radio and television questions. Where all the constituent parts are involved, we might speak of the confederal dimension within federal systems. As a result, neither the institutional experience of the EU nor the practice of national federal systems provide us with clear indications about how to solve our problem. The EU is likely to enter into a new form of cooperation/integration which requires new answers.

The predominant feeling among participants in the IGC was that flexibility cannot be avoided if the EU is to improve its capability for action. They therefore searched desperately for formulae for including flexibility mechanisms in the Treaty, accompanied by as many safety valves as possible. Alternatively, they could have explored further (or could in the next round of Treaty revision) the possibility of cooperation agreements which would work outside the EU and would eventually be absorbed by it. Schengen might be cited as an example of this, although it was introduced the other way round, which is why it is considered as a negative case, an international agreement between member states where the EU as such should have acted. There were certainly shortcomings in the Schengen institutional arrangements, but the negative image seems due more to the circumstances of its creation than to its actual functioning. One might, on the contrary, imagine categories of international arrangements concluded by some member states which might be integrated formally in the EU in pillars I, II, or III once they have 'matured'. By means of this approach, the EU might achieve a much more substantial degree of flexibility than by insisting that the policies in question should be considered to be part of the EU treaty from the outset. However, a formula for providing democratic accountability in such a category of arrangements would still have to be elaborated.

Conclusions

The present situation of the EU is dominated by a reluctance to discuss its end goal seriously. The EU has become a large club where free-traders, federalists, and many others in between can live together happily, so long as they do not require their underlying convictions (if they have any) to be made the subject of a frank and possibly public discourse. Political science has somewhat followed this trend by insisting on the increasing complexity of the construct, the evolution of which reveals less and less evidence of a single master plan, but rather a multitude of sectoral rationales. But if the EU is mainly characterized as a negotiating system, including substantial shortcomings as regards accountability and transparency, we should try to develop our understanding of the functioning within it of classical political notions like representation.

What I have tried to do in this chapter is to discuss a particular problem in this wider context. If we look at the EC treaty, in institutional terms we find representation mentioned mainly in two ways: the very effective representation of member states in the Council (still exercised largely by the national governments), and the representation of the peoples of the member states in the directly elected EP. Ever since its creation, but more dynamically since the introduction of direct elections, the EP has demonstrated an astonishing evolution away from the limitations of its original mandate. Reluctantly, the member states have had to respect this evolution by granting budgetary powers, participation in legislation, enhanced political control of the Commission, and other rights. Internally, the creation of multinational political groups was the main driving force for overcoming national divisions to a considerable extent. The EP can be proud of these achievements.

But in terms of political representation, how far do these improvements go? Are they sufficiently important to maintain that the EP represents the general interest of the EU as a whole? For the time being at least, there is no major challenge to this assumption, but the deficiencies which have accumulated over recent years may one day prove fatal. They concern above all the national political parties, which have failed to create a European dimension for the parliamentary mandate. The selection of candidates and campaign issues are largely dominated by national factors, a possible identification with European leaders has not been pursued, and the various European party confederations play a marginal role in this context. The situation resembles that of the German *Bundestag* or the French *Assemblée nationale* being composed solely of members from regional parties.

As a result, I would argue that there are certain elements within the EP which are representative of the EU as a whole, but that, on the other hand, it seems clear that for both constitutional and attitudinal reasons, the representation of the component wholes is likely to remain stronger than the majority of EP members are prepared to admit. The proof of the pudding lies in flexible integration. If, in the present EU of fifteen members, and the future EU of twenty, twenty-five, or more members, some of the more active and capable ones want to go ahead while respecting certain procedures, would the whole of the EP then be in charge of controlling, legislating, and authorizing credits for the respective policies, or would it only be those MEPs who have actually been elected in these countries?

The EP has repeatedly and clearly said that it will never split up, and that it considers itself in its present composition to have competence for these possible additional policies also. On the other hand, in early 1997, the Dutch presidency indicated for the first time in a public document that it is of the opposite opinion, and that the EP should, like the Council, split up in these cases. A constitutional conflict of some magnitude is therefore brewing.

What is the role of political science in all of this? Perhaps, influenced as it has been by the pluralist tradition, then by neo-functionalist, neo-corporatist, multi-tier network and other approaches, all of which have their merits, it has not insisted enough on the fact that political representation in a democratic system must define its base. In a national state, the national state is the base, which is why so many studies can just concentrate on its component parts and the mediation of interests, some even pretending that the state has largely withered away. In the EU, a comparable framework does not exist. This may be an advantage for day-to-day activities, but it is a serious shortcoming when fundamental problems can no longer be avoided.

This leads to the question, in how far it is possible to democratize the EU, an issue which was already part of the classical discussion about the democratic deficit. But recently, more radical answers have been put forward (see Chapters 6 and 7). To put this argument in a nutshell: There is no chance of a possible EU democracy, because there is no European people, no *demos*. No *demos*, no democracy—quite simple. What we might then be able to secure for the EU at most is some kind of limited legitimacy, either based on a generally agreed set of procedures, and/or on an acknowledged output. There is insufficient room to discuss these assumptions in detail here; I will therefore limit myself to a few remarks. The starting point could be called 'the *demos* trap'; it stems from a holistic, static notion of 'the people' which probably never existed. When analysing the EU, we should avoid the personal mines left over from former generations of constitutionalists. If anything, *demos* should rather be analysed in its classical sense as the totality, the congregation of the citizens, and not in its 19th-century distortion, which puts an abstract 'people' to the forefront and seats the citizen in the second row. In strengthening links with the citizens, the EU is on the right track.

The second point concerns the separation of input and output. The underlying idea is to retain the democratic input where it exists, in the member states, and to separate from it the EU part of the output (Scharpf 1999). The democratic discourse would remain where the peoples are, and EU decisions would be taken in a way which would 'neutralize' questions about democracy in a regime-like situation. A number of guarantees concerning procedures would be added.

It is very doubtful whether such an easy way out is feasible. The EU has already gone too far for that. Too much of the public arena in the member states has been involved to separate the parts again. As a result, whether we like it or not, political representation, democracy, and legitimacy will remain on the EU agenda for the foreseeable future. They are notions that have their origins in the nation state, and they need to be adapted to presently evolving forms of government and governance. If we look closely, there is nothing fundamentally new in this, because these notions were never static. What is new is the acceleration of the changes in our living conditions, in terms of space, time, and intensity among others, which is reflected in our societies and public institutions. As far as the EU is concerned, political representation, together with democracy and legitimacy, is one of the key notions that present a major challenge, and which need to be analysed more closely.

PART III

Flexibility and the Challenge of Enlargement

9

Negotiating Flexible Integration in the Amsterdam Treaty

ALEXANDER C.-G. STUBB

In the early hours of 18 June 1997, the Amsterdam European Council concluded the 1996–7 intergovernmental conference (IGC) of the European Union (EU). This chapter will focus on the negotiations which led to the institutionalization of closer cooperation or flexible integration,[1] that is, the possibility for a number of member states to cooperate more closely in specific areas using the institutional framework of the EU. Although it might not be used in the short term, flexibility is an important legal and political issue, influencing all aspects of EU activity in the long term. The notion of flexibility is not new to the EU, but the Amsterdam Treaty provides the first institutionalization of this concept as a basic principle in the Treaties. This chapter tries to determine how the subject was approached in the negotiations. It is divided into four parts:

(1) a description of the flexibility clauses in the Treaty;
(2) the agenda-setting stage, which lasted from June 1994 to June 1996;
(3) the drafting stage, which ran from July 1996 to December 1996; and
(4) the negotiating stage, which lasted from January 1997 to October 1997.

This chapter contains parts of the author's Ph.D. thesis: 'Flexible Integration and the Amsterdam Treaty: Negotiating Differentiation in the European Union', submitted in December 1998 to the International Relations Department of the London School of Economics and Political Science under the supervision of Professor William Wallace.

The views presented in this paper are strictly personal, and do not necessarily reflect those of the Finnish Ministry for Foreign Affairs, by whom the author was employed before and during the IGC. The assessment is based on public documentation of the Conference. References to the negotiations were obtained from a number of anonymous interviews with other participants in the IGC. The author was a member of the Finnish negotiating team during the negotiations.

[1] It is interesting to note the evolution of the general terminology of differentiation between 1994 and 1997. When the IGC debate was launched in 1994, Schäuble and Lamers, among others, referred to a 'hard core' of member states, and the academic community began talking about 'differentiated integration'. Next, the Reflection Group preparing the agenda for the IGC talked about 'flexible integration', and finally, the Amsterdam Treaty institutionalized the most politically correct and least ideologically charged term of 'closer cooperation'. This chapter will use 'flexibility' as the over-arching term, because it is the broadest one signifying all forms of differentiation. Closer cooperation only covers what can be called 'enabling clauses'.

Both internal and external factors influenced the end result of the IGC negotiations on flexibility. Internally, the negotiations were difficult because flexibility meant different things to different people. For Germany and France, for instance, flexibility was a means by which to deepen the integration process, whereas for Britain it was a way of opting-out from further integration. From the publication of the Schäuble and Lamers paper in 1994 to the final stages of the negotiations, there seemed to be an unusually high level of confusion and, on occasion, ignorance about the subject being negotiated. For this reason, the new Treaty provides a rather random set of rules for the management of flexibility.

Externally, there were three hidden agendas in the negotiations, each of which was addressed before the end of the IGC. First, there was the aim of driving the integration process forward without the awkward, unwilling member states. This problem partially solved itself through the British elections on 1 May 1997, when a more pro-European Labour government was elected. Second, there was the prospect of enlargement to over twenty-five member states. This challenge was met by the Commission's Agenda 2000 document, and a consensus among the member states that the enlargement negotiations would begin with 'five plus one' applicant countries. Third, there was the prospect of a small Economic and Monetary Union (EMU). When the IGC began, it appeared that the convergence criteria would be met by only a limited number of member states, and that EMU would therefore go ahead with only a few countries. By the time the IGC negotiations drew to a close, it had become clear that a total of eleven member states would be likely to join the third stage of EMU, with the result that the need for institutionalized flexibility seemed less acute.

This chapter is the story of the flexibility negotiations as seen through the eyes of a practitioner. The analysis is heavily actor-based but, for the sake of streamlining the analysis, member states are presented as unitary actors.

The Flexibility Clauses in the Amsterdam Treaty

The new treaty provides for three basic forms of flexibility: enabling clauses; case-by-case flexibility; and pre-defined flexibility.

Enabling Clauses

The enabling clauses are the main flexibility innovation of the Amsterdam Treaty. They enable the willing and able member states to pursue further integration in a number of policy areas within the institutional framework of the EU, subject to certain conditions set out in the Treaties. Examples include a general flexibility clause and clauses specific to the first and third pillars.

TABLE 9.1. Main forms of flexibility in the Amsterdam Treaty

Form of flexibility	Definition	Example
Enabling clauses	Enables willing and able member states to pursue further integration (subject to certain conditions set out in the treaties) in a number of policy areas within the institutional framework of the Union	• General flexibility clause (Articles 43–45 TEU) • Clauses specific to the first pillar (Article 11 TEC) • Clauses specific to the third pillar (Article 40 TEU)
Case-by-case flexibility	Allows a member state to abstain from voting on, and to formally declare that it will not apply, a decision which will nonetheless commit the Union	• Constructive or declaratory abstention (Article 23 TEU)
Pre-defined flexibility	Covers a specific field, is pre-defined in all its elements including its objectives and scope, and is applicable as soon as the Treaty enters into force	• Protocol No. 2 integrating the Schengen *acquis* into the framework of the EU • Protocol No. 3 on the application of certain aspects of Article 14 TEC to Britain and Ireland • Protocol No. 4 on the position of Britain and Ireland in the new Title IV of the TEC • Protocol No. 5 on the position of Denmark in Schengen

A general flexibility clause to be inserted as a new Title VII into the Treaty on European Union (TEU) (Articles 43–45 [K.15–K.17]), sets out the general conditions and institutional arrangements for the enabling clauses. The aim is to preserve the basic principles of the Treaties, and to safeguard the interests of any member state which is outside the framework of closer cooperation. Eight conditions are laid down, which set the framework for closer cooperation. Flexibility must:

• further integration
• maintain the single institutional framework
• constitute a measure of last resort

- involve the majority of the member states
- preserve the *acquis communautaire*
- protect outsiders
- be open to all
- comply with the additional criteria laid down in the pillar-specific enabling clauses.

The clauses applicable to the first and third pillars (Articles 11 [5a] TEC (Treaty of the European Community) and Article 40 [K.12] TEU) set out the specific conditions and decision-making mechanisms in each of those areas. In the first pillar, flexibility is restricted by a so-called 'negative list', which states that flexibility can be established so long as the proposed cooperation:

(1) does not concern areas which fall within the exclusive competence of the Community;
(2) does not affect Community policies, actions or programmes;
(3) does not concern the citizenship of the Union, or discriminate between nationals of member states;
(4) does not go beyond the limits of the powers conferred upon the Community by the treaty; and
(5) does not constitute a discrimination or a restriction of trade between member states, or distort the conditions of competition between them.

The decision triggering flexibility in the first pillar is taken by a qualified majority vote (qmv) in the Council. If, however, a member state declares that, for important and stated reasons of national policy, it opposes the granting of the authorization of a flexible measure, the matter is referred to the European Council for decision by unanimity (the so-called 'emergency brake'). The initiative for a flexible solution originates in a request to the Commission from the member states concerned. The Commission then submits a proposal, and has the final say as to whether or not a particular flexible solution will be pursued. The possibility of joining a flexible solution is also dependent on a decision by the Commission.

In the third pillar, two conditions apply for flexibility. The cooperation proposed should respect the powers of the European Community and the objectives laid down in the third pillar, and must have the aim of enabling the Union to develop more rapidly into an area of freedom, security and justice. These conditions are in line with the more specific conditions set out in areas covered by pre-defined flexibility (see below). The trigger mechanism is the same as in the first pillar (qmv and the 'emergency brake'). The difference from the first pillar is that, instead of a binding proposal, the Commission gives only a non-binding opinion on the initiative put forward by the member states. In addition, instead of the Commission's approval being required, it is the participating member states who decide whether a non-participating member state may join the flexible solution.

Case-by-Case Flexibility

This allows a member state to abstain from voting on, and to formally declare that it will not apply, a decision which will nonetheless commit the Union. This so-called 'constructive' or 'declaratory' abstention is a cross between a decision-making mechanism and flexibility, and is provided for in the second pillar (Article 23 [J.13]).

Constructive abstention is not new to the Treaties. Article 205(3) [148(3)] TEC states that: 'Abstentions by members present in person or represented shall not prevent the adoption by the Council of acts which require unanimity'. Article 23 [J.13] now contains almost exactly the same wording: 'Abstentions by members in person or represented shall not prevent the adoption of . . . decisions'. The difference between the two forms of declaratory abstention is that, in the first pillar the decision binds the EU as a whole, including the abstaining member states, whereas in the second pillar, the decision does not bind the abstaining member state. Nevertheless, Article 23 of the Amsterdam Treaty includes a mutual solidarity clause similar to that of Declaration 27 of the TEU. Article 23 states that: 'In a spirit of mutual solidarity, the member states concerned shall refrain from any action likely to conflict with or impede the Union action . . . '.

Pre-defined Flexibility

This covers a specific field, is pre-defined in all its elements (including its objectives and scope), and is applicable as soon as the treaty enters into force. In the Amsterdam Treaty, pre-defined flexibility is primarily laid down in the protocols and declarations. Examples include:

1. Protocol No. 2 integrating the Schengen *acquis* into the framework of the European Union.
2. Protocol No. 3 on the application of certain aspects of Article 14 of the TEC to Britain and Ireland.
3. Protocol No. 4 on the position of Britain and Ireland in the new Title IV on visas, asylum, immigration, and other policies related to the free movement of persons.
4. Protocol No. 5 on the position of Denmark in Schengen.

The most obvious previous examples of pre-defined flexibility are the British opt-outs from the Social Protocol and EMU, and the Danish opt-outs from EMU, defence, citizenship, and police cooperation.

The Agenda-setting Stage: June 1994–June 1996

The first stage in the negotiations which resulted in the institutionalization of closer cooperation was the agenda-setting stage, when the agenda for the 1996

IGC was established and some of the most important questions on flexibility were raised. It began with the Corfu European Council in June 1994, included the opening of the IGC at the informal Turin European Council on 29 March 1996, and ended with the Florence European Council in June 1996. It can be further divided into four subphases.

From Corfu (June 1994) to Messina (June 1995)

The Corfu European Council established 'a Reflection Group to prepare for the 1996 Intergovernmental Conference' to be headed by Carlos Westendorp of Spain, and asked it to begin its work during the Italian Presidency (European Council 1994a: 15). The heads of state and government further invited the institutions of the EU to submit reports on the functioning of the Maastricht Treaty by the spring of 1995, which they duly did (Council 1995; European Parliament 1995b; Commission 1995a; European Court of Justice 1995; Court of First Instance 1995; Court of Auditors 1995; Economic and Social Committee 1995; Committee of the Regions 1995). The mandate for the Reflection Group did not make a direct reference to the examination of flexibility. Nevertheless, the Group was urged to examine measures 'deemed necessary to facilitate the work of the institutions and guarantee their effective operation in the perspective of enlargement' (European Council 1994a: 16).

Although there had been extensive debate on the issue of flexibility since the publication of the Schäuble–Lamers paper on 1 September 1994, only two of the eight reports submitted to the Reflection Group contained specific references to the notion of flexible integration. The Commission's report suggested that further enlargement would force the Union 'to look more closely at the possibility of different speeds of integration' (Commission 1995a: 6). The Commission was anxious to ensure that the single institutional framework be preserved, and that any form of flexibility would aim to achieve the Community's common objectives. The report made it clear that the Commission was 'utterly opposed' to any form of à la carte integration which would allow the member states to pick and choose areas of policy preference.

The European Parliament (EP) had clarified its thinking on flexibility since its somewhat contradictory 'Resolution on a multi-speed Europe' of 28 September 1994. In its report to the Reflection Group, the Parliament noted that the increase in diversity might well require flexible arrangements in the future. Following the same general line as the Commission, the EP said that flexibility should not lead to a Europe à la carte, and should not undermine the principle of equality of all states and citizens of the Union. In specifying the first strict conditions of flexibility, the EP emphasized that flexibility 'should not undermine the single institutional framework, the acquis communautaire or the principles of solidarity and social cohesion throughout the European Union' (European Parliament 1995a: 8).

At first sight, it seems somewhat surprising that the Council's report made no mention of flexible integration. After all, at a later stage it was the Council Secretariat which provided the impetus for the institutionalization of flexibility as a treaty principle (see below). The reason is that the Council's report differed from those of the Commission and the EP in as much as it had no political preface. It focused, as requested, on the experiences relating to the implementation of the Maastricht Treaty, whereas the other reports were policy papers with a clear political agenda and vision, which sought to influence the debate in the Reflection Group.

The Dutch government released an important early contribution to the flexibility debate in 1994, in which it argued that flexibility should be temporary. This Dutch intervention was important in that it provided the first set of conditions for flexibility introduced by a member state. On 2 March 1995, the Spanish government elaborated on these conditions in a White Paper dealing with the IGC. This document introduced the idea of non-exclusion in relation to flexibility, by stating that no member state should be excluded from closer cooperation. More importantly, it provided a second set of conditions on flexibility to be introduced by a member state. These conditions were later to be found, virtually unchanged, in the report of the Reflection Group, which was chaired by Carlos Westendorp of Spain, who was involved in the drafting of both the Spanish White Paper and the report of the Reflection Group. The language of the document clearly shows that Spain was on the defensive about flexibility, believing that decisions should be made by unanimity, and cohesion should be safeguarded.

From Messina (June 1995) to Madrid (December 1995)

The Reflection Group was set up in Messina on 2 June 1995. It was composed of the personal representatives of the Foreign Ministers of each of the member states, a representative of the Commission and two representatives of the EP. The group met fourteen times between June and December 1995, and the discussions revolved around five separate topics: (1) challenges, principles, and objectives; (2) the institutional system; (3) the citizen and the EU; (4) the EU's external and security policy; and (5) the instruments at the EU's disposal. The meetings were usually structured around a set of questions which had been sent out to members of the group in advance. The notion of flexible integration was discussed nine times, not as a separate topic but mainly under the heading of challenges, principles, and objectives. It was to become a separate topic only when the IGC began.

The Reflection Group submitted its final report to the Madrid European Council in December 1995. After the publication of the report, it became clear that the institutionalization of flexibility would be a permanent part of the IGC's agenda, with the result that the EU capitals began considering the issue more carefully. Many member states advocated limits and restrictions on flexibility, and stressed the importance of cohesiveness. The notion of restricted flexibility had its roots in the reactions of the member states to the proposal, set out in the Schäuble–Lamers paper of 1994, of the creation of a core of member states which would drive the integration process forward, namely, Germany, France, and the Benelux. This put many of the other members on the defensive, since they were afraid of being excluded. It is also important to note that the Reflection Group rejected flexibility in the first pillar, and only saw it as a viable option in the second and third pillars. This shows a certain bias and prejudice on the part of some members of the group, who viewed the new member states as prospective troublemakers in the second pillar. Flexibility could overcome this problem, they thought. It was also clear that Britain, Ireland, and Denmark would have problems adopting new provisions relating to the third pillar in general, and the Schengen agreement in particular, and it was thought that flexible solutions could solve this problem too. The first pillar, however, was considered sacrosanct, a notion which was emphasized by the Commission in particular.

By December 1995, the debate on flexibility had come a long way. In enabling the ideas of Schäuble and Lamers to find their way into the conference documentation, the Reflection Group had performed an essential role in setting the agenda for the flexibility debate in the IGC.

From Madrid (December 1995) to Turin (March 1996)

During the time between the end of the work of the Reflection Group, and the beginning of the IGC on 29 March 1996, the member governments worked on their positions for the IGC. The political impulse for the flexibility debate was established in two Franco-German documents which were published before the IGC. The first was a letter produced by Chancellor Helmut Kohl and President Jacques Chirac on 7 December 1995, born out of a Franco-German summit in Baden-Baden. The underlying idea on flexibility was that willing and able member states should not be prevented from closer cooperation so long as that cooperation remained within the established institutional framework, and was open to all members of the EU. The second document was also a joint Franco-German paper, published by Foreign Ministers Klaus Kinkel and Hervé de Charette, and stemming from a seminar held in Freiburg on 27 February 1996. This document referred to the Kohl–Chirac letter, and added that a possibility for opt-outs should be linked to the new proposed flexibility clause, so as to prevent any member state being forced into a particular area of cooperation.

The member states and the EU institutions set out their positions on flexibility in a number of papers on the eve of the IGC. Most of the member states' reports outlined their general IGC positions, and gave a brief overview of the issues pertaining to flexibility. Without going into detail about the individual reports, Table 9.2 outlines some general observations about their content. It is equally useful to outline what the member states and the institutions said about the conditions for flexibility; these observations are outlined in Table 9.3.

TABLE 9.2. Content of the member states' and institutions' intergovernmental conference reports

Issue	Member state/Institution
Mentions flexibility	Commission 1995c, 1996a; Belgium 1995; Benelux 1996; Denmark 1995a, European Parliament 1995c; Germany 1996b; Greece 1995, 1996; Spain 1995, 1996; France 1996; Ireland 1996; Italy 1995a,b, 1996; Luxembourg 1995; Netherlands 1994, 1995a,b,c, 1996; Austria 1995, 1996; Portugal 1996; Finland 1995, 1996b; Sweden 1995a,b, Britain 1995, 1996
Does not mention flexibility	European Parliament 1996b; Denmark 1995b; Netherlands 1995b
Is generally progressive about flexibility	Commission 1996a; Belgium 1995; Benelux 1996; Germany 1996a; Spain 1995, 1996; France 1996; Ireland 1996; Italy 1995b, 1996; Luxembourg 1995; Netherlands 1994, 1995a, c, 1994; Austria 1995, 1996; Finland 1995, 1996b
Is generally open about flexibility	Sweden 1995a,b; Britain 1995, 1996
Is generally hesitant about flexibility	Denmark 1995a; Greece 1995a,b, 1996; Portugal 1996
Pegs flexibility to enlargement	Commission 1996a; Spain 1995, 1996; Italy 1995a; Netherlands 1994, 1995c; Austria 1995; Finland 1996b
Pegs flexibility to the slowest member state	Commission 1996a; Belgium 1995; Spain 1995; Austria 1996
Rejects à la carte as a viable option	Commission 1996a; Belgium 1995; Benelux 1996; Spain 1996; Luxembourg 1995; Netherlands 1994, 1995c; Finland 1996a; Sweden 1995a,b
Supports à la carte	No one
Mentions constructive abstention	Luxembourg 1995; Netherlands 1994, 1995a
Mentions the willing and the able	Commission 1996a; France 1996
Lists conditions and principles	Commission 1996a; Belgium 1995; Benelux 1996; Spain 1995, 1996; Italy 1995b, 1996; Netherlands 1994; Austria 1995, 1996; Finland 1996b; Sweden 1995a,b; Britain 1996
Does not list conditions and principles	Denmark 1995a; Germany 1996b; France 1996; Ireland 1996; Netherlands 1995c, 1996; Finland 1995; Sweden 1995b; Britain 1995

TABLE 9.3. Conditions for flexible integration

Condition	Member state/Institution
Flexibility as the last resort	Commission 1996*a*; Belgium 1995; Benelux 1996; Spain 1995; Spain 1996; Austria 1995, 1996; Finland 1996*a*
Maintaining the single institutional framework	Commission 1996*a*; Benelux 1996; Spain 1996; Italy 1995*b*, 1996; Austria 1995; Finland 1996*b*; Sweden 1995*a,b*
Compatibility with the objectives of the treaty	Benelux 1996; Netherlands 1994; Finland 1996*b*
Open to all member states	Commission 1996*a*; Belgium 1995; Benelux 1996; Spain 1995, 1996; Italy 1995*b*, 1996; Netherlands 1994; Austria 1995, 1996; Finland 1996*a*; Britain 1996
Safeguarding the single market	Commission 1996*a*; Belgium 1995; Benelux 1996; Spain 1995, 1996; Italy 1996; Netherlands 1994
Safeguarding the *acquis communautaire*	Benelux 1996; Spain 1995, 1996; Italy 1995*a*, 1996; Netherlands 1994; Finland 1996*b*
Control of the European Court of Justice	Commission 1996*a*
Trigger by other than unanimity	Belgium 1995; Netherlands 1994
Key role for the Commission	Belgium 1995; Benelux 1996
Supporting measures for outsiders	Spain 1995, 1996; Finland 1996*b*
Flexibility should be temporary	Spain 1996; Austria 1996; Finland 1996*b*
Flexibility judged on a case-by-case basis	Spain 1996
Flexibility should not distort competition	Austria 1995

The following observations can be extrapolated from these reports. First, by the end of March 1996 (just before the opening of the IGC), it had become clear that flexibility would be on the agenda. Each of the member states mentioned the subject in their reports. Second, all the member states and the institutions seemed to reject the notion of an *à la carte* Union—or at least no member state advocated a pick-and-choose form of flexibility. Third, a group of hesitant member states began to emerge; it included Sweden and Britain (both of whom were open to flexibility but did not advocate it), Greece, Denmark, and Portugal. Somewhat surprisingly, Spain saw itself as a core country, and seemed to support some institutionalization of flexibility. Fourth, it is also interesting to note that, although many member states seemed to support the notion of flexibility, almost all of them suggested 'tight strait-jackets' for its application. This was a clear indication of the general feeling that, although flexibility was desirable, it should be managed in such a way that it would not get out of hand.

From Turin (March 1996) to Florence (June 1996)

The Turin European Council of 29 March 1996 provided the mandate for examining flexibility in the IGC by asking it

> to examine whether and how to introduce rules either of a general nature or in specific areas in order to enable a certain number of member states to develop strengthened cooperation, open to all, compatible with the Union's objectives, while preserving the *acquis communautaire*, avoiding discrimination and distortions of competition and respecting the single institutional framework.   (European Council 1996a: 5)

From the start of the negotiations, it was clear that flexibility would be one of the most difficult and sensitive areas of discussion. Between the European Councils of Turin and Florence in March and June 1996, respectively, the member states began discussing their general positions on flexibility. During that time, the Italian presidency submitted two background documents on flexibility (CONF 3821 1996 and CONF 3860 1996) which were, by nature, rather general, in that they asked questions rather than provided answers. Among other things, the member states were asked whether they would prefer a general flexibility clause or flexibility on a case-by-case basis. At this stage, an interesting coalition of willing and able member states emerged: the six founding countries and the three newest member states preferred a general flexibility clause, whereas the rest suggested that a case-by-case approach would be sufficient. The reason for these preferences was grounded in the assumptions, current at the time, about which countries would be eligible to participate in the third stage of EMU. The oldest and newest member states believed they would form the core, whereas the remainder assumed they would be left out on the periphery. As will be shown, these attitudes changed as the IGC progressed.

The German and French delegations were the first to speak on flexibility in the first meeting where the subject was discussed. Both delegations alluded to the Kohl–Chirac and Kinkel–de Charette letters, and explained that they had been working together on the subject. Despite this, the parameters for the application of flexibility came from the so-called 'Ten Commandments of Flexibile Integration', a non-paper presented by the Finnish government on 30 May 1996. These 'commandments' comprised a number of rules intended to help govern the application of flexibility, such as the single institutional framework. The creation of these commandments constituted a milestone for the new articles on flexibility in the Amsterdam Treaty since, in one way or another, each of them played a part in the new treaty provisions.

The Florence European Council, 21–22 June 1996 asked the IGC to continue to examine the notion of flexibility. By this stage it had become clear that all the member states wanted strict rules regulating flexibility. Nevertheless, flexibility was discussed on a rather general level, and few delegations wanted to reveal their true position. Indeed, none of the member states seemed to have a clear set of answers to all the questions posed by the presidency documents. This was hardly surprising, since the position papers issued by the member states before the IGC began had been abstract, not only because the member states did not want to reveal their positions, but also because they were not sure what their actual positions were. (This supports the idea that IGC negotiations are a learning process.) Despite the vagueness of the positions of the member states, however, the agenda for flexibility had been set, and issues of decision-making, form, and control had been raised. It then became the task of the Irish presidency to draw up the first, concrete draft article on flexibility.

The Drafting Stage: July 1996–December 1996

The Irish followed the advice of the Florence European Council, and put flexibility on the agenda at an informal meeting of the representatives of the Foreign Ministers in Cork, 5–7 July 1996. The discussions were based on a non-paper questionnaire circulated by the presidency, which dealt with the arguments for and against flexibility, the conditions and principles of flexibility and the methods and instruments of flexibility. The debate was not conclusive at this stage, but it was nevertheless helpful in mapping out the more concrete positions of the various member states.

On 25 September 1996, the first draft article on flexibility was introduced by the Irish presidency (CONF 3914 1996). A general flexibility clause (without specific conditions) was accompanied by three specific flexibility clauses which set out the conditions for flexibility in each pillar. The first trigger mechanism for flexibility was outlined. In the first pillar, the decision to seek a flexible solution was to be made by qmv, whereas in the second and third pillars unanimity would be required. The debate on the draft article at the level of the representatives on 30 September demonstrated that flexibility had become one of the most difficult issues under negotiation. Most delegations thought that the flexibility issue would be solved in the final stages of the negotiations. A feeling of indecisiveness reigned, along with a belief that there were far more questions than answers. At this stage, a majority of the member states were of the opinion that flexibility was more suitable for the second and third pillars than the first, an assumption which was to be overturned later by the Dutch presidency. It should be noted that the article was not drafted by Irish civil servants, but rather by the Legal Service of the Council, whose influence in IGCs is a much neglected issue in the literature on European integration. Given the fact that it provided over 90 per cent of the draft articles which were used as the basis for negotiation in the 1996–7 IGC, its role should not be underestimated.

After the informal Dublin European Council in early October 1996, the general positions on flexibility began to change. By the spring of 1996, nine member states had advocated a general flexibility clause, and six member states had supported a case-by-case approach to flexibility. By October 1996, flexibility was being seen as a necessity, everyone accepted that both general and specific flexibility clauses would be inserted into the new treaty, and the remaining differences in opinion concerned how, rather than whether, these clauses would be incorporated.

The political impulse for flexibility was further strengthened by a third Franco-German memorandum, presented on 17 October 1996 (CONF 3955 1996). The document supported a general flexibility clause for the first pillar, so long as the institutions retained their regular role and the *acquis communautaire* was preserved. This was the first time that flexibility in the first pillar emerged as a viable option. The document was diplomatic about the trigger mechanism for flexibility, suggesting that no member state should have the right of veto on this point. It is interesting to note that the subject of the document was defined as 'closer cooperation with a view to increased European integration', a clear indication that, throughout the IGC, France and Germany viewed flexibility as a way forward towards deeper integration.

Flexibility was discussed at ministerial level on 25 November 1996. The discussions were not based on a draft article; instead, ministers were asked to discuss a set of questions (CONF 3985 1996). This highlights the self-evident: drafting is seldom done at ministerial level, at least not in the early stages of the negotiations. Most ministers stressed the importance of keeping flexibility within the treaty framework, both before and after the next enlargement. Many emphasized the importance of safeguarding the objectives, the *acquis communautaire*, and the institutional framework of the EU. However, the ministers were not willing to discuss specifics, such as the decision-making mechanisms of flexibility. At this ministerial meeting, Portugal announced that it would submit a draft article on flexibility, but when it appeared it was defensive in character, and was never really discussed at ministerial or representative level (CONF 3999 1996). The main aim of the document was to ensure that any decisions on flexible arrangements would require unanimity.

The legacy of the Irish presidency was a Draft Treaty, published in December 1996 (CONF 2500 1996). It did not propose a draft article on flexibility, but rather outlined a number of issues where a degree of common agreement seemed to have emerged: for example, flexibility should not be regarded as an alternative to the normal decision-making process, it should only be used subject to precisely defined conditions, it should be open to all member states, and the rights of non-participating member states should be respected. Nevertheless, the Irish presidency had carried out very important groundwork for the final stage of the negotiations. The parameters and models of flexibility had been defined in earlier draft articles at the level of the representatives. With hindsight, it could be argued that flexibility was a less sensitive issue to negotiate than many had been led to believe. When looking at the articles on flexibility being discussed before the Irish Draft Treaty, it is clear that they do not differ much from those which were negotiated in the final stages of the IGC. The rather timid approach of the participants can, however, be explained by the fact that none of the three 'hidden agendas' of the flexibility negotiations—awkward member states, EMU, and enlargement—had been resolved by the time of the Dublin European Council of 13–14 December 1996.

The Negotiating Stage: January 1997–October 1997

The first draft article on flexibility proposed by the Dutch presidency was released on 11 February 1997, following a discussion about flexibility at ministerial level on 20 January 1997. The Dutch document was influenced by five other documents which had been released in the previous weeks. The first of these was a non-paper (SN 639 1996), distributed on 20 December 1996 before the end of the Irish presidency. It contained a general flexibility clause, supported by three specific flexibility clauses. The second document was a questionnaire released on 8 January 1997 (Non-Paper SN 500 C1 1997) and again on 16 January 1997 (CONF 3802 1997), which asked the member states to indicate their positions on flexibility, ranging from enabling clauses to pre-defined flexibility. The third document was a draft article on flexibility, circulated by the Italian delegation on 15 January (CONF 3801 1997). The fourth was a paper distributed by the Commission on 23 January (CONF 3805 1997), and the fifth, dealing with the incorporation of Schengen, was released on 4 February by the presidency. These documents, and the ministerial debate on flexibility held on 20 January 1997, were important in moulding the Dutch presidency's thinking on flexibility. The Commission document was particularly important, in that it gave a 'green light' to the idea of an enabling clause, provided that it was accompanied by safeguards.

The first Dutch draft article (CONF 3813 1997), mentioned above, had an important impact on the final version of the flexibility clauses included in the Amsterdam Treaty. It was based on the premise that a general flexibility clause and three specific clauses could be incorporated into the new Treaty. The need for a flexibility clause in the second pillar was questioned by the presidency, however, which suggested that constructive or declaratory abstention combined with the 'old' Articles J.4(4) and J.4(5) would provide sufficient flexibility for Common Foreign and Security Policy (CFSP) matters. The reason for this stems from the fact that the president of the group of representatives, Michiel Patijn, was personally very sceptical about any form of flexibility in the second pillar. He believed that questions with defence implications would be better taken care of by the North Atlantic Treaty Organization (NATO) than by any flexible arrangement which might eventually lead to the incorporation of Article 5 of the Treaty of West European Union (WEU) into the EU. Patijn's influence on flexibility in relation to the Schengen agreement was equally important.

The representatives' meeting of 17–18 February 1997 witnessed the first detailed discussions on flexibility, indicating that the real negotiations had finally begun. The member states began to reveal their positions on questions relating to decision-making mechanisms, the budget, the number of participants and the involvement of the institutions, and a new set of coalitions began to emerge. At this stage of the negotiations, the member states could be grouped as follows:

(1) the *progressive* member states: those able and willing to pursue closer co-operation (Germany, France, Italy, Belgium, Luxembourg, Netherlands, Austria, Ireland, and Finland);
(2) the *hesitant* member states: those able but not necessarily willing (Britain, Sweden, and Denmark); and
(3) the *reluctant* member states: those not able but willing (Portugal, Spain, and Greece).

The reluctant member states were aiming to limit flexibility, because they knew they would have difficulty in participating in every flexibility measure proposed. The hesitant member states, on the other hand, wanted to put the brakes on flexibility, because they knew they did not want to participate in all the proposed areas of closer cooperation. Perhaps most surprisingly, it was not the big member states (i.e. Germany, France, and Britain) who were leading the movement for the institutionalization of flexibility. Even though the political impulse had come from the Franco-German axis, it was the progressive quintet of Italy, Ireland, Finland, the Netherlands, and Belgium which was orchestrating the process.

By this stage, the three different forms of flexibility—enabling clauses, case-by-case flexibility, and pre-defined flexibility—had been clarified. In the very early stages of the IGC, in April 1996, the governments had been asked to choose between three different models of flexibility. The first was a multi-speed model, which corresponds to transitional clauses, for example in relation to enlargement. The second was a variable geometry model, which corresponds to enabling clauses, and the third was an *à la carte* model, which corresponds to both case-by-case flexibility and pre-defined flexibility, where a member state can pick and choose in which policy area it wants to participate.

The more ideologically charged terminology had gradually given way to more practical and concrete examples of various possible forms of flexibility. As a result, only the enabling clauses, case-by-case, and pre-defined flexibility were left on the agenda at this stage; transitional clauses were no longer being considered by the IGC. Interestingly, there was a slight contradiction in terms in the position of those member states which rejected the à la carte model, but supported case-by-case and pre-defined flexibility, since they are essentially the same thing. Nevertheless, by February 1997, the negotiators finally had a clearer picture of what was meant by flexibility.

At the end of March, the Dutch presidency circulated a revised draft of some of the issues in the Irish Draft Treaty (CONF 2500 ADD1 1997), in which a draft article on flexibility was also proposed. The trigger mechanism (i.e. unanimity or qualified majority) in the first pillar was left in square brackets, indicating that agreement had not as yet been reached on this issue; pillar two required unanimity; and flexibility in pillar three could, interestingly enough, be triggered by qualified majority voting. The document drew on suggestions from a revised version of the first Dutch draft article on flexibility (CONF 3835 1997), two Irish non-papers—one on the third pillar (3–4 March 1997) and the other on the first pillar (7 March 1997)—and a presidency progress report on the state of play of the Conference on March 19 (CONF 3848 1997). In the ministerial meeting held on 25 March, commemorating the 40th anniversary of the signing of the Treaties of Rome, the presidency's draft article was generally well received. Nevertheless, Britain, Greece, and Portugal were still sceptical about the enabling clauses, and noted that if they were incorporated into the new treaty, any decision based on them should require unanimity. Ireland and Austria, on the other hand, were sceptical about an enabling clause in the second pillar, and suggested that constructive abstention would be sufficient for CFSP matters. On the eve of the ministerial meeting, the Greek delegation had submitted a proposal on flexibility which, much like Portugal's suggestion in 1996, was defensive in character (CONF 3866 1997).

By the time the representatives met on 14–15 April, the negotiations had moved to the stage of drafting articles. The comments from delegations were detailed and technical in nature, confined to proposing changes to the draft article. The delegations were happy by and large with the general enabling clause, and the enabling clause relating to the third pillar. However, there were two specific problems in the first pillar flexibility clause: the first concerned the decision-making mechanism, and the second related to the number of participants in any given flexible arrangement. The hesitant and reluctant member states wanted decisions to be taken by unanimity, while having at least three-quarters of the member states participating at any given time. The progressive member states, on the other hand, sought a qmv mechanism, and argued that half of the member states were enough for any given flexible arrangement. In the second pillar, the debate revolved around whether an enabling clause was necessary for CFSP matters. Here, the reluctant and hesitant member states were joined by Ireland and Austria in supporting constructive abstention in place of an enabling clause. Finland was the odd man out among the ex-neutral countries, because it did not object to a general flexibility clause in the second pillar. Spain, on the other hand, did not support constructive abstention. Interestingly, all the member states who supported an enabling clause in the second pillar suggested that the trigger should be qmv.

The mid-April meeting of representatives preceded the final stage of the negotiations. Three more documents were submitted before the Amsterdam Treaty was concluded. The first was a non-paper (SN 2555 1997), called a 'Compilation of texts under discussion' rather than a draft treaty, because the presidency wanted to keep the debate as objective as possible. The document was discussed in a ministerial conclave on 20 May, at an informal European Council on 23 May, and at the level of representatives on 26–28 May. The second document, a 'Consolidated Draft Treaty' (Non-paper SN 600 1997), amended as agreed in the preceding meetings, was not very different from the first. It had two options for negative lists (i.e. areas that would not be suitable for flexibility) in the first pillar, one more specific than the other. The document was discussed by the Foreign Ministers on 2–3 June, and by their representatives on 5–6 and 9–10 June. The third document, the Draft Treaty published on 12 June 1997 (CONF 4000 1997), was drafted on the basis of these discussions; it included a more restrictive negative list, and the trigger mechanism for pillars I and III was qualified majority, while pillar II required unanimity.

Throughout May and early June, negotiations on flexibility appeared to lose the heat of the previous months, and a mood of indifference prevailed. As mentioned earlier, this was mainly due to the election of a pro-European government in Britain, and the fact that the EMU and enlargement questions had been implicitly agreed. There no longer seemed to be a pressing need for enabling clauses. This was the explicit message from the Franco-German grouping, which seemed to have little passion for enabling clauses, particularly when compared to their positions in the early stages of the negotiations. Also, the fact that the principle would in any event be included in the new treaty was enough for the progressive member states, who must have implicitly believed that the instruments of flexibility could be perfected in future IGCs. In addition, it had become clear that the enabling clauses would not be sufficient in third pillar matters, or in matters relating to the incorporation of the Schengen Agreement and the new Community provisions on visas, asylum, and immigration. Consequently, Britain, Ireland, and Denmark would have to be dealt with in the traditional way, that is, through pre-defined opt-outs.

On the eve of the Amsterdam European Council, only three open questions concerning the flexibility provisions remained. First, what should be the trigger for flexibility? Second, who should have the final say in initiating flexibility in the first pillar? Third, should there be an enabling clause in the second pillar? The debate about flexibility at the Amsterdam summit took less than ten minutes. First, France and Britain suggested that the trigger mechanism for flexibility should be qualified majority, with a so-called emergency brake similar to the Luxembourg Compromise. This idea had been discussed in relation to the second pillar in earlier representatives' meetings, but had not received much support. At the European Council in Amsterdam, however, no one objected to the idea, and the institutionalization of the Luxembourg Compromise in relation to flexibility became a reality. Second, Portugal, supported by Italy, Greece, Belgium, and Austria, suggested that the Commission, in its role as the guardian of the treaties, should have the final say in triggering flexibility in the first pillar. The change was accepted, and the Commission retained its central role in first pillar flexibility. Finally, Britain, Greece, and Austria suggested that the enabling clause in the second pillar be dropped in favour of constructive abstention. The presidency agreed, and the enabling clause was dropped without any objections from other member states.

For those who had been involved in the flexibility negotiations, it all seemed rather anti-climactic. Over thirty months of preparations and negotiations were concluded in less than ten minutes. In retrospect, however, this rather suggests that the subject had been well prepared. Only a few issues were left open before Amsterdam, and the heads of state or government were able to come to an agreement about the new provisions on flexibility relatively easily.

Conclusions

The IGC discussions on flexibility took place at two levels: an abstract political level (prominent during the agenda-setting stage); and a concrete legal one (during the drafting and negotiating stages). As with all IGCs, the focus was on legal detail, rather than political reality. During the conference, the debate focused mostly on the institutional as opposed to the political implications of flexibility; no one asked what flexibility was really needed for, whom it would benefit or in which areas it should be employed.[2] So it is no surprise that although the Reflection Group suggested that flexibility be applied in the second and third pillars but not the first, the end result was that the new treaty institutionalized flexibility in the first and third pillars, but not the second. Nor is it surprising that, although all the member states had rejected the à la carte model at the beginning of the negotiations, it became the central plank of flexibility as institutionalized in the Amsterdam Treaty, in the form of case-by-case and pre-defined flexibility.

---

[2] Admittedly, the Dutch presidency circulated a so-called 'positive list' of areas in which flexibility would be applied, but this list was considered too restrictive.

The documentation clearly shows that the evolution of flexibility was typical of any new concept developed in an IGC. First, the idea was launched; second, the concept was defined; third, a draft article was provided; and finally, the draft article became subject to interpretation and negotiation. No one, however, expected that the flexibility negotiations would continue after the Amsterdam Summit, up until the signing of the new treaty on 2 October 1997 (see below). For an illustration of the evolutionary stages of the debate on flexibility, see Table 9.4.

Much of the flexibility debate revolved around 'what should not' as opposed to 'what should be done'. This approach was evident throughout the IGC, from the agenda-setting stage with the Reflection Group's conditions and Finland's 'Ten Commandments', to the European Council in Amsterdam. Flexibility was not about allowing, it was about disallowing. The reason for this 'defensive' approach to flexibility was that the Schäuble–Lamers paper of September 1994

TABLE 9.4. Evolutionary stages of the flexibility negotiations

Stage	Evolution
Preparatory stage: June 1994–June 1996	• Political impulse from Franco-German letters • Conditional outline by the Reflection Group • Mandate from the Turin European Council • Definitions and forms of flexibility outlined • Conditions for flexibility established • Enabling clauses introduced • Florence European Council announces that flexible provisions will be included in the new treaty
Drafting stage: July 1996–December 1996	• First draft article on flexibility introduced by the Irish presidency • First trigger mechanism introduced • Political impulse strengthened by Franco-German initiative on flexibility • Irish Draft Treaty does not provide a draft article
Negotiating stage: January 1997–October 1997	• Italian draft article focuses the debate • Commission's outline of flexibility in the Community pillar • Doubts on enabling clause in the second pillar cast by Dutch presidency • Enabling clause in the second pillar dropped at Amsterdam European Council • Flexibility institutionalized in the new treaty

suggested that a hard core of five member states (Germany, France, and the Benelux) would drive the integration process forward. A majority of member states saw flexibility as a means of exclusion. In addition a plethora of terms (multi-speed, variable geometry, *à la carte*, and so on) emerged to exacerbate the confused debate (Stubb 1996: 283). The flexibility debate could have been very different if the Dutch government paper of November 1994 had been published earlier. This paper focused mainly on multi-speed integration, and established conditions on the basis of which it could be pursued. However, the stir caused by the Schäuble–Lamers paper ensured that not much attention was given to the Dutch document.

It was during the drafting stage, which occurred under the Irish presidency in the latter half of 1996, that the debate began to gain focus. The presidency, pushed by the Council Legal Service, introduced the first draft article, which was mostly discussed at the level of representatives. In fact, the Irish were not too keen to deal with flexibility and procrastinated for some time. Despite its hesitancy, the Irish presidency should be given credit for the way in which it conducted the flexibility debate. It was wise to make the ministers debate the principles, and to leave the discussion of the draft articles to the representatives. It was equally wise to insist that much of the outcome of the flexibility clauses in the new treaty should depend on how much progress had been made in the IGC in general. This approach maintained the pressure for reform in other areas. It is also important to note that all of the early flexibility articles were drafted by the Council Legal Service, which serves as a reminder of the multitude of players which influence an IGC process: member states, EU institutions, and the presidency. However, although some scholars have argued that interest groups also influence an IGC process (Mazey and Richardson 1997), from personal experience I must disagree. Their influence is more apparent than real, especially in institutional matters. The opposite, of course, is true in the day-to-day business of the Community.

The negotiating stage—from January 1997 to October 1997—was not as exciting as had been expected. The Dutch presidency had prepared the issue well, and by the time of the Amsterdam European Council, it was clear that flexibility would not take centre stage at the summit meeting. Other issues, such as the reweighting of votes in the Council and the number of Commissioners, were competing for that privilege.

But perhaps the most interesting negotiations on flexibility took place after the Amsterdam summit. The question of what had actually been decided on the decision-making mechanism for incorporating the Schengen agreement into the Treaty proved problematic. The post-Amsterdam version of the treaty (CONF 4004 1997) stated that unanimity was required, whereas the pre-Amsterdam Draft Treaty (CONF 4002 1997) suggested that qmv would be sufficient for deciding whether an outsider could adopt legislation which was based on the Schengen *acquis*. The Irish, Danish, and British governments claimed that the original formulation (qmv) had not been changed at Amsterdam, but the Spanish disagreed. After a review of the informal notes and the tapes from the Amsterdam meeting, it was concluded that a change *had* been agreed. Consequently, a unanimous decision will be required of the Schengen members, if Britain, for example, wants to adopt Schengen legislation.[3]

During the course of the IGC, a clear difference emerged between the member states' policy papers and their actions in the negotiations. This was inevitable, since the initial policy papers needed to be sufficiently vague in order to provide the necessary room for manoeuvre and for error during the course of the negotiations. Consequently, the member states' positions changed throughout the IGC, following the mood of the negotiations. Sweden, for example, started with a positive view of enabling clauses, but ended up as one of the most fierce advocates of unanimity as the trigger for flexibility. Positions in IGCs swing for many reasons, but rational choice and calculation are rarely among them. IGC negotiations are a messy and often confusing learning process, where the basic positions of the member states show some continuity, but the specific positions of the negotiators fluctuate in line with the dynamics of the negotiations.

This chapter categorized the positions of the member states as progressive, hesitant or reluctant, but EU negotiations are too complex and fluid to fit neatly into boxes; these simplified categorizations should therefore be treated with caution. The position of a member state is not that of a unitary actor; it is adopted by the government in power, and mediated through ministers or representatives. The ministries in a particular member state can differ more over the national position than the actors at ministerial or representative level in Brussels. During the Dutch presidency, for example, cleavages emerged in the positions on flexibility advocated by the Foreign Ministry and the Ministries of Finance and Social Affairs and Employment in The Hague. Nevertheless, these simple categories do help to shed light on the complex policy developments which took place during the IGC.

The new treaty provisions do not correspond to the form of flexibility advocated by Schäuble and Lamers in 1994 because, in the end, there was no need to push flexibility to the extreme. The most awkward member state had a new pro-European government, the EMU countries had implicitly been chosen and the enlargement question had been solved. By the late spring of 1997, it was clear that flexibility would not be an issue over the next ten to fifteen years, or at least not before the applicant countries' long transitional periods run out. This should not, however, hamper long-term research on flexibility, and indeed some studies of post-Amsterdam flexibility have already emerged (Shaw 1998c;

---

[3] The background to the tension relates to the ongoing debate between Spain and Britain over the status of Gibraltar.

de La Serre and Wallace 1997; Ehlermann 1997; Edwards and Philippart 1997; Philippart and Edwards 1999; Stubb 1997, 1998, 1999).

Expansion leads to diversity, and the greater the diversity, the more the issue of flexibility comes to the fore. The institutionalization of flexibility marks a new phase in the process of European integration. Up until the Amsterdam Treaty, common objectives were sought in unison; now a mechanism for permanent differentiation has been established. In the end, the effects of flexible integration will depend on the desire and the ability of the member governments to apply the policies and the objectives established in the Treaties.

10

Flexibility: A Tool of Integration or a Restraint on Disintegration?

HELEN WALLACE

'Flexibility' emerged as one of the key words in the practitioners' discourse during the intergovernmental conference (IGC) leading to the Treaty of Amsterdam in 1997. The term became part of the new Eurospeak of the process, and shorthand for a broad-ranging debate on the institutions and politics of the European Union (EU). In a way, the term surfaced much as 'subsidiarity' had done in the negotiations leading to agreement at Maastricht in 1991 on the Treaty on European Union (TEU). Subsidiarity had then appeared to provide both a rationale and an operating tool for rearranging the division of labour between the European and national policy arenas. Similarly, flexibility, according to its proponents, promised a new principle and a new tool for responding to differences in the enthusiasms and capabilities of the member states of the EU to take on new tasks of policy integration. In the period following Maastricht, it had become evident that subsidiarity was both a contested concept and a muddled guide for practice. In the previous chapter in this volume, Alexander Stubb explained how notions of flexibility were developed in the IGC, and incorporated into the new treaty. Yet, as Peter Leslie argues in the next chapter, these notions can be interpreted as efforts to address fundamental asymmetries in the integration process. In the aftermath of Amsterdam, flexibility needs to be examined both for its role as a potential principle in the integration process, and for the scope it might offer for resolving problems of practice.

The Inheritance

The history of Western European integration is littered with attempts to provide the means for the more integration-minded governments to forge

Special thanks are due to Beate Kohler-Koch and Alexander Stubb for their probing comments on an earlier draft of this chapter. The revised version provides them with only partial answers. This chapter relies heavily on Françoise de La Serre and Helen Wallace, *Flexibility and Enhanced Cooperation in the European Union: Placebo rather than Panacea?* Research and Policy Papers No. 2, 'Notre Europe', Paris, September 1997.

ahead more quickly than the hesitant in creating tools for intensive policy coop-eration. The European Community (EC), with its precursor the European Coal and Steel Community (ECSC), is the obvious example, embraced only by the integration-minded governments of the day. The then hesitant governments preferred looser arrangements for more limited cooperation, less ambitious both economically and politcally (Wallace 1999).

A variegated pattern also emerged in the field of defence and security through the Brussels Treaty Organization and later the North Atlantic Treaty Organization (NATO) and the Western European Union (WEU), with their differing memberships and tasks. The members of the military alliances thus became separated from the neutral and non-aligned countries. We should, however, note here that the choices made for neutrality or non-alignment by some Western European countries should not be viewed as necessarily reflecting absence of ambition or commitment. Rather, they represented the particularities of the situations of the countries concerned. It can also be argued that there was a valuable synergy in these differentiated security arrangements.

Moreover, the history of relationships between European countries is also one of often vigorous regional groupings and intense special partnerships between neighbours. Some fell within the borders of the EC/EU (e.g. the Benelux grouping and the Franco-German partnership), the two being com-bined in the original formulation of the Schengen Agreement to manage land borders between these adjacent countries; others fell outside or across the boundary of the EC/EU, notably the Nordic family. In addition to relationships based on geographical connection, we have also witnessed a proliferation of groupings of countries based on shared functional agendas. The European Space Agency is one such example, with several others existing in the defence procurement field. The 'normality' of transnational institutional arrangements in Europe is thus one in which there have been diverse groupings, with their memberships and intensity of common action varying over time and accord-ing to circumstances.

It is only quite recently that the argument for conceiving of the EU as all-encompassing in terms both of countries and of functional cooperation has gained momentum among practitioners and the lobbying groups supporting integration. Thus, by the early 1990s, it had begun to be imaginable that the EU might include the whole of Western Europe (more or less), and potentially Central and Eastern Europe as well. In the defence field, a debate began on the prospect of NATO as an eventually 'pan-European' organization or, in some quarters, on the potential for the EU also to become a forum for a 'common defence'. In addition, some practitioners began to argue that the EU should also absorb some of the historically separate European forums for specific func-tional cooperation. In particular, the idea of incorporating the Schengen Agree-ments dealing with border controls began to gain currency.

As the 1996–7 IGC approached, two parallel transitions were clearly taking place. One was a set of moves, started in the Maastricht IGC, by the protagonists of the EU as an all-embracing framework which would subsume other arenas of cooperation. The other was the opening of a debate about how then to handle the different levels of engagement from the participating countries within the EU. The new debate carried many echoes of earlier debates about managing diversity (Stubb 1996; Wallace and Wallace 1995), which had been described by a complicated and confusing vocabulary, with different terms being coined periodically to capture the debate of the moment. In 1996–7, 'flexibility' emerged as the modish term, alternating in the practitioners' discourse with the French-derived term 'enhanced cooperation', signifying the bid to create an avant-garde grouping.

Factors of Change

There were five important factors in 1996–7 which marked this debate out from its predecessors. The first was the well-defined plan to develop an economic and monetary union (EMU), the first flagship project in the EU which had deliberately envisaged the participation of only some of the EU members—a core of the willing and able, within a larger circle of adherents to the other EU regimes. The second factor was that successive enlargements of the EU in Western Europe had brought within the EU membership more countries which were able, but not willing, to extend the shared agenda, as well as countries which lacked some of the capabilities to attain certain policy objectives. Third, the development of the EC into the EU had raised expectations that two different projects of integration might be elided, namely, the political economy project, developed through the EC, and the defence and security project, hitherto organized through NATO and the WEU. Fourth, both the EU and NATO were contemplating Eastern enlargement and the prospect of developing pan-European frames of reference. Fifth, the preoccupation with the consequences of the permeability of borders as regards the free movement of persons had brought new issues onto the integration agenda.

Stubb (1999) argues that flexibility, or a proxy for it, has been debated in the EU whenever discussion has turned to one of the following issues: EMU, foreign and security policy, border management, enlargement or whether and how to exclude 'awkward' countries. As he elaborates, what was distinctive about the 1996–7 IGC was that it had all five of these issues before it, directly or indirectly. Another way of expressing the same point would be to view this recent period as a kind of reprise of the debate in the early 1950s, when discussion veered between plans for an all-embracing framework (at the time only in Western Europe), and those for an exclusive and intimate grouping of the most integration-minded countries. The ECSC and the European Economic

Community (EEC) were, of course, a product of a decision in favour of the latter.

In combination in 1996–7, these factors raised major questions about the recasting of the European integration model and its methodologies. As we shall see in subsequent sections, these questions included how to deal with: *numbers* (from EC6 to a pan-Europe of twenty-five to thirty countries); *dissidents*, with various countries waxing and waning as blockages to consensus—Greece, Denmark, and Britain were the most frequently invoked as 'problems', but others, perhaps especially Spain and Sweden, were also partly in the frame; *stronger differences of characteristics*, with wide ranges of social, economic, and geographical features of a more or less objective kind distinguishing countries across the continent from each other; *new constellations of power*, given both the changed configuration of united Germany and the prospect of enlargement to include many more smaller countries; *resort to cooperation outside the Treaties*, in so far as some European governments practised cooperation outside the main institutional arrangements, with the Schengen Conventions the most frequently cited case; and *new challenges*, in so far as the new Europe presented different issues for potentially shared solutions.

It was asking a great deal to address all of these questions through a single device, and of course the IGC as a whole was concerned with finding a larger collection of new tools that would permit the EU to adapt to its changing context, membership, and policy demands. Yet, flexibility was variously articulated as addressing each of these questions in one way or another. In the event, the IGC did introduce formulae to encourage flexibility, although these formulae were much more constrained than some of those involved had hoped.[1] Other sections of the Amsterdam Treaty were also formulated so as to generate some of the adjustments sought in the IGC. However, several of the difficult issues were deferred, reflecting both differing views on what institutional remedies were appropriate and the imprecise time-line for Eastern enlargement.

It should be noted here that the listing of the factors of change outlined above is derived from the discourses and propositions of the practitioners. Analytically, however, some further distinctions need to be made. Bundled together in the vocabulary of flexibility were: changes in the context and conditions for integration; variations in the objectives of the actors involved; differences in the interests of the actors; controversies about which values and norms should be embedded in the process; debates about the feasible and desirable policy scope for shared regimes; and questioning of the institutional rules and practices through which to develop policy regimes. It is thus hardly surprising that the debate on flexibility became so complex.

---

[1] See Ch. 9.

In this respect, too, there was a stark difference from the Maastricht discussion of subsidiarity. This latter was at least partly rooted in a wider intellectual debate, and backed by a body of literature which gave some insights into the analytics of sharing powers between different levels of government. Different normative preferences could also be located in relation to a familar and articulated set of analytical arguments. In the case of flexibility, the practitioners were operating much more in the dark. Although the underlying issue of managing asymmetries is present within countries, and especially within federal or quasi-federal polities, the analytical literature on asymmetry is much less well developed.

In the following sections, the factors of change that impacted on flexibility are reviewed. Some comments are offered on how far the formulation of flexibility at Amsterdam deals with them, and on the questions which remain to be addressed.

Dealing with Numbers

Two arguments were present in the practitioners' debate about the increasing number of member states in the EU. One held that an institutional framework developed initially for only six participating countries had already been stretched to its limits with the extension of EU membership since 1995 to include fifteen countries. Not surprisingly, this argument was most frequently heard from practitioners and commentators from the early members of the EC, as well as from those practitioners and advocates keen to portray their countries as very integration-minded.

The second argument, widely articulated by both practitioners and commentators, asserted that Eastern and Southern extension to accommodate an as yet unspecified additional number of countries involved so radical an increase in numbers that quite different kinds of institutional arrangements would be needed. The underlying assumption was that there might have been a kind of optimal number of 'like-minded' EU members at some stage in the past, which permitted sufficient intimacy and alignment of interests and values for common policies and a shared legal regime to be viable. However, that optimal cooperation circle had reached its limits—or so ran much of the conventional wisdom.

Such views could draw support from a more analytical discussion of the transaction costs involved in managing cooperation among a large number of actors or units (see for example Olson 1965 and Scharpf 1997). Temptations to defect, to freeride, or to extract side-payments typically either obstruct agreement or burden the negotiators. In the absence of either a strong agreement on solidaristic norms or acceptance of majority-decision rules, large numbers can indeed lead to inefficiency or ineffectiveness of outcomes.

Nonetheless, we should be a little wary before taking this problem as insoluble. It is the kind of problem which the developers of the US federation had to address in the 19th century, as the number of states grew. American experience—a federation of now fifty states—has demonstrated that numbers *per se* may not be the critical variable (in the American case, the issue of whether 'applicants' were slave states or free states, and of how to strike a balance between the two groups was crucial). More important are: first, the extent and nature of differences in characteristics and values; and second, how far linking political mechanisms can bind even quite different states into a single polity.

Hence, in the EU context what may be at least as important as the number of countries involved is how far a shared value set and similar characteristics can be established, and whether or not transnational political and social connections are robust.[2] In the 1996–7 IGC, the articulation of the debate about how many member countries can be managed in a single negotiating set may instead be seen as anxiety about the diffuseness (whether actual or feared) of values and characteristics, as well as about the weakness of transnational links. It is perhaps hardly surprising that the numbers argument seems so compelling for practitioners in the Council of the EU and the European Council, since it is precisely in these forums that the member states as such are represented, and that the aggregating mechanisms are weakest. It is here that the number of participating units acquires primary importance. Those most worried about the consequences have sought solutions in terms of either a stronger rule of majority decision (more qualified majority voting), or ways of reducing the numbers of participants for certain purposes (flexibility mechanisms).

The more socialized and most experienced of the member governments are, not surprisingly, those which are the most disturbed by the prospect of numerous new and inexperienced countries joining 'their' club. The 'old' member states, in particular, expended a lot of effort to push forward the argument that an antidote was needed. Hence, buried in the argument that the number of members as such is the problem is a strong strand of nostalgia about lost intimacy. One meaning of flexibility, therefore, was as a code for reversion to an old inner core of the EC pioneers. This nostalgia gained cogency for much of the period of the 1996–7 IGC, because it seemed as if that same old core group would, more or less (Italian participation was the one most in doubt), be coterminous with the first group of full EMU members.

Evidence on the way the Council of the EU operates does indeed suggest that socialization does occur within this forum, and contributes considerably to the negotiating process (Hayes-Renshaw and Wallace 1997; Lewis 1998*b*). We should, however, be wary of the way in which the argument has been put among the practitioners. In part, it reflects a nervousness from the

---

[2] For a longer version of this argument, see Wallace (1997) and Wallace (1999), which set out the distinction between deep and shallow integration in the context of the EU and its Eastern enlargement.

'old' member governments about their potential loss of influence compared with earlier years. The argument here is more about relative position than about numbers as such. In part, the discussion also represents a recognition that, within a larger and differently constituted group, new behavioural norms, styles, and interests might have to be accommodated. Here, we should note that some late-joining countries have become socialized into the prevailing norms and behavioural codes relatively easily; Ireland and Finland are good illustrations, and their positions in the 1996–7 IGC reflect this (McDonagh 1998; Stubb 1999). Some other member states, as we shall see in the next section, have appeared rather as 'dissidents'.

As the IGC proceeded, however, the nostalgic argument for facilitating pioneer intimacy started to lose force, as it became clear that the first group of participants in the single currency was likely to be rather larger. While EMU might be the key expression of the most important vanguard group, if constituted as ten or eleven members (with Ireland and Finland among them), it would be very different from the core Europe of the Schäuble–Lamers proposal (essentially construed as only five countries). Moreover, this large vanguard would have a rather strong shared characteristic as an inducement to achieving coherence, and a shared value set. In addition, the pressures would then be strong for initially non-participant countries among the EU membership to join EMU.

The other part of the argument about numbers related to further enlargement. Here, the worry about numbers was fuelled by the assumption of persistent differences in characteristics, which would separate new (post-communist) countries from 'West' Europeans. The differences would, it was implied, mean that new members would either not align themselves to the existing coalition pattern within the west European EU, or would destabilize this coalition pattern. Enlargement would bring to the table quite different preoccupations, as well as the inexperience of the not yet socialized, and it would tilt the balance of numbers towards the poorer cohesion countries. Thus, it would be the multiplication of numbers and differences which would defeat the institutional system.

An odd loss of self-confidence within the EU made this line of argument seem compelling in the mid 1990s, as had been the case earlier, at the time of Portuguese and Spanish accession, and subsequently when faced with the accession of some members of the European Free Trade Association (EFTA). Then, as again recently, the European Council concluded that if only two or three new members joined, the institutional system would remain robust. The institutional protocol added to the Treaty of Amsterdam states that

> At least one year before the membership of the European Union exceeds twenty, a conference of representatives of the governments of the Member

> States shall be convened in order to carry out a comprehensive review of
> the Treaties on the composition and functioning of the institutions.

There is no magic about the number twenty. The implicit assumption is that if
new members were to arrive in smallish numbers they might be manageable,
because they could be socialized into the system. Here, we should acknowledge that both rational actor and institutionalist analysts would concur in
acknowledging that experience of negotiation and learning processes would be
likely to facilitate cooperative behaviour, though not to guarantee it, as we shall
see in the next section.

Uncertainty about the multiplication of obstructions which might follow
from a larger number of members made flexibility seem a prudent form of
insurance. What the flexibility proposals at Amsterdam sought to do, *inter alia,*
was to legitimize meetings and decision-making on some issues by fewer
members than the full group. The claim was that smaller groups would be
more 'progressive' and more adventurous, but would act as a kind of magnet
for the tail of doubting governments. As Stubb's categories in the previous
chapter suggest, some adroitness was demonstrated by the advocates of flexibility in appearing to capture the integrationist high moral ground for their
cause.

Yet the corollary risk was that exclusion of the less progressive would inhibit,
rather than encourage, integrationist behaviour by the potentially excluded
member states. The parity principle (or, as Leslie argues in the next chapter, a
form of symmetry) was therefore retained, in that a proposal to act on a more
restricted basis would still be open to challenge, and subject to veto by a
member state 'if a very important and stated reason of national interest' could
be plausibly adduced. An inclusive rule based on the possible recourse by any
member to veto is thus set in tension with the opportunity for an exclusive
group to define a convincing case for going ahead with a line of action on its
own. In one sense, it could be argued that there is nothing new about this since,
in the pre-Amsterdam EU, recourse to the Luxembourg Compromise was in
theory available to a member state which judged its core interests to be vulnerable. All that the Amsterdam negotiation did, so the argument runs, was to
formalize the implicit and hardly used Luxembourg Compromise, perhaps
taking comfort from the fact that it had been so little activated. Yet to encap-
sulate such behaviour in treaty form is to invite and to legitimate its exercise.
There is a real risk that these provisions may have precisely the opposite effect
from that which the proponents of flexibility intended.

Dealing with Dissidents

In tracing the history of the emergence of flexibility in the EU debate, a rather
clear correlation can be found with rising irritation by some member govern-

ments and other EU actors at the 'awkwardness' of some member states. Some late-joining countries have settled into EU membership more smoothly than others. Three are widely cited as having repeatedly caused systemic or policy conflicts: Denmark, Greece, and Britain, each for different reasons. In anticipation, General de Gaulle had blocked British entry twice, and the Commission had counselled against Greek accession in its opinion of the Greek candidature. Some insiders would add Spain and Sweden as also being, in some senses, awkward member states. In an institutional system in which, for some purposes, member states have a form of parity, any member state has the opportunity to be disruptive, and on some issues to veto or fail to deliver ratification of a collective agreement. Flexibility mechanisms might provide an escape from single country vetoes, or so it was argued.

An underlying question here concerns the nature or cause of dissident behaviour by some member states. Several different elements were conflated in the practitioner debate. Singularity or particularism of individual country (or incumbent government) interests prompted some claims of exceptionalism, self-evidently justifiable in the relevant countries, but frequently misunderstood or disliked by other members. Sometimes it has been different norms or values which have prompted governments from particular member states to react differently to proposals for collective EU policies. Sometimes other structural properties of a member state have led to its isolation—or tough demands—in EU negotiations. Here, we might note that we lack thorough evaluative and comparative studies across the member states. Much of the literature on the adaptation of individual countries to EU membership presumes a single trajectory of adaptation (see for example Rometsch and Wessels 1996). Hence we need to keep in mind the question of how far dissident behaviour arises from within the relevant country, and how far it may be prompted or aggravated by insensitive or inelastic behaviour on the part of the prevailing majority.

Distinctive Greek positions have been perceived by other member states as most troublesome on external policy issues, a situation that is derived as much from political geography as from value preferences (Featherstone and Infantis 1996). These have exhibited themselves in EU discussions of relations with Cyprus, Macedonia, and Turkey. Versions of such geographical idiosyncracy are attributed to several, perhaps all, of the current candidate countries, leading to fears of a multiplication of problems in so far as the EU would acquire more difficult and localized interfaces between neighbours with troubled bilateral relations. Much of the debate about flexibility vis-à-vis the common foreign and security policy (CFSP) pillar lay here, although it was also driven by recognition of Danish distance from WEU, and the then British resistance to ambitious extensions of EU powers in the defence and security field. The new British government has since emerged as the leading proponent of European defence autonomy.

The adoption at Amsterdam of 'consensus minus one—or two—or three' as the solution was a pragmatic approach to permit movement. Here, significantly, the principle of inclusion of all member states in the discussion was retained, allowing some member states to dissociate themselves from a majority preference, except when key interests of theirs were at stake. This rather common sense approach is not a *portmanteau* solution to all the problems of dissent about CFSP, but interestingly it preserves the scope for the forum to act as a means of socializing or educating governments with distinctive positions about emerging majority preferences.

In other areas of EU business, the problem of dealing with 'dissidents' has been less adroitly resolved by the Amsterdam provisions. For most of the business of the first pillar, it was recognized that isolation of dissidents was no solution, in that the unity of the single market had to be fostered, and 'opt-out' arrangements from individual policy regimes might cause as many problems as they solved. It was a relief to all the practitioners to be able to end the opt-out for social policy that had been devised for the British Conservative government at Maastricht, and there was little appetite for extending such arrangements. Nonetheless, in two areas of policy new formulations were under consideration: the development of EMU, and the issues surrounding justice and home affairs (JHA).

EMU was the one area where it was already established ground that those member states participating in the single currency regime would have privileged arrangements for closer cooperation, but Maastricht had left some of the definitions contested as to what these arrangements embraced. The Amsterdam formulas for flexibility addressed these, in so far as some scope would thereby be found for decisions agreed to by less than the full membership which might be taken within the EU institutional framework and subject to the normal legal rules. The question of how much scope was not laid down, and it became clear later in 1997 that the harsh political contention between insiders and outsiders would remain. Arguments about the role of the Euro-X club (the group of finance ministers from only those EU member states participating in the single currency) also showed that the Amsterdam provisions on flexibility would not prevent temptations to establish smaller groupings outside the EU's formal framework.

The debate on JHA carried echoes of concerns about what was perceived as, in particular, British dissidence or exceptionalism arising from the persistent refusal of the British government to embrace Schengen. As we shall see below, there was strong pressure to bring the Schengen arrangements within the EU framework. Yet, the exceptionalism of the British, which spilled over to include Ireland because of the long-established Anglo-Irish Free Travel Area, could not be ignored. At Amsterdam, somewhat contradictory conclusions were reached. The special positions of Ireland and Britain were acknowledged, but in very strangely formulated Protocols, which were soon afterwards to give rise to considerable criticism and operating confusion. Denmark was also awarded special status to implement Schengen under international rather than European law, and sympathy for the Nordic arrangements permitted Iceland and Norway to be awarded special 'good neighbour' status of association. On the other hand, blindness (whether wilful or ignorant) about the problems of borders in Central and Eastern Europe entrenched an extraordinarily rigorous insistence in the Amsterdam text that new members must take Schengen commitments on 'in full', whatever the nature of the prior border regime with neighbouring countries not joining the EU. Here we should note the difficulty of understanding the reasons for, and the consequences of, exceptionalism already influencing practice ahead of ratification of Amsterdam and ahead of Eastern enlargement. As examples we should note the delicacy of Hungarian border relations with several of its neighbours, and the adverse results of Poland's imposition of stronger controls over free movement of persons from Belarus and Ukraine under pressure from the EU.

As a general observation, we should here bear in mind a tension about how the integration process should be construed. One definition involves the establishment of 'club membership' with strict rules and privileges, and with high thresholds to separate the club members from the outsiders. Part of the flexibility debate at Amsterdam was about defining club membership as less than the full EU membership for certain purposes, because of the dissident behaviour of some member states. An alternative definition of integration has to do with spreading the values and practices of the members to neighbours, in order to give greater strength and solidarity to the region as a whole, and to surround the EU with a co-opted 'near-abroad'. But co-option requires inclusion in EU regimes and in the socializing institutions which govern them, and it requires some softening of the boundary between members and non-members.

Managing Differences of Characteristics

Much of the history of the EU has been about efforts to find formulas, institutions and policy regimes which weave forms of unity out of diversity. Even in the small founding membership, significant differences marked out individual countries and regions in socio-economic terms, and in relation to physical and geographical endowments. As the membership has expanded, so the range of heterogeneity has grown, always testing the capacity of the EU process to respond, and always questioning the willingness of negotiators and national policy-makers to promote forms of convergence. Further enlargement promises yet more challenges of heterogeneity. To summarize a much longer story (see Wallace and Wallace 1995), the EU has rather an impressive record of adroitness in bargaining, in legislation, and in selective programmes to handle those forms of heterogeneity which result from more or less objective differences of social, economic, and geographical characteristics. This experience provides assets on which to draw in developing mechanisms which might address objective differences in new member states. In other words, differentiation of policy might be a viable strategy for dealing with many of the practical problems of Eastern and Southern enlargement. The flexibility debate points, however, towards an alternative approach, by suggesting that differences of objective or quasi-objective characteristics among the member states might be dealt with by their exclusion from some policy regimes, rather than by aided inclusion.

Several strands in the current debate in the EU add weight to this possibility. First, the move towards EMU and the disciplines associated with its management will quite likely lead to a more doctrinaire approach to what might be the corollaries of monetary alignment, perhaps inducing less sympathy for the less convergent member state economies on some of the softer policy issues. Second, as we hinted above, the development of EU measures for managing JHA, now retitled as an 'area of freedom, justice, and security', are leading towards a much sharper definition of what differences can be tolerated by the EU and its regimes, even in objective circumstances. Third, the line between 'objective' differences of characteristics and 'subjective' differences of taste or political and cultural preference is, in practice, very hard to draw.

Past experience in the EU indicates that the adoption of policy regimes to accommodate differences of characteristics, and especially extremes of relative wealth and poverty, has depended on a strong norm of solidarity as a basis for generosity of treatment and, where appropriate, redistributive mechanisms. Current signals tend rather towards the erosion of solidarity norms. Flexibility, in the sense of opening a space for the able to integrate more quickly, has as its potential corollary an endorsement of the view that it is up to the laggards to help themselves. Here we might note a paradox in the vocabulary of flexibility, since, if differently construed, it could mean allowing to the laggards or less convergent a more elastic form of application of some EU rules and regimes.

The IGC did not address this set of issues explicitly. However, the legitimation of flexibility as a mechanism for a vanguard group to separate itself for certain purposes and to define the ground of future policy regimes could be interpreted as tilting the EU away from solidaristic norms and practices.

Changing Constellations of Power

Discussions of power relationships within the EU have historically been much masked. The character of the bargaining process and some skill of institutional design have diffused and softened the exercise of power. The inclusion of all member states in the negotiating process, combined with the retention of the parity principle for certain purposes, has been a vehicle for facilitating broad endorsement of most collective decisions, whatever the key impulses which have driven particular propositions forwards. Earlier suggestions in the 1970s and 1980s that there should be a governing leadership group, for example in the form of a *directoire*, received little support. The decision rules were inversely structured to protect the weaker members of the EU and to accommodate the outliers. The shared institutions, notably the Commission and the European Court of Justice, also provided mechanisms of inclusion. Thus, the decision rules were developed to prevent particular member states from exercising too much influence, and to foster coalitions as the route to winning an argument.

During the 1990s, these features of the EU system came under increasing strain. The unification of Germany, the prospect of serial enlargement, the tensions between the more integrationist and less integrationist governments (especially as projected by the EMU debate), and the pressures on the Community budget combined to sharpen the distinctions between different categories of members. One manifestation of this was the discussion of the relative weights of larger and smaller member states in the formal voting arrangements of the Council. Another was the debate over the size and distribution of seats in the college of Commissioners. These two issues were discussed without resolution in Amsterdam. We should note that these issues arose less because of concerns about the total number of member countries, and more because of concerns about the relative weight of particular member states.

A third reflection of the debate over the distribution of power was the discussion of flexibility or closer cooperation. To collectivize the reordering of power relationships by developing a group of apparently integrationist countries would, it was felt, soften the exercise of directing roles. The precaution, expressed in the texts at Amsterdam, that other countries could join the vanguard group as and when they were ready was designed to reassure. If successful, the creation of a vanguard group would simultaneously address several issues. The increased weight of Germany within the EU would be counterbalanced by the engagement of other group members. The integrationist vocabulary would be an insurance against complaints of bias and privilege. The presumed predominance of the 'old' member states would help to protect the EU system against dilution and diversion, as new and mostly smaller countries became more involved. The anchoring of the inner group to the EMU project would facilitate the so-called deepening of the EU. If the same spearhead could be used to intensify moves towards a common foreign and eventually defence policy, there would, in the minds of the advocates, be a virtuous circle with its own dynamic.

Although many of these aspirations were not explicitly articulated, they were reflected in some of the surrounding discourse about strengthening the 'little Europe', in order not to be too diverted by the 'large Europe'. Hence, the flexibility debate had some elements of institutional and political creativity, in sharp contrast to the rather clumsy debate about changing voting weights in the Council, or altering the college of Commissioners to the more representational basis of one per member state. However, the constraining of opportunities for the vanguard group to have a clear identity also showed the efforts of those member governments likely to be excluded from this vanguard group to put a brake on its development. In this sense, the outcome of Amsterdam—limited scope for flexibility and deferred decisions on the operations of the Council and Commission—leaves the power issue for later.

Restraining Cooperation outside the Treaties

Over the years, European governments have developed a variety of means to cooperate on shared concerns outside the framework of the Treaties, both bilaterally and multilaterally. By the 1990s, permissive acceptance of such arrangements had been succeeded by anxiety lest such other forms of cooperation might weaken the EU or be a means of escaping the political and legal disciplines of the EU, or else might set up contradictions with EU regimes. But these other arrangements seemed to exist precisely because they had not been accepted by the full membership of the EU, and were built around subjects known to be especially contentious for some EU members. Flexibility looked as if it might provide a pathway to bring these other arrangements within the EU framework, even if some EU members did not (immediately or eventually) want to participate.

Three policy areas seemed particularly relevant. One was EMU, where it became increasingly expected that EMU participants might want to develop flanking policies. A second was in relation to the free movement of persons, where a plurality of links grouped different EU countries (sometimes, as in the Nordic case, with non-EU members), of which the enlarging Schengen group was viewed as by far the most important, and with the most direct connections with areas of EU policy. Schengen was a particularly provocative case, because its classical intergovernmental character meant that it escaped from the EU disciplines of relative transparency, legal guarantees, and due process, and some mechanisms for exercising democratic scrutiny. The third area concerned foreign policy and defence, where the old differentiated arrangements of the Cold War era were being supplemented by new European defence partnerships (the Euro-corps and such like), and *ad hoc* groups containing only a minority of EU members (e.g. the contact group on Bosnia).

It was thus a strategic objective for some member states and the Commission in the 1996–7 IGC to increase the incentives for making the EU framework predominant, even if the price was to accept partial participation by only some EU member states in the short to medium term. The outcome of Amsterdam was to tilt the balance towards the EU, but not unambiguously. In the EMU case, it has probably become harder for EMU members to reinforce the club of single currency adherents by developing other policies alone, at least to the extent that they require formal and legislative or quasi-legislative decision. This does not, however, rule out the temptation or the opportunity for EMU participants to caucus or to collude in one way or another.

In the Schengen case, Amsterdam looks on paper like a major victory for EU inclusiveness, in so far as the texts envisage the Schengen *acquis* being incorporated within the EU process, and a good deal of it within the first (and stronger) pillar. It remains to be seen how this works out in practice. The advocates hope that history will judge Schengen to have been a valuable pioneering experiment, which opened up a critical area of policy for development as a regular EU regime. Critics, less impressed by the prior experience of Schengen, fear that the result may be the ill-considered importation into the EU of uncertain and unstable arrangements.

As for foreign and defence policy concerns, much remains to be seen. The Amsterdam formulation contains some elements designed to make the EU framework more attractive and more capable as a means of focusing both debate and a shared infrastructure for common actions. But it also contains few penalties for, or deterrents to, cooperation among smaller groups of EU members faced with particular events or policy developments. What seems to be evident from the discussions over both NATO and EU reform is that it will be hard to resolve the questions of which EU members are involved in, or committed to, which formula for cooperation as an abstract institutional question. However, the pace of the discussion on European defence autonomy was extraordinary in 1998–9. The British reversed their position to become the keenest proponents of a strong collective European framework and capabilities, working closely with the French. By the time of the Cologne European Council of June 1999, it was more or less agreed that WEU would be folded into the EU, and a cooperative division of labour established. This shift was prompted much more by substance (including the Kosovo war), than by procedure.

Responding to New Challenges

Part of the momentum behind the flexibility debate grew out of dissatisfaction with the so-called 'heaviness' (or *lourdeur*) of the EU institutions, perhaps especially when faced with new challenges. If this was already a problem within an EU of fifteen members, then by analogy it could be expected to become even more of a problem in an EU of, say, twenty-five members. Two different threads wove into the discussion: one was the persistent advocacy of extended qualified majority voting in the Council, which seemed stymied by those who were attached to unanimity as the preferred decision rule; and the second was impatience with the actual practice of consensus formation (under both unanimity and qualified decision rules). The opportunity to construct a vanguard group of the more committed integrationists seemed to deal with both parts of the argument. The vanguard would be constituted by those member states who would have been the majority anyway, but liberated from the blocking minority or stray vetoes of the less integrationist, and by definition, it seemed, the vanguard group would be more committed to integration and in practice operate consensually.

The negotiations over flexibility became the focus for the tension between, on the one hand, attempts to proceed with the earlier logic of institutional development towards a more majoritarian system and, on the other, a re-appraisal of the underlying institutional process by separating the vanguard from the laggards. Neither argument scored a clear victory in the resulting formulations of the Amsterdam provisions. The tension between the two approaches persists, and remains to be tested against the critical issues which had provoked the IGC debate. It remains to be seen what will follow in practice. The constraining of flexibility by a series of conditions and qualifications will not make it so easy for the purported vanguard group to run ahead and pick up new challenges. The late insistence of Helmut Kohl at Amsterdam on retaining the unanimity rule in so many sectors has also dashed some of the hopes of quick progress, even within the presumed leading group.

New Wine in Old Bottles or Old Wine in New Bottles?

Amsterdam, as we have seen, produced some contradictory results which point in different directions. Many of the arguments, both implicit and explicit, echo old debates. But the new context, and the prospects of both EMU and pro-tracted enlargement negotiations, leave many questions still to be addressed, and much ground still to be tested. Flexibility provides no magic solutions to any of the issues. By opening up the space for some institutional experimenta-tion, a different opportunity structure is perhaps offered for the participants to exploit. Yet the poverty of debate on 'the institutional problem' facing the enlarging EU suggests that a great deal more needs to be thought through, if the EU is to refashion its institutions to address its potential agenda and the requirements of its diverse membership. As an operating tool, flexibility can hardly be expected to substitute for other institutional changes on which, by the time of the Cardiff European Council in June 1998, it had already become clear that further deliberations would follow. What then of flexibility as a prin-ciple to guide decisions about the development of the EU integration model? The asymmetries in the construction of the EU, especially faced with eastern enlargement, will persist and could well become more sharply defined. These asymmetries have different implications, depending on what dimension of the integration process is being addressed.[3]

---

[3] For a stimulating analysis of the different implications of asymmetries, see Ch. 11.

Two other elements have emerged from this chapter: one is an issue about 'club membership', and the other relates to the distinction between 'deep' and 'shallow' integration. As regards club membership: it is a strong feature of the EU that it has the characteristics of a club, designed to promote and to extend the privileges of membership for its adherents, and governed by strict rules and codes of conduct among the members. Both the institutional arrangements of the EU and the *acquis communautaire* are versions of the obligations (and benefits) of membership. Each enlargement negotiation can be viewed as being focused on determining whether and how other countriers might meet the EU club's eligibility criteria. Necessarily, the club concept involves forms of discrimination against non-members, and hence, necessarily, associated countries on the outside cannot expect to attain the privileges (or the voice) of a full member. There is thus a tension between, on the one hand, the consolidation of the club and, on the other, political or economic policies on the part of the club to spread the values and practices of the members to other neighbours.

The idea of creating a vanguard group through recourse to flexibility can be viewed as the creation of a club within a club. For a combination of reasons to do with numbers, differing degrees of 'like-mindedness' and socio-economic or political diversity, the membership of the extended EU club may have been deemed to have outstripped the capacity of the club to retain coherence, discipline, and solidarity. A vanguard group might rediscover these features, or so some of those involved seem to believe. The more analytical point to note is that it is possible that the flexibility debate might unleash the instruments and a dynamic that could give an identity and a legitimation to the club within the club. In parallel, one might therefore see the wider membership behaving differently, as one might also see some weakening of the distinction between the outer circle of club members and the inner ring of neighbours.

The second element, which follows on directly, relates to the distinction between 'deep' and 'shallow' integration. Historically, the EU has been *the* example of deep integration in Europe, and the Union project was itself designed to reinforce deep integration. Yet the EU has found itself with some member states that are less than fully committed to deep integration. The tendency to recognize forms of exceptionalism is one evidence of this; and the other strong signal is the creation of an EMU smaller than the EU. The willingness to address sensitive issues of citizenship and border management collectively, but only among some member states of the EU, seems a particularly important illustration here. The creation of a 'social union' is a particularly contested concept in the European integration process. The flexibility debate alerts us to a possible recasting of the tension between deep and shallow integration patterns *within* the EU now, rather than defined by the boundary between members and non-members.

11

Abuses of Asymmetry: Privilege and Exclusion

PETER LESLIE

The Amsterdam Treaty creates, for the first time, a framework for the future development of the European Union (EU) as an asymmetrical form of political organization, that is, a political structure in which some of the member states participate more fully than others. Although it is not known what use will be made of the relevant features of the treaty, it is almost inevitable that the issue of asymmetry will present some thorny dilemmas for the member states over the years to come. Asymmetry, or debates over its acceptability, will very probably be an important feature of the unfolding process of European integration—the Europe that lies 'beyond Amsterdam'.

The historical context in which the Amsterdam Treaty was negotiated makes this clear. The late 1990s have been a time of swelling integrationist ambition within some of the member states, manifested by the launching of Economic and Monetary Union (EMU), and the desire to develop simultaneously the social and political aspects of the Union. These years have also been a time of rising scepticism about the European project within other member states. Above all, these years have been a time in which newly emancipated states in Eastern and South-Eastern Europe have sought to chart a politically democratic and economically liberal future for themselves, either within the EU or in close association with it. These developments, taken together, have posed fundamental challenges to the EU: its institutions, its finances, its internal political (and social and economic) cohesion, and its policies towards its neighbours, many of them clamouring for entry.

In this context, it becomes important to see the EU not only in itself, with its current fifteen members, but also as the core of a larger European regional system with indistinct boundaries or fuzzy edges. This is a system whose development is being driven forward by a complex process of interaction between forces internal to the EU (forces that certainly do not all pull in the same direction), and external events. It is evident, though, that not all states are able to advance along the integration path at the same speed, and of those that are able to keep up with the leaders, not all wish to do so. There are divisions both within the existing membership, and certainly within the larger European system, comprising the EU itself and a penumbra of neighbouring states.

Asymmetry, or what some have called 'differentiated integration' (Stubb 1996), is already a feature of the European regional system. The distinction between full members and associate members, notably within the European Economic Area (EEA),[1] is a clear instance of this. However, in the pre-Amsterdam period, there was only *ad hoc* accommodation for the concept of asymmetry applying to the member states themselves. New members were expected to incorporate the full *acquis communautaire* in their policies after a period of transition. The Schengen Accords, originally signed by only six states, were reached outside the framework of the treaties, and by the late 1990s had still not been signed by all the members (whereas Norway, an EEA state but not a member of the EU, is a signatory). Britain's self-exclusion from the Social Protocol of the Maastricht Treaty (Treaty on the European Union—TEU), was another case of asymmetry, accepted by the other member states apparently under the assumption that Britain would come in later, as has occurred. An even more high-profile case of asymmetry arose with the TEU's clauses on EMU, and the 1998 decision of the European Council to launch EMU with eleven member states—Britain, Denmark, and Sweden choosing to stay outside, and Greece not qualifying. However, in all these instances of asymmetry, there has been the assumption or the prospect, however remote in time, that all member states will eventually come to assume fully the privileges and obligations that membership offers and entails.

Two features of the Amsterdam Treaty depart from this assumption, and make provision for the future development of the EU in a form that permits (and may even require) different levels of participation by different member states. Most dramatically, the new Treaty does this through Article F.1, under which a member state that persistently violates the basic principles of the Union—liberty, democracy, and respect for human rights—may be sanctioned by a unanimous vote of the other members, which may deprive the offending state of certain rights of membership, including the right to vote in the Council. Such an action would clearly bring about a crisis, certainly in the state thus sanctioned, and quite possibly throughout the Union; there would obviously

---

[1] The European Economic Area (EEA), launched in 1993, comprises the EU states and the member states of the European Free Trade Association (EFTA), except for Switzerland. Since the accession of Austria, Finland, and Sweden, the non-EU members of the EEA are Norway, Iceland, and Liechtenstein. These states have full access to EU markets, as a condition of which they must apply the *acquis*. While they are consulted by the Commission when it formulates legislative proposals, they are not represented in the Council of Ministers. For a description and analysis of the EEA, see: European Commission (1992a), Heidensohn (1995), Hosli (1993), Kux and Sverdrup (1997), Laredo (1992), Laursen (1993), Norberg (1992), Pedersen (1994), Reymond (1993).

have to be very extreme circumstances if this clause were to be invoked. The other feature of the Amsterdam Treaty potentially leading to new forms of asymmetry is the flexibility provisions, as analysed by Alexander Stubb and by Helen Wallace elsewhere in this volume (Chapters 9 and 10). Stubb points out that these provisions may not be used in the short term, but that they have the potential to influence all aspects of Union activity in the longer run; as Wallace suggests, they have the potential to consolidate a 'vanguard group' in the EU, or a 'club within the club'. Specifically, they offer the potential for a majority of member states to achieve closer cooperation among themselves while not involving others (e.g. a set of directives might apply to some but not all of the member states). Thus, as Stubb points out, by contrast with earlier cases of differentiated integration, '. . . the Amsterdam Treaty provides the first institutionalization of the concept of flexibility as a *basic principle* in the Treaties'.

Any recourse to Article F.1 or the flexibility provisions, and indeed any proposals to invoke either of these, will occasion controversy. Also, relations with non-members, especially applicant states, are inherently controversial; part of the controversy will be over limitations on membership rights, even if applying only to a transition period. Some people will see asymmetry within the EU as essential, if the integration process is not to be slowed to a pace manageable by the economically weakest, or acceptable to the most politically recalcitrant, of the member states. Others will see asymmetry within the EU itself as inherently dangerous, provoking division and threatening disunity; or they may see it as inherently unfair. Against this backdrop, several different questions arise. What forms of asymmetry are there: what is the concept and what are its variants? What forms of asymmetry are acceptable, or under what conditions (historical circumstances) might certain forms of asymmetry be acceptable? Who, in asymmetry matters, is to be the umpire? If asymmetry of any kind can ever be tolerated—as clearly the drafters of the Amsterdam Treaty, and indeed the architects of the Maastricht Treaty, believed—then what are the limits of its acceptability?

These are the questions that are the subject of this chapter. As befits a conceptual discussion with strong normative overtones, these questions are addressed in general terms, applying to the whole genus of compound political systems—supranational or confederal systems, federations, and unitary states with a regionalized or quasi-federal structure. In all such cases, of course, there are governmental institutions at the Union level, and political decision-making within the system involves various forms of interaction among institutions at two (or multiple) levels. Our analysis focuses especially on the economic aspect of such compound systems—or more specifically, on different aspects of economic union, and the political arrangements necessary to support them. The main empirical referents are the EU and the Canadian federation;[2] some reference is also made to the North American Free Trade Agreement (NAFTA).

Two Forms of Asymmetry

Asymmetry, as the term is employed in this chapter, may be of two broad types: functional and political.

Functional Asymmetry

This is defined here as a condition in which the powers or competences of central institutions do not apply uniformly throughout the system; political processes at the union level, or linking various levels within the system, cover a wider set of functions in some parts of the territory than in others. I argue below that some degree of functional asymmetry, sometimes not even noticed, is present in all compound systems. However, the more interesting cases are ones where there is an explicit agreement to accommodate it. In a historical process of economic and political integration, formal recognition of functional asymmetry may arise in several ways: first, because some of the participating states have gained an exemption from certain rules applying to the rest; second, because some have opted out of (or never opted into) certain aspects of the union, and the others have agreed to this; or third, because—as in the EU, with its convergence criteria for monetary union—some states do not meet stipulated conditions for participating in some aspect of an integration process. It should be noted, though, that functional asymmetry is not solely about uneven participation in a process of integration, as for example in the EU. It may arise also in those federal systems where some of the constituent states are making claims for an increase in their powers (as in Canada, in relation to Quebec and several other provinces), and in unitary states undergoing a process of

---

[2] The analysis of asymmetry offered here reflects in part the author's personal involvement, over a period of more than 20 years, in political debates in Canada about the future of the country. Many of the relevant issues have been placed on the agenda by demands from Quebec that it should gain additional constitutional powers. One proposal has been to gain 'special status' within the federation; a second proposal has been for 'sovereignty-association' (a political formula prescribing political sovereignty for Quebec, while also affirming its full participation in the economic union); a third proposal is for outright political independence. On special status, there is a classic (hostile) analysis in Trudeau (1968); compare this with much more favourable presentations in Canada, Task Force on Canadian Unity (1979) and Lenihan et al. (1994). On sovereignty-association and similar formulas, see: Charbonneau (1978), Leslie (1979), Québec, Ministère des affaires intergouvernementales (1978), Québec, Conseil exécutif (1979), Resnick (1991), Soldatos (1979). On EC/EU analogies, see: Demers and Demers (1995), Leslie (1996b). On federalism and constitutional reform issues in general, see: Cairns (1991); Fafard and Brown (1996, and other vols in this annual series), Russell (1992), and Trent et al. (1996).

federalization or devolution of powers to autonomous areas or regional communities (as in Spain, Italy, and Britain). In all these cases, functional asymmetry denotes that decentralization or devolution occurs more rapidly, or goes further, in some parts of the territory (or in relation to some identifiable groups of people) than applies generally.

Whatever the origins of functional asymmetry, a consequence of it is that 'membership' is not a uniform category; a state may be 'half-way in', or 'in' for some purposes and 'out' for others. Thus functional asymmetry denotes departure from a one-size-fits-all concept of membership. The result is that, at any one time, some of the constituent (or member) states are more pervasively constrained by central decision-making (or joint decision-making) than others.

Political Asymmetry

This denotes uneven or unequal participation of some entities (territorial units or communities) in governmental processes that are at play across the system as a whole. It implies difference of political status, or disproportionate power within the system. However, what is 'disproportionate' is a notoriously subjective matter; perceptions of equal/unequal status reflect expectations, and to say that there is asymmetry, or unequal status, is close to saying that an important group rejects the compromises inevitably built into any political structure. Thus, within a compound system, the larger units may endorse or demand a rule of representation where every individual person has a formally equal voice, while the smaller units may claim that each of them should have equal weight in decision-making, regardless of size. Similarly, ethnic or cultural minorities may claim that equality means equality among social collectivities; they may affirm that each identifiable community—each sociological 'nation'—is entitled to an equal voice in decision-making (or perhaps, at least, that the smaller communities deserve a relatively loud voice). A further complication arises when system boundaries are indistinct, as is the case with the larger European system. Here, the EU states are (collectively) 'rule-makers', while the rest (the associate members), are 'rule-takers'.

Nowhere is this more clearly illustrated than in the cases of Norway (an EEA member), and Switzerland (whose voters rejected the EEA in a referendum). Stefan Kux and Ulf Sverdrup (1997) have described in detail the adaptations that these two states have made, both in policies and governing structures, in order to gain access to EU markets. They question the conventional assumption that non-member states experience less pressure for adaptation than members do. They point out that both Norway and Switzerland

> . . . have developed strong administrative and institutional linkages and
> deepened their cooperation with the EU. Yet, short of full membership,

their relationship remains strongly asymmetric. In everyday politics in Brussels, these countries get limited attention and have restricted access to policy-making. Since they are out of sight they are also out of mind and out of the formal and informal decision-making processes in the EU. . . . Facing a strong domestic opposition against European integration, the Norwegian and Swiss governments are pursuing a strategy of substantial adaptation and intensive participation without full integration.

Of course, the two cases are different, because Switzerland rejected membership in the EEA

For political reasons, the [Swiss] administration insists that the unilateral adaptation—and the content of the bilateral agreements under negotiation—remains just below the EEA level. The scope and the speed of Europeanization of Swiss legislation differs, however, little from that of most EEA countries [including Norway], at least in the more technical fields of norms and regulations. The main difference is that Switzerland transposes on a voluntary basis and in an informal way, while the EEA countries are subjected to treaty legislation, participate in the joint institutions, contribute financially, and face legal supervision and sanctions in case of non-compliance.

A similar process of adaptation to European Community (EC) market norms has occurred in the Central and Eastern European countries (CEECs), to some extent formalized in the Europe Agreements that have been negotiated with ten of these states (Müller-Graff 1993). It is clear that in all these cases (the EEA states, Switzerland, and the CEECs), access to EU markets has been conditional on modelling national legislation and administrative practice to EC market rules. In varying degrees, but most clearly among the EEA states, such adaptation has been mandated by international agreement. They do not make the rules, but they have to observe them.

In all such cases, political asymmetry is obvious; one might say it is explicitly recognized in legal instruments. The situation is much muddier within political entities, especially compound systems, in which there are well-established mechanisms of political representation, but these are claimed by some to be biased or inadequate. Objective measures or indicators of political asymmetry in these cases are lacking, or at least contested. One might say that, in general, any system where one state or group of states (by virtue of size, wealth, or cultural dominance) exercises control, while others feel themselves to be effectively voiceless, is—from the perspective of these groups—politically asymmetrical. The problem for an outside observer is that although the people involved may regard themselves as voiceless, others may well regard them as full participants.

Attitudes towards Asymmetry

The analysis that follows is about the interplay between functional and political asymmetry. Attention is focused on the former, at least to begin with. I ask why functional asymmetry is sometimes unacceptable (to political elites and to voters) in most of the constituent states in a compound system, whereas in other instances a majority of states may agree to, or even require, asymmetry. In thinking about this, it is important to be clear where the proposals for asymmetry are coming from. In some cases, there will be states—let us call them the 'autonomists'—that seek to maintain policy control over matters which other states have agreed should lie within the competence of the union. With respect to these matters, the autonomists seek to preserve their independence or autonomy in a variety of ways: through simple non-compliance with agreed rules, through non-implementation of joint decisions, or through formal derogations, opt-outs or selective opt-ins. In other cases, proposals for asymmetry may be made by a group of states leading a process of integration—let us call them the 'integrationists'. These are the states that, in Europe, have led the way to differentiated integration; Helen Wallace refers to them as a 'vanguard group'. They have wanted to advance further themselves (e.g. by creating a common currency), but have wanted (in this case) to avoid jeopardizing this new initiative by admitting states they have considered to be fiscally too undisciplined.

When proposals for asymmetry are made, whether by autonomists or by integrationists, the outcomes vary. In some cases, asymmetry is rejected; in others, it is conceded; and in a further set of cases, it may be imposed. What explains these outcomes, or the variability among them? An answer may be given at three levels:

- *level one* is the level of economic calculation: if there is asymmetry, does it involve costs for some of the states, and if so, which ones?
- *level two* links economic issues with non-economic ones: here, membership in, or admission to, certain aspects of an economic union may be made conditional upon adherence to certain social and political norms; and
- *level three* links functional asymmetries to political ones: here, opt-outs applying to one or several states may be matched by limitations on its/their participation in political processes at the union level.

Whether functional asymmetries are rejected, conceded, or imposed, the outcome may be experienced subjectively as involving either privilege or exclusion. Both terms imply normative evaluation, perhaps by an observer, almost certainly by participants in a political negotiation over the acceptability of proposed asymmetries. Participants who do not regard asymmetry as inherently objectionable, or do not reject it without consideration of its practical effects, may nonetheless be alert to its potential abuses: permitting it may involve privilege, and imposing it may involve exclusion; these are both, though clearly in opposite ways, 'abuses of asymmetry'.

The acceptability of asymmetry is obviously a political question, one in which subjective judgement is inescapable. In order to highlight this, I enquire in this chapter into abuses of asymmetry, or those forms of asymmetry which some participants in a political negotiation may regard as abusive. One of the difficulties in discussing this subject is that there is no single umpire to rule on such questions; decisions on asymmetry are reached through negotiation, and people, indeed countries, have different views as to what constitutes privilege on the one hand, or exclusion on the other. A large part of the difficulty for the analyst, then, is to try to see issues from the perspective of participants in an ongoing political process, leading potentially to substantial asymmetry, but possibly to its rejection in all but the most compelling circumstances.

Functional Asymmetry within Economic Unions: Calculations of Cost and Benefit

A first approach to exploring the asymmetry puzzle is to look for evidence of free-riding, or opportunities for free-riding. The question here is whether a state can gain the benefits of common policies, or benefits flowing from the implementation of principles underlying an economic union, without incurring corresponding costs. Membership in an economic union entails commitments to the other members, and if some of those commitments can be evaded through opting out or simple non-compliance with joint decisions, while the advantages of membership remain, this amounts to free-riding. The state(s) concerned gain a privileged position *vis-à-vis* the others: there is not only asymmetry, but abuse of asymmetry.

Aspects of Economic Union

To analyse situations potentially giving rise to free-riding and, more generally, privilege or exclusion, it is necessary to identify and distinguish between various aspects of an economic union. An economic union may, itself, be conceptualized as one element of a compound system, which may also have other elements, notably ones dealing with social (or social policy) issues, and with security issues (internally: criminal matters and the maintenance of order; externally: military affairs and matters of 'high politics').

Within compound systems, the economic, social, and security-related elements may be developed to differing degrees, and may be supported by a political or institutional framework designed to formulate and implement policies in each of these various domains. Neither the political/institutional structure, nor any of the functional elements, may be said to characterize the system as a whole; the economic, social and security-related elements may each be classified in their own way, as political structures also typically are.[3] For distinguishing forms of political union, there are widely accepted categories, though disagreement persists on how to define them, or where to 'place' a particular system within a more or less standard typology. Thus, it is common to distinguish federations from unitary states, as well as from more loosely linked groupings of states (confederal, supranational, intergovernmental); but consensus is not always to be found when it comes to fitting actually existing systems into these widely employed categories. For example, it has quite frequently been asserted that one compound system, the EU, fits none of them.[4]

In the present section of this chapter, we abstract from the complexities inherent in actually existing entities such as the EU. Our concern is with the specifically economic element of compound systems, or with various aspects of economic union, in which the states comprising the system may participate to differing degrees. A useful point of departure for this discussion is Bela Balassa's (1961: 2) classic typology of forms or stages of integration

[3] On the security side, it is likely that Karl Deutsch's (1957) concept of a 'security community' provides the best basis for developing a typology of what might be called 'security unions'. However, to this basic concept would have to be added other categories, notably to take account of the EU's third pillar (justice and home affairs, including the policing aspect of the Schengen agreement).

The appropriate starting place for developing a typology of 'social unions' is less obvious. As far as I know, no one has attempted to develop such a typology—a set of categories identifying different types of social union, or different aspects of social union. However, discussions of citizenship rights, notably as pertaining to the EU, would be pertinent to developing such a typology. Concretely, fleshing out the concept of an EU citizenship that complements national citizenship would contribute significantly to developing the somewhat rudimentary social union already comprised within the EU. Theoretically or conceptually, the task would be to generalize from this and other cases, in order to create a typology of forms of social union. The steps taken so far towards developing the social aspect of European integration suggest that, in creating a general purpose typology, one useful distinction to make would be that between a social union that creates rights associated with employment (health and safety, unemployment insurance, retirement benefits, collective bargaining, etc.) and a social union that also creates rights inherent in the individual, without regard to present or past employment status (rights, e.g. to education and health care, public pensions, social assistance, etc.). Portability of benefits across jurisdictional boundaries would be one feature of a social union; another would be redistribution with a strong territorial dimension (in this respect contrast, e.g. the EU with Germany or Canada). While attempts have been made to distinguish between types of welfare regime, notably by Esping-Andersen (1990), and while the coalescence of distinct welfare regimes (built up on a national or subnational basis) would be a very significant feature of a social union within a compound system, I am not aware of attempts to develop a typology of types of social union on this basis. For an interesting example of the 'citizenship' approach, however, see Ch. 15.

[4] Thus, Jacques Delors once described the European Community as an 'unidentified political object'; others have stressed that it is *sui generis*. Such refusals-to-categorize seem to me to be evasive; when one examines the details, every system is unique.

Economic integration . . . can take several forms that represent varying degrees of integration. These are a free-trade area, a customs union, a common market, an economic union, and complete economic integration. In a free-trade area, tariffs (and quantitative restrictions) between the participating countries are abolished, but each country retains its own tariffs against nonmembers. Establishing a customs union involves, besides the suppression of discrimination in the field of commodity movements within the union, the equalization of tariffs in trade with nonmember countries. A higher form of economic integration is attained in a common market, where not only trade restrictions but also restrictions on factor movements are abolished. An economic union, as distinct from a common market, combines the suppression of restrictions on commodity and factor movements with some degree of harmonization of national economic policies, in order to remove discrimination that was due to disparities in these policies. Finally, total economic integration presupposes the unification of monetary, fiscal, social, and countercyclical policies and requires the setting-up of a supra-national authority whose decisions are binding for the member states.

Balassa's list has been used or adapted subsequently by many writers. His categories (or variants of them) have become conventional—so much so that they are frequently used without attribution in both the academic literature and public discourse.[5] Moreover, Balassa's conceptualization of the integration process as a set of discrete though cumulative steps (each higher stage of integration is built on the ones below) has become standard in the literature.[6]

---

[5] Some recent examples from the academic literature are: Armstrong (1995: 25), El-Agraa (1994: 1–2), Healey (1995: 4–9), Hitiris (1994: 2), Jovanovic (1992: 9—a slightly expanded Balassa list), Molle (1997: 10–12—a modified Balassa list), Pomfret (1997: 4–5—no explicit reference to Balassa, but the terms are used), Preston (1997: 147—refers only to 'customs union', 'Single European Market', and 'full economic union'), Swann (1996: 3–6). Of special interest is a series of publications by Pelkmans (1980; 1986a,b), in which he proposes a substantial elaboration of the Balassa list. He argues that, whereas Balassa's categories incorporate the distinction made by Tinbergen (1954) between negative integration (removal of barriers) and positive integration (policy co-ordination or the implementation of common policies), such a distinction is possible, in practice, only in the purer forms of market economy. In mixed economies, by contrast, some degree of policy co-ordination is needed to bring into existence even a free trade area. Despite Pelkmans' path-breaking contribution, however, it remains conventional to follow Balassa in regarding a free trade area, customs union and common market as instances of negative integration (removal of barriers). Under this supposition, only Balassa's 'economic union' (typically linked with monetary union in conception and in practice) and 'total economic integration' involve positive integration as well.

[6] In this sense, Balassa's typology contrasts with typologies of political entities, which are mutually exclusive. For example, in the Balassa scheme, a customs union is a free trade area with, in addition, a common tariff vis-à-vis third countries; by contrast, a unitary state is not a federation plus something else, it is a political form that negates the essential features of federalism.

For a discussion of asymmetry, however, it becomes necessary to adopt a different approach, as I do in this chapter. The minor change is that I adopt a different set of categories, using 'economic union' as a generic term for the whole set, rather than (as in Balassa) as a particular stage of economic integration. I believe that the new terminology corresponds better than the still-standard list to the realities of economic relations among states and other political entities, whether globally or within compound systems. The major change is that I suggest it is important to think of integration as involving not so much a set of sequential stages as a kaleidoscopic mix of aspects, in constantly changing configurations. The cumulative feature of the Balassa typology either presumes completion of one stage before the integration process moves on to the next, or implies simultaneous completion of several stages, the higher necessarily comprehending the lower. This may be called 'the cumulation hypothesis'; it is fundamentally called into question by the very idea of asymmetry. This is why I believe it useful to identify several aspects of an economic union, each of which may be developed in some degree but not necessarily 'completed'. Various aspects, each partial or imperfect, may thus be combined in multiform ways, or interwoven in distinct patterns, making each actually existing case of economic union unique, but also understandable in terms of the categories developed below. The categories (aspects of economic union, rather than stages of integration) are as follows:

• A *trade and investment union* (*TIU*) involves some degree of integration of markets for goods and services, and of capital markets, or the partial removal of barriers affecting trade and investment beyond what has been accomplished under the international (global) trading regime. Given the existence of the World Trade Organization (WTO)—which supervises not only rules on trade as such, but also on capital markets and investor rights—the existence of a TIU necessarily implies a degree of integration among participating states beyond that which arises from membership in the WTO alone.

• A *labour market union* (*LMU*) involves some degree of commitment to freedom of movement of labour, perhaps supported by appropriate social provisions (linkages to a parallel social union), as well as a compatible regulatory framework based on mutual recognition or harmonization of regulations in keeping with common or joint decisions.

• A *foreign economic policy union* (*FEPU*) involves vesting the conduct of trade and investment negotiations in some joint authority (in a supranational political structure) or a common government (in a federation). It should be noted that, under a FEPU, the distinction between 'trade' matters and domestic economic policy is an artificial one, since almost any aspect of economic policy can be declared to be 'trade-related'. This is true, for example, of market regulation and competition laws, all forms of subsidy, intellectual property laws, product standards, worker safety regulations, environmental standards, and measures to safeguard the health of people, plants, and animals.

• A *monetary and fiscal union* (*MFU*) involves the creation of a common currency and perhaps the co-ordination of fiscal policies. The fiscal side of an MFU may, of course, be developed *before* a common currency is introduced, and indeed may be seen—as a strict application of the convergence criteria written into the TEU would have implied—as a prerequisite of monetary union. However, there are cases of monetary union (notably in both Canada and the United States) where it has not been deemed necessary to co-ordinate fiscal policies at all.

• A *structural/developmental union* (*SDU*) involves joint action among the participating states to promote economic development. It is likely that it will be necessary to create central institutions having authority to engage in sectoral policies and policies affecting the location of industry (and therefore of population too). This implies a policy role that fundamentally affects the distribution and redistribution of resources and wealth across the territory.

Functional Asymmetry as Tolerated Non-compliance

Within each of the aspects of economic union, the opportunities for functional asymmetry are considerable if common rules are not observed or common policies are not implemented. This form of asymmetry may be described as tolerated non-compliance. The motives for it are not obscure: each aspect of an economic union has its attractions or its anticipated benefits for participating states, and entails obligations to the others. States are likely to try to reap full benefits while minimizing their obligations to each other; that is, they are likely to try to retain what powers they can to manage what they see as their own affairs, resisting central control or adherence to common policies or rules.

It is an important question to what extent states are allowed, in practice, to get away with this. When they do so to different degrees, functional asymmetry is the result; and if such asymmetry is sufficiently obvious to come to widespread attention, there is potential for free riding, which creates privilege. Hence the importance of seeing that, under each heading, each state that reaps the benefits of union plays by agreed rules and meets its obligations to the rest.

The attractions of economic union, or the benefits that various aspects of it may offer, are summarized in Table 11.1, which also identifies the obligations or commitments that each aspect of economic union may entail. It is not possible to be categorical about the latter; as has been emphasized above, each aspect may, according to the case, be developed only to a certain extent, or implemented with various exceptions, exemptions or imperfections. Some degree of 'slippage' is especially likely when common policies are mandated at

TABLE 11.1. Aspects of economic union: benefits and obligations

Attractions/Benefits	Commitments/Obligations
Trade and investment union (TIU) Enhanced economic efficiency; lower consumer prices and enhanced market access (export of goods and services); wider investment opportunities and better access to capital.	Open markets reciprocally for goods and services (remove barriers); offer mutual recognition of regulations (product standards and industrial processes) or adopt common regulations; ensure non-discrimination towards partners in the union; adopt similar or common policies regarding competition, including state support for industry.
Labour market union (LMU) Broader labour market offers workers enhanced employment opportunities and geographical mobility rights; employers gain access to new or additional supplies of labour.	Relax controls on immigration, at least for purposes of employment or business; harmonize regulation of labour markets; ensure portability of social benefits; perhaps adopt similar policies for social protection.
Foreign economic policy union (FEPU) Further increases in efficiency (closer-to-optimal allocation of resources); added clout in international economic negotiations.	Implement international trade and investment agreements, as regards market-opening, regulation of markets (products and processes), definition of property rights, and so on.
Monetary and fiscal union (MFU) Lower interest rates and easier access to capital; stability in investment and trade (reduction of risk); greater efficiency in allocation of resources.	Adhere to common rules (if any) for the conduct of fiscal policy, and for the regulation of financial markets.
Structural/developmental union (SDU) 'Created comparative advantage', or ability to implement a strategic trade policy at the union level; some states (generally the weaker ones) become net recipients of development assistance.	Formulate and implement common industrial or sectoral policies; provide support for education and training, and for research and development, throughout the union; some states (usually the stronger ones) required to offer development assistance to others.

the union level, with the states being responsible for implementation. This is notably the case within the EU, where policy decisions frequently take the form of directives issued to the states, and enforcement is variable—it is dependent upon some combination of good faith behaviour by the states, pressure from the Commission, and decisions of the European Court of Justice (ECJ). The fact that alleged infringement of European laws results, in the first instance, in negotiation between the Commission and the supposedly offending state, is indication enough that a degree of tolerated non-compliance is endemic to the system.

The question is, at what point does non-compliance with common rules, more within some participating states than among the others, become politically unacceptable? While no categorical answer to this question is really possible—certainly no *a priori* answer can be given—the principle of routine compliance remains valid. Infringement of this principle, which may be described as covert or unacknowledged asymmetry, confers privilege in the sense that a flagrantly non-complying state may reap the benefits of union without fulfilling its normally reciprocal obligations to the others. Such a state becomes a free-rider, unless the benefits usually offered by membership are curbed in some way, perhaps through retaliatory action by the others. This raises the spectre of increased internal barriers to the movement of goods, services, capital, or labour (or some combination of these), which, if arising generally, will lead to an overall downgrading or impairment of the union. Thus, both by the criterion of fairness, and by the threat posed to the principles of economic union, any significant degree of covert asymmetry is inherently abusive. Effectively, then, the union has two choices: to enforce uniformity, or to formalize and perhaps extend functional asymmetry, thus creating different classes of membership.

Formal Asymmetry: Opt-outs and the Question of Privilege

With formal asymmetry, there can be no equivocation or concealment: here, there are aspects of an economic union (or more generally, of a compound system) in which some states participate, while others do not. In this section, it is assumed that the initiative for this comes from autonomists—states that wish to exercise policy control over subjects that the others have transferred (or envision transferring) to the union level. The autonomists want to opt out of, or prefer not to opt into,[7] aspects of the economic union to which the others are committed; the question is whether the others will (or should) let them participate *à la carte*.

The term 'participation *à la carte*' is, of course, pejorative. However, I have used it because it pinpoints the issue at hand: whether selective participation in an economic union creates privilege for those who pick and choose. There are several reasons why opting out of some aspect or aspects of an economic union

[7] The difference between opting-out and not opting-in is sometimes insisted on. The distinction implicitly raises questions about what is fair or equitable; it certainly points to strategic considerations (the relatively strong bargaining position of a state that refuses to participate in some new aspects of an economic union). However, the effect of opting-out is about the same as that of not opting-in. In both cases, some members of the union participate in it on a selective basis. For the sake of simplicity, unless the distinction is germane to the argument at that point, I shall refer in what follows to 'opting-out' to cover both situations.

could be viewed in this way. One is that, if most states commit to a particular form of union, a state that wants to make a more limited commitment—to opt out of some aspect of the union—cannot effectively be excluded from benefits inherent in membership. This is the free-rider problem, applied not to each of the aspects of economic union individually, but to all together. Is it the case that no one aspect can be effectively disentangled from the others? A second reason is that the integrationists may insist that the economic benefits of membership should be available only to states that make commitments in other areas as well, for example, to democracy and the protection of human rights, or to common defence goals. And a third reason is that the political arrangements necessary to govern the economic union may be all of one piece, incapable of being split up into different segments; if so, a state having autonomist preferences could not extract itself politically from individual aspects of the economic union. In consequence, that state would necessarily have a voice in making rules that did not apply to it, or conversely, if it did not participate in governance processes at the union level, it would have to accept that rules applying to it would be made without its effective input. In the first case there is political privilege, and in the second, political exclusion.

In this section, I deal with only the first of these three issues: necessary linkages among aspects of economic union. I have argued that the imperfections of a trade and investment union need not prevent the development of other aspects of economic union, and that these aspects need not be developed all to the same extent. However, whatever form of economic union does emerge is likely to be the result of ongoing bargaining among the states. Some states may decide to participate in a TIU *only if* market outcomes are modified by sectoral policies and regional subsidies. (This, for example, was the position taken by France during the negotiations leading up to the establishment of the European Economic Community—EEC.) If, as a result, most of the others agreed to create some form of SDU, all would have to belong. It would scarcely be acceptable that an individual state—an existing member, or an applicant for membership—should gain or retain full access to the others' markets, while standing aloof from joint policies. A common foreign economic policy might also be part of the 'package', especially since sectoral policies may be ineffectual without an external trade dimension: one sees this clearly in the case of agriculture within the EU.

If the elements of economic union are thoroughly imbricated in the ways that the history of the EC/EU suggests, no state could reasonably be allowed to select only those aspects of a union that it found advantageous. For one state to be 'part way in' would not be acceptable to the others. This, indeed, was Britain's discovery during the early stages of the emergence of the EEC, especially with the two de Gaulle vetoes on its membership. To some extent, the dilemma still exists: Britain has constantly been forced to buy into a larger package than it has really wanted, on pain of finding itself excluded from continental markets.

Of course, Britain has not been alone in finding itself in this situation. It has been typical of some other states on the fringes of the EC as well, notably Switzerland and Norway and, until recently, Sweden. Opposition to EC/EU membership in these countries has been based on a range of issues, by no means all of them economic. However, the economic issues have been important ones: prominent among the opponents of membership have been representatives of economic sectors and regions that have felt threatened by European-level policies; so far, the electorates of Switzerland and Norway have been unwilling to make the necessary economic adjustments and political commitments. On the other hand—paradoxically—some of the states that have had to make the greatest economic adjustments, both Mediterranean and Eastern European states, have been strongly committed to membership. They have apparently been ready to assume its obligations as well as being anxious to obtain its benefits. Their enthusiasm can probably best be explained as the result of the aspirations of domestic economic and political elites, who have understood that the transformation of their countries (the twin transitions to liberal democracy and to liberal capitalism) could only be brought about by membership of the EC/EU.

Formal Asymmetry: Admission Criteria and the Question of Exclusion

The opposite of opting out is imposed asymmetry: the practice of limiting participation in an economic union, or in various aspects of economic union, on the basis of eligibility criteria. This subject, reviewed by Helen Wallace in Chapter 10, is at the forefront of the EU's agenda today, and indeed has been for several years. In a first set of cases, the issue is enlargement: are applicant states to be admitted as members, or to be limited to associate membership (however defined), or to be kept out altogether? On what basis can such decisions fairly be made? In a second set of cases, typified by EMU and the convergence criteria, the issue is selective admissibility: should all existing members automatically be eligible to participate in any proposed new aspect of economic union? The range of relevant considerations, especially with regard to enlargement, is by no means limited to economic matters. However, I would like here to abstract from the larger set of issues, and to focus on a narrower set, specifically those having to do with calculations of economic cost and benefit.

Whether the issue is that of enlargement or selective admissibility, the members of an economic union may be concerned that some states would not, and perhaps could not, meet all the obligations that the union, in all its existing or contemplated aspects, reasonably entails. Their solution may be to differentiate among different classes of membership, denying some states admission to certain aspects of the union, or perhaps limiting the benefits associated with, say, membership in an SDU. This 'filtering' stance is paradoxical because, as noted at the beginning of this chapter and as underscored in the immediately preceding section, in some instances a state's adherence to only those aspects of the union that it chooses may be unacceptable to most or all of the others. The various aspects of economic union may, in the view of most states, form a single package, and opting out arrangements may appear to confer privileged status. Observably, however, states do sometimes take the opposite view; they argue that fairness—balancing the benefits and obligations of union—demands splitting up the package, and admitting states on a piece-meal, subject-to-exceptions basis. Why this apparent inconsistency?

From an economic point of view, the basic issue involved in *enlargement* (not the only issue, but the one where the stakes are largest) is whether applicant states are to gain full access to EU markets. Eligibility is conditional on adher-ence to the *acquis communautaire*. States that are unwilling or unable to observe the market rules formulated as the *acquis* are ineligible for membership; they must have a 'functioning market economy', as well as the capacity to cope with competitive pressures and market forces within the Union'.[8] On the other hand, they may be admitted, through Europe Agreements, as associate members; but the Europe Agreements incorporate various limitations on market access.

Associate members—the countries with Europe Agreements, and EEA members—are partially but not fully admitted to the trade and investment union that is the basic building block of the EU. The extent of their access to EU markets is variable, and depends on the relevant treaties. This is an instance of imposed asymmetry, a phenomenon even more starkly illustrated by the fact that associate members are not allowed to participate in any of the other aspects of the economic union comprised within the EU. Moreover, for those applicant states eventually admitted as members, the possibility exists that there will be a long transition period, during which the rights of membership are conferred only selectively, in ways that will not impose excessive adjustment costs on existing members.

Christopher Preston (1995: 454; 1997) has noted that the 'classical Commu-nity method' of enlargement has thrust most of the cost of adjustment arising from increased economic diversity (notably disparities in living standards, but also structural differences in agriculture) upon the applicants. They have had

---

[8] These phrases are drawn from the declaration adopted at the Copenhagen European Council in June 1993. Naturally, being able to 'cope with competitive pressures' is a matter of degree. Those regions already within the EU that lag behind the others are eligible for support in the form of structural funds; thus, to demand of applicant states that they have the capacity to 'cope' is to insist that they not be an excessive drain on the structural funds. There is also a curious paradox here, or a deliberate refusal to consider the implications of this admission cri-terion: logically, one would have to infer that a country not admitted to the EU will be able to catch up more quickly than if it were already a member state—if not, then as a non-member, a country already too far behind would inevitably fall even further behind.

to accept the *acquis communautaire* in full, without permanent opt-outs; existing members of the Community have been unwilling to return to first principles and rationalize existing policies, redesigning them in ways that would suit the enlarged Community. Instead, new policies have been overlaid upon the existing ones, sometimes creating strains that have had to be worked out after enlargement has occurred. Ostensibly, the same stance was taken at the Copenhagen summit of 1993 with reference to the applicants of Eastern Europe; but Preston (1995: 460, 461) argues that, given the low income levels and large agricultural sectors of the Visegrad states (let alone others)

> Full implementation of the *acquis* involves more problems for incumbents who would have to foot the bill, than applicants. Enlargement would involve unpacking the compromises underpinning the CAP and Structural Funds. . . . Given the interests at stake in any future enlargement negotiations, it would be impossible to proceed to a full accession conference without these issues having been dealt with beforehand. . . . The EU is very conscious of the need to deal with these problems before the momentum for full accession becomes unstoppable. . . .
>
> The superficial attractions of enlarging the EU sooner rather than later, but excluding agriculture and cohesion spending, would be unlikely to satisfy the east Europeans' aspirations to join a Union of notional equals. The IGC [intergovernmental conference] will have to address this issue in developing generally applicable rules that do not create a form of second-class membership. The EEA experience suggests that too much fudging of the boundaries between insiders and outsiders is unsatisfactory for both sides.

Events, however, have so far followed a different track.[9] The IGC has run its course, the Amsterdam Treaty is in force, the Commission has published Agenda 2000 (in 1997), and the accession process has been launched. It is widely believed that the momentum for an Eastern enlargement has become unstoppable, but one could scarcely claim that there has been prior resolution of the thorny policy issues that enlargement will entail for existing members. There appear to be three logically possible outcomes. First, that all existing members will agree, during the enlargement negotiations, to some fundamental revisions of EU policy that have important budgetary implications, heavily burdensome for some. Second, that 'a Union of notional equals' will not be achieved, if at all, until long after formal accession has occurred. Third, that the negotiations will drag out indefinitely because of opposition within (or by) some of the existing member states. In practice, there may well be a combination of these three. The negotiations may take much longer than is currently acknowledged. The

---

[9] I am grateful to Charles Pentland for discussions on the matters addressed in this paragraph.

transition period may be lengthy—indeed, the flexibility provisions of the Amsterdam Treaty could be used in such a way as to transform 'transition' into permanent asymmetry. And finally, existing EU policies (especially on agriculture and structural funds) may be adapted to accommodate an expanded membership, but not so fundamentally redesigned as to permit retention of existing budgetary limits—in which case the allocation of costs will become a major sticking point. Whatever the combination of these three outcomes, it is clear that the EU-15's commitment to the principle that membership of the Union is open to all the countries of Europe that meet the announced criteria (i.e. without claiming a privileged position for the existing members) will come under strain. What is uncertain is whether the delays incurred, and the compromises made, will be perceived by the applicants as unwarranted exclusion.

Similar issues arise in relation to existing members of the Union as integration extends into new functional areas, and *selective admissability* is considered. This has been illustrated by the pre-history of EMU, and the reluctance of the economically most powerful states—the pacesetters of the integration process—to apply the convergence criteria with the strictness that the most financially orthodox would have wished. These criteria were formulated out of concern that the economically weaker states (or the fiscally less resolute, less conservative ones) would be unable to function economically within a common currency regime, unless they obtained special assistance. The European Central Bank (ECB) has been structured in such a way as to ensure this does not happen, and it has been instructed under the EC Treaty (TEC) (Articles 104 and 104a; also Protocol 3, Article 21) not to issue overdrafts to national governments or other public authorities. However, the Council may decide to grant emergency financial assistance to member states under certain conditions (Article 103a para. 2 TEC), and the ECB may open accounts for private and public credit institutions and lend money to them provided adequate collateral is supplied (Protocol 3, Article 18 TEC).

These provisions mean that, if a fiscally weak or improvident state has been admitted to monetary union, there is some risk (dependent in part on the size of the state concerned) of its weakening the Euro. This explains the imposition of the convergence criteria, designed to provide evidence of fiscal orthodoxy prior to entry, and it also underlies the treaty provisions authorizing substantial control over fiscal policy among those member states that have been admitted to monetary union (Article 104c TEC). These provisions, written into the EC Treaty by the TEU, reflect an implicit calculation that there are costs (risks) associated with the creation of a monetary union, and that these risks will be borne more by the fiscally conservative states than by those with lax or expansionary fiscal policies.

This reasoning can also be inverted: the costs of non-participation will presumably be borne especially by the states that have not joined, whether because not admitted, or because of their own self-exclusion. The costs of non-membership may be presumed to be: higher interest rates, less access to foreign capital (investors incur higher risks in countries not within the monetary union), disabilities suffered by financial services industries, and foregone employment.[10] On the other hand, a state that does adopt the common currency must accept substantial limitations on its freedom of manoeuvre in the conduct of fiscal policy, and of course monetary policy then lies outside its jurisdiction altogether. Thus, monetary union creates a dilemma for those states that want to preserve their sovereignty: staying out may impose economic costs, but going in may impose political ones.[11] A further consideration is that monetary union may generate strains that, in a period of crisis, could bring it down.[12] However, if I am right in thinking that, in general, it is the non-participants who will bear the main cost if monetary and fiscal union goes ahead without them, voluntary opt-outs are likely to be temporary.

The EMU convergence criteria seemed, when written into the Maastricht Treaty, to be designed to keep the economically weaker countries out in the cold, although in the end it proved politically impossible to do this, except in the case of Greece. Similarly, the EEA agreements were at first seen as a means of delaying an enlargement to include the countries of the European Free Trade Area (EFTA), but in the end they paved the way for the accession of three of the EFTA states. The Europe Agreements initially had a similar purpose, to hold the CEECs at bay for a while, but they were soon transformed into the

---

[10] A non-member with a strong currency is unlikely to incur such costs: in Europe, the case of Switzerland shows this conclusively. In fact, if the Euro lacks the strength of the erstwhile *mark*, this could strengthen the Swiss *franc*—a mixed blessing for Switzerland, because a currency that is too strong is a liability, as is (for opposite reasons) a currency that is too weak. The case of Britain is arguable either way, and indeed it is argued both ways: that an independent pound is an advantage, and that it is a liability.

[11] Political costs are partly symbolic, especially for a country that associates nationhood with its traditional currency. The other political cost is loss of autonomy in economic policy, especially fiscal policy. However, it is arguable that autonomy thins out anyway, as a result of market integration. Also, with reference to Europe, it should be noted that the EC Treaty declares that all member states 'shall regard their economic policies as a matter of common concern and shall coordinate them within the Council'; the treaty also provides that each member state 'shall treat its exchange rate policy as a matter of common interest' (Arts. 103 and 109m TEC).

[12] Martin Wolf (1998), thereby revealing himself a realist and a sceptic, writes: 'Unhappy history suggests that monetary unions, unaccompanied by a credible merger of sovereignty, do not last, examples being the Latin, German-Austrian, and Scandinavian monetary unions. Long-lasting monetary zones are defined not by whether they are '. . . optimal currency areas' but by the boundaries of a state. . . . The underlying reality is that [under EMU] power will lie with one group of people operating at a supranational level, while legitimacy will remain with another group operating at the national level. The risk that conflict will then emerge between democratic national politics and Europe's inter-governmental order is the greatest threat to the survival of EMU'. One may speculate that, among the reasons that Britain, Denmark, and Sweden have chosen not to join the EMU at its launch is that they prefer to see how it goes before committing themselves.

main instrument of a pre-accession strategy; the process of accession has now been launched for four of the ten signatories. In all these cases, asymmetry—both functional and political—was written into legal instruments underpinning the European regional system, but this *imposed asymmetry* has subsequently been attenuated.

Similar issues have arisen on the other side of the Atlantic, where the NAFTA now underpins a regional system centred on the United States. This agreement (which lacks the superior force, in American law, of a treaty) is an instrument for creating a trade and investment union, and is ostensibly symmetrical. It opens markets reciprocally, it establishes a dispute resolution mechanism, and it provides explicitly that each of the Parties (the United States, Canada, and Mexico) retains full legislative powers (Hoebing, Weintraub, and Delal Baer 1996; Paraskevopoulos, Grinspun, and Eaton 1996; Robinson 1995; Rugman 1994; Smith 1993; Weintraub 1997). However, the question of asymmetry arises in two important respects. The first is that, in practice, Canada and Mexico must adapt to US policy and law in many respects, in order to reduce trade vulnerability—partly to minimize the risk of countervail suits that allege subsidy, and partly to maintain or enhance competitiveness *vis-à-vis* American producers.[13] The second is that the same logic of harmonization under market pressure applies to non-NAFTA states. Consequently, various states in Central and South America (Chile in the forefront) have lined up to gain admission to an expanded NAFTA, or to a Free Trade Area of the Americas (FTAA), a project endorsed by President Clinton, but with little support in Congress. One possible outcome is that the NAFTA will eventually be expanded to include at least some new members, but without giving them rights to invoke the dispute settlement provisions that are very nearly the core of the agreement. In that case, the NAFTA or an FTAA would become openly asymmetrical, and not merely covertly so.

Thus in various ways, and not only in Europe, a state or group of states at the core of a regional system may control access to the economic union that is a primary feature of the system, or may admit applicants only to certain aspects of the economic union. Is this necessarily exclusionary? The very concept of exclusion implies a presumption in favour of opening all of the aspects of an economic union, certainly to existing members, and probably to neighbouring states which want to join in. Do these states appear able to meet the obligations of membership—which is to ask, would the other states (members, or the pace setters in a process of integration), be exposed to unreasonable costs or risks if the membership criteria were relaxed? This is an

[13] The American economy, globally powerful, dominates in North America or in the Americas generally. This means that, to be competitive, neighbouring states have to adopt policies no less favourable to business than US policy is. Conversely, if policy in these states is deemed by US producers to be more favourable to business than US policy, their exporters face the threat of countervailing duties.

unsatisfactory test, because some speculation regarding future events is unavoidable, and 'reasonableness', while subject to argument, is ultimately subjective. Probably the only guideline is to ask whether adding new members, or admitting existing members to some new aspect of the union, would appear likely to alter in a substantial way the balance of benefits and costs to other members.

This is a question that invites a strictly economic calculus, with generous allowance for risk. From a wider perspective, though, economic criteria are insufficient, being too narrow, because every compound system is based on a mixture of economic and other goals—social, cultural, and political. The rest of this chapter is concerned with these other dimensions of compound systems, and their linkages with economic union. The discussion will necessarily be brief, because space is lacking, but an attempt will be made at least to identify some of the relevant issues.

Functional Asymmetry: Linkages among Economic, Social, and Security-related Elements in Compound Systems

Whether one directs attention to the EU or to any of the contemporary federations, it is clear that compound systems are more than a vehicle for creating or sustaining an economic union. The objectives are multiple, and they are typically interwoven in what William Riker (1964) has called a 'federal bargain', a concept that could usefully be applied to other types of compound system as well. Up to now, I have asked what aspects of economic union need to go together if its benefits are to be balanced with corresponding obligations. However, the bargaining processes that created the EU clearly linked economic objectives to political and social ones, and such linkages are probably typical. Indeed, in the case of the European regional system, the linkages have been becoming more obvious: reference has already been made in this chapter to Article F.1 of the Amsterdam Treaty, and to the Commission's 'Agenda 2000' document. In line with the Commission document, the European Council has, in effect, promised the states of Eastern Europe equal economic rights with the states of Western Europe, provided that they not only are functioning market economies, but functioning liberal democracies as well. They must also accept the Schengen *acquis*, and as such adhere to and effectively implement EU immigration policies *vis-à-vis* countries farther to the East. Thus a strong economic inducement is being offered to support overtly political goals; these states will not be allowed to integrate economically with Western Europe while defining themselves politically as they will. They cannot choose to opt in economically but to opt out politically. Similarly, during the EFTA enlargement process, the four applicant states were told that they had to commit to the political or foreign policy obligations that membership entails.

In brief, those most strongly committed to building 'an ever closer union' in Western Europe have adopted goals as far-reaching as those appropriate to any federation, or indeed any nation state. Their strategic objective seems to be to bind existing nation states into a robust political structure. This is not a structure in which existing nation states would disappear; on the contrary, their existence and effective functioning are recognized as being essential to the integration project. After all, member states are, collectively, the most important decision-makers for the EU, and the Union relies on them for finances, and for implementation of policies: without them, the EU would be incapable of doing anything. (The converse is also partly true: without the EU, member states would arguably be much less effective in performing their vastly expanded functions, given a world economic context marked by transnationalization and globalization: hence the concept of pooled sovereignty, as against sovereignty given away.) The point I want to make here is that the EU is a compound system created by a process of integration that reconstitutes some of the elements of nation states as they had taken shape during (in Samuel Beer's (1965/1969) expression) 'the collectivist age'. What has emerged has not supplanted nation states, but has incorporated them into a larger structure which nonetheless, in its compound form, is state-like. And the model is, seemingly, the nation states that preceded the EU's creation.

Asymmetry challenges this vision. Those who propose asymmetrical political arrangements are saying, in effect: 'Let us build a set of new political structures that parcel out the traditional functions of the state in different ways, among a variety of organizations of different memberships: with different territorial boundaries, or with indistinct boundaries, or simply non-territorial'. The concept of asymmetry—not to mention the concept of a 'post-modern state' (Caporaso 1996)—invites one to consider whether an economic union need necessarily be combined with a social (or social-policy) union, and with a political one. The question here is whether an economic union and/or a social union need be supported by an organization, the state, with traditional ('Westphalian') functions. These have been: to create and preserve public order and safety within a clearly defined territory; to defend that territory and its inhabitants against external threat; and (under a liberal democratic public philosophy), to define and protect human rights—procedural justice, civil liberties, and political citizenship.

These are questions arising in many parts of the globe. For example, in Canada, the *indépendantistes* of Quebec want to participate fully in the Canadian economic union, and of course in the continental trade and investment union that has taken shape under the NAFTA. On the other hand, they want to get out of the Canadian federation, and they do not think membership in the political union should be a precondition of membership in the economic union. This probably means, in practice, that some features of the economic union are also unattractive to most *indépendantistes*, but that is another subject. What is important here is that issues similar to those facing Canada also arise in Europe, but inevitably in much more complex form. The most salient of these issues is whether there are politically necessary linkages between an economic union, a 'social union' (which, in the Canadian case, is highly redistributive across regions), and a form of political union based on shared goals relating to security, democracy, and human rights. Both in the EU and in Canada, there is deep controversy over the range of policy matters appropriately decided at the Union level; some member states want to participate for some purposes and not for others. In the case of the EU, there has also been the prospect and the reality of imposed asymmetry. Thus, for admission to EMU, states have had to meet a test of fiscal orthodoxy (although, in the end, it was loosely applied). In addition, a longish list of applicant states is being screened for admissibility on the basis of multiple factors, not all of them related to economic performance or structure. In many forms, then, the question arises: what elements of economic, social and political union need necessarily be conjoined within a single institutional framework, and what elements may be dissociated from others?

Again, there is a Canadian analogy. Logically, there seems to be little reason to demand that Quebec either participate in both the social union and the economic union, or that it withdraw from both. However, logic may not count for much in this case. Most non-Quebecers appear to regard the economic union as one element in a larger (federal) package that must be accepted, if at all, in its entirety. This means that a majority of Canadians outside Quebec might well insist, if Quebecers voted for sovereignty in a future referendum, that the new state withdraw not only from the political and social aspects of the Canadian federation, but from the economic union as well. (A looser form of economic union would, though, undoubtedly be preserved, provided Quebec were admitted to the NAFTA—which would be subject more to US decision than to Canadian attitudes.) As in Europe, where EU membership requires commitment to a common (West-)European set of political values, the prospect of economic benefit is being used to further a basically political and (in its broadest sense) cultural project. At issue here is the elemental feeling that economic favours will not be extended to peoples or states not sufficiently 'like us'. It is hard to escape the conclusion that this is an exclusionary attitude, rooted in political and cultural values, which reflect, in the European case, centuries-old definitions of the boundaries of 'Europe'.

Political Asymmetry

Political issues may also be linked in another way—quite directly so—to asymmetries in an economic union. Here the questions of privilege and exclusion arise in a different light, or in a different way.

Simply put, it would scarcely be tolerable from the perspective of most states in a compound system for one or more of them to opt out from the union for certain purposes (say, for social affairs, or for some aspects of an economic union), while retaining an undiminished political voice. Such a state would have a hand in making decisions that would not apply to it—giving it a politically privileged status. If this were too blatant, the other states could scarcely be expected to agree to such political asymmetry. To avoid political asymmetry, though, political institutions would have to be redesigned so that the opting-out state kept a voice only for those matters actually applying to it. Within an institution such as the EU's Council of Ministers, that is not difficult, as the Maastricht and Amsterdam treaties show.[14] However, it is much more difficult to eject a state from an institution like the EP for some purposes, or in relation to some subjects, but not in relation to all. And with a parliamentary system of government such as Canada's or Australia's, the institutional changes required to avoid political asymmetry would be far-reaching. Perhaps it could not be done at all.

The converse situation is one where rules apply to a state that has no voice in formulating them. This is the condition that, in Europe, has been written into the EEA agreement and the Europe Agreements, as earlier discussed. In North America, an analogous situation also seems to obtain. The NAFTA, while it has no institutions or agreed processes for making NAFTA-wide rules or regulations,[15] provides for consultations at the ministerial level when one state wants to modify its trade laws in ways that another state considers potentially damaging. However, after such consultations, normal political or legislative processes play out according to national constitutions. It seems difficult to imagine that, under these conditions, Canada or Mexico would have a substantial voice in American legislation. The same is not true, however, at the other end of bilateral relations within the NAFTA. Thus, the sheer size of the United States, backed up by its right of countervail whenever a trading partner engages in 'unfair' practices, seems likely to ensure that it has a powerful voice in the future evolution of trade law and other 'trade-related' matters in Canada and Mexico. Pursuing this subject, however, would lead us into another line of enquiry, the study of regional hegemony, which works out the implications of severe asymmetries in economic and political power within regional systems (Leslie 1996a).

---

[14] Under the terms of the TEU, states not proceeding to stage three of EMU are given a derogation from its rules, but en contrepartie, they have no vote on those rules. In these cases, the definition of 'qualified majority' is changed correspondingly. A similar narrowing of voting rights in Council is prescribed under the flexibility provisions in the Amsterdam Treaty for opting-out states.

[15] On the contrary, the right of each NAFTA state to amend its own trade laws is affirmed in the agreement.

Conclusion: Fairness, Privilege, and Exclusion

I have argued that some degree of functional asymmetry is endemic to compound systems such as the European Union or any federal state. It seems desirable to accommodate diversity wherever possible by permitting even quite radical forms of functional asymmetry, while being alive to its twin abuses, privilege and exclusion. These arise, at least potentially, in a variety of guises, which this chapter has attempted to identify and analyse. In some cases, functional asymmetry comes about as a result of the demands or aspirations of a participating state that wants to exercise a policy role which for other states is exercised in common, through institutions at the union level. In such cases, it would seem appropriate to allow for functional asymmetry where it does not create undue privilege, either in terms of economic advantage or in terms of disjunction between participation in the economic union, and involvement in its governance. In other cases, asymmetry (functional and/or political) comes about because states belonging to an inner circle, or wanting to create one, exclude other states that 'want in'. This raises extremely difficult questions of fairness, concerning the extent to which the inner circle of states, the vanguard group, have obligations to other member states, or indeed to neighbouring states or aspiring members. 'Exclusion' is a loaded word (as is 'privilege'), implying some standard of fairness. However, judging what is fair is inherently subjective. In practice 'fairness' will likely be defined through political processes, or processes of negotiation among states, in which another form of asymmetry—asymmetries of power—inevitably come into play.

12

East of Amsterdam: The Implications of the Amsterdam Treaty for Eastern Enlargement

ULRICH SEDELMEIER

Although preparing the European Union (EU) for enlargement to the countries of Central and Eastern Europe (CEECs) was presented as the main rationale behind the 1996–7 intergovernmental conference (IGC), the implications of the IGC's limited results are less clear-cut. When the negotiators at the 1991 IGCs decided to write into the Maastricht Treaty that another IGC should be convened in 1996, enlargement was not foremost in their minds. Subsequent events, however, *de facto* established institutional reform as a precondition for the CEECs' accession process. Any reform of the EU's institutional structure would have to ensure the efficiency of decision-making in an enlarged Union, while providing for 'fair' representation as well as democratic transparency. Yet it was precisely in this respect that the IGC failed to live up to what had been expected of it. Essentially, the Amsterdam Treaty postponed critical institutional decisions to a later date. How, then, should we assess the implications of the lack of progress in the Amsterdam Treaty for the accession prospects of the CEECs?

Many commentators and policy-makers fear that the IGC's results confirm pessimistic predictions that the EU's internal difficulties might make it impossible to find the unanimity needed to agree on the adjustments required for the CEECs' accession (see for example Baldwin 1994). More cynical observers regard the postponement of institutional reform as an expression of the EU's lack of commitment to enlargement, and of the member states' unwillingness to make any concessions for the sake of enlargement which would leave them worse off than under the *status quo* (Planavova-Latanowicz 1998).

Such concerns are not completely unfounded. The member states' collective long-term economic and political interest in enlargement contrasts sharply with the uneven distribution of apparent burdens and benefits among the incumbents, as well as for each of them internally. This becomes even more marked if, in addition to the IGC's questions of institutional representation, the questions of policy adaptation and their budgetary implications, raised by the Commission's document Agenda 2000, are taken into account.

However, an assessment of the implications for enlargement of the IGC's outcome depends crucially on our understanding of the nature of the integration process and of policy-making in the EU. From a rationalist perspective, in which policy-makers defend exogeneously defined material self-interest, and in which policy-making follows a bargaining mode, the prospects for the CEECs' accession is indeed bleak. The member states (as well as the European Parliament—EP) must approve any accession to the EU unanimously. Yet it is difficult to imagine any accession deal which would both be acceptable to the CEECs and yet would leave none of the incumbents worse off (whether in terms of national influence; budgetary contributions or receipts; effectiveness of collective decision-making; or future prospects for 'deep integration'.

This chapter argues, however, that the disappointment over the Amsterdam Treaty and the sheer enormity of the challenges facing the EU need not mean that enlargement will not happen. First, expecting the IGC to agree on far-reaching institutional reform would be to ignore the EU's history of postponing difficult decisions until they become absolutely unavoidable, its bias towards incremental adjustment, and the path-dependency of incremental decisions;[1] the EU is not known for its anticipatory strategic planning. More crucially, however, at the basis of this chapter's argument is the contention that a pure rationalist understanding of the EU as a club that serves only the maximization of its members' narrowly defined self-interest fails to capture important factors which underlie EU policy towards the CEECs.

I argue that an important factor shaping EU policy is its identity towards the CEECs, which includes the notion of a 'special responsibility'. It inclines EU policy towards an accommodation of the CEECs' demands by limiting the range of acceptable policy options—namely, by proscribing a policy that appears purely oriented towards narrow self-interest. It becomes politically salient through the advocacy of a group of policy-makers who are most receptive to this component of the EU's identity. In the case of the association policy, these policy advocates were primarily located inside the Commission, with a loose supportive alliance among the member states' foreign ministries.

Yet, while the EU's identity towards the CEECs might incline the Commission's external relations policy-makers and member state foreign ministry officials towards accommodating the CEECs' preferences, this is not the full story. The association policy (and, for that matter, accession negotiations) are made up of a range of distinctive policies across the range of areas which are part of the association policy or accession negotiations. The above-mentioned group of policy-makers cannot take decisions on these 'meso-policies' autonomously. I argue that the extent to which the CEECs' preferences can be accommodated in these 'meso-policies' is crucially affected by the particular policy paradigms

---

[1] See, e.g. Wallace (1997) with regard to policy towards the CEECs, or Pierson (1996) for EU policy-making more generally.

(Hall 1993) that underpin EU policy in the respective meso-policies, and is not simply a function of the strength of interest group opposition, as interest-based approaches assume.

This chapter proceeds as follows. First, the evolution of the link between the IGC and an Eastern enlargement will be traced, followed by an outline of the main results of the IGC with regard to institutional reform. The following section builds on the observation that the association policy accommodated the preferences of the CEECs to a far larger extent than rationalist approaches would suggest, and argues that the EU's collective identity towards the CEECs played a key role in this process. On this evidence, rationalist predictions that the complexity of the adjustments needed for enlargement will prevent the member states from forging a consensus for reforms might be overly pessimistic, despite the lack of results in the Amsterdam Treaty. The next section turns from the broader principle of enlargement to the detail of policy substance in the meso-policies, and to the role of policy paradigms as crucial factors affecting the extent of accommodation in these meso-policies. Finally, evidence is presented from two meso-policies (liberalization of the steel trade and the regulatory alignment of the CEECs with the internal market) to illustrate how policy paradigms, or rather their amenability to change, can act either as facilitators or obstacles to accommodation, independent of interest group pressure.

The Link between the IGC and the EU's Eastern Enlargement

Enlargement Preparations on the EU Side

Enlargement presents major challenges, not only for the CEECs but also for the current member states. The key challenges relate to institutional and policy adaptation. An EU of more than fifteen members faces pressures on its institutional structure, in terms of both the efficiency of decision-making and institutional respresentation, which must also be balanced with growing demands for increased transparency and accountability.[2] In addition, given the specific economic nature of the applicants (i.e. their low per capita GDP in comparison to the EU average, and the large share of agriculture in their economies), a continuation of the Common Agricultural Policy (CAP), and regional spending in their current forms would either require a substantial increase in the current member states' budgetary contributions or a considerable decrease in their receipts.[3] The latter set of questions was separated out from the IGC's agenda in order to avoid mutual blockages, and because they do not require

---

[2] For a fuller discussion of this point, see Wallace and Wallace (1995) and Edwards (1998).

[3] For a fuller discussion of this point, see Mayhew (1998: 236–311) and Grabbe and Hughes (1998: 90–103).

treaty changes for their resolution. They were dealt with separately in the Commission's Agenda 2000 document, and are not the subject of this chapter, which deals with institutional issues.

This section traces the evolving link between the requirement of institutional reform, the IGC, and enlargement. It notes that, against the background of their interconnectedness in the public perception, the failure of the IGC to agree on the necessary reforms would indeed appear as a major setback for the accession prospects of the CEECs.

The 1991 IGCs on Economic and Monetary Union (EMU) and on Political Union were inward-looking, and inspired by an agenda which largely pre-dated the dramatic political changes in Central and Eastern Europe of the late 1980s. The EU's relations with both the European Free Trade Association (EFTA) members and the CEECs were kept separate, in the form of the European Economic Area (EEA) agreement for the former, and association agreements—so-called 'Europe Agreements' (EAs)—for the latter. The IGC thus avoided (or missed an opportunity for) considering whether, in the changed context, their relations with their neighbours did not present a much more fundamental challenge to the EU's traditional integration project (Wallace 1991).

Not surprisingly, the main reason for including a provision in the Maastricht Treaty to convene a follow-up IGC in 1996 was to assess the operation of the pillar structure and of the new common foreign and security policy (CFSP), rather than to prepare for enlargement (Dinan 1998: 36). Yet by 1995, enlargement was being presented as the main rationale behind the IGC, and institutional reform had become a key agenda item. The two main reasons for this development were the 1995 enlargement of the EU to include Austria, Finland, and Sweden, and the evolution of the EU's policy towards the CEECs.

The 1995 Enlargement to Admit Austria, Finland, and Sweden

Somewhat ironically, it was not the success of, but the problems with, the internal agenda which turned attention to enlargement, as a more positive and morale-boosting project for the EU. The Edinburgh European Council of December 1992 brought the internal agenda back on track by agreeing on the budgetary perspective and on a solution to the problem (created by the Danish referendum) of ratifying the Maastricht Treaty. The European Council thus agreed to the opening of enlargement negotiations with the EFTA applicants.

Already at that stage, the perspective of an increase in membership from twelve to sixteen (including Norway) was causing concern among the existing members. The European Parliament (EP), in particular, threatened to withhold its assent if the EU did not take the necessary measures to ensure efficient decision-making. Eventually, the EP accepted that reform would only take place after accession. The 1995 enlargement thus went ahead under the previous practice of a mere arithmetical projection of current arrangements for institutional representation and the threshold for qualified majority voting (qmv) in the Council. Even so, it led to an internal dispute over the corresponding rise of the threshold for blocking minorities under qmv, which the Ioannina agreement merely papered over (European Council 1994a). Consequently, the Corfu European Council of June 1994 suggested that the IGC should deal with institutional reform

> [The Reflection Group of member state representatives, established to prepare for the 1996 Intergovernmental Conference] will also elaborate options in the perspective of the future enlargement of the Union on the institutional questions set out in the conclusions of the European Council in Brussels and in the Ioannina agreement (weighting of votes, the threshold for qualified majority decisions, number of members of the Commission and any other measure deemed necessary to facilitate the work of the Institutions and guarantee their effective operation in the perspective of enlargement).   (European Council 1994a: 20)

Evolving EU Policy Towards the CEECs and the Link with Internal Adaptation

The separation from the internal agenda of EU policy towards the CEECs was most clearly expressed in the member states' refusal to make an explicit link in the EAs between association and eventual accession, and to commit the EU to an eastern enlargement. However, policy continued to evolve.[4] At the June 1993 European Council in Copenhagen, the heads of state and government declared that those CEECs which met the economic and political requirements of membership could join the EU. Crucially, the European Council also stipulated that the EU itself had to be prepared for enlargement

> The Union's capacity to absorb new members, while maintaining the momentum of European integration, is also an important consideration in the general interest of both the Union and the candidate countries. (European Council 1993: 5)

On a number of occasions, the link between the EU's own preparations and enlargement was reiterated. The Essen European Council of December 1994 announced a pre-accession strategy to prepare the CEECs for future membership. It declined the CEECs' demands for a clear timetable, but linked the timing of accession negotiations to institutional reform at the IGC

> On the European Union side, the institutional conditions for ensuring the proper functioning of the Union must be created at the 1996 Intergovern-

---

[4] For an overview of this issue, see Sedelmeier and Wallace (1996 and 2000 forthcoming).

mental Conference, which for that reason must take place before accession
negotiations begin.   (European Council 1994*b*: 7)

A formal link between the IGC and enlargement was formulated by the
Madrid European Council of December 1995. Having previously agreed to
open accession negotiations with Cyprus and Malta six months after the end
of the IGC, some member states urged that this offer be extended to the
CEECs. The European Council established the conclusion of the IGC as
the main reference point for the presentation of the Commission's opinions on
the candidates (which is the first step in any enlargement process), and for the
opening of accession negotiations

> [The European Council] asks the Commission to expedite preparation of
> its opinions on the applications made so that they can be forwarded to the
> Council as soon as possible after the conclusion of the Intergovernmental
> Conference . . .
>
>   Following the conclusion of the Intergovernmental Conference and in
> the light of its outcome and of all the opinions and reports from the Com-
> mission [composite paper on the impact of enlargement on the EU, par-
> ticularly on the agricultural and regional policies, and on the financial
> framework from 2000], the Council will, at the earliest opportunity,
> take the necessary decisions for launching the accession negotiations. The
> European Council hopes that the preliminary stages of negotiations will
> coincide with the start of negotiations with Cyprus and Malta.   (Euro-
> pean Council 1995: 23)

In the build-up to the 1996 IGC, both the chairman of the Reflection Group
of member state representatives, Carlos Westendorp, and the Commission
presented enlargement as the main rationale for institutional reform. The
Reflection Group identified 'two fundamental reasons [for reform], namely
improving the functioning of the Union on the one hand, and, on the other,
creating the conditions to enable it to cope successfully with the internal and
external challenges facing it, such as the next enlargement' (Reflection Group
1995*a*: 1), and devoted a whole chapter of its report to 'enabling the Union to
work better and preparing for enlargement' (Reflection Group 1995*b*: 6–8). The
Commission included enlargement in the title of its opinion ('Reinforcing
Political Union and Preparing for Enlargement'), which stressed the precondition of institutional reform throughout

> The Intergovernmental Conference is the first stage in a busy timetable,
> which moreover depends on the Conference for its success: within the next
> four years, Europe has to have [among other things] adjusted its polices
> with a view to enlargement. . . .
>
>   [T]he European Union cannot commit itself to this round of enlarge-
> ment without making sure that changes, sometimes far-reaching ones, are

first made in the ways and means of its operation. . . . The Commission expects of the Intergovernmental Conference that it strengthens the Union so as to prepare enlargement around a clear political project. The Union must therefore: . . . adopt an institutional system which will work in an expanded Europe.   (Commission 1996a: 3–4)

On the basis of this overview of the evolving link between institutional reform at the IGC and enlargement, it would indeed seem that an insufficient result at the IGC would be a major obstacle to proceeding with the enlargement process. The following section briefly reviews the IGC's results in this respect, which are indeed disappointing when viewed from an enlargement perspective.

Institutional Reform in the Amsterdam Treaty

Qualified Majority Voting and Institutional Representation

The Amsterdam Treaty did not significantly extend the application of qmv, which had been widely regarded as a condition for continued efficient decision-making. Nor did it take any concrete decisions on the reform of the institutional structure ahead of enlargement, and it postponed dealing with the more fundamental questions until a later date (Avery and Cameron 1998: 140; Grabbe and Hughes 1998: 103; Mayhew 1998; Neunreither 1998b). The two articles in the protocol on institutions (Protocol No. 11 attached to the Amsterdam Treaty) imply two directions for future reforms. Following the next enlargement, each member state will have only one Commissioner, with the larger member states being compensated through a reweighting of votes in the Council. The absolute number of Commissioners may be capped at twenty, suggesting that once this ceiling has been reached, there might no longer be an automatic representative for each member state

> At the date of entry into force of the first enlargement of the Union, . . . the Commission shall comprise one national of each of the Member States, provided that, by that date, the weighting of votes in the Council has been modified, whether by reweighting of votes or by dual majority, in a manner acceptable to all Member States, taking into account all relevant elements, notably compensating those Member States which give up the possibility of nominating a second member of the Commission.
>
> At least one year before the membership of the European Union exceeds twenty, a conference of representatives of the governments of the Member States shall be convened in order to carry out a comprehensive review of the provisions of the Treaties on the composition and functioning of the institutions (Treaty of Amsterdam, Protocol on the institutions, Articles 1 and 2).

Flexibility and Enhanced Cooperation

One area which attracted major attention during the negotiations was the introduction of a clause on 'flexibility', in the sense of permitting a group of member states to develop forms of 'enhanced cooperation' (i.e. for some members to proceed further and faster with integration in certain areas). The final provisions of the Amsterdam Treaty are rather cumbersome, since they can only be used as a 'last resort', and with the consent of a majority of the member states. The latter's reluctance to insert a more ambitious clause into the treaty might, however, turn out to be an advantage rather than a disadvantage for the CEECs. While flexibility was presented both as a solution for a more diverse membership and as a tool to facilitate the accession of the CEECs, it appears primarily as a mechanism to bypass the veto of the more reluctant within the current membership. It is less clear what the CEECs could gain from it, given that, in those areas in which they might require flexible arrangements, this could be dealt with under the existing practice of transitional arrangements. More worryingly, flexibility raises the spectre of marginalization and 'second class membership' which would exclude them from areas where their accession creates pressures on the EU budget (de La Serre and Wallace 1997; for a more in-depth discussion of flexibility, see Chapters 9, 10, and 11).

Implications for Enlargement?

How are we to assess the implications for enlargement of the limited outcome of the IGC? The current arrangements are clearly insufficient as preparations for increased numbers of members. The Italian, Belgian, and French governments have already declared that they will not approve enlargement unless further progress is made on institutional reform. Indeed, another IGC will have to deal with institutional issues before any accessions can occur. The result of the IGC thus seems to confirm rationalist predictions about the likelihood of agreement among the member states. It also suggests that the pessimistic assessments of the CEECs' accession prospects from a rationalist perspective seem well-founded. Grabbe and Hughes (1998: 104) express the concerns of the CEECs when they conclude that: '[i]nstitutional reform, as much as policy reform, could thus be a serious hurdle for enlargement and could easily be used by reluctant member states as a means of delaying enlargement'.

Yet a rationalist account might be unduly pessimistic. In fact, the determination on the part of the member states to conclude the IGC at Amsterdam, despite its inconclusive nature, rather than to continue the negotiations seemed to confirm their commitment to opening formal accession negotiations early in 1998. Certainly, the debates at the IGC exposed some worrying trends for both the CEECs and the current members. However, these arguably relate more to the apparently changing perceptions of the nature of integration in an enlarged Union. First, the inclusion of the Commission in the equation of national representation challenges the notion of the Commission's independence, and reflects a lack of appreciation for Monnet's concern to create a lean, efficient, and cohesive collegial body. Second, the emphasis on the weighting of votes as opposed to the previous practice of very rarely using formal voting seems to reflect a diminishing trust in mutual solidarity, in the ability to cater for minority positions and in building coalitions (Hayes-Renshaw and Wallace 1997: 295; Neunreither 1998b). By contrast, the inability to agree on institutional reform at this early date, albeit desirable, need not be the most worrying feature for the CEECs. I argue that, on the evidence of the evolution of EU policy towards the CEECs, there might be less reason to fear that the EU will stall on enlargement over the complexities of institutional, policy and budgetary reform than interest-based accounts would suggest.

The debates about institutional and policy adaptations within the EU have parallels with the EU's policy towards the CEECs so far (the association policy). EU policy was largely the result of intra-EU debates about the extent of concessions, and their internal distribution. Of course the association policy as such required different types of adjustment from the EU than accessions. The former related primarily to trade liberalization and the latter to institutional and policy adaptation. However, the consideration of these internal reforms already impinged on the debates about the CEECs' eventual membership during the evolution of the association policy. We would thus expect that the factors and dynamics which shaped the association policy will also crucially affect the debates about intra-EU adaptation and accession negotiations. An analysis of the association policy should provide important clues as to the validity of interest-based approaches with regard to current and future intra-EU debates on adjustment and accession negotiations.

The following section argues that the EU's collective identity towards the CEECs was an important factor in inclining the EU to accept the CEECs' membership objective, and to accommodate the CEECs' preferences in the association policy to a greater extent than rationalist approaches would predict. In turn, the explicit commitment to enlargement and the formal opening of accession negotiations in March 1998, while not prejudging the substantive nature of accession treaties, reinforce the identity-related stakes in successful enlargement for the EU.

EU Identity Towards the CEECs and the Limits of a Rationalist Approach to the Association Policy

Most analyses of the association policy are based on rationalist assumptions, and use, at least implicitly, a liberal intergovernmentalist framework

(Moravcsik 1993). In these analyses, the association policy is the result of a strategic bargaining process among utility-maximizing actors in a two- or three-level game involving the CEECs, the member state governments and EU-based sectoral interest groups (Haggard *et al.* 1993; Nicolaïdis 1993; Guggenbuhl 1995; Niblett 1995; Shaffer 1995; Friis 1997). These accounts explain EU policy towards the CEECs on the basis of the relative bargaining power of each group of actors, and the interaction between levels. However, EU policy accommodates the interests of the CEECs to a much larger extent than rationalist approaches would predict, concerning both the question of membership and issues of policy substance.

Accommodation of the CEECs' Preferences in the Association Policy and the Limits of a Rationalist Approach

Rationalist approaches have problems in explaining why the member state governments agreed to enlargement despite full awareness of the difficult compromises on certain of their interests which this would eventually entail. Despite initial reluctance to sanction the CEECs' objective of eventual membership of the EAs, EU policy continued to evolve. The Copenhagen European Council of June 1993 endorsed the eventual accession of the CEECs, and the pre-accession strategy put this principle on a concrete footing, although there was no major change in the security environment. In March 1998, the EU opened accession negotiations which are 'probably the most significant of the different stages of the accession process . . . because opening them implies a willingness to conclude them' (Avery and Cameron 1998: 27). Even if an accommodation of the CEECs' desire to join did serve the broader political and economic interests of the most powerful member states (e.g. the German government), more reluctant member governments could have exercised their veto. The case of the CEECs is in striking contrast to a number of earlier applications, such as those by Britain, Greece, Spain, Malta, or Turkey, when member governments or the Commission had not felt inhibited in openly speaking out against enlargement. Even reluctant EU policy-makers did not deny the legitimacy of the CEECs' demands, and accepted their eventual membership.

Furthermore, the CEECs' preferences on concrete issues of trade liberalization were accommodated to a greater extent than the lowest common denominator of sectoral interests on the EU side suggests. The material bargaining power of the CEECs' is not sufficient to extract such concessions from the EU. Nor are overriding political or security interests on the EU side an entirely sufficient explanation, since it is not obvious to what extent subordination of sectoral interests in particular cases is a requirement for the achievement of such long-term interests. Moreover, German officials, for example, were often among those arguing for restrictive policy outcomes.

Interests and the distribution of power (between the member states, between different domestic groups, and between the EU and the CEECs) clearly affected policy outcomes, but these *alone* seem insufficient to account for the extent of accommodation of the CEECs' interests. Accommodation goes beyond a mere acknowledgement of a 'situational interdependence' (Keohane 1991: 229) between the member states and the CEECs. Analyses which treat EU policy towards the CEECs primarily as a set of trade negotiations, or as a narrow case of joint EU foreign policy to stabilize its 'near abroad', fail to capture an important aspect. I argue that EU policy towards the CEECs is not simply about material interests and the material bargaining assets of the different actors. It is also about the definition and the enactment of the EU's collective identity towards the CEECs.

The Collective EU Identity towards the CEECs

More diffuse norms embedded in the EU's institutional structure which contribute to a collective EU identity towards the CEECs can be traced back to the notion of the broader European vocation of the EU in the Rome Treaty, and its proclaimed role in supporting democratic and market economic development. Statements by EU policy-makers about the EU's role towards the CEECs reinforced these norms, and endowed them with more concrete substance. From the origins of the EU throughout the Cold War period, such statements stressed the EU's solidarity as well as the involuntary nature of the CEECs' exclusion from the integration process. Declarations in response to the changes in the CEECs in the late 1980s reaffirmed this commitment, and pledges of EU support for the CEECs' transformation reinforced this normative discourse. Successive European Council meetings as well as individual officials asserted a 'special responsibility' on the part of the EU towards the CEECs, in that the EU has a 'historical opportunity' to overcome the division of the continent, and an obligation to actively support democratic and economic development in the CEECs and their integration into the EU. The notion of a special EU responsibility towards the CEECs has become a central feature of the EU's policy discourse about its role *vis-à-vis* the CEECs.

This diffuse notion of EU responsibility towards the CEECs constitutes one component of the collective identity of EU policy-makers. Compliance with this self-image is an important aspect of EU policy, in that it suggests that certain types of behaviour are more 'appropriate' than others. The component of EU identity which implies a responsibility for the CEECs is enacted through compliance with a diffuse regulative norm which proscribes purely self-interested behaviour, and prescribes the consideration of the CEECs' interests in policy. The accommodation of these interests is thus not only the result of convergence between dominant EU and CEEC interests, but also an important evaluative standard of policy in its own right.

The norm of EU responsibility and the regulative norm of accommodating the CEECs' interests in EU policy do not determine policy outcomes, but they might structure the 'realm of possibilities' for available policy options by excluding certain options as inappropriate, and reinforcing the legitimacy of others (Price and Tannenwald 1996: 148–9; see also Klotz 1995: 461–2). In this sense, the regulative norm provides the necessary condition, in combination with more self-interested motivations, for EU policy to be defined as needing to accommodate CEEC interests.

However, EU identity and the regulative norm of accommodation resonate more with some policy-makers than with others. The resonance is strongest with policy-makers who represent the EU externally, and towards the CEECs in particular: the heads of state and government and the foreign ministers of the member states, as well as Commission officials responsible for policy towards the CEECs. The resonance is particularly strong for the latter, since identification with an EU identity is a much greater part of their multiple social identities. By contrast, EU identity towards the CEECs is a much less important factor in shaping the preference formation of sectoral policy-makers, both inside the Commission and in the member state governments.

Policy Advocacy and Policy Impact

An analysis of the association policy suggests that the EU's identity towards the CEECs affected policy principally through the advocacy by a specific group of policy-makers of policy options compatible with this identity. These policy advocates were primarily based inside the Commission, including the Commissioners responsible for external relations, and Directorate General (DG) I, in particular the unit dealing with policy towards the CEECs (DG I-E, later DG I-L). They promoted an accommodation of the CEECs' interests not only because of far-sighted self-interest, but also for its own sake. This does not necessarily imply altruism, but rather suggests acting according to appropriate behaviour. This group of policy-makers was most frequently the source of statements acknowledging and asserting a special role for the EU towards the CEECs, and frequently justified policy preferences with reference to norms of accommodation.

Identity and Policy Advocacy in the Association Policy

An overview of the development of the association policy shows that this group of policy-makers was the source of policy initiatives and the firmest advocates of the CEECs inside the EU. The Commission played a key role in the immediate EC policy responses to the unfolding changes in the CEECs in the late 1980s (examples of the Commission's input include the Trade and Cooperation

Agreements, the co-ordination of G-24 aid, the Phare programme, and the EC Action Plan). DG I also reacted very rapidly to the Council's decision of early 1990 to base relations with the CEECs in the framework of association agreements by quickly devising a far-reaching framework for 'Europe Agreements'. During the negotiation of the EAs, and indeed in the internal EC negotiations on the negotiating directives for those agreements and their revision, it was Frans Andriessen, his *cabinet* and the officials in DG I-E who were consistently the strongest advocates of the CEECs' preferences. On a number of occasions, they obtained concessions in the intra-EU negotiations which took greater account of the CEECs' preferences.

The initiative for improving the EAs, namely by accelerating trade concessions in the sensitive sectors, and by committing the EC to the objective of the eventual accession of the CEECs, emanated from the Andriessen *cabinet*. DG I-E officials started to forge a consensus for this immediately after the signing of the EAs. The initiative gained further momentum in 1993 through the personal commitment of Leon Brittan as external relations Commissioner, leading to the declarations of the Copenhagen European Council in June of the same year. The idea of a pre-accession strategy, which put the principle of the eventual accession of the CEECs on a working footing, emerged from close co-operation between the Brittan *cabinet* and DG I-L. Endorsement in the Council was achieved through the close cooperation of the Commission team and the German presidency in the second half of 1994.

One way in which the policy advocates and their supporters obtained influence on policy was by affecting the structure of discourse about EU policy towards the CEECs. References to EU 'responsibility' not only compelled the member states' foreign ministers and heads of state or government into behaviour in accordance with this norm, or into justifying deviation from such behaviour with reference to competing norms rather than idiosyncratic self-interests, but the reinforcement of the discourse of collective responsibility also implied limitations to the perceived legitimacy of arguments relating to the defensive, particularist interests inside the EU for sectoral policy-makers and organized interests.

In this respect, the explicit acknowledgment of the CEECs' membership perspective not only added greater weight to arguments based on the EU's collective identity, it also reinforced the incentive of the policy advocates to pursue such an explicit acknowledgment as an objective in its own right. This discourse did not determine outcomes, but it limited the realm of acceptable policy options to those which accommodated the CEECs' preferences to a certain extent.

The importance of collective self-perceptions and of the terms of policy discourse also seems to be reflected in the apparent sensitivity and vulnerability of EU policy-makers to criticism of the lack of accommodation in the EAs and the association policy. Thus, criticism from the CEECs directly, as well as that from the broader academic community, had an impact on policy, despite not being linked to material resources. In turn, the formal endorsement of the commitment to enlargement reinforced the identity-related stakes, and made it unacceptable to appear to fail the CEECs.

However, an important factor which enabled the policy advocates to influence policy was that they could also draw on arguments relating, and actors receptive, to notions of far-sighted self-interest. The suggested complementarity of norm-led accommodation of the CEECs' interests, and of the maximization of long-term self-interest through support of the transformation processes, are important.

In sum, an analysis of the overall development of the association policy suggests that norms relating to the EU's collective identity towards the CEECs inclined EU policy towards accommodating CEEC preferences to a certain extent. Focusing on the overall development of the association policy provides important insights, particularly with regard to the continued evolution of policy towards a policy of enlargement. However, an exclusive focus on this level fails to capture variations in the extent of accommodation of the CEECs' preferences on concrete issues of policy substance across the range of policy areas, as well as the factors which obstructed or facilitated such accommodation. It is precisely these issues, however, which are crucially important for the substantive results of the accession treaties.

In the following section, I suggest that it is not simply the strength of interest groups in these different policy areas which determines the scope for accommodating the CEECs' preferences, as rationalist approaches assume. The respective policy paradigms underpinning EU policy in these areas are crucial factors which mediate the impact of the advocacy of accommodation on policy.

Policy Substance and Accommodation: The Role of Policy Paradigms

The above-mentioned uneven resonance of a collective EU identity across different groups of EU policy-makers is crucially important for the association policy and, by extension, for accession negotiations. The association policy and accession negotiations are a 'composite policy' which is constituted by a range of 'meso-policies', that is, distinctive policy decisions across the range of policy areas which are part of the association policy or accession negotiations. The member states' foreign ministers and heads of state or government were collectively most receptive to the effect of the EU's identity towards the CEECs, but they cannot take these decisions autonomously. Issues of policy substance are therefore the outcome of a process of horizontal policy co-ordination (i.e. negotiations with those policy-makers who have primary responsibility for the respective meso-policies).

In general, this creates obstacles to accommodation, since these meso-policy-makers are less receptive to the EU's identity towards the CEECs, and might be guided by quite different priorities. Indeed, an analysis of the association policy reveals that the main opposition to a more far-reaching accommodation was not primarily the result of national differences among the member states, but came predominantly from sectoral policy, both within the Commission and within the member state governments.

The observation that the debate about the association policy is characterized by a cleavage between different groups of policy-makers which cuts across national lines has also been made in two other analyses of the association policy (Niblett 1995; Torreblanca 1998). However, while these analyses also challenge liberal intergovernmentalist assumptions of interstate bargaining at the EU level, they share the latter's rationalist approach to domestic politics. They thus identify the source of the meso policy-makers' opposition to accommodation as the pressure of societal interest groups in the respective policy areas.

By contrast, I argue that the meso policy-makers do not simply act according to the interests of the strongest societal groups, but have preferences of their own which they may pursue even against societal pressures (see for example Evans *et al.* 1985). These preferences can be significantly shaped by 'policy paradigms' as a coherent set of ideas which underpins their understanding of policy in their respective areas of responsibility (Hall 1993).

The degree of compatibility between sectoral policy paradigms and policy options advocated to accommodate the CEECs' interests are thus an important factor which mediates the policy impact of such policy advocacy. Policy paradigms might form additional, immaterial obstacles to accommodation. However, to the extent that these policy paradigms are amenable to change, emerging alternative policy paradigms might facilitate accommodation, despite strong opposition from interest groups. An important question is therefore whether advocacy of the CEECs' preferences can challenge dominant policy paradigms, and foster the ascendancy of alternative, more compatible, policy paradigms.

The following section provides evidence from two meso-policies, the steel trade and regulatory alignment, to illustrate in which ways policy paradigms and their amenability to change can act either as facilitators or obstacles to accommodation.

Policy Advocacy and Policy Paradigms: The Cases of the Steel Trade and Regulatory Alignment

Liberalization of the Steel Trade

The case of the EU policy of steel trade liberalization towards the CEECs illustrates how the emergence of an alternative policy paradigm for EU steel policy which is more compatible with the preferences of the CEECs facilitated accommodation, despite opposition from interest groups. In this case, the alternative policy paradigm emerged to a large extent independently of the association policy. But the interplay between those meso policy-makers who promoted a change in EU steel policy and the advocates of an accommodating policy towards the CEECs played an important role in the ascendancy of the alternative policy paradigm.

The EU policy to liberalize the steel trade in the framework of the association policy accommodates the CEECs' preferences for free and unconditional access to the EU market to a considerable extent. Before the negotiation of the EAs, the steel trade was regulated by a highly restrictive regime of Voluntary Restraint Agreements (VRAs), which imposed both quantitative and price restrictions on CEEC exports. The EAs ended the VRAs, immediately eliminating all quantitative restrictions, and the advocates of the CEECs' preferences in the Commission successfully resisted the insertion of provisions to maintain the possibility of re-introducing VRAs. The greater autonomy of the meso policy-makers in the implementation phase meant that, on a few occasions, EU trade defence instruments were used against CEEC steel producers. However, the advocates of the CEECs' preferences inside the EU were able to resist interest group pressure for the wholesale reintroduction of a restrictive regime as part of the 1993-4 EU plan for the restructuring of the steel industry. This outcome contradicts rationalist predictions, since EU producers in the steel sector were strongly opposed to liberalizing trade with the CEECs, and there was no countervailing pressure from consuming industries on the EU side.

The policy paradigm which had dominated EU steel policy since the inception of the European Coal and Steel Community (ECSC) could be described as a 'managed restructuring paradigm'. This paradigm is based on the assumption that, because of the specific production and market structure of the steel industry, the nature of competition in this market differs crucially from other sectors. During periods of depression, the free play of market forces would thus not induce firms to undertake the necessary adjustment measures, but would merely lead to cut-throat competition in which not necessarily the most economically viable firms would survive. Rather, firms would only restructure and cut overcapacity if this was organized as a collective effort, under the guidance of public policy-makers, and in a stable external environment. The accommodation of the CEECs' preferences for liberalization is thus at odds with this dominant policy paradigm.

However, since the early 1990s, an alternative policy paradigm which I call the 'non-intervention paradigm' has emerged (for a somewhat similar argument, see Dudley and Richardson 1997). This paradigm rejects the idea of the steel sector as a special case. In contrast to the dominant paradigm, external competition is regarded as a positive contributing factor to restructuring. This paradigm no longer places the emphasis on the protection of the EU market, but on the need for open markets abroad. It is thus much more compatible with the CEECs' preferences.

The ascendancy of the non-intervention paradigm meant that the policy advocates in the Commission could find support for trade liberalization towards the CEECs among some steel meso policy-makers despite strong opposition from organized interests in the sector. Although this alternative policy paradigm emerged largely independently of the association policy, the interaction between advocates of the non-intervention paradigm for EC steel policy and the advocates of an accommodating policy towards the CEECs also played an important role. The advocates of the non-intervention paradigm provided arguments and a supportive alliance for the advocates of an accommodating policy towards the CEECs to push for greater CEEC access to the EC steel market. In turn, references to the need to open EC markets in order to support the CEECs provided an impetus for the ascendancy of the alternative steel policy paradigm in the steel sector.

The Regulatory Alignment of the CEECs with the Internal Market

The case of EU policy for the regulatory alignment of the CEECs illustrates how accommodation was facilitated through the ability of the advocates of the CEECs' preferences in the Commission to successfully challenge the viability of certain elements of the policy paradigm underpinning the EU's internal market with reference to the specific situation in the CEECs. On the current evidence, this was particularly the case for environmental policy. Yet in the area of social policy, officials in the Commission's DG V resisted accommodation with reference to the EU's internal market paradigm, despite the absence of societal groups which would have pressurized them into doing so.

The process of regulatory alignment is similar to that of regulatory harmonization to remove non-tariff barriers (NTBs) in the single market programme, and to the EEA regime which extended the internal market to most of the EFTA countries. The regulatory alignment of the CEECs, as the economic core of the EU's pre-accession strategy, is based on a Commission White Paper (WP) of 1995, endorsed by the Cannes European Council in June 1995. The WP provides a guide for the CEECs, while final, legally binding decisions in this respect will only be taken in actual accession negotiations.[5]

Essentially, the CEECs' interest in the EU's regulatory alignment policy lies in selective alignment, which would allow the CEECs to delay the adoption of those EU rules which regulate the production process, but do not affect the nature of products and thus do not form NTBs. Such process regulations pri-

---

[5] It should be noted, however, that there is some ambiguity in this respect with regard to the Accession Partnerships, which follow on from the WP (Grabbe 1999).

marily concern measures in the area of EU social policy, such as health and safety at the workplace, and elements of EU environmental policy, such as pollution from stationary sources. Selective alignment thus means implementing those measures during long transitional periods after accession rather than at the pre-accession stage.

Rationalist approaches identify two main sources of opposition to accommodating the CEECs' preference for selective alignment. The first is pressure from EU producers to impose strict compliance with process regulations on CEEC companies from an early stage, in order to reduce the latter's competitive advantage. A second source of opposition could be identified in those member state governments which are more generally reluctant about an Eastern enlargement, and might insist on extensive alignment and the strict and early application of EU regulations as a means of delaying the accession of the CEECs.

Two main elements of the policy paradigm underpinning the EU's internal market militate against accommodating the CEECs' selective alignment. The first is a distinctive understanding of the nature of economic competition, reflected in the endorsement of the 'level playing field' argument, which suggests that 'fair' competition requires not only the harmonization of regulations which concern products, but also production processes. Significantly, this argument is not generally accepted among economists, but dominates the EU discourse on the internal market. The second element is the broad acceptance inside the EU that the internal market is not merely based on a rationale of competition and market integration, but that it also serves the protection of broader public policy objectives, notably high levels of social and environmental protection (Wallace and Young 1996). In sum, both these elements of the EU's internal market paradigm constrain the extent to which EU policy-makers view the CEECs' demands for selective alignment as feasible and legitimate.

However, the assumptions on which the EU's internal market paradigm is based are by no means widely shared among economists. The argument can be made that, for participation in the Single European market, the harmonization of process standards is less important than the harmonization of product standards. While the former affect the competitive position of firms, and thus indirectly affect competition in the internal market, they are not essential for the functioning of the internal market. They do not constitute NTBs, as they do not affect the free circulation of products. Furthermore, it can be argued that there is nothing 'unfair' about competition in the absence of harmonized environmental or social standards (see for example Smith *et al.* 1996). On these grounds, there are strong reasons for granting the CEECs the possibility of selective alignment and for implementing process regulatory measures in the course of long transition periods after accession, rather than at the pre-accession stage.

Despite the fact that strong groups inside the EU, as well as the EU's internal market paradigm, are opposed to selective alignment, the WP accommodates the CEECs' preferences to a significant extent. The EU's regulatory alignment policy was essentially driven by a small team of policy-makers inside the Commission, composed of officials from the CEEC unit in DG I and from the *cabinet* of Leon Brittan, the external relations Commissioner. These policy-makers' understanding of the specific situation in the CEECs led them to question the viability of the EU's internal market paradigm. They convinced the policy-makers of DG XV, responsible for the internal market and the drafting of the WP, to take a selective approach. Thus, the single market measures outlined in the WP essentially concentrate on product regulations and exclude process regulations. This selective approach is most clearly reflected in the area of environmental policy, where such process regulations as the pollution from stationary sources are excluded from the WP.

However, the area of social policy constitutes an exception to the general rule. Officials from DG V insisted on the inclusion of process regulations, such as health and safety at the workplace. Significantly, their opposition to selective alignment was not the result of external pressures. Rather than defending the interests of particularist groups inside the EU, these policy-makers defended the dominant internal market paradigm as an expression of their specific understanding of, and preference for, the operation of the EU's internal market. In turn, the presentation of their arguments with reference to assumptions underpinning the broadly accepted internal market paradigm made it hard for DG XV to deny their legitimacy.

Conclusions

Coming back to the starting point, I noted that a link between the IGC and enlargement had been established, which *de facto* made institutional reform at the 1996–7 IGC a precondition for the accession process. Since the results of the Amsterdam Treaty are insufficient as a preparation for the accession of the CEECs, this chapter has assessed the implications for the prospects of Eastern enlargement.

The sceptical view that institutional reform might make the EU stall on enlargement seems confirmed by the IGC's inability to agree on institutional reform, and must appear even more plausible if the, at least equally difficult, questions of policy and budgetary adaptation are taken into account. However, this chapter has argued that predictions made on the grounds of the constellation of the material interests of the incumbents might be unduly pessimistic. The dynamics that underpin the debates about institutional and policy adaptation are similar to those behind the association policy, and the evidence of the evolution of the association policy so far suggests that the EU's policy has not been purely guided by material interests inside the EU.

In this chapter, I have argued that the EU's collective identity towards the CEECs has inclined it to accommodate the CEECs' preferences to a greater extent than an interest-based approach would predict. By the same token, the EU has an identity-related stake in bringing accession negotiations to a successful conclusion, which might prevent member states from obstructing enlargement with reference to their narrow self-interests. Thus, despite the limited results of the 1996–7 IGC, the principle of Eastern enlargement does not seem in doubt.

Still, for the actual outcome of accession negotiations, the devil lies in the detail of policy substance, which has to be negotiated in co-ordination with policy-makers who are less receptive to this component of the EU's identity. This chapter has argued that it is not merely interest group pressure which might constrain the scope for accommodation, but that the policy paradigms which underpin EU policy in the various policy areas play an important role.

These policy paradigms might form additional obstacles, as current evidence from regulatory alignment with EU social policy reflects. Yet I have also illustrated how policy paradigms might facilitate accommodation despite countervailing interest group pressures. In the area of steel trade policy, this was the case through the emergence of an alternative, more compatible, policy paradigm. Early evidence from regulatory alignment with environmental policy suggests that the argument of the unsuitability of the dominant policy paradigm for the situation in the CEECs seems to have successfully challenged the internal market paradigm through a process of persuasion. Thus, whether the EU can resist the temptation to make the CEECs bear the brunt of the adjustment costs will depend on whether positive dynamics can be struck between internal policy adaptation and alignment of the CEECs. To take account of the specific situation and requirements of the CEECs, EU policy-makers must be prepared to confront some of the idiosyncrasies of Western European integration.

PART IV

Theoretical Perspectives on Constitutional Change

13

Precedents and Present Events in the European Union: An Institutional Perspective on Treaty Reform

ULF SVERDRUP

The 1996–7 intergovernmental conference (IGC), which resulted in the Amsterdam Treaty, was convened to prepare the European Union (EU) for the challenges of the next century, for which a radical review and reform of the EU's institutions was considered to be of paramount importance. During the IGC, issues related to institutional reform ranked high on the agenda, and played a prominent role in the discussions. In this chapter, I investigate and map the organizational factors that constrained and facilitated institutional reform in the EU, and I challenge the liberal intergovernmental perspective (Moravcsik 1993, 1995) which argues that the preferences and power of the member states are the key explanatory factors for such reform. Based on an empirical investigation of the 1996–7 IGC, I suggest that an institutional perspective of governance (March and Olsen 1989, 1995) reveals important aspects of political reform which have previously been neglected.

Formally, an IGC is a conference where representatives of the member states consider amendments to treaties. The outcome of the conference must be agreed upon unanimously and ratified by all member states (Bainbridge and Teasdale 1995: 282). In the history of the EU, a total of six IGCs has taken place, four of which were held between 1988 and 1998. A certain tradition of arranging IGCs in the EU has gradually emerged, encompassing both procedures and practices. The 1996–7 IGC was formally opened during the Italian presidency in March 1996, but the initial preparation had already started some years before with the publication of papers, media coverage, political statements and so on. The formal conference negotiations lasted for fifteen months, and the initial

I would like to thank Johan P. Olsen, Andrew Moravcsik, Karlheinz Neunreither, Peter Leslie, Beate Kohler-Koch, Alexander Stubb, Fabrice Larat, Bjørn Otto Sverdrup, Bent Sophus Tranøy, Antje Wiener, Fiona Hayes-Renshaw, and Ingrid Mohn Sverdrup for their helpful comments on earlier drafts of this chapter.

draft was first agreed upon in Amsterdam during the Dutch presidency, in June 1997. After extensive renegotiations, modifications, and even a renumbering of certain articles in the draft, the final version of the Amsterdam Treaty, as it was named, was officially signed in October 1997. The member states were expected to ratify the treaty during 1998 and to implement it by the beginning of 1999, but by October 1998 this timetable was already in arrears.

Three main theories compete to explain the driving mechanism of European integration, and differ as to how they evaluate the importance of grand bargains. First, the liberal intergovernmental perspective argues that the dynamic of European integration is primarily a result of negotiations between the most powerful member states in key bargaining situations (Moravcsik 1991a, 1993). Second, the supranational approach argues that the transformation of the legal system in Europe is the key motor of European integration. It has been claimed, for instance, that 'the Court of Justice constituted the European Community' and that 'the Court created the present-day Community' (Shapiro 1992: 123). According to this approach, the dynamic of European integration is primarily interpreted as the well-structured and rule-bound activity of the European Court of Justice (ECJ). Third, the multilevel governance approach argues that the main driving forces are the day-to-day processes of negotiation, competition, and co-operation within and between networks at multiple levels of governance. The activity in these networks is often characterized as functional problem-solving among technical experts (Héritier 1994; Jachtenfuchs and Kohler-Koch 1996a). It is argued that the development of policies and institutions is more or less independent of the IGCs and primarily a matter of daily political practice, and that unco-ordinated, decentralized action and uncontrolled shifts shape the living constitution of the EU (Kohler-Koch 1998b: 2).

These three approaches highlight different mechanisms (bargaining, rule-following, and problem-solving), and they emphasize the importance of different actors (the national governments, the ECJ, and the different multilevel networks). It has been argued that there are not only three theoretical approaches, but also three modes of governance in the EU (Weiler et al. 1995a: 25). In other words, various aspects of European integration are driven by different mechanisms, and each theoretical perspective reveals important aspects of European integration (Peterson 1995). If this is so, the theoretical challenge is to eliminate inconsistencies in the existing models, to specify their area of validity and to show the interaction between the different dynamics.

I maintain that there are good theoretical, empirical and normative reasons for an examination of grand bargains in the EU such as an IGC.

First, it is a basic assumption in democratic governance that decision-makers are able to decide on, and to design institutions. It is assumed that decision-makers are neither driven purely by accident nor merely victims of their environment. If the latter were the case, issues related to democratic accountability, transparency, representation, and so on, would be of limited relevance. In order to facilitate democratic governance in a realistic way, we therefore need to specify the set of factors which enable or constrain the decision-makers in the specific historical and institutional setting (Olsen 1997). An investigation of the IGC, therefore, could potentially highlight some of the most pertinent theoretical questions related to democratic governance:

- What are the conditions for institutional reform in a democratic context?
- What are the key driving mechanisms in processes of institutional design?
- How can political systems in a democratic context learn from experience and increase their capacity to govern and to shape political institutions?

Second, the dominant theoretical approach in the field of European integration has been the theory of liberal intergovernmentalism (LI), which focuses particularly on grand bargains, arguing that investigating key bargaining processes is particularly important in developing our theoretical accounts of the EU (Moravcsik 1991a, 1993; Urwin 1995; Wallace 1996a; Laffan 1997a). The aim of the LI perspective is to explain 'the substantive and institutional development' of the EU through the sequential analysis of national preference formation and intergovernmental strategic interaction (Moravcsik 1993: 480). The LI perspective is thought to be particularly well-suited to a key bargaining situation of a constitutional nature, such as an IGC (Weiler et al. 1995a: 24). Although the LI perspective has been the subject of much criticism, it still remains the most consistent and rigorous theoretical approach in the field of European integration today, and its core assumptions are grounded in a strong tradition in the social sciences (Moravcsik 1997: 514–15). The IGC, it seems, offered a unique match between a theoretical model and an empirical situation which is supposed to fit the theory particularly well. This good match gives us a unique opportunity for testing the theory on the basis of a crucial single-case design,[1] that is, a situation where the theory being tested has specified a clear set of propositions and some circumstances within which the propositions are believed to be true (Eckstein 1975). If the theory cannot be applied under such circumstances, clearly it should be modified.[2] Finally, the IGC attracted considerable political, intellectual and administrative attention, capacity and prestige, which in itself makes it an interesting object of study.

This chapter is organized as follows. First, the two theoretical perspectives of institutional reform are outlined. Next, an empirical investigation demonstrates how both the IGC and the outcome of the process were constrained by: (1) the EU's well-defined historical course; (2) a distinct set of organizational

---

[1] We should of course be careful in drawing conclusions on the basis of a single-case test. However, a single-case design is both powerful and fruitful when the case represents a unique situation, and when we are exploring other alternative theoretical approaches (Yin 1994).

[2] Eckstein (1975: 127) argued that a single-case design can 'score a clean knockout over a theory'. Others are more sceptical about single-case design (King et al. 1994).

procedures and norms regulating the decision-making process; and (3) a series of pressing events which were relatively loosely coupled to the IGC itself. I argue that a complete understanding of the IGC is impossible if the analysis is based solely on the preferences and powers of the member states. I argue that the LI perspective is important but not sufficient for an understanding of institutional reform processes. The institutionalist perspective is more illuminating and offers a theoretical framework which is more consistent with some of the empirical observations than is the case with the LI perspective. I suggest that a proper analysis of institutional dynamics and reform processes in the EU requires a dynamic perspective on decision-making. The decision-making process needs to be situated in a distinct historical, institutional and environmental setting, revealing how actors are embedded in a web of structuring elements. By developing our theories and mapping out how history, procedures, and present events constrain and facilitate decision-making, we are also increasing the possibility of successful institutional design.

Two Theories of Institutional Change

Political institutions like the EU are not static; they are continually changing and adapting. Changes in organizations are frequently characterized by small steps and incremental modifications. Continuous processes of change rarely form part of large-scale reform programmes, and they are hardly ever firmly controlled or well co-ordinated. Sometimes, well-planned and precisely timed reform attempts are made in order to review and reorganize the institutional apparatus of a political sector, a nation state, or an international organization. Such large-scale reform efforts might lead to dramatic and significant changes, but experience has shown that most of them fail to make any significant short-term impact (March and Olsen 1983). It is a basic assumption of democratic theory that the *demos* has the possibility to decide and shape political agendas, and to design political institutions, which enable the implementation of decisions (Dahl 1989). However, institutional design in a democratic context is difficult (Goodin 1997; Olsen 1997). In this section I argue that the LI perspective is overly optimistic, while the institutionalist perspective is at the same time more pessimistic and more realistic in evaluating the possibility for design.

In the field of European integration, the LI perspective assumes that the member states are able to design institutions which ensure effective implementation of political decisions. This perspective is based upon three basic premises (Moravcsik 1993: 480–2). First, state action reflects the bounded rational action of national governments, who try to achieve clear objectives, acting and calculating on the basis of an identifiable utility function. Second, the policy objectives of the member states are not stable; they vary according to shifting domestic pressures and alliances. These shifts in domestic opinion are smoothly aggregated through the political institutions in the member states. Their preferences are dependent on the domestic configuration of societal preferences, which are first and foremost determined by constraints and possibilities imposed by economic interdependence (Moravcsik 1993: 488–96). Lastly, an intergovernmental negotiation process involves two consecutive steps: first, the national governments define a set of state interests, and second, they engage in negotiations in order to realize these interests. The outcome of these negotiations is determined by the relative bargaining power of the member states. Consequently, according to the LI perspective, the most important actors for understanding IGCs in the EU are the large and powerful member states, such as Germany, France, and Britain. The logical starting point, therefore, is a detailed analysis of the preferences and powers of the member states. Moravcsik (1993: 498) presents us with four specific assumptions about key bargaining situations. First, key bargains are voluntary bargains, not imposed on any of the governments. Second, the national negotiators have easy access to information about the preferences and opportunities of their counterparts, and they are able to communicate at low transaction costs in an environment rich in information. Third, the negotiations take place within a flexible and protractible period of time, which makes it possible for the member governments to extend numerous offers and counter-offers at a low cost. Finally, it is assumed that it is possible to design efficient institutions which are capable of monitoring and enforcing the agreements made at all levels.

The institutional perspective on design, however, is less optimistic. It assumes that decision-making is embedded in a certain historical, institutional and temporal context which helps to create and constrain the possibilities for deliberate choice. This perspective is also based on three assumptions (March and Olsen, 1989, 1995). First, political life functions according to fairly stable rules and procedures. Decision-making involves finding a match between a particular role on the one hand and, on the other, a set of procedures which are believed to fit that particular role and situation. Decisions are made on the basis of rules and norms accumulated from past experience and learning, rather than on the calculation of preferences and the anticipation of future events. Second, the rules and procedures are institutionalized (i.e. they are taken for granted), and they guide decision-makers in their efforts to interpret and create meaning out of the situation. Certain abiding rules inform the decision-makers' normative judgements and their understanding of appropriate alternatives and actions. Resources and capabilities are linked to certain rules, thereby helping to uphold specific interpretations and world views. Third, institutions evolve in a path-dependent way (i.e. a decision made at one stage creates opportunities and constraints for decision-making at a later stage). In most cases, institutions change slowly and incrementally within the existing procedures and norms. Occasionally, however, a dramatic crisis or external shock can lead to a situation where the existing rules and procedures are unhelpful for interpreting the world and creating meaning. Under such conditions, institutions may change rapidly. Generally speaking, institutional design is a complex process of matching existing institutions, actions, and contexts in ways which are complicated and of long duration.

Most institutions have their own internal dynamic and operate in relatively separate spheres. Over time, institutions gain some autonomy and are able to buffer themselves against their environment. Despite a general tendency towards differentiation, decisions in one field are nevertheless structurally or accidentally coupled with decision opportunities in other areas (Cohen *et al.* 1972; Kingdon 1984). Decisions observed in a particular field are therefore often purely artificial or by-products of decisions made in other fields (Olsen 1972: 48). In general, the more established and institutionalized the political system, the more capacity it has to buffer the reform process. The EU is an adolescent and weakly institutionalized system; it therefore finds it difficult to separate issues and buffer the agenda. Furthermore, we can assume the increased likelihood of interlinkages between different spheres as an increasing number of cross-sectoral issues are addressed. Constitutional issues do not pertain to one particular sphere, but frequently regulate the relationship between different spheres. Consequently, the more issues of a constitutional character dominate the IGC's agenda, the more difficult it will be to buffer that agenda.

These interlinkages may lead to deliberate attempts to pair issues or to sequence events in order to achieve a goal. However, the coupling is frequently accidental and at times structural. The manner in which decision-makers distribute their attention is often determined just as much by the time of the appearance of the problem as by any assessment of its relative importance (Weiner 1976; Cyert and March 1992). Due to the importance of timing, deadlines function as action generators, triggering attention and decision-making activity (Starbuck 1983; Bromiley and Marcus 1987). This does not, however, imply a complete state of anarchy. The timing of the emergence of a particular problem, solution, or choice opportunity is often well organized and structured. Several deadlines are institutionalized and constitute important parts of the political organization at national and European level. For instance, budget and electoral cycles create fairly predictable rhythms of political life (Sverdrup 1996). According to this view, the distinct temporal location of a decision-making process helps to shape the pitfalls of, and possibilities for, reform.

The Path-dependency of the IGC

The IGC was not, as the LI perspective assumes, a voluntary process with few constraints, but a conference structured by past regulations and statements.

Three different mechanisms gave rise to the path-dependency of the IGC. First, the Maastricht Treaty (the Treaty on European Union—TEU) laid down regulations that helped to shape the agenda. The IGC was convened at this particular time because of German, Belgian, and Italian dissatisfaction with the outcome of the Maastricht negotiations in 1991. These countries managed to persuade the representatives of the other member states to agree to the convening of a new IGC in 1996 (Bainbridge and Teasdale 1995), and the agreement was formalized and incorporated into the TEU as Article N. According to this article: 'A conference of representatives of the governments of the Member States shall be convened in 1996 to examine those provisions of this Treaty for which revision is provided, in accordance with the objectives set out in Articles A and B' (Council of the European Union 1993).

The fact that the convening of the IGC was provided for in the treaty was novel. The idea was to bind the parties to meeting within a short space of time to evaluate the treaty and to negotiate further some unresolved elements. However, between the end of the Maastricht conference in 1991 and the opening session of the IGC in 1996, some of the premises for convening the IGC had changed dramatically. The aim of the IGC was to evaluate and improve on the TEU (Laursen 1997), but due to the delay in the ratification of the treaty, by 1996 the member states had had little experience of how it actually worked in practice. For instance, certain aspects of the co-decision procedure had never actually been implemented. To some extent, 'superstitious learning' was therefore possible where the link between past action and outcomes did not exist or was ambiguous (March 1994: 89). Despite these limitations on learning from experience, the IGC was opened as laid down in the treaty because the members states were formally obliged to negotiate a new treaty. A similar self-binding mechanism was inserted in the Amsterdam Treaty, in Article 2 of the 'Protocol on the institutions with the prospect of enlargement of the European Union', in which the parties agreed that a new IGC shall 'carry out a comprehensive review of the provisions of the Treaties on the composition and functioning of the institutions' at least one year before the number of member states exceeds twenty. Declaration 6, signed by Belgium, France, and Italy, requests that the next IGC concern itself with institutional reforms and criticizes the 1996–7 IGC for failing to meet the 'need . . . for substantial progress towards reinforcing the institutions'.

The issues on the IGC's agenda were also structured by the text of the treaties. The TEU listed a number of issues to be included on the agenda of the IGC in 1996 (Council of the European Union 1993). For instance, Article B stated that the conference should discuss the maintenance of the *acquis communautaire* and the extent to which the policies and forms of cooperation needed revision. Article J.4 called for a discussion of the relationship with West European Union (WEU). Article J.10 stated that the conference should examine whether or not any amendments were needed to the provisions relating to the

Common Foreign and Security Policy (CFSP). According to Declaration 1, the IGC should consider whether the EU should extend its competence to include issues related to civil protection, energy, and tourism. In Declaration 16 it was made clear that the IGC should review the possibilities of establishing a hierarchy of different categories of community acts. Most of these issues received considerable attention and played a predominant role in the preparations for, and the negotiations of, the IGC. Furthermore, because the IGC was framed and perceived as a revision of the TEU, the latter had an indirect impact on the IGC. Comparisons were frequently made between the IGC and the negotiations on the Maastricht Treaty, and the IGC was often referred to as 'the Maastricht II negotiations'. For instance, one commentator wrote that 'the Maastricht Treaty looks like it is heading for a 5,000 mile service'.[3] Many of the statements referred implicitly to the TEU by asserting, for example in the 1996 IGC, that the discussions should be more open, it should not surprise, it should be simpler, easier to understand, it should be more inspiring (Laursen 1997: 59–61). These references to the past helped structure the problems, solutions, and causal beliefs of the decision-makers.

Second, national adaptations to past treaties also influenced and eventually structured the IGC's new decision-making process. In the aftermath of the Maastricht negotiations, national institutions made several adjustments to the treaties in order to implement the TEU. Most importantly, as regards influencing European-level decision-making, certain national courts sought to draw and contest the boundaries of European integration by testing the legitimacy of the Europeanization process and the legal status of this transformation. The most influential ruling was that made by the German *Bundesverfassungsgericht* (*BvG*) in October 1993 (Weiler 1995*b*), defining the boundaries of further integration which imposed limitations on the issues on which German politicians could decide during the IGC. In Denmark, the courts also tested the constitutional validity of the Danish ratification of the TEU (Rasmussen 1996).[4] This case occurred during the negotiations and the ratification process, preventing the Danish negotiators from suggesting further transfers of competence or any increase in the use of majority voting. In addition to the legal case, the Danish negotiators were constrained by the referendum to which they had bound themselves on the ratification of the outcome of the IGC. The referendum was held in May 1998, and a clear major-

---

[3] *Financial Times*, 10 May 1995.

[4] The case concerned the conflict between Art. 235 of the Treaty on European Union (TEU) and §20 in the Danish Basic Law, which states that it is only possible to delegate sovereignty in a limited and clearly defined area. The Danish Supreme Court (*Højesteret*), in its 150-page ruling, established the rule that the *Højesteret* has the final say in such issues, and stated that the ratification of the TEU was not in conflict with the Danish Basic Law (*Weekendavisen*, 8–16 April 1998).

ity of 55.1 per cent of the voters supported the ratification of the Amsterdam Treaty.[5]

These two cases show the mutual interdependencies between and within the many levels of governance within the EU. On the one hand, national constitutions and courts respond and adapt to EU decisions, and this response in turn imposes restrictions upon the EU. In the judicial ruling of the national courts, the legal reasoning and decision-making activity in the EU is important. However, the member states also have to anticipate or take into account the structuring effects of national constitutions and rulings on the decision-making process in the EU (Rasmussen 1996: 66; Weiler 1995b). European integration is a large-scale process of mutual adaptation, rather than a one-dimensional process of national adaptation. Constitutional reforms within the member states will alter the system of co-ordination, thereby also necessitating doctrinal modifications at Community level (Llorente 1998: 28). Furthermore, the legal rulings of the national courts are not a direct result of the TEU or of the IGCs. Their history can be viewed as a response to a long-term gradual increase in competence for the EU, as well as the gradual development of legal reasoning and consciousness within the member states, at best triggered by the IGCs. In processes of Europeanization, one can therefore observe layers of adaptation and incremental change, which in turn lead to the triggering of disputes on the distribution of competence and power between the legal and political institutions within and between the member states.

Past political declarations and statements shape future discussions. There is no clear beginning and end to the IGC as a decision-making process. Statements prior to the formal opening of the IGC structured the discussions and the issues on the agenda. The statements on the future enlargement of the EU to admit the Central and Eastern European countries (CEECs) were of particular importance for the IGC. At the Copenhagen European Council in June 1993, it was decided that the EU would be enlarged to include the countries of Eastern and Central Europe, as soon as they were able to satisfy the political and economic requirements of membership (European Council 1993). At the Essen European Council in December of the following year, the heads of state and government concluded that 'the institutional conditions for ensuring the proper functioning of the Union must be created at the 1996 Intergovernmental Conference, which for that reason must take place before accession negotiations begin' (European Council 1994b). Prior to the IGC, it was decided that the formal negotiations on accession should start six months after the IGC was completed. Both statements were repeated systematically during the preparations. These political statements, based on no economic or political analysis, increased the pressure to address certain issues on the agenda, in particular the issue of

---

[5] See http://www.aftenposten.no/nyheter/uriks/d41161.htm.

institutional reform. The issue of enlargement was an underlying element during the negotiations, and even became the criterion for determining whether the IGC had been successful or not.

In the IGC, the course of the decision-making process was structured by the past. This path-dependency challenges the theoretical notion of the conference as a voluntary process, in which member states control the agenda and have leeway to design the resultant institutions. In principle, 'nothing in the assumption or causal mechanism of LI analysis denies the historical and path-dependent quality of integration' (Moravcsik 1995: 613). However, how and to what extent this path-dependent quality comes into force remains unresolved. One argument consistent with the LI perspective entails considering the dominant parties as being capable of planning future steps and designing historical routes. Equally, past decisions lead to an effective change in the preferences and the distribution of power and resources within and among the parties. This implies the creation of new dominant coalitions and, ultimately, new policies and institutions. The empirical evidence of the IGC does not support such a view. For instance, it is virtually impossible to find a vision or position relating to the 1996 conference during the Maastricht negotiations (Laursen and Vanhoonacker 1992; Ross 1995a). The convening of a new conference can instead be interpreted as a by-product of the separation of problems and sequencing of attention in order to reach an agreement during the Maastricht negotiations.

Furthermore, if any of the member states had a clear position on the 1996 IGC during the Maastricht negotiations, these positions reflected a completely different political climate. The understanding of what was appropriate, possible, reasonable, and effective in terms of European integration had changed dramatically since the previous IGC, because of the changes in East and Central Europe, German unification, economic and monetary union (EMU), new applicant countries, a new economic situation, and so on. For instance, after the TEU, Laursen (1992: 259) wrote: '[I]t can therefore seem odd that references to a federal goal for the Community had to be taken out at Maastricht to allow the British to accept a new Treaty. But the "F-word" may be back to haunt the anti-federalists again at the next IGC in 1996'. However, support for federalist ideas was low at the IGC, and it was virtually impossible to find any references to the concept. Finally, for some of the member states, the IGC was certainly not a result of their own previous calculations and voluntary actions. For the new member states—Austria, Finland, and Sweden—the IGC was a review and reorganization process shaped prior to their entry into the EU. Their participation was mandatory and not voluntary.

From an institutional perspective, these factors do not create analytical problems, because adaptation to the past is considered to be less effective and more multifaceted than in the LI perspective. In general, it is assumed that there is a mutual process in which the environment adapts to institutions, and at the same time institutions adapt to their environments (March and Olsen 1995: 42). The cases of the national courts clearly illustrate this web of adaptiveness (Weiler 1995*b*; Llorente 1998). Good matches are difficult to find in processes of continuous adaptation both to and of the environment. Present solutions cannot easily be equated with past ones; there are many equilibrium points, and they are largely dependent upon the internal characteristics of the individual member states and their institutions (March and Olsen 1989). As a political system becomes more complex, these co-evolving processes become more intricate. Consequently, it can be claimed that the leeway for voluntary action is reduced when the ability to shape and control the agenda in key bargaining processes is reduced. It is likely that in previous IGCs the legacy of the past thus played a less structuring role. This path-dependent development does not make decision-makers slaves of the past. The evolutionary development stems from a sequence of choices. Because of the path-dependent character of the development, the impact of small, well-timed interventions can be multiplied by other forces and enabling reforms (March and Olsen 1995: 44). Past decisions are both enabling and constraining factors. As the IGC shows, the scope for interventions in a complex political system like the EU is limited. Treaty texts, the adaptations of national legal institutions and political statements on the future made at top-level political meetings seem to be particularly important in the structuring of the conference. These findings are consistent with the argument that key bargains are important, but they are preceded by more profound changes in the legal, political and cognitive development of European integration (Weiler 1991: 5).

From Closed and Diplomatic to Open and Democratic

Organizations and decision-making situations are not merely tools for achieving certain goals. The belief that the organization of a decision-making process affects its outcome is a basic premise of organizational theory. In any decision situation, certain resources, sets of information, rules and procedures, participants, networks, problems and solutions, technologies, expectations and norms, visions and causal beliefs exist (Scott 1981: 7). The composition of these organizational factors helps to shape the outcome of decision-making. Organizations are not neutral, but rather represent a mobilization of bias (Schattschneider 1975: 30). Three organizational factors shaped the IGC: (1) the procedures for arranging the conference; (2) the increasing number of participants; and (3) the democratization of the method for making treaty revisions in the EU. I argue that the IGC's agenda was overloaded with issues, and the exchange of opinions, contrary to what liberal intergovernmentalists assume, was both costly and time-consuming.

In the history of the EU, committees have been established to prepare the agenda of IGCs. Traditionally, the decision has been made either to set up a 'Committee of wise men' or else to depend on high-ranking staff or politicians. The Dooge Committee, established at the Fontainebleau European Council in 1984 leading up to the Single European Act (SEA), was an example of the first type of committee (Edwards and Pijpers 1997: 8), while the 1996–7 IGC followed the second approach, which required a less clear mandate. These expert committees have been influential in setting agendas, drafting initial texts, and ultimately shaping the outcome of the conferences, whose work they prepared. Experts in the field of European integration and prominent European politicians sat on these committees. At the Corfu Summit in 1994 it was decided, in line with tradition, that a Reflection Group should be created, whose task it would be to manage, protect, and prepare the IGC's agenda.[6] The Reflection Group was chaired by Carlos Westendorp, a Spanish diplomat and very experienced EU expert. The group consisted of representatives from each member state, as well as two representatives from the European Parliament (EP), and one from the European Commission. The members of the group were meant to act as the personal representatives of their Foreign Ministers, and as free thinkers with some autonomy.[7] Their mandate, briefly, was to learn from and correct the errors of Maastricht, and to rethink the institutional set-up of the EU and its future challenges. Even the composition of the group reflected the path-dependency of the IGC. Five of the eighteen members of the group had participated in the Maastricht negotiations, and many of the members were well-known Brussels bureaucrats and politicians, a fact which ruled out any radical reform proposals.[8]

The Reflection Group had high ambitions and addressed some of the fundamental questions regarding the EU, such as—What are the problems facing the organization (i.e. the EU), and are the traditional methods and principles of integration still valid and legitimate? The members used political imperatives like: 'The EU must dramatically adapt and radically change its institutions'.[9] Its opening session was arranged in Taormina, Sicily, coinciding with the 40th anniversary of the Messina Conference. It was overloaded with symbols and references to the success of past treaty-making. Consequently, the IGC was all set to be perceived as a Messina II rather than a Maastricht II, refer-

---

[6] Conclusions of the Presidency, Corfu European Council, 24–25 June 1994a (SN 150/94).

[7] *Agence Europe*, 6 July 1995, interview with Mr Westendorp.

[8] The members of the Reflection Group were as follows (those participants whose names appear in italics also participated in the Maastricht negotiations): *Carlos Westendorp (Spain)*, Michel Barnier (France), Werner Hoyer (Germany), *Silvio Fagiloio (Italy)*, Donald Davis (UK), *Joseph Weyland (Luxembourg)*, Gay Mitchell (Ireland), *Niels Ersbøll (Denmark)*, Stephanos Stathatos (Greece), Franklin Dehousse (Belgium), Michel Patijn (Netherlands), Andre Concalves Pereira (Portugal), Manfred Scheich (Austria), Ingvard Melin (Finland), Gunnnar Lund (Sweden), *Elisabeth Guigou (EP)*, Elmar Brok (EP), Marcelino Oreja (European Commission): *Agence Europe*, 31 May 1995.

[9] *Agence Europe*, 6 July 1995.

ring to the success of the 1957 Treaty on the European Economic Community (EEC) rather than the crisis of legitimacy following the ratification of the Maastricht Treaty. The President of the EP argued that the new IGC should demonstrate 'the same bold political vision and the same strength of political will' as the Messina Conference 40 years before.[10] Despite this and other similar calls for major reforms, when the Reflection Group presented its preparatory report at the Madrid Summit in December 1995, it became clear that the group had failed to create a consistent agenda and a platform for further discussion.[11] The report did not reveal a common understanding of the shape of the future European polity, the problems facing the EU, nor of the proposed solutions. In contrast to previous conferences, the IGC's preparatory group was unable to limit the agenda and to present a set of solutions. The ambiguity of the agenda prevailed during the conference. Even during the Dutch presidency and the work in the Patijn group (a group named after the Dutch Secretary of State for Foreign Affairs, Michel Patijn, who led the final negotiations) during the last weeks of the reform process, it proved difficult for the parties to manage the agenda. During the final negotiations in Amsterdam, which lasted for more than eighteen hours, the agenda shifted. Issues which had been central in the initial stages of the conference were discussed in the final minutes, while issues more or less unrelated to the IGC attracted considerable attention during the final hours.

The ambiguity of the agenda was due in large part to the organization of the IGC. Briefly, the parties met two days each week; the presidency was responsible for preparing the agenda, which was usually circulated among the parties on the Wednesday of the week before the meeting, allowing the delegates a few days for preparations with their national politicians, parliamentary groupings, and different national experts. These work-intensive and time-consuming discussions and preparations lasted for more than fifty weeks. In addition to the regular meetings at administrative level, the EU Foreign Ministers met regularly to review progress and to try to give political impetus to the process. Thus, the IGC engaged a considerable amount of the attention and capacity of the administrative and political systems both in the EU and in the member states.

The methods for discussing treaty revisions had changed since the Maastricht negotiations, during which the parties were presented with a full text, of which they were required to negotiate only the items in square brackets and the footnotes. This method allowed for a gradual accumulation of the number of points on which the parties had agreed and considered settled. The negotiations were aimed at reducing the number of reservations and items in square brackets by means of textual compromises, eventually achieving a final version

---

[10] *Agence Europe*, 3 March 1996.

[11] Report of the Reflection Group: *A Strategy for Europe—An Annotated Agenda* (Brussels, 5 December 1995).

which was acceptable to all (Petite 1998: 3). During the 1996–7 IGC, on the other hand, there was neither an initial agenda nor a draft treaty drawn up by a preparatory committee. Most of the working documents were position papers which were not drafted as legal texts. The first draft treaty was presented to the Dublin European Summit at the end of 1996. Prior to this, the parties had discussed issues without reference to a clearly defined text. Later, the presidency was responsible for presenting a 'Presidency Introductory Note', which was discussed by the delegates while the presidency took notes of the discussions. The proceedings of the next session were based on the previous discussion, and a 'Suggested Presidency Text', which was then discussed by the parties, each of whom could state their opinion and even back out of previous agreements. The IGC was therefore a continuous process of studying proceedings, presenting views, rewriting opinions, and adjusting texts, thus making progress highly dependent on the organizational abilities of the presidency. These new procedures made progress difficult, and it was not possible for the text to be examined closely by legal experts before being presented to the heads of state and government (Petite 1998: 4). It also proved difficult to protect the agenda from relatively loosely coupled issues which were attracting attention.

This increased complexity was also a function of the increased number of participants. Since the previous IGC, the EU had expanded from twelve to fifteen member states. To state the obvious: it is much easier to organize informal discussions and easy communication in a unit with few participants than in a larger unit with many participants. The Reflection Group, for example, consisted of eighteen members, and each member was allowed to bring two assistants. Even the group of eighteen was considered to be too large for the purposes of the discussions.[12] The format of the Reflection Group was a hindrance to personal relations and a trusting, informal atmosphere. The number of participants also reduced the possibility of reaching agreements. If each of the participants were to speak for ten minutes, each session would last more than three hours. Enlargement had increased the flow of information, the number of languages, the amount of issues on the agenda, the number of potential coalitions, and the duration of the meetings. Both the speaking time of each member and the chance of reaching a consensus was thus limited. The EU in general, and the IGC in particular, had become a radically more complex process for effective decision-making and problem-solving.

In addition, the member states and the national administrations had become more Europeanized, and the boundaries within and between the member states had become less clear (Olsen 1995a; Wessels and Rometsch 1996; Hanf and Soetendorp 1998). Today, the boundaries between foreign and domestic policy

---

[12] This view was expressed by the former Secretary-General of the Council, Niels Ersbøll, at a speech in Humlebæk, Denmark.

are blurred, and key bargains in the EU are no longer the preserve of the Foreign Ministries, with representatives from various national and even regional ministries taking part in the negotiations. For example, the German government circulated a questionnaire to all its ministries, in an attempt to determine those fields in which the different ministries would welcome increased majority voting. The Foreign Ministry supported majority voting in most issues, but the questionnaire revealed that a majority of the other German ministries did not.[13] The difficulty of upholding the idea of a single national interest was also apparent in relation to flexibility. During the Dutch presidency, cleavages emerged between the Foreign Ministry and the Ministries of Finance and Social Affairs and Employment in the Netherlands (see Chapter 9). As co-ordinating capacity in the Europeanized administrations is impaired, it becomes more difficult to uphold the analytical assumption outlined in the LI perspective of certain national preferences or dominant national positions in key bargaining processes. Furthermore, ideas, problems, and solutions diffuse across the borders between the member states. National administrations are fused together in a larger European web of administrative bodies, making it difficult to distinguish the position of one member state from another (Wessels and Rometsch 1996).

As is the case with most political processes, the IGC was not solely motivated by its functional outcome; it also helped to create meaning and legitimacy. The member states' view of the IGC differed according to their perception of their ability to influence the agenda. However, they also partly viewed the IGC as a means of increasing their knowledge of the EU system, a way of resolving national political conflicts, and as an opportunity to stimulate the public debate on European issues and thereby educate their citizens. The aim was to initiate research in the field, to stimulate a public debate on the key issues of the conference, and to give the parties an arena for public deliberation and argumentation (SOU 1996: 24, 1).

The manner in which each member state prepared its position was determined by well-established national procedures. In Sweden, for instance, the preparation of the IGC reflected a tradition of extensive public debates and information campaigns, as well as a strong belief in enlightenment and trust in expert analysis regarding political reform processes (Brunsson 1993). A special parliamentary committee, the EU 96-kommitén, was created, which was responsible for making suggestions, analysing the challenges, and contributing to the Swedish position. This committee was perhaps even more important in stimulating the Swedish debate and in educating the public on EU issues. It had a sizeable budget, and arranged public hearings and conferences with representatives from a large number of interest organizations. In addition, the

---

[13] See 'Kreuze beim Nein', Der Spiegel, No. 40, 1996, 22–4. The pattern seemed to be that they were sceptical of majority voting in the fields for which they had responsibility, and supportive of it in other fields.

committee commissioned and published relevant research, and invited foreign scholars and politicians to contribute to the Swedish debate. A large number of free publications and newsletters were available from the committee and were widely distributed (SOU 1996: 19; von Sydow 1997). In responding to the challenge posed by the IGC, the Swedes exploited their traditional procedures for arranging political debates and reforms. This method increased the likelihood of different parties participating and expressing their views, and resulted in an increase in the number of issues on the agenda. Furthermore, as was the case in other member states, the openness of the Swedish government created hindrances for flexibility during the bargaining process in the IGC.

Organizational features at the EU level influenced the IGC as well. The EU institutions had no formal right to participate in the final negotiations, their role being formally limited to the initial stages. For instance, the EU institutions presented their evaluation of the actual working of the TEU prior to the negotiations.[14] These documents were important in structuring the discussions both in the Reflection Group and in the IGC in general. During the IGC, the EP was continually briefed and updated. The EP and the European Commission devoted significant administrative resources to monitoring and influencing the IGC. Both established special task forces and arranged hearings and debates related to the IGC; these bodies also had the administrative power to collect, sort, rank, and reinterpret the position papers presented by the member states. In terms of personnel, the task forces had considerable capacity, and the members enjoyed a high level of legitimacy in EU circles.[15] The information overload and the need for information-processing capacities in the IGC altered the importance of the administrative bodies at the EU level. The greater importance of the EU institutions as regards effective decision-making does not imply that they were necessary, nor that they were successful in their attempts to shape the agenda. Prior to the IGC, the European Commission decided to limit its aspirations and to avoid institutional conflicts. It had not expected or advocated a great leap forward during the IGC towards more competence, and it sought enhanced powers neither for the EU nor for itself (Dinan 1997: 197). However, it should not be forgotten that increased complexity in the EU leads to a greater dependency of the national governments on the administrative and information-processing capacities of the supranational institutions.

---

[14] The Committee of the Regions was the first to present its paper, on 20 April 1995. The European Commission's report was submitted on 10 May 1995, and those of the EP and the ECJ on 17 May 1995. The Court of Auditors also submitted its paper in May. The Economic and Social Committee's paper was the last to be presented, in November 1995.

[15] The Task Forces were composed of prominent persons. The Commission's Task Force was headed by Michel Petite, who had held the same position during the Maastricht negotiations. The former Commission President, Jacques Delors, also had an office at his disposal in this unit.

Changes in organizational procedures and the increase in complexity therefore helped to shape the IGC. From an LI perspective, on the other hand, the preferences and positions of the member states are believed to explain the outcome of the decision-making process. Such interest-based explanations are truly important. For instance, the absence of a shared agenda has been interpreted as a consequence of the scepticism of the British Conservatives.[16] For a long time, the British position of upholding the status quo influenced the IGC (George 1996). At the same time, the delegates were waiting for a joint Franco-German position paper—joint papers from these countries had previously had a strong influence on the agenda (Menon 1996). Between the Franco-German Summit in Baden-Baden in 1995 and the Amsterdam meeting in June 1997, the two countries continually sought to develop a paper which could 'imprint a political impetus on problems of substance'.[17] From May 1996 onwards, the French and German governments met informally every six weeks to address issues related to European integration and the IGC.[18] However, they failed to come up with a final joint position paper. They presented papers in December 1995, February 1996, and a paper on WEU, and they were able, in October 1996, to present an eight-page paper on flexibility or 'enhanced cooperation'.[19] During 1997, cooperation between the two countries intensified, but there was still no Franco-German agreement or solution in sight. The IGC experienced difficulties when the traditional motor of the EU, Franco-German cooperation, ran into issues related to institutional reform, enlargement, and financial burden-sharing.

This suggests that analysing the preferences and power of the member states is insufficient in determining the outcome of the IGC. A systematic analysis of the positions of the member states was undertaken by the Commission's and the EP's Task Forces on the IGC.[20] Furthermore, a group of Austrian political scientists collected and systematically sorted the different views presented by the various member states in their position papers (Griller *et al.* 1996). These extensive documents reveal the enormous amount of issues on the IGC agenda, as well as the complexity of the conference and the difficulty of correctly mapping-out vague positions. Under such circumstances, communication between the parties becomes difficult and costly, and the sequence of the negotiations is unclear. The LI perspective assumes that domestic negotiations occur first, and are followed by negotiations among the European parties. However, the analysis shows that national positions in the IGC were to a large extent

[16] For a typical expression of this view, see *Agence Europe*, 28/9 May, 1996.

[17] *Agence Europe*, 6 June 1996 and 13 June 1996.   [18] *Agence Europe*, 2/3 September 1996.

[19] *Agence Europe*, 23 October 1996. The Franco-German paper was reprinted in *Agence Europe* on 29 October 1996. The idea of enhanced cooperation and flexibility was unclear, and there was no support for a common interpretation of the issue.

[20] 'Summary of the Positions of the Member States and the European Parliament on the 1996 Intergovernmental Conference', Task Force on the IGC, 12 May 1997.

generated in response to the contributions of other member states and of the European institutions. In principle, we would assume that the smaller states, with less capacity and negotiating power, were more responsive to the papers of the larger states than vice versa. However, large states like France (Menon 1996), Britain (George 1996), and Germany (Goetz 1996) also demonstrated ambiguity and uncertainty about their national positions. The uncertainties in the 1996–7 IGC were greater than in previous conferences. This time, the preferences of the member states were not exogenous and decided a long time in advance of the IGC, as suggested by the LI perspective; instead, they were elaborated within a larger process of mutual preference formation. It is thus difficult to uphold the assumption of a clear separation between domestic preference and position formation on the one hand, and negotiation among the parties on the other.

These preference and power-based explanations may be important for understanding the IGC but they are not a sufficient explanation, nor are they able to take into account the important impact of the normative crisis which hit the traditional methods for treaty revision. The need for a new organizational method of treaty revision arose from the changing normative context and the ongoing democratization of the EU. IGCs have traditionally been the domain of diplomats and foreign policy experts, and even more so of legal experts. Treaty revision has thus been conducted within an atmosphere of technicality and secrecy. Media and domestic politicians have paid limited attention to the IGCs, and popular participation has largely been limited to minor debates on ratification. During the Maastricht negotiations, however, this method was challenged. For the first time, documents and position papers circulated in the press, and an increasing number of people and politicians took an interest in the EU. However, the IGC still represented a closed and bureaucratic decision-making process of limited importance for the ordinary citizen. This changed dramatically, however, during the ratification of the Maastricht Treaty, which plunged the EU into a major crisis over legitimacy. From being a celebrated success at its signature in Maastricht, the Treaty was soon regarded as an unreadable and unpresentable fiasco. In Denmark, a small majority of 45,000 voters voted 'no' in a first referendum on 2 June 1992. After the negotiation of a special exemption clause at the Edinburgh summit in December 1992 however, a majority of 56.8 per cent voted 'yes' on 18 May 1993 (Bainbridge and Teasdale 1995: 111). President Mitterand called for a French referendum the day after the first Danish referendum, and the treaty was subsequently accepted by the narrowest of margins: only 51 per cent of french people voted 'yes' in September 1992 (Bainbridge and Teasdale 1995: 245). In Britain and Germany, ratification was equally conflictual, and in the referendums on membership in the new applicant countries—Austria, Finland, Sweden, and Norway—the lack of popular support for the Maastricht Treaty was very marked (Luif 1995).

Several factors contributed to the perceived legitimacy crisis for the EU, evident from the results of the various referendums and the decline in popularity of the TEU. It was partly due to the content of the Treaty itself, and partly to the method of organizing constitutional processes within the EU. As a response to the legitimacy crisis, the IGC was required to address the issue of democracy—in short, to make the EU more 'effective', 'open', 'democratic', and 'responsive to its citizens'.[21] These aspirations were regularly referred to in the preparation of the agenda, and in all the Reflection Group's reports. Similar conclusions were drawn by the presidency at the Amsterdam summit. A democratization of the EU implied that not only the issues but also the procedures regulating the process would have to be adapted in order to respond to this new logic of appropriateness.

In the 1996–7 IGC, both the member states and the EU institutions were considerably more open about their positions than in previous conferences. The European Commission initiated a 7 million ECU programme, called 'Let's Build Europe Together', aimed at increasing public knowledge about the IGC; it sought to develop a permanent dialogue with citizens throughout the negotiations.[22] Most member states had substantial budgets for initiating public debates and discussions on the future of the EU. In addition to governmental initiatives, populist, and professional conferences were held all over Europe, and thousands of publications were produced and distributed widely. An Internet homepage devoted to the IGC kept people informed, making the downloading of documents and position papers possible a short time after their presentation at the IGC.[23] National governments talked readily about their positions, and most major newspapers followed the process closely, publishing their comments and analyses of the IGC.

The character of treaty reform in the 1996–7 IGC was very different to that in the Maastricht negotiations. First, the number of issues on the agenda was greater. An enormous number of domestic, regional, and European institutions, parties, scholars, and interest organizations all tried to gain attention for their respective interpretations, ideas, and interests. Some of the proposals came from powerful and influential organizations, such as the European Union of Employers' Confederations (UNICE) and the European Labour Organization (Euro-LO), others from rather small and marginal interest organizations, such as Animal Welfare; European Disability Forum; and the National Board of Italian Psychologists (Mazey and Richardson 1996). In making these preparations and proposals, an increasing number of interest groups sought an EU in which the citizens would be able to participate in the process of constitution-building, and the development of rights, norms, institutions, and visions in and for the EU (Wiener and Della Sala, 1997: 604). However, as the

---

[21]   Report of the Reflection Group (1995): *A Strategy for Europe—an Annotated Agenda*, Brussels, 5 December 1995 and Presidency Conclusions of the European Council, Florence, 21–22 June 1996b.

[22]   Cited in *Agence Europe*, 30 May 1996.

[23]   See: http://europa.eu.int/en/agenda/igc-home/index.html.

number of issues and expectations increased, it became impossible to maintain firm control of the agenda, because no single unit had an overview of all the contributions. Second, the IGC had to be conducted in accordance with the new and more democratic norm of openness and public deliberation. While the Maastricht process was dominated by legal reasoning, the 1996–7 IGC concerned itself with political and democratic issues, pushing for commitments from the member states. A leading bureaucrat expressed his frustration as follows: 'Gone are the days when we had articles in square brackets, and the processes were purely technical; now decision-making in the IGC is open, unclear, and democratic'.[24] Increased openness made it more difficult for politicians to show flexibility and to change their views during the negotiations, and the increase in information made it more difficult for the national governments to communicate easily and in secret.

The LI perspective pays limited attention to the impact of changes in the normative context on decision-making. For instance, in commenting on the agenda-setting process as regards the French referendum, Moravcsik argued that: '[t]he Maastricht referendum in France is an exception that proves the importance of secrecy and agenda-setting power, in that it demonstrates the potential consequences when governments lose firm control of domestic agendas or take needless risks in ratification' (Moravcsik 1993: 516–17). True, the referendums and the public debates resulting from the Maastricht Treaty represented dramatic breaks with the past, but they also represented an emerging new political and democratic order with increased interest and popular demand for participation in Europe. As students of European integration, we must develop theoretical models which enable us to interpret how integration and disintegration ultimately lead to these changes in the basis of legitimacy and the character of decision-making. By applying a dynamic perspective to the EU, as the institutional perspective suggests, we can interpret the shifts in the mode of decision-making, and show its impact on the dynamics of European integration. Such a reflective perspective on legitimacy and legitimate decision-makers is also consistent with the idea of decision-making as deliberation and argumentative interaction, rather than focusing solely on voting rules, and treating certain actors and their interests as given and legitimate (see Chapter 7).

Present Events and the Temporal Location of the IGC

The 1996–7 intergovernmental conference did not take place within a flexible and easily protracted period of time, as suggested by the liberal intergovern-

---

[24] Michel Petite, European Commission, at a speech delivered in Brussels on 10 July 1997 at the International Political Science Association (IPSA) seminar on the Amsterdam Treaty.

mentalists. Rather, it was situated in a distinct temporal order which affected the content and duration of the conference. In institutional reform, timing is of key importance. In relation to the IGC, expected and unexpected events as well as internal and external occurrences shaped the conditions for design.

First, the IGC was affected, directly and indirectly, by unexpected external accidents beyond the control of any of the decision-makers. It was affected directly in that the events were linked immediately to the agenda, and indirectly in that attention is a scarce resource, and the attention and energy which would otherwise have been allocated to the IGC was drawn to other issues, such as the war in Bosnia, the crisis in Rwanda and Zaire, and the BSE (bovine spongi-form encephalopathy) crisis. The latter, which concerned infected British beef, captured public attention around the time of the formal opening of the IGC, and at a point when the conference badly needed political impetus. Thus, the opening session in Florence more or less ended in a discussion on how to handle the BSE crisis. This issue was also used as an excuse for the British government's refusal to participate in both day-to-day decision-making in the EU, as well as in the negotiations at the conference. During a short period of time, therefore, the adoption of more than seventy pieces of legislation was prevented, and the British also managed to obstruct discussions in the IGC.[25]

Some issues were more predictable than others. Routine internal day-to-day decisions in the EU influenced the IGC's agenda. As a weakly institutionalized system, the EU lacked the capacity to separate out day-to-day issues from con-stitutional ones. For instance, when the ruling by the ECJ forced Britain to agree to a standard 48-hour working week, it was argued shortly afterwards that the British Prime Minister 'should go to the IGC and insist on rewriting this legis-lation'.[26] A few days later, these changes were proposed as modifications to Article 118a.[27] During the IGC, several issues regarding public health, com-petition rules and state aids, which were normally managed within the normal EU procedures for problem-solving, were easily linked to the conference and helped to halt the constitutional process. As long as the decision-makers were unable to separate or buffer ordinary issues from constitutional ones, the agenda tended to be overloaded and crisis-driven, rather than reflecting enlight-ened discussions on a limited set of issues.

The IGC was convened in an environment made turbulent by other impor-tant ongoing reform processes in the EU. Of particular importance in shaping the IGC was the plan to create the EMU by 1999. During the initial stages of the conference, most parties tried to keep the design and institutions of the EMU out of the discussions, but it continually overshadowed the IGC, and the interlinkage between the two was obvious. Towards the end of the IGC, when

---

[25] See the article 'Florence peace talks await UK's cease-fire declaration', *Financial Times*, 21 June 1996.

[26] Cited in *Agence Europe*, 12–13 November 1996.   [27] *Agence Europe*, 16 November 1996.

it was clear that the changes would be marginal, the Commission President, Jacques Santer, even expressed doubt that there could have been an agreement during the IGC negotiations without the French initiative to strike a bargain on employment in relation to the EMU.[28] The EMU also affected the duration of the IGC, as the member states had to find a solution there before they could enter into the final stages of economic and monetary union. In addition, the need to find an agreement on the new budget before the Delors II package ran out in 1999, before the scheduled reforms of the Common Agricultural Policy (CAP) came into force, and before the negotiations with the new applicants began, all pressurized the parties to reach a final agreement.[29] When the IGC ended, it was even explicitly stated that it had been a success because 'after all they had agreed upon the EMU'. Leading politicians were happy to continue with more small-scale and incremental adjustments, and claimed to have avoided the major crisis of failing on all fronts simultaneously.[30]

Election and budget cycles in the member states also structured the IGC's agenda, and determined the amount of attention decision-makers were able to pay to it. During the 1996–7 IGC, a large number of national elections were held, perhaps the most important being the British elections, which took place on 1 May 1997. The Dutch Prime Minister, Wim Kok, argued at an early stage that the British election campaign was interfering with the IGC and creating too many uncertainties.[31] As a consequence of the election, the British negotiators changed, and the new Labour government only had six weeks in office before the new treaty was completed in Amsterdam. During this time, they had to develop new positions in a process that had already lasted for almost two years. Any changes introduced at this stage could have reduced the continuity of decision-making in the IGC, and eventually destroyed any agreements reached.[32] This election directly altered the issues on the agenda; for instance, the intense focus on flexibility during the IGC was linked to a large extent to the desire of the other member states to bypass the 'problem' of the British Conservatives. When Labour won the election, interest in the concept of co-operation and flexibility decreased.

The parliamentary elections in France also affected the IGC, with the date of the beginning of the work of the Reflection Group being postponed until the beginning of the Spanish presidency in order to avoid a clash with the elections (Menon 1996: 242). During the negotiations, the French called for a

---

[28] Jacques Santer at the seminar 'Amsterdam and Beyond' in Brussels, 11 July 1997.

[29] DOC/97/9: 'Agenda 2000—For a stronger and wider Europe', Brussels, Press Release IP/97/660.

[30] See the descriptions of the Amsterdam Summit in *Agence Europe*, 18 and 19 June 1997.

[31] *Agence Europe*, 4 October 1996.

[32] However, in the British case, both the Conservative and the Labour parties had been kept regularly briefed by the Foreign Office. Labour also had an arrangement with a former official from the Committee of Permanent Representatives (Coreper), who travelled around Europe visiting governments and presenting different views on the proposed reforms, making the transition from opposition to government smoother.

modest IGC agenda in order to end the conference rapidly, thereby decreasing the likelihood of any interference with the French parliamentary elections, originally scheduled for 1998.[33] At one stage, the French government also wanted to speed up the IGC by extending the mandate of the negotiating group 'to elaborate draft treaties'.[34] The extraordinary meeting of the IGC held in October 1996 in Dublin was also largely a result of the French politicians' perceived need to speed up the negotiations. However, President Chirac called for an election at the end of May 1997, primarily because of the timetable of the final stages of the EMU. The surprising victory of Lionel Jospin meant that, in the final stages of the IGC, France had a new regime which was inexperienced, but nevertheless held firm positions. By presenting radical solutions during the Amsterdam meeting, they brought employment to the top of the agenda, and insisted on parallelism between economic and monetary policy in relation to the EMU, thereby creating uncertainty and turmoil during the final days of the IGC. The French focus on the EMU distracted the discussion from the issues on the agenda, and shaped the outcome in Amsterdam.

Treaty revisions have to be approved by every member state, and this formal rule also influenced the duration of the IGC. Some member states ratify treaties by parliamentary votes, while others use referendums, and no government wishes to fail. In Denmark, for instance, it was decided that a referendum would be held on the IGC.[35] In general, ratification processes represent an opportunity to express all sorts of ideas, not only of support and frustration. Ratification processes do not necessarily focus on a limited set of issues; other issues which are loosely coupled to the issue itself frequently come to dominate the discussions. Consequently, the interlinkage between ratification and national elections, as well as other important reforms such as the EMU, made it difficult to extend the duration of the IGC.

The above discussion shows that timing and temporal location were important in structuring the IGC. However, it is difficult to conceptualize the importance of timing and the significance of a certain temporal order. Ideas differ as regards the importance of timing and the role it plays in decision-making. For instance, the sequencing and ordering of decisions can influence outcomes, while the distribution of costs and benefits of being a first mover in strategic bargaining or of being a copycat, the use of filibustering tactics and the more trivial but nevertheless important dynamic of the 'iron trouser phenomenon'[36] are all determined by timing (Goodin 1995). The issue of timing in relation to the IGC has been addressed by several scholars, for instance Patterson, who

---

[33] See 'Showdown Time' and 'IGC Timing', *Financial Times*, 18 September 1996.

[34] *Agence Europe*, 22 June 1996.

[35] The idea of a Danish referendum was confirmed a short time after the completion of the Draft Treaty.

[36] The 'iron trouser phenomenon' is mentioned by the 'insider', Christopher Matthews, who argued that 'whoever can hold out longest before having to go to the toilet can dictate terms to the others' (Goodin 1995: 12).

wrote: 'There is now much talk in Bonn of agenda management, that is, pre-venting the timetables for enlargement and EMU colliding with one another and designing decision points at the most propitious times' (Patterson 1996: 174). The underlying idea here is the possibility of designing and sequencing events in a manner that maximizes expected utility, consistent with the LI perspective. However, sequencing events and designing the timing of political decisions is very difficult, and many of the temporal structures cannot be manipulated.

The institutional perspective focuses less on the possibilities of design and more on how a decision-making process is embedded in a distinct temporal order. Two issues are thus important from an institutional perspective: first, protecting the agenda from unpredictable, loosely coupled issues; and second, operating in accordance with the predictable, well-established, and demanding rhythms of political life. Several temporal structures, such as elections and budget cycles, are beyond the control of national governments; in fact, tem-poral orders are often written into constitutions precisely in order to prevent their manipulation. Furthermore, these temporal orders function as deadlines, in that they help to focus attention, and to create meanings and frames of ref-erence. Fixed and structured deadlines limit the possibilities for searching for new and acceptable solutions, with final solutions tending to be close to exist-ing ones, thereby largely maintaining the status quo (Bromiley and Marcus 1987). The IGC was a process where the demanding internal rhythms of the nation states had a significant impact on the content and duration of the con-ference, and the fixed temporal location limited the search for solutions to ones close to existing institutional arrangements, thereby making radical reform less likely.

Conclusions

This examination of decision-making in the IGC has shown that three mecha-nisms were particularly important in structuring the conference. First, past decisions created the framework for the IGC. This path-dependency dictated the issues on the agenda, and determined the manner in which they were framed, limiting the possibility of radical solutions to existing problems. Instead of an adaptation to the future, therefore, the IGC represents an adaptation to the past. Second, the increase in the number of member states and the changes in the procedures for handling the IGC increased the complexity of the bar-gaining process, and made information and communication more costly and more complicated. The very model of intergovernmental bargaining was chal-lenged, because of the importance of organizational factors at both European and national levels. The Europeanization of the nation state has made it difficult to maintain the idea of a clear separation between domestic position formation and international negotiation. The logic of the two-level game is therefore problematic. Furthermore, the normative crisis concerning the democratic deficit in the EU has ultimately transformed the mode of institutional reform in the EU. The gradual democratization of the EU makes the dynamic of institutional and constitutional design different to that of secret bargaining within a system of technocratic diplomacy. Finally, a series of other pressing events, as well as the location of the conference in a distinct temporal order, affected the distribution of attention and the issues addressed during the treaty revision process.

In conclusion, this examination has questioned the basic assumptions of institutional reform processes according to the LI perspective, that is, that key bargains in the EU are characterized by their voluntary nature, easy communication, and flexibility as regards time. I have shown that the IGC did not represent a voluntary process, the processing of information was difficult, and it was not flexible in time. This chapter has demonstrated that a careful analysis of the constraints and possibilities created by the path-dependent development of the EU, the internal dynamics and the decision-making procedures in the IGC, and a distinct temporal location help to increase our understanding of the EU. The institutional approach reveals important aspects of decision-making which have all too often been ignored in the past.

The LI perspective is fruitful, but it is not sufficient to explain the dynamics of key bargains in the EU. By enriching our theoretical dimensions and categories, we can improve our understanding of the dynamics of institutional reform in general, and of the EU in particular. This analysis has suggested an alternative approach, based on institutional theory. The EU is currently facing new institutional reforms related to Agenda 2000 and the enlargement to include the countries of Eastern and Central Europe.[37] The institutional perspective outlined here suggests that successful design is more likely if reformers understand some of the most important dynamics which constrain and enable them to design effective institutions in a democratic context, and in particular if they can exploit the possibilities related to path-dependency, organizational factors in decision-making, and the importance of timing and a distinct temporal location

[37] On Agenda 2000, see: http://europa.eu.int/comm/agenda2000/index_en.htm.

14

A Blairite Treaty: Neo-Liberalism and Regulated Capitalism in the Treaty of Amsterdam

MARK A. POLLACK

> *The conservative tide is on the wane. We must not let Europe be bogged down in an excessive neo-liberal, monetarist model.*
>
> Lionel Jospin, at the Congress of the Party of European Socialists, Malmö, Sweden[1]
>
> *The centre-left parties now have a majority in Europe, giving us a great opportunity. But we will quickly be rejected if we go back to our old ways. We must modernize or die.*
>
> Tony Blair, at the same congress[2]

This chapter rests on three basic assumptions. The first, following Simon Hix (1994), is that the politics of the European Union (EU) can be theorized in terms of a left–right cleavage, as well as the more familiar cleavage between national independence and European integration. As Hix points out, students of international relations have traditionally analysed the main events (and indeed the minutiae) of EU history in terms of whether these events increased or decreased the level of supranational integration in the EU. Yet such an emphasis on integration *per se* tells us little or nothing about the implications of European integration for domestic politics, including the traditional left–right conflict between free market neo-liberals and more interventionist christian or social democrats. Indeed, Hix and Lord (1996a) argue that the EU political system is a two-dimensional political space, with an 'integration' dimension and a 'left–right' dimension, neither reducible to the other, and they examine the nature of partisan contestation in such a two-dimensional space.

The second assumption of the chapter, following Liesbet Hooghe and Gary

The author is grateful to Kathleen McNamara, Jo Shaw, and the editors for helpful comments on earlier drafts of this chapter, and to the World Affairs and the Global Economy (WAGE) programme of the University of Wisconsin–Madison for research support.

[1] Quoted in Conradi (1997).   [2] *Idem.*

Marks, is that, in the context of Hix's two-dimensional space, the political debate in the EU today can be theorized as a right–left struggle between neo-liberals on the one hand, and proponents of what they call 'regulated capitalism' on the other. In their words

> The *neoliberal project* attempts to insulate markets from political interference by combining European-wide market integration with the fragmentation of authority among national governments. The neoliberal project rejects democratic institutions at the European level capable of regulating the market, but seeks instead to generate competition among national governments in providing regulatory climates that mobile factors find attractive.   (Hooghe and Marks 1997: 3)

By contrast

> The *project for regulated capitalism* proposes a variety of market-enhancing and market-supporting legislation to create a social democratic dimension to European governance. This project attempts to deepen the European Union and increase its capacity for regulation by, among other things, upgrading the European Parliament, promoting the mobilization of particular social groups, and reforming institutions to make legislation easier (i.e. by introducing qualified majority rule in the Council of Ministers). (Hooghe and Marks 1997: 3)

'These projects,' according to Marks and Hooghe, 'are coherent, comprehensive packages of institutional reforms around which broad coalitions of political actors at European, national, and subnational levels have formed' (Hooghe and Marks 1997: 3).

There are, to be sure, problems with Hooghe and Marks' classification scheme, which is both too narrow and too broad. The scheme is too narrow in the sense that both the neo-liberal and regulated-capitalism projects focus almost exclusively on 'first pillar' economic issues, leaving out a number of politically important aspects of EU politics, such as the second and third pillars (common foreign and security policy—CFSP; and justice and home affairs—JHA), which have left–right political implications in the member states as well as at EU level. Yet, I would argue, the concept of regulated capitalism is also too broad, in that it overestimates the coherence of the project and its supporting coalitions, and underestimates the number of cleavages cutting across the two projects. More specifically, I will argue below that the supporting coalition for the project for regulated capitalism can be further subdivided into a coalition of left and centre–left parties on the one hand, and a separate 'cohesion' coalition of poor states (regardless of political colour) on the other. The former group, I will suggest, won some significant victories in Amsterdam; the latter did not. Furthermore, as we shall see, the European left was itself divided at Amsterdam about the precise nature of its European 'project', which was not as self-evident as the ideal-type of regulated capitalism might suggest. Nevertheless, despite these weaknesses, Hooghe and Marks' categories are a useful heuristic device with which to analyse the left–right implications of European integration in general and EU treaties in particular, and this chapter will therefore begin, but not end, with the use of the Hooghe–Marks classification.[3]

The third basic assumption of the chapter, following the institutional analyses of Douglass North (1990) and others, is that institutional design—including the creation and amendment of the EU's constitutive treaties—is not politically innocent, but rather facilitates or hinders the adoption of specific political programmes. That is to say, as rational actors, the participants in the EU's various intergovernmental conferences (IGCs)—including member governments, supranational organizations, and private interests lobbying from the outside—prefer and bargain for those institutional configurations which are most likely to facilitate the adoption of their substantive political programmes, be they left or right. The outcome of any given IGC, therefore, represents not only an advance or a setback for the process of integration *per se*, but also for the projects of neo-liberalism and regulated capitalism, respectively.

With these three assumptions in mind, this chapter examines the 1997 Treaty of Amsterdam, asking whether the new Treaty represents an advance or a setback to the respective projects of neo-liberalism or regulated capitalism. Before moving to the Treaty of Amsterdam, however, I begin by very briefly surveying the three most important constitutive treaties in the history of the European Community / Union, namely the Treaties of Rome (1957), the Single European Act (1986), and the Maastricht Treaty (1992). The basic argument here is straightforward. From Rome to Maastricht, the fundamental thrust of the treaties has been neo-liberal, in the sense that each of the Community's constitutive treaties facilitated the creation of a unified European market, while setting considerable institutional barriers to the regulation of that same market. The Treaty of Rome, for example, featured important powers for the then European Economic Community (EEC) in the areas of free movement, competition policy and external trade policy, while granting the Community few powers of positive regulation and only a modestly redistributive Common Agricultural Policy (CAP). The Single European Act (SEA) picked up on this basic theme, focusing primarily on the completion of the internal market by 1992, and largely limiting institutional reforms to this goal. The Maastricht Treaty on

---

[3] A final flaw of Hooghe and Marks' categories is less important, but deserves mention here. In their paper, Hooghe and Marks argue that the relationship between the national/supranational and the left/right dimensions is orthogonal, i.e. that those on the left prefer a supranational Europe, while those on the right prefer strictly national competences. In fact, however, we can usefully disaggregate supranationalism by issue area, so that neo-liberals prefer supranational powers in market-making areas such as the internal market, trade, competition, and monetary policy, while proponents of regulated capitalism advocate supranational powers in areas such as social policy, industrial policy, employment, and environmental and consumer protection.

European Union (TEU), in its turn, focused primarily on the project for Economic and Monetary Union (EMU), which has turned out to be a neo-liberal project in effect, if not in its original conception.

The Treaties of Rome, the SEA and Maastricht were not, of course, uniformly neo-liberal documents. Because European treaties must necessarily be signed and ratified by all EU member states in order to take effect, reticent member states were in each case able to demand institutional reforms to facilitate the adoption of some elements of the regulated capitalism project, including both regulatory competences for the Union and redistributive transfers from some member states and regions to others. Hence, we shall also see that, accompanying the EU's central neo-liberal project, we also find a growing regulatory capacity for the Union across the three treaties, as well as a growing element of redistribution in the EU's cohesion policy in the SEA and Maastricht.

In the context of this institutional history, I argue, the Treaty of Amsterdam represents an outlier. By contrast with the earlier treaties, the Amsterdam Treaty features no central neo-liberal project comparable to the common market, the internal market, or EMU, all of which are left essentially unchanged in the new treaty. Rather, the Treaty of Amsterdam, which was negotiated by governments controlled overwhelmingly by the left and centre–left, addresses many of the central issue-areas of the regulated capitalism project, including employment, social policy, women's rights, human rights, the environment, and the powers of the European Parliament (EP). Yet, if the Amsterdam Treaty represents a modest turn to the left in the EU's institutional history, it does *not* represent the victory of Hooghe and Marks' model of regulated capitalism, and that for two main reasons. First, in keeping with the critique of Hooghe and Marks offered above, the centre–left majority at Amsterdam remained entirely silent on the subject of cohesion, which was put off for later negotiation as part of the Santer Commission's Agenda 2000 exercise. Second, and for our purposes more importantly, the final negotiations leading up to Amsterdam revealed a split in the European left regarding its 'project' for European integration. In the weeks prior to the Amsterdam European Council, a traditional socialist agenda for an interventionist, regulatory Europe championed by the French Prime Minister, Lionel Jospin, collided with a new centre–left project promoted by the British Prime Minister, Tony Blair, which accepted the traditional socialist goals of employment and social welfare but was more sceptical of binding regulation and intervention at EU level. The final version of the Treaty, I argue, most closely reflects the new centre–left programme of Tony Blair, which seems likely to dominate the Union's social agenda in the years to come.

The organization of the chapter is straightforward. In the next section, I briefly analyse the central provisions of the Rome Treaties, the SEA, and the TEU, assessing both the development of the Union's neo-liberal project, and the regulatory and redistributive elements added to that project over time. The aim here is not to provide a detailed negotiating history of these Treaties, which is far beyond the scope of the current chapter, but simply to analyse these familiar treaties from the unfamiliar perspective of left and right. In the third section, I turn to the negotiation and content of the Amsterdam Treaty, analysing the treaty provisions in terms of Hooghe's and Marks' categories, and suggesting that the European project of the left has become more complex and fractured than the ideal typical project of regulated capitalism put forward by those authors. In the final section, I conclude by characterising Amsterdam as a 'Blairite Treaty', which reflects Blair's effort to find a 'third way' between the traditional projects of neo-liberalism on the one hand, and regulated capitalism on the other. Throughout the chapter, my primary aim is analytical, not causal: the aim of the chapter is to provide a theoretical lens through which to *analyse* the left–right implications of the EU's constitutive Treaties, rather than a causal theory to *explain* these Treaties. I will nevertheless hazard a few tentative hypotheses to explain the weak left turn of the Amsterdam Treaty, focusing in particular on the unusual dominance of the left and centre–left in the member governments of the Union in June 1997. I begin, however, four decades earlier, with the Treaties of Rome.

From Rome to Maastricht: A Neo-Liberal Project

Neo-liberals and supporters of regulated capitalism advocate different institutional configurations for the EU, in keeping with their substantive policy preferences. Thus, neo-liberals have historically favoured strong EU institutions only with regard to market liberalization, in areas such as the internal market, competition policy, external trade policy and, since the triumph of monetarism in the 1980s, monetary policy. Outside these areas, however, neo-liberals advocate a minimal institutional agenda, placing strict limits on qualified majority voting (qmv) and on supranational delegation in areas of social regulation. By contrast, proponents of regulated capitalism favour qmv and supranational delegation, particularly in areas of social regulation and cohesion policy. In terms of these criteria, I argue, the European Treaties from Rome to Maastricht constitute, on balance, a neo-liberal project.

The Treaties of Rome and the Triumph of Free Movement

To understand why, consider first the 1957 Treaties of Rome, which established the EEC (now the European Community—EC) and Euratom, respectively. The Rome Treaties were signed during the golden age of the Keynesian welfare state, and were often portrayed by neo-functionalists as the result of a cross-class and cross-party consensus on economic issues in the Western Europe of the 1950s and 1960s (Lindberg 1963; Haas 1964). However, if we examine the historical record of the negotiations which produced the Treaties, we find a stark cleavage between the liberal advocates of free trade on the one hand, and the primarily French advocates of a less liberal, more regulated Europe on the other.

After the failure of the European Defence Community in 1954, European liberals generally rallied around a 1953 Dutch proposal for a European customs union among the 'Six', which was later revived as a project for a common market, featuring free movement of goods, services, labour, and capital, as well as binding European rules for competition and a common external trade policy (Küsters 1987: 82). The supporters of this liberal view included the governments of the Benelux countries and Germany (with the exception of the liberal Economics Minister, Ludwig Erhard, who advocated global free trade rather than a regional trading bloc); the Italian government, which strongly favoured the proposed provisions regarding the free movement of labour; and finally a small group of liberal French ministers and officials in the centre–left government of Guy Mollet, who served as Prime Minister from January 1956 through the signing of the Rome Treaties in March 1957.

By and large, however, the overwhelming majority of French officials and business elites were fervently opposed to the common market proposal. In the view of these French critics, French industry was simply unprepared for the competition which would accompany a common market, in particular because the social and fiscal charges on business were higher in France than in the other five states. In addition, critics of the common market also pointed out the potentially devastating effects of free trade on French agriculture, and the potential conflict between the common market and France's commitment to her overseas territories. In place of the common market, therefore, the French government advocated a new atomic energy community, or Euratom, which had been proposed by Jean Monnet as the centrepiece of a revived European integration process, and which appealed to Paris as a way of spreading the costs of nuclear research and development (Marjolin 1989: 281–97; Lynch 1997: 169–78).

Thus, when the Belgian Foreign Minister, Paul-Henri Spaak, drafted a Benelux proposal for the relaunching of the European integration process in May 1955, he proposed a linkage between the common market (designed to appeal primarily to the liberal governments of the 'five') and Euratom (designed to appeal primarily to the French). This linkage was agreed to by the Foreign Ministers of the Six at the Messina Conference in June of 1955 despite the reluctance of the French delegation, and was maintained later in the meetings of the Spaak Committee and the IGC, leading to the simultaneous signing in March 1957 of two Rome Treaties: the EEC Treaty, and the Euratom Treaty, respectively.

Throughout these negotiations, the cleavage between market-oriented liberals and the *dirigiste* French establishment was once again dominant, especially over the terms of the common market. Indeed, the predominantly liberal French negotiators in Brussels, faced with hostility to the common market within the French bureaucracy and the National Assembly, were forced to demand a series of revisions to the report of the Spaak Committee, including most notably: a pause after the first stage of trade liberalization, after which a unanimous vote would be required to move onto the second and final stage; temporary safeguard measures for specific industries; special arrangements providing explicit protection for agriculture in the common market; special arrangements for the French overseas territories; and most controversially, upward harmonization of social and fiscal regulations in order to mitigate or remove the competitive disadvantages which France suffered as a result of her domestic social regulations (Küsters 1987: 89–90). These demands, which would have severely compromised the common market, were summarily rejected by the other five member states in the negotiations, in which the French delegation eventually agreed to compromise on most of their demands.

Overall, the Treaties of Rome bear the imprint of the liberal vision. The central element of the EEC Treaty is, of course, the common market, which is in essence and intent a liberal, market-making project. According to the terms of the Treaty, the common market would be an area characterized by the free movement of goods, services, labour, and capital; moreover, the transition to the final stage of the common market, on 1 January 1969, was made automatic, and not subject to a further vote as the French government had originally demanded. In addition to this central element, the Treaty also included several flanking policies favoured by the advocates of the liberal vision, including most notably competition and external trade policies. The provisions for competition policy are based on liberal, American-inspired views of antitrust policy, and provide the Commission with some of its strongest supranational powers to police cartels and concentrations, abuse of dominant positions, and state aids to industry; for this reason, the competition policy laid out in the EEC Treaty has been characterized aptly as 'the first supranational policy' in EU history (Wilks and McGowan 1995). Finally, the Treaty also provided for a common external trade policy *vis-à-vis* the rest of the world, and authorized the Commission to represent the common market countries in international trade negotiations. In short, the clearest, most automatic provisions of the Treaty, and those providing for the greatest supranational competences, are those which provide for the creation of a liberal, free-trading area with significant supranational powers in competition and external trade policy.

By contrast, the few elements of regulated capitalism present in the Treaties were inserted largely at the insistence of the French, and are weak and vague by comparison. Euratom was, of course, the great *dirigiste* counterpart to the common market, but turned out to be less significant than expected in the decades to follow. Within the EEC Treaty, the most striking exception to the liberal project was the CAP, reflecting the general conviction in *all* of the member states that agriculture would continue to be protected in the common market; yet the Treaty provisions on the CAP were left quite vague, leading to a string of political struggles between de Gaulle and the other five during the 1960s to secure permanent EC funding for French agriculture (de Menil 1977). The Treaty also included a French-inspired Article 141 [119 EEC] on equal pay for men and women, which remained a dead letter until its activation by litigation in the late 1960s and 1970s (Hoskyns 1996).[4]

Finally, in response to French concerns about competitive distortions caused by France's advanced social regulations, the Treaty also includes provisions for the 'harmonization' of national regulations, most notably in Articles 94 [100 EEC] and 308 [235 EEC]. Once again, however, these provisions for regulatory harmonization were watered down significantly from the original French proposals, in which successful harmonization of social regulations would be a prerequisite for the final, definitive stage of the common market. By contrast, the final draft of the EEC Treaty simply provides for the possibility of harmonization of social legislation, by a unanimous vote of the Council of Ministers. These provisions are not, of course, insignificant, and later served as the legal basis for a broad range of EC regulatory policies (Pollack 1994: 123–6). Nevertheless, the harmonization process proved in practice to be slow and inefficient, and a decade later John Pinder (1968) would note the difficulty of so-called 'positive integration' in the EC in comparison to 'negative integration' or market liberalization. Indeed, by the mid-1980s, the slowness of the harmonization process had led to a proliferation of non-tariff barriers which frustrated the market-making aims of the EEC Treaty. It was this situation which the SEA of 1987 was designed to address.

The SEA and the Primacy of the Internal Market

The literature on the SEA and the '1992 programme' is immense, and bears no repetition here (see for example Corbett 1987; Green Cowles 1993; De Ruyt 1986; Gazzo 1986; Moravcsik 1991b; Pelkmans 1988). The centrepiece of the SEA is, of course, the commitment to complete the internal market by the end of 1992, through the adoption of the 300-odd directives outlined in the Commission's 1985 White Paper 'Completing the Internal Market' (Commission of the European Communities 1985). The 1992 programme was, of course, a quintessentially neo-liberal project, and was, in Moravcsik's terms, the outcome of a long process of convergence among national preferences. Over the course of the 1980s, Moravcsik argues, the key member states of the Community— first Thatcher's Britain, then Kohl's Germany, and finally the post-Keynesian,

---

[4] Throughout this chapter, and at the risk of anachronism, I follow the volume's practice of listing treaty articles according to the numbering system of the new consolidated treaties. The original article numbers, and the specific treaties in which they appear, follow in brackets.

post-1983 Mitterrand government in France—embraced the neo-liberal goal of a single European market, which would provide Europe with the economies of scale necessary to compete against the rival economies of the United States and Japan (Moravcsik 1991*b*). It was in this context of neo-liberal consensus that Jacques Delors, the new President of the European Commission from 1 January 1985, proposed the 1992 programme, together with a series of institutional reforms designed to facilitate the rapid adoption of the Commission's proposed directives (Sandholtz and Zysman 1989; Cockfield 1994).

The SEA itself is—at least in comparison to the later Maastricht and Amsterdam Treaties—a spare document, which faithfully reflects the aims of its neo-liberal project. The heart of the SEA can be found in Article 18 [8A EEC], according to which: 'The Community shall adopt measures with the aim of progressively establishing the internal market over a period expiring on 31 December 1992 . . .'. In order to facilitate the rapid adoption of the Commission's proposed directives, the SEA also provided for limited institutional reform, most notably the adoption of qmv for internal market issues, and in particular the new Article 95 [100A EEC], which provides for the Council to adopt, by qmv, 'measures for the approximation of the provisions laid down by law, regulation or administrative action in the Member States which have as their object the establishment and functioning of the Internal Market'. The decision rule of qmv is, of course, listed by Hooghe and Marks as one of the hallmarks of the regulated capitalism project; yet, as Andrew Moravcsik (1991*b*) points out, the extension of qmv in the SEA is limited largely to the internal market provisions of the treaty. The SEA, therefore, gave Europe the institutional means to establish an internal market but, as with the EEC Treaty, set a higher threshold for the adoption of social regulation within that market.

However, despite the overall neo-liberal thrust of the SEA, the requirement of unanimous agreement meant that certain aspects of the regulated capitalism project made it into the text of the Single Act. For the sake of brevity, I focus here on three of these aspects. First, at the insistence of Italy, Germany, and the Benelux countries, the Single Act enhanced the powers of the EP by creating a cooperation procedure which gave Parliament the right to propose amendments to EC legislation; these amendments, if accepted by the Commission, could then be adopted by the Council of Ministers by qmv, but rejected only by unanimity. This new cooperation procedure, by enhancing the powers of the directly elected Parliament, was a clear step in the direction of the regulated capitalism model, but its scope was limited by the treaty to internal market issues (De Ruyt 1986: 125–6).

A second aspect of the regulated capitalism project was the creation of new sectoral competences for environmental protection, worker health and safety, and research and technological development. These provisions gave the Community explicit competence to adopt Community-wide regulations which were not necessarily tied to the internal market, and to engage in a modest industrial policy aimed at encouraging cross-border research and development (R&D) collaboration. Yet these provisions essentially codified policies which had previously been adopted on the basis of Articles 94 [100 EEC] (internal market) and 308 [235 EEC] (the Community's 'flexible clause'), rather than creating policies *de novo*. Furthermore, most of these new competences remained subject to the old decision rules of unanimous voting and consultation, rather than qmv and cooperation with the EP. Finally, a new Article 139 [118b EEC] was adopted to promote a 'social dialogue' between employers and industry at the European level, but was rarely used prior to the Maastricht Treaty. Hence, only the provision in Article 138 [118a EEC] for the adoption of worker health and safety regulations by qualified majority represented a significant advance in the Community's regulatory capacity.

Third and finally, however, the SEA did take a major step towards the ideal of regulatory capitalism in its provisions for a Community 'cohesion policy'. Economic and social cohesion was a crucial part of Delors' vision for an *espace organisé*, in which the wealthier member states and regions would demonstrate solidarity with the poorer, and Hooghe and Marks therefore include cohesion alongside regulation as part of their ideal type of regulated capitalism. Among the member states, however, the core cleavage on the issue of cohesion was not between left and right, but rather between the richer and poorer member states of the Community. Thus, the key *demandeurs* in the negotiations were the Socialist government of Greece and the Christian Democratic government of Italy, which were supported by Ireland and by the incoming member states of Spain and Portugal. The demands of these states were resisted, however, by both the right-wing and left-wing governments of northern Europe, which would become net contributors to any enlarged Structural Funds. In the end, the conference agreed on a series of five new articles for the treaty (Articles 158–162 [130A–E EEC]), which specified the general objective of economic and social cohesion, called for its integration into other Community policies, and codified the existence of the European Regional Development Fund (ERDF), which had hitherto been based on the catch-all Article 308 [235 EEC]. The new provisions also called for the comprehensive reform of the Structural Funds, to be decided by a unanimous vote of the Council on the basis of a Commission proposal, to be submitted immediately after the entry into force of the SEA.

On the central issue of financing, however, the northern states resisted the demands of the south for an explicit commitment to greater expenditure, opting instead for a non-binding declaration according to which: 'The financial resources of the funds . . . shall be substantially increased in real terms so far as funding possibilities allow'. Subsequently, the size of the Structural Funds was doubled in February 1988, in a major intergovernmental bargain in which Spain and the other southern states linked the issue of structural financing to the completion of the internal market programme (Pollack 1995). Thus, cohesion emerged as the central element of the regulated capitalism project in the Single Act, but its core constituency among the member states consisted not of the European left, but rather of the poorer member states of the south, regardless of their political colour. Indeed, it was the willingness of these southern member states to block the neo-liberal objective of the internal market which gave them the leverage to demand major redistributive transfers—a pattern we shall see repeated at Maastricht.

The Maastricht Treaty and the Institutionalization of Monetarism

Once again, the literature on the Maastricht Treaty is extraordinarily rich and detailed, and I will not attempt to summarize it here (see for example Cloos *et al.* 1993; Corbett 1994; Duff *et al.* 1994; Grant 1994; Laursen and Vanhoonacker 1992; Ross 1995*a*). Put simply, the Maastricht Treaty encompassed the existing European Communities in the framework of a new European Union, in which the existing EC would constitute the first pillar, while the second and third pillars would involve intergovernmental cooperation in the areas of the CFSP and JHA, respectively. Within the EC pillar—which is our main concern in the context of the struggle between the neo-liberal and regulated capitalism models—the central element of the treaty was clearly the provision for a neo-liberal economic and monetary union informed by monetarist economic views and based on the model of the German *Bundesbank*. Indeed, as Kathleen McNamara (1998) argues in her recent book, the Maastricht provisions on EMU represent the culmination of an 'historic economic policy convergence' in the Western Europe of the 1980s, as governments of the left as well as the right sought to emulate the economic successes of the *Bundesbank*, embracing the monetarist project as the most promising answer to the economic policy failures of the late 1970s.[5] In terms of the institutional history of the EU sketched above, the Maastricht Treaty therefore represents the extension of the European neo-liberal agenda from the internal market to the realm of economic and monetary policy.

Nevertheless, the Maastricht Treaty also includes a number of institutional changes and specific policy competences which reflect elements of the regulated capitalism project, largely at the insistence of the French and German governments, both of which were eager to develop European 'political union', thereby binding the newly united Germany more firmly into the institutions of Western Europe. In the area of institutional reform, for example, the Maastricht Treaty facilitates positive social regulation by expanding the use of qmv for areas outside the realm of internal market policy, including the environ-

---

[5] For detailed analyses of the EMU provisions of the treaty, see e.g. Eichengreen (1993) and Kenen (1995).

ment, consumer protection, and a number of areas in social policy. Similarly, and again reflecting Hooghe's and Marks' ideal type of regulated capitalism, the Maastricht Treaty increased the powers of the EP by extending the use of the cooperation procedure, and creating a new co-decision procedure which gives the Parliament veto power in areas such as the internal market, the environment, and consumer protection.

In terms of sectoral competences, the Maastricht Treaty created explicit EC competences for a number of new policy areas, including consumer protection, public health, education, and even culture (although the latter three areas specifically ruled out harmonization, opting instead for recommendations, co-ordination of national provisions, and modest financial 'incentive' programmes). The new Treaty also included symbolically important provisions on 'European citizenship', although the rights attached to such citizenship were limited in comparison to the rights of national citizenship (see Chapter 1). By far the most important new competence in the negotiations, as well as the most controversial, was social policy, which had been largely absent from the EEC Treaty, and had featured only indirectly in the SEA under the rubric of worker health and safety. The latter provisions had been extensively used since the entry into force of the SEA, but in general the adoption of social regulations had lagged far behind internal market liberalization in the late 1980s. Consequently, the Delors Commission proposed a revised social chapter, providing the EC with the competence to adopt harmonized social regulations in a wide range of areas, mostly by qmv. These proposals led to a bitter debate between John Major's Conservative government in Britain, which was the most neoliberal in orientation and opposed any provision for social policy in the treaty, and the other eleven who, to varying degrees, favoured a social chapter with at least some qmv. This basic conflict led to a year-long, eleven-to-one deadlock in the 1991 IGC on political union, and emerged as the single greatest obstacle to agreement at Maastricht. In an effort to break the deadlock, the Dutch Prime Minister, Ruud Lubbers, proposed watering down the social chapter, but Major rejected this as well, telling his colleagues that: 'Just as for you, signing this treaty without the social provisions creates problems, for me it is the other way round. I would not get the support of the British parliament or business' (quoted in Gardner 1991).

At this point, Delors came forward with the idea of an eleven-member 'opt-in', whereby all of the member states other than Britain would agree to a binding Social Protocol to the Treaty, under which the eleven would adopt social regulations within the framework of the EC institutions without British participation. This compromise proved acceptable to all twelve member states, and so a Social Protocol was added to the Treaty. Under the terms of the Protocol, the eleven signatories could adopt social policy provisions by qualified majority and in cooperation with the EP in the following areas: improvement of the working environment; working conditions; information and consultation of workers; equality of job opportunities and treatment of work between men and women; and the integration of persons excluded from the labour market. In addition, the Protocol also allowed for harmonization in a number of other areas, including: social security and social protection of workers; protection of workers where their contract is terminated; worker representation; conditions of employment for third-party nationals; and financial contributions for the promotion of employment and job creation. However, the Protocol expressly excluded the following from the scope of EC competence: pay, the right of association, the right to strike, and the right to impose lock-outs from the scope of EC competence. Finally, the Protocol allowed for the possibility for European employers and unions to negotiate agreements directly through the social dialogue, subject to the approval of the Council of Ministers (Ross 1995a: 191; Cloos *et al.* 1993: 307–15; Corbett 1994: 49–51; European Social Observatory 1993: 52–7). Thus, the Maastricht Social Protocol increased the regulatory capacity of the Union in social policy, but to varying degrees depending on voting rules, and excluding Britain.[6]

Finally, at the insistence of the 'poor four' member states, the 1991 IGC took up the issue of cohesion once again. The primary *demandeur* this time was Spain, which came to the IGC with a long list of cohesion-related demands including: an increase in the funding allocated to the Structural Funds; a revision of the Community's own resources system, which would better reflect each member state's ability to pay; and the creation of a new 'Interstate Compensation Fund' to help the less prosperous member states to meet the rigorous convergence criteria for EMU. Not surprisingly, as Ibanez (1992: 108) points out, '... these ideas were not very well received in the Member States of northern Europe'. With the exception of a few minor changes to Articles 2 [2 EEC] and 158–162 [130A–E EEC], all of the major Spanish demands were rejected by the northern net contributors, and ignored in the draft treaties prepared by the Luxembourg and Dutch presidencies. Realizing, however, that their bargaining leverage would be greatest before the new treaty was signed, the Spanish Prime Minister, Felipe Gonzalez, and his European Affairs Minister, Carlos Westendorp, hardened their demands, and the cohesion issue was finally resolved at the Maastricht summit itself in a deal between Kohl (the largest net contributor) and Gonzalez (the largest net recipient). In the end, the Treaty provides for the creation of a new Cohesion Fund for the southern member states, provided that these states adopt national programmes to meet the EMU convergence criteria laid down in the Treaty (Grant 1994: 200; Cloos *et al.* 1993: 158). Thus the Maastricht Treaty, like the SEA, codified the European commitment to economic and social cohesion, and created a new instru-

---

[6]   For good discussions of the Social Protocol and its subsequent use, see Pierson and Leibfried (1995), Kim (1997).

ment for financial redistribution. Once again, however, the successful coalition was not a coalition of the left, but a coalition of the poor, exploiting the interest of the northern member states in EMU to secure a redistributive side-payment. In both treaties, cohesion was the price to be paid to pursue the neo-liberal core project of the Union.

The Treaty of Amsterdam

Summing up the previous section, the three major treaties in the history of the EC/EU demonstrate a clear trend. In each case, the treaty is dominated by a neo-liberal market-building or monetarist project, married to some regulatory or redistributive elements designed to secure the unanimous consent of reluctant member states. Nevertheless, the overall thrust of each treaty, and of the European integration project as a whole, is strikingly neo-liberal, particularly considering the need for unanimous agreement among six, ten, or twelve member states.

In this context, the Amsterdam Treaty is an outlier. Unlike the Rome Treaties, the SEA, and Maastricht, the 1996 IGC was convened not to advance any particular policy goal, but rather to review the provisions of the Maastricht Treaty five years on, and to reform the institutions of the Union in preparation for its impending enlargement to the east and south.[7] Thus, at the heart of the Amsterdam Treaty we find no central neo-liberal element, but rather a mostly silent affirmation of the status quo on neo-liberal issues such as the internal market, competition and trade policy and EMU. By contrast, however, the treaty records modest progress on many elements of the regulated capitalism project—except cohesion policy, which is not mentioned at all. Let us explore each of these elements in turn.

Neo-Liberalism: The Status Quo Preserved

If one examines the negotiating history of the 1996 IGC—available to an unprecedented degree on the Commission's *Europa* website (Commission of the European Communities 1998) and in the pages of *Agence Europe*, European Report, and the *Financial Times*—the striking fact is that most of the EU's neo-liberal *acquis* was kept off the negotiating table. The internal market provisions of the Treaty, for example, were scarcely discussed at the conference, and the only major change to these provisions was the extension of the EP's

[7] Analysis of the Amsterdam Treaty has been a growth industry in the year since the Treaty was agreed. For excellent general accounts of the 1996 IGC and the Amsterdam Treaty, see e.g. Devuyst (1997), Duff (1997), Edwards and Pijpers (1997), European Policy Centre (1997), European Social Observatory (1997), Petite (1998).

co-decision powers to areas such as the right of establishment and the rules governing the professions.

In the areas of competition and external trade policy, efforts were made early on in the negotiations to amend the treaty provisions in a more liberal direction, but these mostly failed. In competition policy, Germany in particular campaigned for the creation of a European Cartel Office (modelled on its own *Bundeskartellamt*), which would take over the Commission's responsibilities in competition policy, and which would presumably be more stringent and less open to political pressures in the application of EC competition law (Wilks and McGowan 1995). These demands were, however, rejected early on by a number of other member states. In a similar vein, the Commission pressed for an amendment to Article 133 [113 EEC] on external trade policy, which would bring services and intellectual property issues within the realm of the EC's common commercial policy, and make them subject to qmv in the Council of Ministers. The effect of such a change would be not only to enlarge the Community's legal competence, but also to remove national vetoes from these areas of trade policy, giving the Commission greater flexibility to negotiate liberal trade agreements with third countries. Once again, however, a majority of member states, led by France, rejected the Commission's proposals, although the new treaty does provide for a future incorporation of services and intellectual property into Article 133 [113 EEC] by a unanimous vote in the Council of Ministers (Petite 1998: III.2).

Finally, with regard to EMU, the conference made an extraordinary effort to keep the subject off the agenda entirely, lest the conference call the project or its deadline of 1 January 1999 into question; and indeed, the Treaty of Amsterdam is entirely silent on the question of EMU. Nevertheless, the subject of EMU was extensively and unexpectedly discussed at the Amsterdam European Council itself, as a result of the election of the new French Socialist government of Lionel Jospin two weeks earlier. Elected on a wave of protest against EMU-induced austerity measures, Jospin and his Economics Minister, Dominique Strauss-Kahn, immediately denounced the German-inspired Stability Pact, which committed EMU members to fiscal austerity after the transition to the Euro in 1999. They insisted that the pact be renegotiated to stress the importance of growth and employment, and the need for an 'economic government' alongside the new European Central Bank (ECB). However, the German Chancellor, Helmut Kohl, constrained by the *Bundesbank* and by a hostile German public opinion, resisted any renegotiation of the Stability Pact, as did most of the other member states. In the end, the Jospin government agreed at Amsterdam to sign the Stability Pact unaltered, in return for a non-binding Resolution on Growth and Employment, a proposed European summit on unemployment to be held the following November in Luxembourg, and finally, an Employment Chapter written into the text of the Amsterdam Treaty itself (Vernet 1997).

Regulated Capitalism: Reforms at the Margins

Despite the last-minute electoral convulsions in France, therefore, the neo-liberal core of the Union—centred around the internal market, EMU, and the flanking policies of competition and external trade—were left essentially untouched in Amsterdam. But to what degree was this neo-liberal project challenged by the competing vision of regulated capitalism? Following the outline of the previous sections, in this part of the chapter I examine the provisions and the negotiation of the Treaty of Amsterdam, beginning with the general institutional reforms undertaken at Amsterdam, and then moving on to the new and enlarged competences for the Union agreed in the treaty.

Institutional reform was, of course, the great weakness of the 1996–7 IGC, which failed in its attempt to reform the EU's institutions in preparation for the next enlargement to the East and South. Most notably, the conference failed to agree on the reweighting of votes in the Council of Ministers and on the size of the Commission in an enlarged EU, both of which will be the subject of a future IGC.

This highly publicized failure should not, however, obscure the significant institutional changes which were made by the Amsterdam Treaty, several of which advance the cause of the regulated capitalism project, in particular by strengthening the powers of the EU's supranational institutions. The big winner of the treaty in this regard was the European Parliament, whose legislative powers were increased substantially through the extension of the co-decision procedure to twenty-three new areas, including public health, the environment, equal opportunities and equal treatment, incentive measures for employment and combating social exclusion, and other areas of social policy. With the exception of the articles concerning EMU, which were left untouched, the cooperation procedure has now been eliminated entirely in favour of the co-decision procedure. The latter procedure, moreover, has been simplified through the removal of the Council's so-called 'third reading', in which the Council could previously, by unanimous vote, adopt legislation which had been rejected by the Parliament. Thus, under the new treaty, the EP will participate as a co-equal legislator in most areas of substantive social regulation. In addition to these key provisions, the EP also gained the right to approve the appointment of the Commission President (Petite 1998: IV.1).

The role of the Commission itself was 'scarcely questioned at all in the Amsterdam discussions' according to Petite (1998: IV.3), and the Treaty amendments in this area are minor, relating primarily to the 'presidentialization' of the Commission, which will henceforth operate 'under the political guidance of its President' (Article 219 [163 EEC]). The President will also have a role in selecting individual Commissioners 'by common accord' with the member governments, and is granted the right to reshuffle Commission portfolios. More generally, Petite points out, the Commission's right of initiative is strengthened in several ways: by the creation of new Community competences, several of which feature qmv; by the incorporation of asylum, immigration and visa issues into the first pillar; and by the creation of a shared right of initiative between member states and the Commission for the remaining third pillar issues.

The European Court of Justice (ECJ), whose powers had been assailed early on in the conference by the Conservative government of the British Prime Minister, John Major, in fact benefited from a grudging and complex expansion of its jurisdiction in the 'communitarized' areas of asylum, immigration, and visas, and—subject to even greater restrictions—in the remaining third pillar issues.

Finally, with regard to the Council of Ministers, the IGC famously failed to agree upon any generalized move to qmv, largely because a weakened Chancellor Kohl was forced by domestic opposition to veto the extension of qmv to areas of *Länder* competence, such as culture, industry, and the professions. Even here, however, the situation is not entirely bleak, as qmv was accepted for new competences dealing with equal opportunities for men and women, as well as for public health, incentive measures for employment, and to combat social exclusion, and other issues relevant to the regulated capitalism project (Petite 1998: IV.2). It is to these specific competences that we now turn.

In addition to the general institutional reforms mentioned above, the Amsterdam Treaty also introduces or expands *specific Community competences* in areas such as employment, social policy, equal opportunities, environmental protection, consumer protection, public health, and human rights. These new and enlarged competences, like the general institutional reforms reviewed above, move the Union in the direction of the project for regulated capitalism. Yet the specific provisions and the negotiating history of the treaty reveal a growing tension within the European left between the traditional socialist vision of a regulatory Europe, held most notably by the government of the French Prime Minister, Lionel Jospin, and the more market-oriented, centre–left vision of the British Prime Minister, Tony Blair. To understand the nature of this tension, let us consider briefly a few of the treaty's provisions.

The issue of employment policy in Europe is, of course, a central question for the project of regulated capitalism, which might easily be expected to advocate a centralized, or at least centrally co-ordinated, policy to reduce unemployment. In this context, it is striking that the member states agreed unanimously on the inclusion of a new Employment Chapter in the Amsterdam Treaty, in line with the project of regulated capitalism. The idea for a new Employment Chapter had been broached early on in the conference, in particular by the Commission and the Swedish delegation, and had attracted the support of many member governments eager to demonstrate the Union's attentiveness to the central concerns of their citizens. Furthermore, the election of the Jospin government in France gave the Employment Chapter an additional impetus, as it was clear that the French would make some movement on employment a precondition for the adoption of the Stability Pact; yet the *content* of the Employment Chapter was fundamentally contested not only between left-wing and right-wing governments, but within the left as well.

The pivotal figure in this debate was the new British Prime Minister, Tony Blair. Elected just a month before Jospin, on 1 May, Blair had immediately reversed a number of the long-standing neo-liberal negotiating positions of the previous Conservative government, agreeing to negotiate new Treaty provisions on social policy, the environment, the powers of the EP, and employment.[8] Indeed, the elections of Blair in May and Jospin in June signalled to many the ascendance in Europe of the political left, which now participated in government in thirteen of the fifteen member governments, leaving only Kohl's Germany and Aznar's Spain controlled by the political right.

The diversity of views within the European left was revealed, however, at a meeting of Socialist Party leaders in Malmö in Sweden from 5 to 7 June, just two weeks before the Amsterdam European Council. The meeting was the first foreign appearance for Jospin since his election, and in his speech he attacked the neo-liberal, monetarist thrust of European integration in recent years. 'Market forces', he argued, 'if there is no attempt to control them, will threaten our very idea of civilization' (quoted in *Reuters* 1997). France, according to Jospin, remained in favour of European integration. 'But today, with high unemployment, low growth and increasing poverty, Europe can no longer be built on the back of its citizens', he maintained. More specifically, Jospin laid down a series of four demands regarding Economic and Monetary Union. First, the Euro should not be overvalued against the dollar and the yen, which Jospin believed provided the United States and Japan with an advantage in export markets. Second, Jospin (supported by Jacques Delors, in attendance at the conference) demanded an 'economic government' to co-ordinate economic, taxation, and wage policies, and to provide a counterbalance to the ECB. Third, Jospin called for the inclusion of Italy and Spain in the first stage of EMU, which would have the dual advantage of avoiding competitive devaluations by those countries as well as diluting the hard core of monetarist countries within the Euro zone. Fourth and finally, Jospin demanded an explicit EU commitment to growth and employment, including the expenditure of EU funds to stimulate job creation (de Bresson 1997; Marlowe 1997).

By contrast, Blair's message at Malmö represented a new, centre–left agenda which stressed the fundamental principles of European social democracy, but differed on the details of policy and of institutional reform. Like Jospin, Blair

---

[8] Interestingly, Blair's policy reversals were limited entirely to the first (economic) pillar of the Union. In the other two pillars—namely, on the issues of foreign and defence policy, and on the incorporation of Schengen and the third pillar into the European Community—Blair's negotiating positions were virtually identical to those of John Major.

argued that employment should be placed at the centre of the EU agenda. 'The most immediate challenge facing the Union is tackling unemployment— finding work and keeping work is a key priority for Europe's citizens and making that happen must be a priority for the EU', Blair wrote on the eve of the conference (quoted in Clare 1997). Yet the tone of Blair's remarks was far less interventionist than Jospin's. Indeed, in Malmö, Blair lectured the other socialist leaders on the need for reform, telling them that, like the British Labour Party, European socialists must 'modernize or die'. In place of the statist policies of the old left, Blair argued, the left and centre–left in Europe should adopt new policies emphasizing flexible labour markets, worker retraining and a reformed welfare state. 'Our task', he argued, 'is not to go on fighting old battles but to show that there is a third way, a way of marrying together an open, competitive and successful economy with a just, decent and humane society' (quoted in Shrimsley 1997). On the specific provisions of the draft Treaty, Blair indicated that he would accept an Employment Chapter and a Social Chapter in the treaty, but only if these emphasized labour market flexibility and avoided over-regulation of the European labour market

> We must make sure that in taking action to create jobs we do not do any-
> thing which would damage Europe's competitiveness. To be unemployed
> because of a government's good intentions does not make the situation
> any more pleasant. The risk that the employment chapter might backfire,
> putting in jeopardy more jobs than it creates, is not one that I am prepared
> to take.   (quoted in Clare 1997)

Blair also rejected any additional expenditure of EU funds to deal with unemployment (Royle 1997). The difference in emphasis between Blair's message and Jospin's was stark. As Klaus Hänsch, former President of the EP, put it: 'European social democracy has to make a choice between Blair and Jospin, between new Labour and old socialism' (quoted in Barber 1997).

On the issue of employment, the member states opted for Blair's version. The Employment Chapter agreed to in Amsterdam and incorporated into the treaty (Articles 125–130 [109n–109s EEC]) formally makes 'a high level of employment' an EU objective, and provides for co-ordination and monitoring of national employment policies, and the creation of an advisory committee on employment. However, at the summit, Blair and Kohl joined together to rule out any harmonization in the area of employment policy, and to block any major new EU spending on employment programmes, which are restricted to pilot projects of limited scope and duration.[9] In short, the new Treaty provisions place employment clearly on the EU agenda, and require member states to account for their national employment strategies on an annual basis in a way

---

[9] For detailed analyses of the Employment Chapter, see Devuyst (1997:9), Petite (1998: II.1), European Parliament (1997a,b).

that would have been unthinkable just a few years earlier; yet the approach is voluntaristic and falls short of granting the Union any significant regulatory or redistributive capacity. As one British government official commented after the Amsterdam European Council: 'There is a very clear British stamp on the employment chapter and the summit conclusions. Flexible labour markets, welfare reform, the refusal to put more costs on business, these are very much on the agenda. . . . [Blair] does feel that there is an argument being engaged here and it's one that he can win'. Blair himself struck a similar tone in his assessment of Amsterdam: 'The summit as a whole focused in a very, very important way on the issue of jobs and economic reform, the focus being on education, skills, flexible labour markets *rather than old-style state intervention and regulation*' (quoted in Smart and Coman 1997, emphasis added).

The Amsterdam provisions on social policy tell a similar story. The key issue here was the reform of the Maastricht Social Protocol, which the Commission had proposed incorporating into the body of the EC Treaty, with the support of the fourteen member states which had signed the Protocol. This initiative had been blocked by the Conservative government of John Major throughout most of the IGC, but soon after the British elections, Blair announced that Britain would agree to sign the Social Protocol, which was incorporated into the EC Treaty as Articles 136–143 [117–120 EEC] and thus became binding on all the member states. As we have seen, however, Blair also argued at Malmö against over-regulation of the European economy, and on the eve of the Amsterdam European Council, the British delegation indicated that it would oppose any extension of qmv under the Social Protocol, which was therefore incorporated into the EC Treaty without any changes in the Council voting rules (Helm and Jones 1997). The revised social chapter nevertheless contains a few moderate advances in the EC's regulatory capacity, including an upgrading of the EP's role to co-decision for all measures decided by qualified majority in the Council; an explicit reference to fundamental social rights (which are not, however, directly effective); and a new provision allowing the adoption, by qualified majority and with co-decision, of incentive programmes to combat social exclusion. Perhaps most significantly, the new treaty includes a substantially revised Article 141 [119 EEC] reaffirming the principle of equal pay for equal work or 'work of comparable value' (in line with the case law of the ECJ), and providing for the adoption of legislation aimed at equal treatment and equal opportunities for men and women in the workplace, by qmv and with co-decision for the EP. These provisions have been criticized by women's rights advocates, who argue that the effect of the new treaty provisions is limited to women as participants in the workplace, and does not guarantee equality between men and women more generally (see for example Commission of the European Communities 1997b). Nevertheless, within the limited sphere of the workplace, the new treaty provisions should facilitate the adoption of equal opportunities and equal treatment legislation in the future, and in this regard the new Article 141 [119 EEC], like the communitarization of the

Social Protocol more generally, represents a modest increase in the regulatory capacity of the Union.

In addition to the core competences of employment and social policy, the provisions relating to the environment, consumer protection, and public health were all the subject of modest revisions, strengthening the EU's regulatory capacity to varying degrees. In the case of the environment, the major change was an alteration of Article 95 [100A EEC], which now allows member states, on the basis of new scientific evidence, to introduce new environmental standards (rather than simply retain existing ones) which are stricter than those of Community legislation. This new provision, inserted at the insistence of the northern European countries, instructs the Commission to examine these new national provisions and to issue a ruling within six months; in the absence of such a ruling, the new national standard will be deemed to have been approved. In addition to this central provision, the IGC also agreed to strengthen the EP's role in environmental policy from cooperation to co-decision; the Commission's proposal to adopt qmv for all environmental legislation was, however, rejected. Finally, the language on sustainable development and the integration of the environment into other policies was strengthened as well (Europe Environment 1997). The result of these changes is not revolutionary, but the new treaty will nevertheless allow the EP a greater say in environmental regulation, and will leave individual member states with greater leeway to adopt stricter standards after harmonization, both of which are in keeping with the agenda of regulated capitalism.

In the case of public health, the new Treaty calls for high standards to be adopted at European level for human organs, blood, and blood derivatives; it also provides for the use of the co-decision procedure in the case of veterinary and plant health measures for the direct purpose of public health protection, which had previously fallen under Article 37 [43 EEC] and consequently the consultation procedure. The changes in consumer protection are more modest, simply clarifying the objectives of the Community, and making mention of consumers' rights to information and education; in comparison to Maastricht, the Community's regulatory competence is not significantly enhanced.

Finally, the Amsterdam Treaty substantially strengthens the Union's commitment to human rights in a number of ways. First, the Treaty empowers the ECJ to review the actions of the Community institutions as regards the respect of fundamental human rights. Second, in anticipation of EU enlargement to new member states with only short histories of human rights protection, the Treaty creates a new mechanism to penalize member states which persistently or seriously violate fundamental human rights; in particular, the Council may decide by qmv to suspend the rights of a member state in violation. Third and finally, the treaty includes a general non-discrimination clause which allows the Council, by unanimous vote and after consulting the EP, to adopt legislation to outlaw discrimination on the basis of sex, racial or ethnic origin, religion or belief, disability, age, or sexual orientation. This is an extraordinarily broad statement of non-discrimination, going beyond the narrow labour market provisions of Article 141[119 EEC], but the treaty nevertheless stopped short of creating a directly effective right to non-discrimination which could be claimed by individuals and enforced in the courts, settling instead for a relatively demanding competence to legislate at the European level in the future (Petite 1998: I.1).

In sum, the Treaty of Amsterdam modestly increases the regulatory capacity of the Union in most of the key issue areas of the regulated capitalism project, subject to the limitations imposed by Blair's less interventionist approach to employment and social policy. The major exception to this trend is the issue of cohesion, on which the treaty is silent. Indeed, in contrast to the 1985 and 1991 IGCs, the subject of cohesion was barely discussed in the 1996–7 IGC, and this for several reasons. First, most of the delegations, including the traditional *demandeurs*, such as Spain and Greece, accepted that the real bargaining over the future of cohesion policy would occur in 1999, when the Union was scheduled to adopt the financial perspectives for the period 2000–6. Second, in contrast to the SEA and the Maastricht Treaty, the Amsterdam Treaty contains no core neo-liberal project, and hence no opportunity for the cohesion countries to demand redistributive side-payments from the wealthier member states in return for their agreement. More generally, the lack of any significant provisions on cohesion in the Amsterdam Treaty demonstrates that economic and social cohesion, while a central part of Delors' intellectual project for an *espace organisé*, finds its constituency in the poor countries of Southern Europe regardless of their political colour, and not in the political left. Hence, the left and centre–left majority at Amsterdam embraced much of the project of regulated capitalism, but remained silent on the issue of cohesion.

Conclusions

The EU has implications for the left–right dimension of European political life. These implications can be theorized, in ideal typical terms, as a struggle between the competing projects of neo-liberalism and regulated capitalism. International treaties are not politically innocent in this struggle, but rather facilitate or hinder the adoption of these respective projects. In this context, I have argued that the core project of European integration from the EEC Treaty to the Maastricht Treaty has been neo-liberal, focusing on the twin goals of the internal market and monetary integration. The Treaty of Amsterdam left in place the bedrock of this neo-liberal project, which had become the object of consensus among the member governments of the EU, both left and right. As we have seen, however, the Amsterdam Treaty also went beyond the EU's neo-liberal core, adding to it a series of more or less significant changes in institutional provisions and sectoral competences, and moving the Union subtly to the left in comparison to the neo-liberal thrust of the previous Treaties.

How might we explain this leftward turn, however modest, in the Amsterdam Treaty? Once again, it should be stated that the aim of this chapter is analytical rather than explanatory, and that I do not intend to put forward a new theory of intergovernmental decision-making here. A thorough explanation of the outcome at Amsterdam would no doubt have to consider multiple factors, including the difficult experience of the Maastricht ratification debates, the economic context of high unemployment rates throughout Europe, and the accession in 1995 of new member states with a long tradition of open government and social regulation. Taken together, such factors take us some way towards explaining the increased emphasis on issues perceived to be important to ordinary citizens, such as employment, social policy, the environment, and the free movement of persons.

Perhaps most importantly, however, the brief account of the 1996–7 IGC offered above points clearly to the partisan composition of the governments at Amsterdam as an important causal factor in explaining the outcome of the conference. In June of 1997, an astounding thirteen of the fifteen EU governments included socialists or social democrats among the governing coalition, including the pivotal British, French, and Italian governments; nine of these countries were led by socialist or social democratic prime ministers. Germany, moreover, was led by Helmut Kohl's CDU which, despite sniping from its liberal FDP partners, has historically been a proponent of the model of regulated capitalism. In the context of the negotiating record of the conference, it seems clear that the emphasis on social issues in the Amsterdam Treaty can only be explained in terms of the last-minute victories of leftist governments in France and, especially, in Britain, where the Blair government reversed long-standing British vetoes on key issues such as the Social Protocol, the Employment Chapter, environmental policy, and the EP. In Andrew Moravcsik's (1991*b*) language, the preferences of EU member governments converged—by electoral mandate. The Treaty of Amsterdam was negotiated principally by governments of the left and centre–left, and bears their imprint.

Yet, the Treaty of Amsterdam does not represent the triumph of a traditional socialist or social democratic ideal of regulated capitalism. Rather, I have argued, the Treaty of Amsterdam, and in particular the key sections of the Treaty dealing with matters of employment and social policy, were shaped largely by the new government, and the new governing philosophy, of Tony Blair. As the leader of New Labour, and currently as Prime Minister, Blair has accepted the central elements of the neo-liberal status quo he inherited from Margaret Thatcher, seeking only modest regulatory and redistributive changes around the margins of Thatcher's neo-liberal legacy. Similarly, the Treaty of

Amsterdam accepts and incorporates the fundamental neo-liberal thrust of the earlier Treaties, while superimposing on these Treaties a number of provisions which indicate a commitment to traditional social democratic principles such as employment and social protection, without significantly increasing the ability of the Union to adopt binding European policies in these areas.

What, then, are we to make of this Blairite Treaty? I see two possible interpretations. In the first interpretation, Blair—and, by extension, the Amsterdam Treaty, which reflects his views—represents the capitulation of the European left, which has swallowed the neo-liberal prescription of free trade and monetarist economics, and offers only weak, symbolic treaty provisions to address questions of employment and social policy without actually providing the Union with the institutional means to act in these areas. The second interpretation, most prominently offered by sociologist Anthony Giddens, is that Blair is in the process of defining a third way, a new radical politics 'beyond left and right', based not on state intervention and regulation but rather on preparing individuals to survive and prosper in the new global economy (Giddens 1994, 1996, 1997). It is still too early to judge whether Giddens' interpretation holds water: Blair's third way is as yet poorly defined, especially at the European level, and the Amsterdam Treaty has not been in force for long. Yet, it remains an intriguing and ironic possibility that, just as scholars like Hix, Hooghe, and Marks are exploring the left–right implications of European integration, centrists like Blair and Giddens claim to be transcending a left–right distinction which is too blunt, and too outdated, to serve as a guide to policy in the new global economy.

15

Constitutional Settlements and the Citizen after the Treaty of Amsterdam

JO SHAW

This chapter focuses on two related questions: the construction of the citizen as a constitutional figure in the European Union (EU); and the interpretation of the new constitutional settlement for the Union after the Treaty of Amsterdam. The two issues are related in the following way: 'citizenship' in this chapter is less an object of study in itself, and more an optic for understanding the development of institution-building and polity formation in the Union context.

The chapter is in two parts. The first part amplifies the following five assumptions underpinning my study of 'the citizen' after Amsterdam

- *Citizenship* in its EU context is to be understood as a form of post-national membership, the relevance and scope of which extends beyond the formal terms of the treaty provisions establishing the category of 'Union citizens'. Issues of democracy and polity-formation form important contextualizing reference points for understanding citizenship in the constitutional sense. More specifically, there are two central elements in a conception of citizenship which focuses on the EU dimension: the problem of identity in a transnational polity, and the challenge of identifying a form of 'full membership' in the specific socio-economic and geopolitical context offered by the EU at its present stage of development. One way of understanding these elements is to feed them into the characteristic dualist approach to citizenship, comprising aspects of 'identity' and 'rights'. The dualism does not stand alone, however, as there

This paper was written while the author was EU-Fulbright Scholar-in-Residence and Visiting Professor at Harvard Law School in 1998. She would like to express her thanks to Harvard Law School and the Council for the International Exchange of Scholars for supporting her stay. Earlier versions of this paper were presented as lectures at the Fletcher School of Law and Diplomacy, Tufts University, and to the Law and Globalization Program of the Institute for Legal Studies, University of Wisconsin–Madison; the author is grateful to participants for their useful comments and criticisms. She is also grateful to the following for helpful comments on earlier drafts, and for discussion on these topics: Gráinne de Búrca, Nigel Evans, Peter Leslie, Joanne Scott, Joseph Weiler, and Antje Wiener.

continues to be an ongoing tension between the sometimes competing and sometimes congruent aspects of identity and rights within citizenship. This is negotiated in the ongoing 'experience' by individuals of 'their' citizenship, and the on-going 'practice' of citizenship by institutional actors such as the Commission and the European Court of Justice (ECJ).

• The European Community (EC)/EU must be studied as a transnational polity-in-the-making, characterized by shifting and dynamic forms of multilevel *governance*. However, much legal and political scholarship points to the key role played in this polity by legal institutions and the transnational 'rule of law' policed by the ECJ, thereby constituting a system which locks the member states in. One characteristic means of revealing some of the contradictions inherent in the emergent polity has been by reference to an ongoing tension between its 'hard' legal core and its 'soft' political contours.

• In this polity-in-the-making, *democracy* remains both a conceptual problem and a practical challenge, requiring multilevel and multi-actor solutions that are 'beyond the state' and, perhaps, also beyond the conventions of Western-style representative liberal democracy.

• *Intergovernmental conferences* (IGCs) and treaty-making moments may highlight those times when the EC/EU is quintessentially the creature of the member states. But IGCs and treaties must themselves be seen in context: they are framed by periods of prior debate and negotiation which involve actors other than national governments; once in place, they are subject to interpretation by courts (especially—and authoritatively according to its dictates—by the ECJ) and 'management' by the institutions as well as the member states. They are 'owned' then by a broader interpretative community.

• The final assumption concerns the question of method: I suggest that the best way to study the Treaty of Amsterdam and its context in the light of these comments is as one step in an ongoing process *of constitutional settlement* (or indeed unsettlement). It enhances constitutionalism in the EU, by adding to the body of rules and basic principles needed to make a political system work and to control the exercise of political power.

It will be clear, therefore, that this chapter is written from the perspective that, although modest in ambition and conception, and lacking the single 'big idea' which has driven the agenda of earlier IGCs such as Maastricht, there are aspects of the Treaty of Amsterdam that require consideration and categorization within a constitutional frame of reference. What remains unclear is the extent and significance of the changes it brings about. How far has constitutionalism now carried the Union? Do the existing rules and principles cover mechanics and function alone, and eschew issues of content, such as the question of the nature of a 'European' society or political community based on the EU? What role does the 'citizen' play in this emerging constitution?

In the second part of the chapter, using this frame of analysis, I shall argue that it is possible to derive from the Amsterdam Treaty some evidence of a gradual move from a form of constitutionalism covering just basic rules of design and operation, to a more substantial constitutional conception that delivers a clearer (but still incompletely formed) picture of the content of the EU polity. For these purposes, the constitution of the citizen in legal and political discourse is a vital tool for constructive analysis. Constitutions are clearly about more than just citizens and citizenship, but in many respects the shifting nature of the EU as a polity increasingly emphasizes the role of the citizen. This is especially so as a matter of rhetorical commitment— 'getting the citizen involved', 'giving the citizen a stake'—but in addition I would also suggest that what might be termed a 'thicker' conception of Union citizenship is emerging, which is central to the development of the EU's constitutional frame. I use the term 'thicker' not in order to make a distinction between process and substance in the context of the management of polities (Walzer 1994: 11–15), but in order to distinguish between a minimal set of universalist prescriptions, essentially of a moral nature, and a maximal set of particularist values. Thus, while we will probably all agree that we are for freedom and against tyranny, a community of interest which shares a view as to exactly *why* we have these views and *what outcomes* we want to see would be of a more particularist and therefore maximal nature. Positing the figure of the citizen as central to the evolution of the integration process is motivated partly by the normative preconception that 'good' constitutions are not imposed from above, but emerge from a conjunction of top-down and bottom-up forces involving institutional design and citizen participation. It is also driven by the observation that the correct frame of reference for studying 'European integration' should not be limited by the formal EU institution-building process, but should also comprise 'the multiple social processes that have promoted the integration of economic, political, and social life within the larger European framework' (Klausen and Tilly 1997: 4).

Hence, the second part of this chapter examines four main aspects of the constitutional settlement after Amsterdam relevant to the dynamic constitution of the citizen. The first concerns practical and theoretical problems resulting from the proliferation of polities which the increasingly differentiated Union now envisages. The 'hard' legal core is called into question by the attempted 'constitutionalization' of flexibility or differentiated integration. This extends across the first pillar enabling arrangements, the new third pillar, and especially the newly communitarized old third pillar and Schengen arrangements. Can there be citizens or members of the multiple polities which the flexible arrangements may in the future give rise to? Second, in the citizenship provisions themselves, one key change is made: Union citizenship is confirmed as *complementing* rather than *replacing* national citizenships.[1] This small change may seem commonplace to students of Union citizenship, and may be intended as a reassertion of national sovereignty in the sense of the power of definition. Paradoxically, it simultaneously confirms the open-textured nature of Union citizenship which is its greatest conceptual strength. Third, like other EC/EU treaties before it, the Treaty of Amsterdam appears ambiguous as to whether it implies 'more' or 'less' Europe—the traditional cleavage in the context of European integration between intergovernmentalism and supranationalism/federalism. I shall argue that what emerges in the Treaty of Amsterdam is a greater awareness of other competing models for socio-economic development, for example, between the competing perspectives offered by regulated capitalism and market capitalism. More relevant to our purposes, I examine the very different visions of the citizen and notions of political community evoked by the 'area of freedom, security and justice' and the 'European social model'. What implications does this have for the future of an ideal type of 'full membership' of the EU, for the practice of EU citizenship, and for the emergence of some form of European political community which supports a notion of membership? Finally, we shall conclude by looking at the rights dimension of EU citizenship, which has been given a considerable amount of not always very flattering attention in the literature thus far. Turning to the Treaty of Amsterdam, formal changes in the status of individuals as holders of rights under EC law are, I would argue, more limited than might at first blush appear: the transparency provisions are concerned with the institutional economy and interinstitutional balance; so far as they affect individual citizens, the fundamental rights provisions essentially restate ECJ case law; and the much lauded non-discrimination provision is merely a tightly worded law-making power which may never be exercised. What significance should we now ascribe to the rights core of Union citizenship?

Assumptions

Citizenship Union-style

Citizenship of the European Union was institutionalized by the Maastricht Treaty on European Union (TEU). A new provision was included in the treaty (Article 8 EC) proclaiming that

---

[1] There are two other changes which should be mentioned, but are not discussed further: Under Art. 18 [8a] EC, the legislative procedure for implementing the free movement principle is changed from assent by the European Parliament (EP) to co-decision. Unanimity in the Council is retained. Under Art. 21 [8d] EC, a third political right of access for Union citizens is included: 'Every citizen of the Union may write to any of the institutions or bodies referred to in this Article or in Article 7 [the EP, the Council, the Commission, the ECJ, the Court of Auditors, the Economic and Social Committee (ESC) and the Committee of the Regions] in one of the languages mentioned in Article 314 and have an answer in the same language'.

> Citizenship of the Union is hereby established. Every person holding the nationality of a Member State shall be a citizen of the Union.

Simple words—and also, perhaps, empty gestures. The formal rights and duties conferred on Union citizens in the provisions which follow are few, and are primarily linked to residence in a member state other than the one of which the citizen is a national. They are limited to a right of residence in other member states (which is not absolute, and may be limited by Council legislation), residence-based electoral rights in local and European parliamentary elections, consular and diplomatic protection in third countries, petitions to the European Parliament (EP), and complaints to the European Ombudsman. Only the last two are not directly linked to free movement, or at least movement away from the home state. This emphasis highlights the primary heritage of Union citizenship, which lies in a conception—fostered principally by the Commission and the ECJ—that the free movement of persons implies more than merely economic rights under the treaties and secondary legislation. The predominant emphasis of the citizenship rights is to constitute the strong transnational citizen who holds and exercises rights *vis-à-vis* the member states, which are set up as the obstructive parties. It does nothing, on the face of it, to constitute either a vertical relationship between the EU and 'its' citizens, or a horizontal relationship between the citizens *inter se*. It suggests little or nothing about the essentially reciprocal nature of citizenship.

It is wrong, however, to study the citizenship question in the EU wholly or even primarily by reference to the formal rights established in the second part of the Amsterdam Treaty. A fuller but still incomplete perspective on the scope of citizenship is given if it is described by reference to some sort of ideal type of citizen with 'full membership' of a given community, following many standard definitions of the concept of 'citizen'.[2] Paradoxically, the message to be derived from such an exercise in EC law is that the progress from civil, to political and thence to social rights is, to a large extent, flipped on its head in the EU context. The legacy of market citizenship embedded in the treaty provisions on free movement of commodities and factors of production strongly marks the present status quo of EU citizenship rights (Everson 1995). Thus, what emerges is less a purely 'social' status than a broader socio-economic status combining elements of market, industrial, and welfare citizenship. The other elements of the rights of citizenship remain underdeveloped: EU citizens are alienated from the enjoyment of political sovereignty in relation to the EU, and there is no meaningful public space within which they can operate as political actors. Furthermore, their civil status (that is, their enjoyment of classical liberties) is largely constituted by reference to rights anchored in national constitutions or in a different type of 'European' frame of reference—the Euro-

---

[2] A fuller exposition of my approach to Union citizenship can be found in Shaw (1997, 1998*a*).

pean Convention on Human Rights and Fundamental Freedoms. The scope and nature of Community fundamental rights remains profoundly problematic, and a contested terrain.

Notwithstanding this gloomy prognosis, let us assume that Raymond Aron's classic statement that there can be no European citizens no longer holds—if it ever did (Aron 1974). At one level, it is not difficult to see the normative imperative that some attention must be paid—after more than thirty years of development—to the 'affective' dimension of European integration (Laffan 1996). The widely recognized legitimacy deficit of the 'Monnet method' has placed demands upon the political process—and the changes introduced by the TEU, not to mention the Treaty of Amsterdam, represent one form of response to this issue. Conceptually speaking, many would suggest that citizenship, while historically linked to the vocation of the nation state, is not inextricably bound to notions of nationalism or indeed attempts in the state context to distinguish between citizen insiders and alien outsiders. Citizenship remains a means for setting the parameters of inclusion and exclusion of any given community, as well as postulating the ideal type of membership of and participation in that community. But identity, loyalty, and community-based fellow-feeling can operate in different ways and to different degrees at many levels, including the local, regional, national, and supranational. Identity is not a zero sum game. There are no a priori reasons why a form of 'community' could not emerge at EU level, based on more than simply the holding of a set of legal rights, although so far any such 'community' has proven to be more imaginary than most. Moreover, there are equally no a priori reasons why the boundaries of membership must be set by reference to the category of nationals of the member states, although political realism might suggest that it will be some time before that national reference point is abandoned—if it ever is—to include, for example, lawfully resident third country nationals.

To achieve this conceptualization of Union citizenship, however, we have to draw more widely on the rich intellectual heritage of citizenship studies. At one level, David Held's (1991: 20) description of citizenship simply as 'membership of a community' involving a reciprocity of rights against and duties towards that community is evocative. But we need to examine its individual elements more closely. So we must also focus on the political element of citizenship, where citizenship constitutes the political community, or indeed vice versa. Citizenship, according to this view, constitutes a 'community of concern and engagement' (Kostakopoulou 1996), and offers the space in which political claims can be articulated and resolved (Everson 1996). Another possibility is to focus more on personal rather than purely political identities, and on the competing claims of individuals and groups. For example, Charles Tilly (1996: 6) identifies citizenship as 'a set of mutual, contested claims between agents of states and members of socially-constructed categories: genders, races, nationalities and others'. One might conclude that citizenship comprises not only the well-established dual elements of identity and rights, but also elements of access, experience, and practice (Wiener 1998: 21–30). These emerge not only through individual experience, but also through institutional practice. The negotiation of these elements is a historical, dynamic, and indeed geographically contingent process. The combining of these elements reminds us that citizenship is not just an object of study in itself, but also a frame of reference for making sense of other aspects of the human condition, and in the context of the EU, the 'European condition'.

Perhaps more pertinent than the theoretical *possibility* of a form of postnational membership emerging independently of pre-existing notions of state citizenship or national definitions of affinity is the more pragmatic observation that the practice of citizenship in the EU has in fact become deeply embedded in what the Union *does* and *is*. This is not to suggest that a citizenship perspective should be used as a prism of analysis for every aspect of EU law, policies, and politics, although many facets of the 'European condition' can be nicely illuminated by such a perspective. Thus, for example, if the optic is that of studying the challenge of democracy in an emergent non-state polity, then the 'claim' of the citizen to be politically sovereign—banal in a state context, novel perhaps in the supranational domain—needs to be taken seriously and dissected in respect of its constituent elements (individual rights and principles of collective representation). Moreover, while it is right to say that citizenship is more than a legal status, the dominance of the ideology of the transnational rule-of-law polity demands that some emphasis be placed on observing the gradual accretion (or diminution) of formal legal rights guaranteed by judges and courts at the national and EU levels. These observations about democracy, polity formation, and law will shape many of the comments made in the next two subsections of this chapter. But above all, as the last subsection of this part will show, IGCs and new treaties are only part of the overall picture of the European polity-in-the-making, and this is highly relevant to the constitution of the citizen, not only as a figure in IGCs and treaties, but also in the day-to-day practice of EU governance.

Governance and the EU: The Hard Legal Core and the Soft Political Contours

To use a description of the EU as an emergent non-state, a transnational polity-in-the-making, or a multilevel supranational governance system as a starting point for analysis could, of course, be said to beg the question of precisely what is being studied. Equally, it could be regarded as a virtue, in that it makes no *a priori* assumptions about the nature of the EU, avoiding descriptions by reference to misleading specified categories such as the (nation) state, the federation or even the international organization. Moreover, it emphasizes the point that the key issue is to identify *how* we are studying the governance process in the

EU, not *what* we are studying when we examine governance issues. The study of governance in the EU, therefore, is a constructive rather than a deductive process. It is also a multifaceted process, since EU governance, like the EU polity itself, is not a unitary phenomenon. In certain respects, the policy-making process *is* a principally intergovernmental exercise. In other cases, it lies largely in the hands of the relatively autonomous supranational institutions. In yet other instances, what Weiler has described as the characteristic of infranationalism holds, where the dominant governance mechanism is the 'committee' ruled by experts and 'faceless bureaucrats' (see for example Weiler 1997*a*, and Neyer, Chapter 7). In each case, the study of governance faces different challenges, and a single theory of how the EU works and why it changes seems to elude articulation.

Methodologically, there have been deep cleavages between legal and political approaches to the EU (Wincott 1995*b*). Legal scholarship on the EU is often criticized because it favours a rule-bound conception of the 'progress' of integration over an understanding of the underlying political or economic dynamics (Caporaso 1996). In similar terms—positing a continued and essentialist separation of the two lines of argument—Bellamy and Castiglione (1997: 444) have recently argued that legal means and institutions must be subordinated to political practices of mediation and reconciliation, 'for democratic deliberation has a capacity that legal mechanisms lack to build new allegiance and identities, and to negotiate workable compromises when a consensus on new forms of common life cannot be achieved'.

Yet, as Obradovic (1996) has shown, far from the legal nature of the EU needing to be seen as somehow separate from the EU's political development, it is in fact one of the key building blocks of the 'Community of law'—the 'rule-of-law bargain' promoted by the ECJ—which has become central to the projection of what limited legitimacy the Union can in fact claim. Indeed, the project of 'government under law', as well as the conferring of rights on individuals, has almost become a fetish in the EU context, perhaps because of the prominent position which the ECJ was able to take in the early years of the Community with its rule of law discourse.[3] Burley and Mattli (1993: 44) have argued convincingly about the role of law as a mask for politics. I would argue that the member states are sensitive to these issues. Over the course of a number of IGCs, it is notable that they have eschewed most opportunities to interfere directly with that rule-of-law bargain, or to undermine in any significant way the claimed authority of the ECJ in its constitutionalization of the treaty and of individuals as the subjects of EC law. The hard legal core locks the member states in in a manner which offers a guarantee of reciprocity on a dyadic or contractarian model, and which suggests the presence of favourable conditions for a process of judicialization and triadic dispute resolution (Stone Sweet forthcoming; Stone Sweet and Brunell 1998). Even so, some of the

---

[3] The best example is Case 294/83 *Parti Écologiste 'Les Verts'* v. *Parliament* [1986] ECR 1339.

apparent certainties of the EC law/national law relationship from the early years of the Community legal order have themselves been 'softened' through the Court's increased sensitivity to national regulatory competences, and perhaps the influence of the principle of subsidiarity (Armstrong 1998). In the context of market regulation, the ECJ has developed a more nuanced principle of pre-emption in determining the extent to which EU measures displace national measures, matching also the legislative tendency to allow a greater degree of national regulatory discretion and freedom (Weatherill 1994).

Equally, the principle of limited powers (Article 5 [3b] EC)[4] simultaneously empowers and constrains the EC/EU, guaranteeing the legal status of Community competence, but purporting to mark its outer contours. The conventional wisdom in the past has been that the ECJ has played fast and loose with the boundaries of Community competence. This is a charge which is barely sustainable in the light of two recent Opinions of the Court on external trade competence and the conclusion of the GATT (General Agreement on Tariffs and Trade) Uruguay Round, and on the possibilities of acceding to the European Convention on Human Rights, where the Court sharply marked out the boundaries of what the Community institutions can do.[5] An IGC and treaty amendments would be needed to effect the necessary changes in the scope of Community competence. Moreover, the interpretation of powers in the political domain itself has not always been entirely strict, as the example of the early anticipation of the ratification of the Treaty of Amsterdam at the Luxembourg Employment Summit of November 1997 shows quite neatly. For the purposes of constructing a supranational employment policy, the member states were prepared to treat the Treaty of Amsterdam as if it were already ratified, and to 'apply' these new provisions (although formally 'old' powers needed to be found to undertake the 'new' tasks). The point precisely highlights how much of the development of the EU governance structure is about ongoing negotiations and interdependencies between political and legal constraints and possibilities.

Democracy: A Normative and Practical Challenge

Just as the EU escapes easy categorization by reference to established types of political entity, so there are no simple 'quick-fixes' to the pressing conceptual and practical challenges of envisioning democracy within the EU. Let us assume that democracy is a worthy goal, whether as an end in itself or as a means towards promoting human virtue and decency. If that is so, then Curtin (1996) is correct in saying that the EU remains 'in search of a political philosophy' with the help of which the democracy gap, which appears when powers

---

[4] The numbers used for treaty provisions are those in the consolidated texts; the numbers appearing in the square brackets are the pre-consolidation numbers.

[5] Opinion 1/94 [1994] ECR I-5267; Opinion 2/94 [1996] ECR I-1759.

are shifted from one (national) forum to another (the supranational), may be at least partially closed (see also Chapters 6 and 8). But to return to the constitution of the citizen in Article 17 [8] *et seq*. EC: it is very relevant to this conundrum that these provisions provide no real guidance (*pace* complaints to the Ombudsman and petitions to the EP) as to the nature of the relationship between the EU as a political authority and 'its' citizens as a political community, which would be an essential substratum to a debate about democracy.

Not surprisingly, no clear solutions to the democracy challenge are as yet visible, but the outcome is very unlikely to be the straightforward reapplication at the supranational level of a single variant of liberal/representative, republican/deliberative, communitarian, or even associative approaches to democracy. This is precisely a field in which the statist paradigm risks limiting the institutional imagination of those responsible for constitutional design. The supreme irony of the crisis of democracy at EU level—and indeed what might be anticipated to be impending crises of a not dissimilar, but less acute, nature which will arise in the not too distant future as other trade-relations organizations of a regional or multilateral nature, such as the North American Free Trade Area (NAFTA) and the World Trade Organization (WTO), acquire the capacity to challenge the regulatory autonomy of nation states through trade liberalization—is that it comes at precisely the same time that the global spread of democracy (if not always in its classic 'liberal' guise) at nation state level has seemed most assured. But it is important to remember that the problem of democracy at EU level is not simply a single-stranded EU problem. It is a problem with multiple strands, evident within the individual member states, as well as a challenge to intergovernmental relations more generally. Resolutions of the democracy conundrum must therefore respond to the multilevelled, multifaceted, and continually changing nature of governance in the EU.

Governance: An Ongoing Scenario

IGCs, the debates which feed into and off them, and their primary outputs (in the form of new treaties), are moments of high political and legal importance, not to say drama, in the life of the EU. Changes to the treaty framework may institute or formalize new types of relationships between old and new actors (e.g. the insertion of the European Council into the institutional system by the TEU), or disrupt old relationships based on previous provisions, or convention and practice evolved over several years. After the conclusion of new treaties, the ratification process offers the one moment when *some* electorates are given the opportunity to express themselves directly upon the acceptability or otherwise of the integration process. Such (limited) possibilities for citizen 'participation' in the act of treaty-making are themselves constitutive of citizenship in its Union context (Wiener and della Sala 1997), along with pressure group or similar activities which seek to make the agenda-setting stage for an IGC less of an intergovernmental or institution-dominated affair.

Overall, the significance of IGCs, understood as constitutionally defining moments for all parties involved, should not be overstated. As Caporaso (1996: 30) comments: 'Viewed from a long-term perspective, the 1996 conference is likely to be but one punctuation mark in a long, meandering, often messy process of political change'. The tendency is to assume that IGCs and treaties give the member states the invariable 'last say' (Dahl 1956: 38, quoted in Chryssochoou 1997: 522). Is it in fact the case that, through intergovernmental conferences and new treaty provisions, the member states recapture and redirect the integration process? Or rather, is it that the new ongoing rhythm of conferences and amendments visible throughout the 1990s, where one IGC led onto the next, has allowed the institutions, which are the real repeat players in the context of European integration, to 'capture' and 'direct' the will of the member states?

IGCs occur alongside the ongoing and routinized governance processes of the EU. The management of the internal market, the customs union, and the common agricultural policy does not cease during an IGC. Treaties, once ratified, escape the exclusive control of the member states. One notable feature of the legal development of the Union has been the dramatic expansions or changes in meaning resulting from interpretations placed on individual treaty provisions such as Article 28 [30] EC (on non-tariff barriers to trade) or Article 141 [119] EC (on equal pay for equal work) by the ECJ, in particular changes which have resulted in conferring 'new' legal rights on individuals as subjects of law. These developments—once seen as revolutionary—have now been absorbed into the overall legal *acquis* of the Union. New legal powers agreed in a treaty lead into a legislative process where those powers may or may not be exercised, and where the precise substantive outcomes cannot be predicted by reference to the contents of the treaty or the *travaux préparatoires* of the IGC alone. Treaty powers have to be managed, and the Council of the EU, comprising the representatives of the member states, is just one of the institutions involved in the management process. Hence, while the focus of the second part of this chapter is on changes instituted by the Treaty of Amsterdam which are significant from the perspective of the constitution of the citizen at EU level, it takes 'Amsterdam in context' as its primary point of reference.

Studying a Constitutional Settlement

Constitutional development can be seen as a conventional response to problems of human organization and disorganization, and the study of the constitution need not necessarily presuppose the type of political entity which is being settled. We can study the basic rules of the game, understood in a more formalistic or procedural sense, which tells us most of what we need to know about *how* things happen, but very little about *why* or *what for*. In the next part of this chapter, we will look to see whether the Treaty of Amsterdam does in fact tell us rather more about the *why*, even though in many respects it continues a trend in such EU treaty instruments of concentrating on the *how*.

Much of the history of constitutionalism in the EU so far has been marked by two key features. First, it has been predominantly a form of 'top-down' constitutionalism, driven by institutions, governments, and states rather than citizens; and second, it was dominated in the early years by the discourse of the ECJ. The first big 'constitutional' debate concerned the relationship between EC law and national law, and the establishment of the crucial characteristics of EC law (notwithstanding the absence of any relevant provisions in the treaty), whereby EC law is considered—by the ECJ at least—to be both part of national law, and also a superior source of law, even *vis-à-vis* national constitutions. The Court established the basic principle that individuals may derive rights from EC law which national authorities and courts must respect, and it has since buttressed that conclusion by finding, for example, that there is a general principle of state liability under which member states can be required to make good any loss caused by their failure to observe their Community obligations. This form of constitutionalization of the treaty, if not of the polity, remains one of the Court's most important contributions to the development of the EU overall, but as a rules-based conclusion it tells us little or nothing about what the rules are *for* (Armstrong 1998), other than the self-evident objective of securing and strengthening the authority of EC law, which is not necessarily co-terminous with the political authority of the EC/EU as a whole. On the contrary, the work of the Court needs precisely to be read in the context of the market-building activities of the EU as a whole—including the Commission and the Council—before it becomes more understandable.

Top-down constitutionalism continues to be the *leitmotiv* of EU polity-formation, but it is hampered by the limited extent to which such processes can in fact deliver meaningful statements about the type of society that 'Europeans want', and the type of political community which would engage their involvement. And yet the elements of 'bottom-up' constitutionalism in the Amsterdam process are also extremely weak. In themselves, they represent a decisive change from previous IGCs, with a 'louder' noise being made by a number of organizations purporting to represent the interests of vulnerable and not so vulnerable groups, and the more diffuse interests of civil society and citizens generally. While the democratic credentials of many such groups are unlikely to stand up to close scrutiny, they remain a vital surrogate for the expression of citizen interests in any imperfectly organized political community. They represent a continual reminder that supranational institutions and supranational legal and political authority will inevitably have a substantive content. If treaties themselves pay little or no attention to issues of content, then that will be delivered by some other means, such as through the legislative process or executive decision-making—the 'constitutional' credentials of which may be even more tenuous than the treaty-making process involving the governments, the institutions, and the national ratification procedures. The second part of this chapter argues that a greater (if still rather slight) degree of attention to issues of content is evident in the Treaty of Amsterdam, and the events and debates which surround it; moreover, changes which posit the citizen as a constitutional entity within the treaty—but one which escapes the bounds of national-type classifications—and as an increasingly active participant in an embryonic transnational civil society, are the key elements within this shift. The key shifts in the ongoing European integration process emerge out of the tensions between these elements of top-down institutional design and bottom-up struggles and claim-making.

Reading the Amsterdam Constitutional Settlement

The discussion which follows picks out just four aspects of the constitutional settlement agreed at Amsterdam—flexibility and differentiated integration; the complementarity of Union citizenship; modelling a thicker form of EU citizenship; and the rights deficit/surplus—and discusses them in the light of the five assumptions exposed above. It makes no claim to be comprehensive, or to represent a rational choice of issues. It does not discuss, for example, the shift towards a greater degree of bi-cameralism in the legislative process, which lies behind the widespread removal of the cooperation procedure from the treaty and its substitution with co-decision, even though this is clearly relevant to the development of internal EU conceptions of democracy and therefore citizenship.

Flexibility and Differentiated Integration

The relevance of the flexibility debate and the 'closer cooperation' provisions for the constitution of the citizen in the EU might not seem immediately apparent. It lies, in fact, in the close link between the conception of citizenship and the rule-of-law bargain based on the authority of the legal order which sustains much of the EU's claim to legitimacy at the present time, and thus feeds on the assumptions about the hard legal core of the EU. The Domesday scenario highlighted by those in favour of preserving the current degree of uniformity, and who therefore oppose the introduction of the 'canker' of flexibility into the constitutional framework of the EU, suggests that it will destroy the unity of the Community legal order. Philip Allott (1997)—with a different agenda—

opposes the complexity and impenetrability of the new treaty with a rather apocalyptic vision:

> The Amsterdam Treaty will mean the co-existence of dozens of different legal and economic sub-systems over the next ten years, a sort of nightmare resurrection of the Holy Roman empire . . .

This vision can be contrasted with one based on the core of the rule-of-law bargain, positing a unitary and authoritative Community legal order based on a single organizing principle for the legal domain, under which state legal orders have become subsidiary, notwithstanding their claim to be authoritative according to the conventional rubric of the international system of states and the dictates of (national) sovereignty. Of course, problems exist here as well (Walker 1998), since the EC was always in reality a two-dimensional, not a one-dimensional system (there remain Community and national legal orders). There are extensive boundary problems and many of the mechanisms for resolving these or for bridging the gaps—the doctrines of supremacy, pre-emption and effective remedies—all tend in one direction, namely that of reinforcing the authority of EC law. Yet in systemic terms, the Community and national legal orders may simply be irreconcilable, each claiming supreme authority according to paradigms of legal theory that recognize one-dimensional orders alone (Eleftheriadis 1998), although versions of legal pluralism suggest that the problem may be more about the nature of law than about the implications of a systemic conflict (MacCormick 1995). Consequently, there is no simple answer when a national constitutional court claims, as the German Federal Constitutional Court has done since its 1994 decision on the Maastricht Treaty[6] that, notwithstanding the way in which the ECJ has constituted itself in relation to national courts and national legal orders, as well as the Community legal order, it has in fact no 'Kompetenz-Kompetenz' to declare authoritatively the limits of its own jurisdiction. The resolution of difficulties has previously lain largely in a willingness, mainly on the part of national courts, to pull back before taking the final step which might destroy the convention of national court acceptance of the ECJ itself together with its dictates on the nature of EC law.

It is an interesting move in legal scholarship to link the development of a 'flexible Europe' in terms of 'circles of integration' to the vertical reach of EC law and its relationship to national law. But as Walker (1998) has shown, the problems arising from boundary disputes in the event of multi-dimensional orders arising in the context of differentiated integration and multiple systems of closer cooperation under the Treaty of Amsterdam are potentially much greater.[7] Referring to the threat of 'fearsome legal complexity'[8] in the

---

[6] *Brunner* [1994] 1 CMLR 57. See also the decision of the Danish Supreme Court on the constitutionality of Denmark's transfer of powers to the European Community, 6 April 1998.

[7] See also the detailed discussion of the possibilities for flexibility in Ch. 9.

[8] This is a reference to Weatherill (1995: 178).

management of the Social Policy Agreement incorporating the United Kingdom's opt-out from post-Maastricht social policy-making, a threat which never in fact materialized, Walker (1998) argues that, under enhanced differentiation

> The development of adequate bridging mechanisms presupposes forward regulatory planning and a willingness to devise and apply these mechanisms in a spirit of mutual accommodation . . . these qualities are likely to be in less plentiful supply than they have been in two-dimensional Europe.
>
> In suggesting that the day-to-day mutual articulation of legal orders would be less manageable, these considerations also imply that fundamental boundary disputes would be more likely to break out under a three-dimensional configuration of authority.

I would suggest, therefore, that it is no more theoretically difficult to imagine the citizenship of such multiple polities than it is to envision the dual arrangements between the individual nation states and the EU currently emerging in relation to citizenship and national sovereignty. But the practical problems, as these comments show, are likely to be immense.

In assessing the measures adopted at Amsterdam, it seems important to draw a clear distinction between, on the one hand, the organizing principles governing the idea of future closer cooperation under the first pillar, and the arrangements for free movement and Schengen on the other, which are both legally more complex and politically more expedient. Under the first pillar, the combination of Articles 43–45 [K.15–17] TEU and Article 11 [5a] EC not only appears to restrict the practical utility of the enabling provisions, but also to impose a strong and disciplining central core of constitutional principles which must be observed. One of the so-called 'commandments' governing such future flexibility is that it should not 'concern citizenship of the Union' (Article 11(1)(c) [5a(1)(c)] EC).[9] The unity of the order is preserved by making differentiated integration legally possible, but constitutionally limited and practically virtually unimaginable. However, the constitutional debate on flexibility may also be about opening up new political agendas (Shaw 1998b). In deciding on the pre-emptive early application of the new Amsterdam employment provisions, the member states also opened the agenda for new claims for flexibility, in relation to 'targets' on reducing unemployment. While the guidelines eventually adopted by the Council[10] ascribed flexibility to all of the member states, in terms of using their respective starting points as the basis for calculating a reduction in unemployment, press reports ahead of and after the Employment Summit of November 1997 itself were dominated by claims for flexible treat-

---

[9] It is probably correct to assume that this means 'citizenship' in the narrow legalistic sense defined by the scope of Art. 17 [8] *et seq.* EC.

[10] Resolution of the Council on the 1998 Employment Guidelines, OJ 1998 C 30/1.

ment, particularly from Germany and Spain, who were both facing particularly high levels of unemployment.[11]

In contrast to the first pillar enabling provisions, the arrangements agreed for Britain, Ireland, and Denmark in relation to the partial communitarization of the third pillar and the incorporation of the Schengen *acquis* into the Union and Community systems are quite different, and in themselves do not appear to satisfy the requirements laid down for future flexibility. These arrangements, based on a combination of political expediency and some geographical rationality applying very differently to the two cases of Britain and Ireland on the one hand, and Denmark on the other, come close to a system of pick-and-choose. Coupled with the incomplete structures provided for both democratic scrutiny and accountability of executives, the insufficient provision for transparency and restricted possibilities for independent and accessible judicial review at the instance of citizens, non-citizens, and even institutions and states, the creation of a complex set of overlapping legal orders seems inimical to the development of even a 'thin' constitutional framework for civil liberties for citizens with adequate protection against the arbitrary exercise of power. In that context, a 'thick' conception of active citizenship in relation to the crucial issue of borders seems thus far a chimera. It also leaves as yet untouched one crucial political challenge for Union citizenship, namely, the resolution of the legal position of lawfully resident third country nationals, who are implicated in the economic project of European integration, but appear to be largely excluded from the political and socio-cultural projects.

Citizenship Amsterdam-style: The Complementarity of Union Citizenship

The Treaty of Amsterdam introduces a small textual amendment to Article 17(1) [8(1)] EC. A new sentence is added, as follows

> Citizenship of the Union shall complement and not replace national citizenship.

It would be possible to dismiss this change as simply codifying or consolidating the previous legal position. This very point was made explicitly for the Danes in the aftermath of the first Danish referendum on the Treaty of Maastricht in the Edinburgh Summit communiqué. On that reading, the formal change in the Treaty of Amsterdam is no more than the continuation of the time-honoured practice of legal formality catching up with political reality. It is also possible to interpret the insertion of this new sentence as the member states recalling a vision of the EU as (only) a union of nations, and as a

---

[11] See James (1997); Bremner and Pierce (1997); European Report No. 2269, 19 November 1997; European Report No. 2270, 22 November 1997.

reassertion of national sovereignty in relation to the citizenship question by claiming a crucial power of definition.

It has not been seriously suggested in either academic or popular literature that EU citizenship in fact replaces national citizenship. The issue of 'complementarity' is, however, more complex. The constitutional settlement of the EU does not take place in isolation. Once inserted into the Treaties, provisions elude the tight control of the member states, and can take on their own institutionally defined logic and meaning. At the conclusion of an IGC, the doors open to a much wider interpretative community, comprising the EU institutions, national governments and other public bodies, judicial institutions at a variety of levels, social movements and interest groups, and even the wider 'European' electorate and public opinion. The interventions of members of that community validate a more contextual approach to EU citizenship, which steps outside the constraints of the formal treaty-based figure. The Treaty of Amsterdam has also been agreed in a broader context of the transformation of the nation state, for reasons that are not solely related to the European integration process, but also have to do with internal and external pressures of a socio-economic and cultural nature. It must be correct to assume that national citizenship is changing as well, although that is not to say that, as a cypher or signifer of national identity, it is necessarily diminished. But that still begs the question: if Union citizenship is indeed complementing national citizenships, then precisely what job(s) is it doing? Complementarity does not assume unchanged national citizenships.

To this end, what is still needed is a fuller political theory of Union citizenship as a form of post-national membership, and to construct such a theory we must look elsewhere in the Treaties and at other contextualizing materials. Other innovations within and around the new Treaty suggest that such a theory must contain both 'thin' and 'thick' elements to provide the glue for a political community of 'Europeans'. But by confirming its complementary nature, the member states are also reinforcing both the quality of Union citizenship as an open-textured concept, and also precisely the transformatory capacity which they may have thought they were closing off. That might then open the door to creative interpretation or application by the ECJ or even the Commission. The following discussion of the area of freedom, security and justice, and the notion of the European social model is intended precisely to put some flesh on these bare bones, by building schematic models for understanding a thicker form of EU citizenship.

Modelling a Thicker Form of EU Citizenship

I have already suggested that Amsterdam signals a gradual shift towards a more content-oriented model of the EU as a transnational political entity. The nature of that content, I would argue, remains highly ambiguous and substantially unsettled. Some argue that this treaty reveals a general social democratic tendency (e.g. see Pollack, Chapter 14). The provisions on employment also seem to suggest an embryonic engagement with the contrasts between Rhineland or regulated capitalism on the one hand, and Anglo-American market capitalism on the other, in relation to the key issue of flexibility and labour market management. In relation to citizenship, two clear models are evident in the Amsterdam Treaty and in materials submitted during the antecedent negotiations. I shall briefly examine these models, and consider the extent to which they are competing alternatives or complementary elements of an emergent thicker form of EU citizenship.

The models I examine in this section concern the shaping of citizenship along 'social' or 'civil' lines: the so-called 'European social model' or 'European model of society', details of which can be drawn from the Commission's policy initiatives in the citizenship and social policy spheres, as well as its Opinions on the issue of possible amendments to the Union treaties put before the IGC (Commission 1995a, 1996a); and the concept of an 'area of freedom, security and justice' which underpinned the draft amendments to the current Treaties put forward by the Irish Presidency in December 1996,[12] and which finds clear expression in the revised Treaties. As an idea, it also originated in the Commission, specifically in the IGC Task Force.

The 'area of freedom, security and justice' encapsulates provisions on fundamental rights and non-discrimination, free movement of persons, asylum and immigration, and the safety and security of persons. The invocation of 'security' comes close to, but falls just short of, Karl Deutsch's notion of a 'security community', understood as a zone dominated by a converegence of basic values such as those of the rule of law and human rights, as well as the renunciation of violence as a means of resolving conflicts (Deutsch 1957). The use of the word 'area' is notable: this is not a 'community', with all the important historical associations which that term now has within the EC/EU (Weiler 1994). It is an inadequate rendering into English of the more evocative French term *espace*, which has previously been used informally in contexts such as *l'espace sociale européenne*. It is also to be an 'area' for the reason that the issues addressed cut across the existing first and third pillars of the Union, and are thus subject partly to the Community method, and partly to a variant of the intergovernmental method. This will remain the case even after the partial 'communitarization' of the third pillar, as the field of police cooperation and judicial cooperation in criminal matters remains outside the first pillar. On ratification of the Treaty of Amsterdam, the 'area' became a Union objective, under Article 2 [B] TEU.

The idea of organizing this Title and the other elements of the area, particularly the provisions on non-discrimination and on fundamental rights and liberal democracy (the latter as a general principle, not in itself bringing about

---

[12] 'The European Union Today and Tomorrow. Adapting the European Union for the benefit of its peoples and preparing it for the future', Dublin II, CONF. 2500/96, 5 December 1996.

any fundamental change in the interinstitutional balance or enhancement of the formal or social legitimacy of the Union's institutional structure), is perhaps to lend some intellectual and political coherence to a number of highly controversial aspects of the development of the outer limits of the Union's competence. Among the new provisions are procedures allowing for action to be taken against member states for persistent breaches of fundamental rights—seen as essential in the light of the projected arrival of new members from Central and Eastern Europe—and measures to ensure that individuals have adequate protection of personal data in relation to the institutions. In other words, it is a diverse *pot pourri* of issues.

It is worth reflecting in more detail on what this area means since, as a political initiative, it displays a sure grasp of craft, providing just a small degree of ambiguity about the issues of 'whose freedom?', 'whose security?', and 'justice for whom?'. Lying behind the proposal for a new Title III [Title IIIa] of Part Three of the EC Treaty on 'visa, asylum, immigration and other policies related to free movement of persons' was dissatisfaction with the operation of the provisions of the third pillar on Cooperation in Justice and Home Affairs, and the issue of border disputes between the scope of the first and third pillars, particularly in relation to issues of free movement. The new Title should, in the medium term, offer a greater degree of consistency of approach. The successful completion of a single travel area may substantially improve the status of third country nationals.

Another reading of the area of freedom, security and justice evokes a vision of a liberal 'freedom-from' polity. It is closely linked to the negative freedom-oriented dimension of the market ideology of the Union, under which Union citizenship is a minimal framework of protections against member state interference in private economic activities, and so derives force from the limited market citizen of the Union's market-building vocation. This seems to suggest a minimally 'thin' conception of self-interest holding together the political community of EU citizens (freedom and the rule of law). That is not the only message it delivers, however; the identity of the citizen is also constructed through the 'other', the foreigner who needs to be excluded or at least controlled to make the citizen 'secure'. This is a different type of exclusionary 'thickness'. The 'security-oriented' vision of the area of freedom, security and justice inevitably feeds the profound disquiet on civil liberties grounds, which has long been held in some quarters, about the implications of the secretive third pillar and Schengen operations. Chalmers (1998) suggests, for example, that the project of making the Union secure comprises a strong element of population control. It is not a project of empowerment, regardless of the rhetoric of freedom, security, and justice; at best, it is a project for greater institutional efficiency. Moreover, the bringing of the Schengen *acquis* within the Community framework has not suddenly wiped out its deep-rooted undemocratic heritage. Overall, much of what constitutes the 'area' will remain primarily under member state control, with intergovernmental methods and limited democratic control at EU or national level, and limited possibilities for judicial review (den Boer 1997).

The area of freedom, security and justice, therefore, delivers a mixed message about developing a 'thicker' form of Union citizenship and political community. The notion of a European Social Model, on the other hand, provides a sharp contrast. In its Work Programme for 1997, the Commission summarized how it views the general outlines of the 'citizen dimension' of the Union

> The single currency and the single market are by no means objectives in their own right but instruments intended to serve the needs of the population as a whole and the overriding goal of employment in particular. However, the Commission wants to go further still and build a Europe of solidarity with a human face faithful to its own model of society and closer to each individual's concerns.   (Commission 1996b)

The notion of a European social model also emerged as a powerful part of Commission IGC rhetoric, and it can be traced back through a number of generations of Commission documents. A good starting point for this analysis is the 1994 (Flynn) White Paper on social policy (Commission 1994; see also Commission 1993a), although a longer-term perspective on this aspect of Commission policy-making would undoubtedly stretch back to the Community Charter on Fundamental Social Rights for Workers (adopted in December 1989 at Strasbourg), and beyond to the debates on the emergent social dimension of the internal market held during the late 1980s. The general frame now used by the Commission for its discussion of social policy is this notion of a 'European social model', which is intended to suggest the essential elements of the 'sort of society' which Europeans 'want'. The Commission's model is shaped around certain shared values which it claims to have identified

> These include democracy and individual rights, free collective bargaining, the market economy, equality of opportunity for all and social welfare and solidarity. These values . . . are held together by the conviction that economic and social progress must go hand in hand. Competitiveness and solidarity have both to be taken into account in building a successful Europe for the future.   (Commission 1994: para. 3)

A clear echo of this statement is to be found in the Commission's Opinion to the IGC (Commission 1996a: para. 8). It asserts that

> Europe is built on a set of values shared by all its societies, and combines the characteristics of democracy—human rights and institutions based on the rule of law—with those of an open economy underpinned by market forces, internal solidarity and cohesion. These values include the access for all members of society to universal services or to services of general benefit, thus contributing to solidarity and equal benefit.

The point is reiterated in the conclusion (Commission 1996*a*: para. 47)

> The Conference should be the occasion . . . to demonstrate that the Union has clear objectives and the instruments to achieve them: that Europe—united in its diversity—is prepared to uphold and develop its model of society and to make growth and competitiveness work for a social and cultural ideal. . . .

Caitríona Carter (1997) has shown that the European Social Model is an attempt to appeal—as a slogan—to elements of commonality, and that this appeal comprises three key facets: a system of industrial relations based on collective bargaining; the framework of a welfare state system of social protection; and principles of social partnership and consensus underlying decision-making about the allocation of resources and public goods, and the creation of employment. It might also be a defensive turn: this 'appeal to Europe' is the result of a failure to maintain precisely this model at national level in the face of global competitiveness and a disintegrating taxation base with which to fund an ever-growing set of public welfare payments to an ageing population. That which is no longer capable of maintenance in practice at a national level can still be asserted in abstract terms at the level of the EU.

It follows that the extent to which the principles of a European social model are in reality in the process of being achieved, either through a European social policy outside the Treaty or in the Treaty itself, is very doubtful. Furthermore, even though all such statements are articulated at a level of considerable generality, the notion of a 'social model' for Europe is likely always to be controversial, given the extent to which social policy has been used as an arena for national politics, and the use which many member states have often made in this context of discourses of sovereignty rather than those of solidarity (Whiteford 1995; Lange 1992). The controversy over the model becomes clearer the closer it moves towards sensitive issues, such as the role of collective bargaining, redistribution and the provision of public goods such as welfare. As Carter has shown, it is the crisis in the 'social bargain' which underlay the original treaties (market integration at EC level, market-correcting welfare at national level) which raises the stakes for a European social policy responding to the ever-increasing inability of nation states under pressure from globalization and economic integration to deliver such welfare policies (Carter 1997; Leibfried and Pierson 1995). It is not the case, as some critics of European social policy progress have argued, that the 'failures' of this policy are failures to follow a preordained path towards a more federalist-type social policy, the inevitable consequence of which is the transfer of market-correcting welfare policies to the supranational level.

Despite such necessary scepticism, it is still possible to see a number of echoes of the 'European social model' in those parts of the Treaty of Amsterdam dealing with social and related policies. Important initiatives or events outside the conference meeting rooms provided crucial triggers for many of the changes. The British general election of May 1997 and the consequent change of government led directly to the United Kingdom agreeing, outside the Treaty framework, to the non-binding Community Social Charter of 1989. Following on naturally from this was agreement on reincorporating the so-called Social Chapter back into the mainstream of the treaty, and the consequent amendments to the EU social provisions (Articles 136–45 [117–22] EC). A similar analysis applies to the emerging Employment Policy, a field where progress towards European social policy goals has taken place to a large extent outside the framework provided by intergovernmental conferences. The Commission President, Jacques Santer, chose to make employment his '*grand projet mobilisateur*', and pressed for concrete responses to the 1993 (Delors) White Paper on 'Growth, Competitiveness, Employment: the Challenges and Ways Forward into the 21st Century' (Commission 1993*b*) and the Essen European Council declarations of 1994 on employment. Notably, the Commission persuaded the Social Affairs Ministers to adopt its proposal for a Committee on Employment and the Labour Market, without waiting for the conclusion of the Amsterdam negotiations, where such a committee was already on the agenda. From the time of the Dublin draft treaties onwards, there appears to have been reasonably widespread agreement across the member states on the desirability of including some sort of new title on employment in the treaties—even if its contents were still not the subject of agreement.

All of these initiatives and more appeared in a section of the draft treaties headed 'The Union and the citizen'[13] although, as with the area of freedom, security and justice, the process of 'tidying up' the drafts undertaken by lawyers and linguists prior to signature has undermined much of the conceptual simplicity of the original political texts. Provisions are now scattered as amendments or amplifications across the original Treaties, and it is only in non-binding explanatory instruments such as the 'Descriptive Summary' appearing on the Council website that we can still see the traces of the original organizing concepts.[14]

At one level, therefore, the European Social Model offers a different vision of 'thick' Union citizenship, based perhaps on the possibilities, however tenuous, of solidarity in the face of the challenges of globalization, competitiveness, and the dissipation of the solidity of the welfare state. Unlike the area of freedom, security and justice, it evokes the 'freedom to' polity, as well as securing the role of the supranational method against intergovernmental

---

[13] The focus of this chapter precludes the discussion here of provisions on the environment, public health, and subsidiarity—part of the *pot pourri* of changes under the heading 'The Union and the Citizen'.

[14] See: http://ue.eu.int/Amsterdam/en/treaty/main.htm: 'This summary is for information purposes only in order to provide an easily understandable overview of the content of the new Treaty; . . . [it] does not form part of the outcome of the conference, is not relevant to the process of ratification, and does not commit the Presidency or any Member State government or have any legal relevance'.

interests. But it is perhaps more than just a different vision imposed or proposed from 'above', and indeed more than just a defensive manoeuvre. This is apparent if one draws in other contextualizing material, especially the report of the (independent) *Comité des Sages*, established under the Commission's 1995 Social Action Programme (Commission 1995b) to examine what might become of the 1989 Community Social Charter, in the context of the review of the Treaty of Maastricht in 1996–7. This material also suggests a link between the thicker substantive concept and the means or process whereby it might be attained, through a form of bottom-up constitutionalism.

The Committee's report of early 1996 put a number of options of varying degrees of originality onto the negotiating table. It linked social policy and identity through 'a renewed, original social model' along very similar lines to the Commission's own proposals, and made a number of proposals on the incorporation of fundamental civic and social rights into the Treaties. Some rights, it maintained, should be incorporated immediately, including a general right to non-discrimination, and the right to a minimum income for those who cannot find paid work and have no other source of income. Other rights of an essentially aspirational nature might be included, in the form of objectives to be achieved (e.g. the right to education, the right to work, the right to health and safety at work). The Committee also called for the initiation of an important constitutional process, involving a bottom-up constitutional debate. It called for the inclusion of an article in the new Treaty

> . . . to set in motion a wide-ranging, democratic process of compiling, at Union level, a full list of civic and social rights and duties. Initiated by the European Parliament, on a proposal from the Commission, this process, which must closely involve the national parliaments and which would require input both from the traditional social partners and from non-governmental organizations, should culminate in a new IGC within five years' time. (*Comité* 1996: 10)

These are proposals—yet to be adopted in a formal sense—for the future of constitution-building in the Union. In certain small ways they have already been set in motion, as a result, largely, of informal bottom-up pressure. As was already noted, more than ever before, a wide range of national and Union-level organizations operating in the very broad social policy sphere sought to influence the IGC agenda, often by sending in 'shopping lists' of the 'more-rights-for-citizens' nature. The Commission brought together many NGOs, for example, by holding meetings at national level to allow them to discuss the *Comité des Sages* proposals.[15] Such events have opened up a new and more important partnership role for a range of new collective players from the

---

[15] For example, a meeting on 'Basic Needs, Basic Rights' was held in Birmingham on 3 March 1997.

voluntary sector and the public services, alongside the more 'traditional' social partners (the so-called 'third sector').

These developments are of particular interest from the perspective of the evolution of Union citizenship, beyond the possibility that the substantive (and procedural) agendas of the IGC may have been changed by these inputs. This is an important and dynamic example of active social citizenship exercised through collective representation processes, which could be taken much further if the *Comité des Sages* proposals were taken up. In other words, the structural conditions for the emergence of a thicker bond between citizens would be created, although what that bond might be would have to be negotiated. Indeed, it becomes clearer in the light of contextualizing materials, such as the *Comité des Sages* report, that the Commission's adoption of the 'European social model' as an organizing principle probably had as much to do with developing notions of identity and citizenship as with attempts to widen the scope of Community competence for social policy.

The Union after Amsterdam contains elements of both models sketched here. The contrasts between them are strong, but for an embryonic political community of EU citizens it is perhaps important that no avenues of future development are closed off at this stage. Indeed, it is possible that both models may acquire new meaning in the context of the next enlargement to include within the Union states where both 'security' and 'solidarity' have quite con-trasting meanings. I have sketched the two models schematically, in order to emphasize the contrasts between them, rather than any possible middle ground based, for example, on a liberal commitment to the utility of rights. In general, the evidence to be derived from Amsterdam indicates a gradual strengthening of the concern for content over procedure and formal legal status. That shift in itself is probably more important at this stage than the difficult challenge of fixing the boundaries of what it is which binds the community of Union citizens together.

Amsterdam and the Rights Deficit (or Surplus?)

Closely related to the question of the vision of citizenship delivered by the Treaty of Amsterdam is the continuing rights agenda within the EU. It is in fact wrong to suggest that the legitimacy or democracy deficits in the EU can be cured simply by confronting a perceived rights deficit. Most citizens of the EU (as opposed to third country nationals) are not noticeably short on rights as such, *pace* calls for greater protection of the fundamental rights interests of ethnic/racial minority, gay and lesbian, transgendered, and disabled citizens. What are more frequently absent are the mechanisms to ensure that rights which exist in principle are, in fact, effectively enforced, and in the specific EU context, a general lack of awareness about what rights actually exist (Weiler 1997b). The deficit, therefore, is one of effectiveness.

Rights in themselves are unlikely to contribute to the construction of a political community. Their liberal heritage makes them fundamentally individualistic, both in inspiration and in respect of normal methods of enforcement through individual litigation (for a recent discussion, see Fredman 1997). However, rights struggles as opposed to rights themselves can be formative in relation to communities, as the examples of sex discrimination in relation to the EU and gay rights campaigns in many parts of the world have shown (Stychin 1998). Historically, struggles over rights have been one of the core processes helping to establish a link between citizens and governmental institutions in the process of modern state-making (Tilly 1975). But rights struggles can be a double-edged sword: in conceptualizing a claim for recognition in terms of a predetermined legal framework (e.g. trying to push sexual orientation-based claims into a framework designed for sex discrimination), control over issues of definition pass from those bringing the claim to the legal institutions within which it is to be decided (Armstrong 1998; Herman 1994, 1996).

In any event, the advocate of 'more rights' for EU citizens who turned to the Treaty of Amsterdam for support would be largely disappointed by what he or she would find, whether in the domain of civil, social or political rights. The new Treaty makes few concrete changes in the rights status of the subjects of EC law. A guarantee of fundamental rights protection, incorporating also the provisions of the European Convention on Human Rights and Fundamental Freedoms, is formally rendered justiciable before the ECJ, at least so far as pertains to the acts of the institutions.[16] This partially restates (but also significantly understates) the scope of existing ECJ case law on fundamental rights which requires the member states, when implementing EC law, also to act according to the Community doctrine of fundamental rights (Shaw 1997: 188–95). Provisions concerned with sanctions against delinquent member states for persistent breaches of fundamental rights are enshrined in the TEU (Article 7 [F.1] TEU) and they will operate—if they are ever used—essentially at the intergovernmental and interinstitutional level, without reference to the claims or legal status of individual citizens.

Great anticipation preceded the proposal for a non-discrimination provision, but it is in fact a law-making power which was very carefully drafted in order to exclude any possibility of direct effect—although ultimately the choice was made not to state this point specifically in the actual text. The task of crafting a non-discrimination instrument is left to the institutions, assuming the political choice is made to make use of the new power. In fact, the final version of this provision escaped a number of attempts during the course of early 1997 to water down its content and scope. The original proposal provided for a law-making power allowing the Council to act unanimously, on a proposal from the Commission and after consulting the EP, to adopt appropriate measures 'to

---

[16] Art. 46(d) [L(d)] TEU, extending the jurisdiction of the ECJ to Art. 6(2) [F(2)] TEU.

prohibit discrimination based on sex, racial, ethnic or social origin, religious belief, disability, age or sexual orientation'. By February 1997, a retreat appeared to be beginning. In the first drafts of its 'non-papers', the Dutch presidency removed any mention of disability, age, social origin, and sexual orientation from the clause. The presidency commented on ongoing opposition from certain delegations, and asked whether the Conference, instead of a non-discrimination clause for those social categories, could consider addressing their concerns 'in the context of the existing substantive policy provisions (e.g. social policy, education, vocational training and youth (*sic*), public health)'.[17] While many would be sceptical about the practical utility of more rights for citizens in the Union treaties, there can be little doubt about their symbolic importance in creating benchmarks for the treatment of individuals, as well as for the development of state and society. Removing certain categories of discriminatory treatment from the status of 'rights-bearing' would have sent a clear, and unfortunate, message. Consequently, it is of considerable significance that these elements of the original proposal reappeared in later drafts and in the consolidated proposed amendments gathered together by the Dutch presidency,[18] as well as in Article 6a [13] EC when it was finally agreed at the Amsterdam summit. The final text refers to discrimination on grounds of 'sex, racial and ethnic origin, religion or belief, disability, age or sexual orientation'.

In fact, closer inspection of the Amsterdam Treaty reveals that the only field in which individual civil/social rights were actually strengthened was in relation to the already highly developed field of sex discrimination. A second paragraph has been added to Article 3 [3] EC (the activities of the Community) requiring that 'in all the activities referred to in this Article, the Community shall aim to eliminate inequalities, and to promote equality, between men and women'. In this way the policy objective of sex equality has been mainstreamed. A Treaty-based exception to the principle of equal treatment is carved out in a new provision (Article 141(4) [119(4)] EC) allowing member states to maintain or adopt measures 'providing for specific advantages in order to make it easier for the under-represented sex to pursue a vocational activity or to prevent or compensate for disadvantages in professional careers'. This provision has the dual purpose of both reversing an 'unpopular' line of case law heavily restricting national use of positive action measures which the Court appeared to be developing after the *Kalanke* case,[19] and also reinforcing the discretion of the member states in formulating local, regional, or national

---

[17] Non-paper No. 6 'Fundamental Rights and Non-Discrimination', Conference of the Representatives of the Governments of Member States, Secretariat, Brussels, 26 February 1997, CONF/3827/97. (These were made available on the internet, on the Dutch Green Party site, under the auspices of the Dutch Member of the European Parliament (MEP) Nel van Dijk; e-mail: http://www.xs4all.nl~nelvdijk/nonpaper6.html.)

[18] Consolidated Draft Treaty Texts, 30 May 1997, SN 600/97.

[19] Case C-450/93 *Kalanke* v. *Freie Hansestadt Bremen* [1995] ECR I-3051; but see now Case C-409/95 *Marschall* v. *Land Nordrhein-Westfalen* [1997] ECR I-6363, where the Court itself appears to give greater freedom to member states to design their own responses to these societal problems.

responses to problems of systemic sex-based inequalities, often after lengthy and fraught political battles (Barnard and Hervey 1998). It might be argued that the additional developments in relation to sex equality are simply a natural consequence of the existence of legal provisions and interpretative case law, which themselves demanded a response at intergovernmental level. However, they might also signal the strength of the specific lobby on these issues within a number of national governments, the Commission, and the EP.

In the field of political rights, there was some anticipation that the status of the citizen would be enhanced by some sort of 'right' to open government, or at least right to information. Transparency was a debate fanned by the post-Maastricht crisis of legitimacy. In fact, a more specific right of access to Council, Parliament, and Commission documents was established by Article 255 [191a] EC, although subject to both general principles and public and private interest limitation to be laid down by the Council and the Parliament in co-decision, and specific procedures elaborated by each institution in their respective internal Rules of Procedure. This is hardly a charter for freedom of information, or for casting greater light upon what have hitherto been largely secretive negotiating procedures in the Council. 'Openness' as a general idea is consigned to Article 1 [A] TEU, which enshrines a political commitment to take decisions 'as openly as possible'. This seems to signal little change from the pre-Amsterdam position. This had been elaborated by the ECJ and the Court of First Instance in a number of cases,[20] building on Declaration 17 annexed to the Final Act of the Treaty of Maastricht, a Commission/Council interinstitutional agreement of December 1993 taking the form of a code of conduct for those institutions, and, for the Council, amendments to its internal Rules of Procedures and a Decision setting out a procedure for scrutiny of requests and for the taking of decisions. There seems to be a tension between treating transparency as an issue of the institutional economy and as a question of fundamental rights. As Deirdre Curtin (1996: 103) puts it, there is an ongoing dispute about

> ... the legal nature of the principle of freedom of information in the Union context: the Dutch emphasise the fundamental (at least from the perspective of democratic philosophy) nature of the principle and maintain that the primary purpose of the [Council] Decision was to regulate the openness of the administration for third parties. On the other hand, the other members of the Council (with the probable exception of the Danes) are convinced that the Code of Conduct and the Council Decision constitute a simple policy orientation adopted by the Council in the

---

[20] Case T-194/94 *Carvel and the Guardian* v. *Council* [1995] ECR II-2765; Case C-59/94 *Netherlands* v. *Council* [1996] ECR I-2169; Case T-105/97 *WWF (UK)* v. *Commission* [1997] ECR I-313; Case T-124/96 *Interporc Im- und Export GmbH* v. *Commission* [1998] ECR II-23 Case T-83/96 *Van der Wal* v. *Commission* [1998] ECR II-0545.

interests of its own good administration, subject as a matter of course to the other rules of its Rules of Procedure as well as the stringent and discretionary exceptions outlined in the Decision itself.

Kenneth Armstrong (1996: 588) relates this conclusion directly back to the construction of the citizen within the EU political system

> There is . . . a paradox at the heart of the concept of Union citizenship. The concept of citizenship has been invoked as a counterbalance to the seemingly remote institutions of the EU in order to attach political legitimacy to EU governance. However, the essential inter-institutional nature of EU governance has not changed leaving the Union citizen as a rather ambiguous identity within the Union's political and legal systems . . . At no point does John Carvel as a Union citizen ever become constructed in the Court's mind.

Transparency becomes, on this reading, an issue of the institutional economy, not the construction of the citizen.

Conclusion

This chapter has sought to contribute to both the general literature on Union citizenship by offering more evidence of its constructive and contextual nature, and also to the more specific task of understanding and explaining the Treaty of Amsterdam. It has employed methods which take seriously both the legal framework and the political opportunity structure of the EU. It has used a constructive approach to citizenship which goes beyond the identity/rights dichotomy to envision the tensions negotiated through the practice and experience of citizenship, which operates as one of the crucial elements in polity formation. It has suggested that the best way to understand the Treaty of Amsterdam is as the next step in an ongoing process of constitutional settlement, which is gradually moving towards a more substantive conception of the 'European constitution', in which thicker concepts of citizenship are crucial. Above all, it gives a mixed evaluation of the Amsterdam *acquis,* suggesting that the major impact of this new treaty in the citizenship domain may lie in the future, as the broader interpretative community of European integration continues to interact on a day-to-day basis with the new provisions.

This reminds us that, in studying the EU, the focus should always be more on the process than on the end-product, since the ulterior objectives of European integration are not to do with creating particular types of state forms or non-state entities, but rather with more fundamental goals covering human sociality and organization, and even idealism and decency. Union citizenship is, and will continue to be, an essential part of the process of what the EU is becoming, whatever that might be.

16

The Embedded *Acquis Communautaire*: Transmission Belt and Prism of New Governance

ANTJE WIENER

Currently, liberal democracies are undergoing major changes that are causing much debate about the appropriate political procedures and conceptual frameworks for the organization of a polity. The legitimate authority of governments is increasingly being undermined by the 'de-bordernization' of politics and policy,[1] resulting in a 'thinning-out' of the mechanisms of majoritarian rule (Held 1992). These changes have been met in two ways. The first is a conceptual struggle among social scientists over the heritage of experience with, and expectations of, modern state politics. The second is much more closely linked to practices on the ground, involving such day-to-day processes of policy-making as agenda-setting, deliberation, and conflict-solving. Both approaches, however, address the central question of how to maintain a democratically legitimized political order in a context which has been dubbed 'governance without government' (Rosenau and Czempiel 1992). Consequently, 'governance' has come to be widely accepted as a term which includes practices of governing that are not exclusively performed by state actors (Schmitter 1998).

This chapter is a slightly revised version of an article published in the *European Law Journal* **4** (3): 294–315. For comments on earlier versions, I am grateful to Vincent Della Sala, Karin Fierke, Andreas Føllesdal, Carol Harlow, Knud Erik Jørgensen, Yves Meny, Susanne Schmidt, Uli Sedelmeier, Jo Shaw and, in particular, an anonymous referee. For invaluable editing, I am most grateful to Fiona Hayes-Renshaw. Responsibility for the final version is the author's. This final version benefited much from the logistics and intellectually stimulating environment provided by the Robert Schuman Centre, while the author was a Jean Monnet Fellow at the European University Institute in Florence.

[1] The term 'de-bordernization' has been introduced into international relations theories to characterize processes of politics and policy-making across national borders. It challenges such core realist assumptions as states being the sole sovereign actors in global politics, as well as the concepts of power and territory being firmly based on Weberian state systems. See Albert and Brock (1995) and Neyer (1995).

Despite the broad application of the term, however, the meaning of governance still appears to be based on state-centric assumptions about the organization of democratic politics. This conceptual caveat has been highly troublesome in the most interesting case of 'governance beyond the nation-state' (Jachtenfuchs 1995), namely the incremental construction of the Euro-polity. In this chapter, I argue that the European Union (EU) offers crucial insights into the gradual shift from a Weberian form of modern 'government' towards the institutionalization of post-Weberian 'governance'. In contrast to the discussion of governance within international relations—or, more specifically, within regime analysis, which has continued to work with the assumption that state action will be democratically legitimated—the process of European integration has profoundly challenged this core idea. Indeed, in the case of the EU, it has been suggested that the process of governance beyond the nation state has produced a degree of institutionalization which attains a certain degree of statehood (Hobe 1993).

This chapter further argues that the emerging 'polity of polities' context not only threatens the constitutional basis of democratic rule, as the German Constitutional Court's Maastricht judgment has suggested, but also raises the questions of what exactly the new institutions of governance beyond the nation state are, and what they imply for the functioning (rules of the game) and legitimacy (democratic processes) of the political order. In an effort to elaborate on these questions, two themes are developed in this chapter. First, critical questions are raised about the conceptual boundedness of 'governance' in the discussion of constitutional and policy studies within the field of European integration. Second, a methodological access point for the study of the institutionalization of governance in the Euro-polity is advanced. It suggests situating the legal concept of *acquis communautaire* at the boundary of legal studies and politics, and then applying it to a case study of citizenship policy in the EU, in order to demonstrate how the *acquis communautaire*—or more precisely, the 'embedded *acquis communautaire*'—facilitates methodological access to the study of the institutionalization of governance beyond the state and despite states.

The main body of the chapter is divided into three sections. The first discusses the term 'governance' in the context of European integration; the second examines the concept of the 'embedded *acquis communautaire*', and the third provides a summary of citizenship policy as a social practice since the early 1970s, taking the European Summit meetings at Paris, Fontainebleau, Maastricht, and Amsterdam as major turning points in an ongoing story. The conclusion summarizes the major changes in the citizenship *acquis communautaire,* and the interrelated transformation of EU governance.

New Governance Beyond the State and Despite States

An increasing institutional density beyond the territory, level and/or scope of national government and policy procedure has led many contributors to European integration theory to use the term 'governance' when writing about the framework of policy-making and politics in the EU (Bulmer 1997; Jachtenfuchs and Kohler-Koch 1996*b*; Wallace 1996*b*). Much of this literature displays an interest in the substance of European integration, and thus moves beyond a debate on the likely outcomes of the integration process. It has therefore introduced a shift from a theoretically informed debate about the arguable merits of grand theory (and, more specifically, neo-functionalist versus inter-governmentalist approaches) for explaining integration, towards an examination of the details of the policy process in the light of negotiation, agenda-setting and implementation problems (Richardson 1996*a*; Wallace *et al.* 1983; Wallace and Wallace 1996). The focus on policy substance has thus helped to highlight an emerging 'pattern of rule' which had largely been overlooked by theoretical debates in the 1960s and 1970s. This pattern has been pragmatically labelled 'governance' (Bulmer 1997).

By bringing this pattern of rule into focus, governance literature has been crucial for the evolution of an understanding of the Euro-polity as 'a polity in-the-making,' as well as a polity 'beyond the nation state'. A study of the complexity of 'policy substance' (i.e. entailing administrative procedures and policy content) has led to the identification of institutional changes which has enabled market actors to improve policy implementation. Governance in this sense accordingly encompasses sharing an acknowledged set of rules and procedures of social interaction for market purposes, or 'the establishment and operation of social institutions—or, in other words, sets of rules, decision-making procedures, and programmatic activities that serve to define social practices and to guide the interaction of those participating in these practices' (Young 1997).

It has thus long been argued that polity formation in the EU is market-driven and leads, first and foremost, to market-making, not state-building (Streeck 1995). Yet, 'while markets must be 'insulated' from social 'policy', they should never be seen in isolation from social/ethical 'regulation' and political processes (Everson 1998: 196). It is thus the latter processes which distinguish the political and potentially conflictual process of governance from mere functional cooperative administration.[2] However, it has also been convincingly argued that the 'political' aspect of (market) governance is particularly complex once post-national models of governance are the subject of inquiry (Everson 1998). While ultimately the important questions for such a transformation of governance are *who* gets to influence

---

[2] Alec Stone Sweet's distinction between 'dyadic' and 'triadic' models of interaction makes a similar point; see Stone Sweet (1996).

the institutional terms of the political in the Euro-polity and *how*, this chapter tackles the questions of *what* the institutional basis for political intervention is, and *how* it is constituted.

The former issue involves the definition of a 'legitimate third party' to solve conflicts within this polity, as well as the political values transmitted by it. The so-called 'Comitology Decision'[3] is but one example of such political queries underlying a form of EU governance which seeks to govern a new polity in which there is no politically acknowledged centre akin to the nation state polities' unitary administrative structure, which has traditionally preserved the influence of national states. The effort to accommodate the political interests of the EU member states within the otherwise 'highly administrative' committee task of overseeing policy implementation has turned the committees into 'mini-Councils' (Everson 1998), representing an attempt to avoid clear shifts of power and authority. This form of political involvement by national actors in the process of governance beyond the nation state is an interim solution, which demonstrates the modern political actors' ongoing struggle for survival in an increasingly postmodern or, for that matter, medieval political environment (Ferguson and Mansbach 1996; Ruggie 1993).

The latter institutional and constitutive issue, however, seeks to open up a perspective on actors other than state actors. It is of particular importance, in the case of the EU, that this political struggle is taking place over and on the emergent turf of a new polity. Crucially, post-Maastricht, this political space has been invaded by new actors, in particular interest groups, who have demanded access to equal rights for residents and citizens.[4] The case of citizenship policy, for example, suggests that the process of policy implementation is indeed highly political. Beyond 'administration' it involves ethical/social concerns. It pertains to the 'civilization' of what was once perceived of as a market polity (Everson 1998). It is therefore not devoid of ethical concerns and historical experiences, which in turn inform normative expectations and, subsequently, influence policy objectives. It follows that the process of policy-making has become the key locus for establishing the patterns of EU governance, since it is in fact the deliberations over policy objectives, agenda-setting and policy implementation which substantiate and structure that governance (Richardson

---

[3] Council Decision 87/373/EC OJ L197/87 of 13 July 1997 is also known as the 'Comitology Decision'. Joerges and Neyer (1997*a*) point out that this decision on the implementation of the White Paper on the Single Market represents the rejection of 'the idea of a supranational central implementation machinery headed by the Commission, and thus indirectly forces national governments into a co-operative venture'.

[4] For example, hearings which were organized in Brussels by the EP's Institutional Committee on 18–19 October 1995 'with a view to preparing the Dury and Maij–Weggen Reports on revision of the Maastricht Treaty' (*Agence Europe*, 18 October 1995, 4) were attended by 'dozens of Non-Governmental Organizations (NGOs)', while 'over 300 NGOs had asked to take part' (*Agence Europe*, 18 October 1995, 4 and 19 October 1995, 4).

1996*b*). Accordingly, a reference to governance in this sense entails 'thick' governance.[5]

To summarize: the implications of applying the notion of 'governance' without problematizing its state-centric roots 'are twofold: first, market-management, a political process, is not a matter for classic administration and administrative law; and secondly, national polities—and not isolated European citizens—remain the legitimate source of European ethical/social values' (Everson 1998: 210). In other words, while administrative discourse has sought to move beyond state-centric terms, in practice the political remains attached to 'state' politics.[6] Equally it follows that, if we are to assess governance beyond the nation state, changes in policy substance have a greater indicative power than do the preferences of state actors. After all, this is a period when 'the state' is losing power, the political centre has become weaker, and other actors such as, for example, policy networks, have gained an important influence on politics.[7] Following the insight that governance is a process which thrives on conflict (Stone Sweet 1996), we therefore need to both deconstruct core modern concepts, and identify key sets of practices to act as markers in the effort to reassemble them. As the next section suggests, this method is particularly valuable given the constitutional implications of the *acquis communautaire*.

Conceptual remnants are state-centric and all too often misleading when applied as tools in the debates over politics and policy-making in polities other than modern nation states (Ferguson and Mansbach 1996; Ladeur 1997). In the light of these changes to and within modern political entities, the concept of 'governance' has become a fashionable term throughout the social sciences. However, while the popularity of the term indicates an inclination among scholars to move away from state-centric assumptions about modern government, its inflationary use has, so far, been detrimental to its precision (Rhodes 1996). Recently, it has been observed that the discursive shift from the term 'government' to that of 'governance' represents an effort to 'distance modern *governance* from traditional *government*' (Armstrong and Bulmer 1998: 25). However, a *discursive* shift from 'government' to 'governance' must remain superficial unless it is matched by a *conceptual* shift. It has been pointed out that as long as this conceptual shift remains pending, governance remains a concept with a 'rigid adherence to traditional notions of the national polity' (Everson 1998). Subsequently, analyses of governance beyond the nation state that

[5] Legal perspectives in particular have sought 'to identify practices within the decision-making process which challenge the analytical and normative assumptions upon which the majority of integration research rests' (Joerges and Neyer 1997*a*: 274).

[6] Not surprisingly, the term 'governance' has so far been predominantly applied with reference to the regulatory state; see Majone (1994*a*, 1997).

[7] In contrast, actor-oriented approaches to European integration often assume particular characteristics of actors which were true in one particular period of time, but not in another. This neglect of time is expressed by the emphasis on actor preferences instead of substantive policy change (i.e. institution-building).

operate with a discursively altered, yet conceptually steady, concept of governance are open to precisely those conceptual pitfalls of modernity which they
seek to overcome.[8] The political scope of the discursive shift from 'government'
to 'governance' therefore requires much closer perusal.

To avoid the pitfalls of the conceptually limited discursive shift towards the
term 'governance', I propose to focus on the underlying practices of new governance beyond the nation state which themselves contribute to building the
resources of governance. As I will seek to demonstrate, such a middle-range
perspective provides an avenue for assessing the process of institutionalization
which allows for a contextualized and hence historically specific assessment of
the terms of governance, without presupposing the final product of the
process. Empirically, this type of analysis explores policy-making as a practice.
The empirical part of the chapter highlights the citizenship debates in the EU,
and reflects the conceptual problems which arise if the underlying sets of practices which contribute to the construction of meaning are neglected. By applying the methodology of 'embedded *acquis communautaire*' in order to study the
institutionalization of governance in the field of citizenship policy, this chapter
shows that, once the informal resources which inform processes of policy-
making (and which are, in turn, altered by the same process) have been taken
into account, the impact of citizenship policy reaches far beyond the legal provisions of the treaty.

The Embedded *Acquis Communautaire*: Resources and Routinized Practices

This section seeks to point out alternative routes for approaching governance
beyond the nation state, that is, new governance. It argues that the concept of
the *acquis communautaire* (or the shared legal and institutional properties of the
EU) offers an invaluable access point for this enterprise. As the institution which
contains the governance resources which have been created over decades of
European integration, the *acquis communautaire* in fact mirrors the result of legislative, policy, and political practices over time. It is crucial to note, however,
that beyond its role as a legal concept, and hence a guiding set of rules for
European governance at any one time—including its yardstick function for the
entry of new candidates for EU membership—the *acquis* also represents the
continuously changing institutional terms which result from the constructive

---

[8] Armstrong and Bulmer's (1998: 255) distinction between '*modern* governance' and '*traditional*
government' suggests that the 'modern' represents progress compared to the 'traditional'. This
is particularly confusing with reference to other work on European integration, which has begun
to refer to new types of governance as 'postmodern' (see Caporaso 1996; Ladeur 1997; Ruggie
1993).

process of 'integration through law'. This chapter stresses the importance of this link between the practices which underlie the ongoing process of construction and related changes in the *acquis*. I argue that, for analytical reasons, this link is best conceptualized by distinguishing between formal and informal resources, both of which are influential in the construction of the *acquis*. While both sets of resources are clearly not comparable on either legal or political terms, both contribute to the substance of governance, in that they are instrumental in setting 'the rules of the game' in the Euro-polity. Equally, this chapter proposes a new way of conceptualizing the *acquis* which allows for the acknowledgement of both types of resources. In other words, the legal body of the *acquis communautaire* is perceived of as being linked to social practices. It is therefore best conceptualized as the 'embedded *acquis communautaire*'.

The argument builds on the insight that 'routinised practices' (Tilly 1975; Koslowski and Kratochwil 1994) contribute to the meaning of the European Union's *acquis communautaire*.[9] The argument further builds on research which has begun to consider the *acquis communautaire* as an increasingly important and institutionalized reference point within the constitutional framework of the Treaties, as well as within political practice (Gialdino 1995; Joergensen 1998; Michalski and Wallace 1992). Indeed, the treaty requires its addressees 'to maintain the *acquis communautaire* and build on it', and so 'create an ever closer Union among the peoples of Europe'.[10] Consequently, the *acquis communautaire* amounts to a key institution of governance within the Euro-polity. In its efforts to assess the resources entailed in the *acquis*, this section comprises three nested steps. The first raises the critical question of state-centred concepts and principles (i.e. sovereignty, citizenship and democracy), which underlie the European intergration literature on governance. The second suggests deconstructing the concepts involved, according to their component elements and sets of practices. The third involves the analysis of policy-making as a process which includes, on the one hand, making practices routine and, on the other, the impact of these routinized practices on the institutionalization of new terms of governance. In a nutshell, this chapter demonstrates that the practice of policy-making is not only conducive to the institutionalization of legal provisions, but also contributes to the institutionalization of socially constructed norms. The example of the practice of citizenship policy-making exemplifies this socially constructive understanding of the *acquis* and how it

---

[9] According to the European Commission, the *acquis* is understood as 'the contents, principles and political objectives of the Treaties, including the Maastricht Treaty; the legislation adopted in implementation of the Treaties, and the jurisprudence of the Court; the declarations and resolutions adopted in the Community framework; the international agreements and the agreements between member states connected with the Community's activities' (Michalski and Wallace 1992).

[10] See Art. B(5) of the Treaty on European Union (TEU) and Article A TEU, respectively.

contributes to the reconfiguring of the resources of the *acquis communautaire*, to the extent that it influences the substance and structure of 'thick' governance.

The *acquis communautaire* is understood as an institutional framework which is embedded in socially constructed meaning (Kratochwil and Ruggie 1986; Kratochwil 1988; Young 1989). As such, it works as a prism of the substantive dimension of governance. According to this approach, the conditions and meanings of the *acquis* are not fixed but flexible; they depend on constitutive practices (Kratochwil 1988). To date, European integration literature has not completely overlooked the impact of constitutive practices. Instead, the *acquis* has been applied in either a descriptive or a normative fashion. The descriptive use of the *acquis* is commonly applied in the event of enlargement, and more recently, in the event of 'opting out' from the *acquis* at intergovernmental conferences (IGCs). In the event of enlargement, new EU member states are expected to accept the political, procedural and institutional conditions entailed in the *acquis communautaire* at the moment of accession. The 'accession' *acquis* was the oldest concept of *acquis* which defined 'the whole body of rules, political principles and judicial decisions which new Member States must adhere to, in their entirety and from the beginning, when they become members of the Communities' (Gialdino 1995). Yet, while constitutive incrementalism is undoubtedly a part of the *acquis communautaire*, the Maastricht Treaty nonetheless provides reason for caution, given that a 'number of protocols to the Union Treaty [. . .] damage the *acquis communautaire*' (Curtin 1993). Equally, the procedure of 'opting out' is a more recent phenomenon which allows member states to opt out of specific obligations, duties and/or entitlements of the *acquis communautaire* at the time of treaty revisions, which usually occur at IGCs.

The normative application of the *acquis* has been identified as a constructive 'push factor' in constitution-making (Weiler 1993). The concept of 'integration through law', for example, shows how the integration process was driven by institutionalized norms and the European Court of Justice's application of these norms (Weiler 1986; Meehan 1993; Wincott 1996).[11] However, not only is the substance of the *acquis* often difficult to pin down, since it is like 'something that everybody has heard about [. . .], but nobody knows what it looks like' (Michalski and Wallace 1992), it is also not immediately obvious how the *acquis* came about. Why does the *acquis* entail what it does? Viewed from a his-

---

[11] On the importance of regulative and constitutive norms for international regimes, see in particular Kratochwil (1988). On the concept of the embedded *acquis*, the ECJ's informal or formal adherence to the concept of binding precedent, which has a particular importance for common law legal cultures, is another dimension which requires further theoretical elaboration, but which lies beyond the scope of this chapter. (Thanks to Jo Shaw for this observation.)

torical perspective, the *acquis* is an institution which forms part of an ongoing process of constructing meaning and applying knowledge. This process may be informed by past experience and future expectations, based on world views and/or ideas (Hall 1989; Jachtenfuchs 1995). The *acquis* is therefore best perceived of as being embedded in structures of governance, while at the same time contributing to its substance. This embedded structure is distinguishable according, on the one hand, to informal resources such as shared values, ideas, and world views and, on the other, to the routinization of practices which lead to agreement on policy objectives. The formal resources of the *acquis* thus depend on the preceding processes.

In order to make these resources visible, I suggest that informal resources and the routinization of policy be included in the assessment of the *acquis*. According to Fig. 16.1, the *acquis* builds on informal resources such as ideas and values, routinized practices and policy objectives, as well as formal resources such as rules, regulations, and procedures. Informal resources entail ideas and world views which inform debates over policy substance and agenda-setting. They may, but do not necessarily need to become a formal resource. Indeed, more often than not, they form that part of a proposal which has been deliberated on for a relatively long time. While certain aspects of such a proposal may be routinized as a policy objective through frequently discussed and rewritten proposals, they are not necessarily formalized according to a fixed mechanism, procedure, or time-frame. For example, the proposal to establish the right to vote for Community

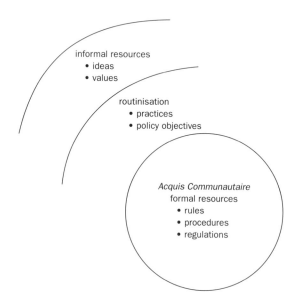

Fig. 16.1. The embedded *Acquis Communautaire*.

'foreigners' (i.e. citizens of a member state residing in another member state)[12] was not formalized in regulations or directives for a long time. However, the underlying ideas continued to be a push factor for a certain form of policy over an extended period of time. During this time, the ongoing policy negotiations contributed to the routinization of the approach to voting rights. Thus, for example, in the case of citizenship policy, the underlying idea for putting citizenship on the agenda in the early 1970s was that citizenship would lead to the creation of a 'European' identity, and the routinization of approach involved step-by-step policy-making, dusting off or, for that matter, revising proposals on long-standing policy objectives (Wiener 1998). As the following case study shows, these informal resources influence the formal resources of the *acquis* on the one hand, and the expectations of a variety of political actors on the other.

By identifying three sets of resources, this model seeks to take account of the 'unintended consequences' of a policy (Pierson 1996). That is, it does not presuppose a policy process which develops on a straight line from point A (informal resource—i.e. idea) to point B (formal resources—i.e. treaty change). Instead, it allows for a systematized perspective on the development of the policy process by offering a way of identifying different layers and at varying speeds. While the embedded *acquis* entails both informal and formal resources, it is important to note that not all informal resources such as ideas and practices immediately form part of the *acquis*. This model suggests that they are only considered to be a part of the *acquis* once they have acquired a degree of routinization which produces a structuring effect on the policy process. The formal resources of the *acquis* have been voted on by the Council, and control over their enactment lies with the European Court of Justice and the Commission. In turn, the informal resources are likely to be contested. They are therefore often debated in the formal and informal forums of the Euro-polity, such as committees and working groups, or networks and interest groups, the particular fora depending on the policy's link with one of the three Community pillars. By debating such issues, these groups contribute to the process of contesting and possibly changing the meaning of the informal resources.

Changes in the *acquis* occur over time and are expressed in the debates which

---

[12] The crucial documents in the policy-making process which led up to the drafting of Art. 8b of the EC Treaty were: the Commission's report on special rights (*Bulletin of the EC*, Suppl. 7, 1975); the Scelba Report of the European Parliament on the 'Granting of Special Rights to Citizens of the Community' (European Parliament 1979); the Commission's report on 'Voting Rights in Local Elections for Community Nationals' (*Bulletin of the EC*, Suppl. 7, 1986); Commission proposal for a Council Directive on the right to vote and stand for election in European and municipal elections at one's place of residence (COM(88)371 fin.); see also Official Journal, No. C246, 20 September 1988; and Commission proposals for voting rights in European Parliament elections (SEC(93) 1021 fin., 23 June 1993) and for voting rights in municipal elections (COM(94)38, 23 February 1994.

take place between 'history-making' Council decisions (Peterson 1995). The dynamic of these debates flows from the often contradictory interests between two largely differing approaches to the process of European integration, i.e. the distinction between integrationists, who will mostly push for the adoption of a proposal, and intergovernmentalists, who will attempt to maintain the status quo. Equally, the resources contribute crucial information for policy-makers because they may be mobilized (the formal resources) or changed (the informal resources) once the opportunity is right. Providing opportunities and constraints, they thus 'invisibly' structure governance. It follows that a change in the *acquis* potentially involves two processes. One includes the expansion of formal resources (changes in the treaty, directives, regulations); the other encompasses a formalization based on routinized practice or the constitution-alization of informal resources (ideas, shared principles, and practices as sug-gested by EP resolutions and Commission proposals or other documents). It is important to emphasize, however, that the three aspects of the *acquis* are not linked in any linear fashion. Instead, the model's attempt to encompass the con-stitutive nature of political conflict is based on the conceptualization of the embedded *acquis* as a form of 'transmission belt' between political processes and constitution-making.[13]

Institutionalizing New Governance: The Case of Citizenship Policy

This section provides an insight into the story of 'European' citizenship prac-tice. To that end, it disentangles the citizenship package and highlights its indi-vidual parts: 'special rights' and 'passport' policy. It specifically seeks to point out the policy-makers' use of informal resources, the routinization of practices and their impact on the changes in the formal resources of the citizenship *acquis*.[14] The case study suggests that shared values, normative ideals, and func-tional perspectives were all crucial factors affecting the policy objectives, which in turn shape the legal framework and rights, and hence impact on everyday policy-making. These elements changed according to four historical stages at four 'history-making' European summits in Paris (1974), Fontainebleau (1984), Maastricht (1991), and Amsterdam (1997).

Within European integration studies, citizenship policy has not received much attention as a practice, notwithstanding its acknowledged contribution in the context of state-building (Bendix 1964; Marshall 1950; Turner 1990; Tilly 1975). Instead, the literature has predominantly focused on legal assess-ments of Union citizenship, thus correctly shedding light on the limitations

---

[13] I am grateful to Karin Fierke for alerting me to the importance of non-linearity for this par-ticular model of the policy process.

[14] For greater detail, see Wiener 1998, chs. 4–12.

of supranational citizenship (Closa 1995; Lyons 1996; O'Leary 1995; d'Oliveira 1995; Weiler 1997c). In contrast, policy-oriented studies of Community citizenship have focused upon a wide variety of aspects of citizenship policy. They have explored the legal problems and political aspects associated with legal innovations which were most evident in the pre- and post-Maastricht debates. Thus for example, while Union citizenship may be distinguished from national citizenship with reference to the rights it entails, the reference to rights alone does not say enough about the character of this new supranational citizenship (Wiener and Della Sala 1997). Instead, Union citizenship has innovative potential, not only in EU polity formation but also as a non-state model for citizenship in general (Benhabib 1997; Wiener 1998). How does this finding relate to the problem of state-centric approaches of governance, however?

Critical theorists have suggested deconstructing such core concepts as sovereignty and citizenship in the modern international state system by desegregating them according to their social dimensions. This method builds on the observation that social practices contribute to the political meaning of such concepts (Benhabib 1997; Biersteker and Weber 1996). In other words, if we are to establish the dynamics which characterize Union citizenship as a newly emergent type of citizenship, analyses need to allow for a means of appreciating the historical variability of the context and content of citizenship. Case-studies, then, need to explore the resources of citizenship. It remains to be demonstrated that normative and functional perspectives have been crucial push factors in the process of creating Union citizenship. To that end, this chapter deviates from the familiar conceptual approach to citizenship based on the dualism of identity and rights (Kymlicka and Norman 1994; Soysal 1994), and takes a broader historical perspective of citizenship as a relational and historically contingent practice (Somers 1994; Tilly 1995).

The broader interest underlying the case study is focused on institution-building as an evolutionary and potentially contested process. Understood in a socio-historical sense, the process of institution-building encompasses the routinization of practices, norms, rules, and procedures, which help to establish a discernible form of citizenship practice. The focus is thus on the resources created through citizenship practice. It is important to note, however, that this focus on citizenship practice does not necessarily mean that civil society actors are involved. In fact, as historical analyses of state-building processes suggest, more often than not it is *either* the state *or* civil groups which dominate the conflictual process of establishing the institutional terms of citizenship (i.e. citizenship practice). The concept of the embedded *acquis* establishes a link between the mutually reinforcing practices of the policy process on the one hand, and institution-building on the other. The constitutional role of the *acquis* thus acquires social meaning by its embeddedness in the social context. The case study illuminates this process.

Paris 1974

During the first historical stage, the lack of a clear political concept of Community development was, according to Belgian Commissioner Etienne Davignon, a yawning gap. This was particularly problematic because the EC was required to act and speak with one voice at that relatively early stage in the development of its polity. As Davignon explained

> one of the difficulties of European construction is that historical stages have to be missed out. It is necessary to behave as if Europe already existed, as a political entity. In history, all countries passed through a phase of exclusively national development. Yet in this instance Europe has to act and intervene at the international level before having completed the phase of its internal development.[15]

Institutional changes were necessary in order to provide the proper means for achieving this end. Referring to the lack of support from European citizens, Davignon used a discourse of identity, stressing belonging. He stated that

> [p]eople should not be able to say: all we know of Europe is the VAT (Value Added Tax) and the increase in the price of vegetables, but we don't feel that we belong to a new entity. *Europe should be personalised* (emphasis added).[16]

The Belgian Foreign Minister, Van Elslande, pointed to the missing link between citizens and the Community as one reason for the crisis at this time. His discourse was also one of identity, this time emphasizing access and rights. As he observed

> [t]he priority being given to setting up the customs union, the difficulties of political union, the weariness that is caused by so many marathons and vague decisions, have gradually eroded away public opinion; the building of Europe is liable to cease being a common ideal, but rather an objective sought after by those who will profit directly from it. In other words, Europe cannot be monopolised by economic and technological achievements and neglect, under penalty of losing essential support, the aspirations of its citizens.[17]

European citizens, therefore, needed to be better linked to the project. The search was on for a policy which would aid in establishing this link by creating

---

[15] *Agence Europe*, No. 713, 5 January 1973, 7.   [16] Ibid., 3–4.

[17] Europe Documents No. 752, 17 July 1973; speech by Foreign Minister van Elslande on 27 June 1972 to the House of Representatives at the end of Belgium's six-month presidency of the Council of Ministers.

a sense of belonging. Van Elslande continued to stress that the Belgian presidency should aim at creating the 'first concrete stage towards establishing European citizenship'. This first stage would include mobility for students, exchanges of teachers and harmonization of diplomas, with a view to giving 'young people [. . .] the chance of feeling truly part of a vast network covering the whole of the Community'. His primary emphasis, however, was placed on the crucial importance of establishing an identity-based link among citizens and the Community since, in his view '[t]hese targets cannot be set on a technical basis. The political commitment must be a real one and each citizen must be able to grasp the significance of what has been decided'.[18] The Italian Commissioner, Altiero Spinelli, demanded that the upcoming Paris Summit focus on the central question of 'what must be done to equip Europe at last with personality, identity, or, in short, that European Government of which it stands in need?'[19]

At this time, the normative ideal consisted of the EC's need to act and speak as one political actor on the international stage. The policy objectives of special rights and passport policy were aimed at the creation of a political Union, beyond functionalist economic organization. Citizenship practice hence consisted of promoting a 'European identity' among the citizens of the member states, based on a common heritage and common external action. Passport policies, special rights for citizens of the member states, and voting rights for EP elections were framed as aspects of citizenship-building. Thus, in the early 1970s, the formal resources of the *acquis* did not include any legal provisions in the EEC Treaty to act on political citizenship rights, although Article 235 EEC Treaty allowed for the possibility of constitutional change based on an IGC. At the same time, the informal citizenship resources involved the idea of a European citizenship as an identity-generating concept, and the routinized resources entailed the policy objectives of special rights and passport policy according to the conclusions of the 1974 Paris *communiqué*. The policy objectives of special rights were partially transformed into formal resources with the introduction of universal suffrage in European elections by means of a Council decision on this subject.[20] The passport policy objectives were turned into a resolution on the introduction of a common passport.[21] In the 1970s, EC policy-makers were interested in maintaining the then current *acquis communautaire*. As some suggested, this could only be achieved on the basis of the EC improving its image in global politics, and thus presenting a united position in the face of the then global crisis. As Henry Kissinger's query (Who speaks for

[18] Europe Documents No. 752, 17 July 1973, 1–2.

[19] Europe Documents No. 775, 3 December 1973, speech entitled 'A Programme for Europe', delivered by Altiero Spinelli, Member of the European Commission, Rome, 23 November 1973.

[20] Official Journal EC, No. L 278, 8 October 1977, 1–11.

[21] Official Journal EC, No. C 241, 19 September 1981, 1 (Council Resolution of 23 June 1981).

Europe?[22]) in the middle of the crisis made clear, the EC lacked representation on the global stage. The discourse of the time reveals that politicians saw this void as being in part due to the lack of a European identity. While drawing on its quasi-constitution, EC politics were legally legitimized, but the EC still did not speak with one voice; its speech remained 'fairly scanty' as Etienne Davignon had rightly noted.[23]

Fontainebleau 1984

During the second stage, the normative ideal which structured governance was the creation of an internal market without frontiers. The policy objectives of that time were the rights of free movement and voting for economically active citizens. Citizenship practice encompassed the extension of voting rights to introduce 'belonging' as a means of integrating European 'foreigners' (passport holders of one member state who were resident in another member state). The enhanced market-oriented integration and the increasing possibilities for workers' movement had created a potentially conflictual situation. As the Commission put it

> [T]his situation—seemingly incompatible with the idea of European Union—has given rise to two conflicting positions. [One is that] foreign residents are campaigning for voting rights in the municipality or residence since they have the same duties and obligations as national residents . . . [The other is that] member states are refusing to drop nationality as the essential criterion for granting the right to vote.[24]

One way of catching up with the pace of economic integration was to redefine the right to vote to include those citizens whose status had been reduced to one of market citizen. According to the Commission, the establishment of voting rights in the country of residence was 'consistent with the logic of a People's Europe'.[25] Indeed, it reiterated that this political dimension of the debate needed to be placed in sharper focus, if the tension between integration on the European level and marginalization on the individual level were to be resolved. Not only democracy, but also belonging to a Community was at stake. The Commission raised the question whether

> [I]n a democratic society, does the fact that people are disenfranchised, even at local level, marginalise them still further when the aim should be to integrate them? Or to put it in another way, could the grant of voting rights contribute to the integration of foreigners?[26]

[22] Henry Kissinger asked this question when a Danish representative of the EC spoke in the name of the Community in Washington in September 1973 (Dinan 1994: 85).

[23] The full citation reads: 'I have at times compared Europe with Tarzan. It has a relatively advanced morphology but its speech is still fairly scanty'; *Agence Europe*, No. 713, 5 January 1973, 7 (interview in *La Libre Belgique*, 28 December 1972).

[24] *Bulletin of the EC*, Suppl. 7, 1986, 6.   [25] Ibid., 5.   [26] Ibid., 7.

The concept of community which dominated EC discourse at that time was, according to the Commission, too closely drawn from the 'purely economic [concept defined] in the Treaties'. It was therefore time to take on 'a new dimension in the context of a People's Europe [because] the concept of community which is purely economic in the Treaties, raises the question of whether or not a People's Europe necessarily involves the granting of political rights, at least at the local level'.[27]

This normative perspective facilitated a fresh view of the actual exclusion (rather than integration) of mobile (border-crossing) Community citizens from enjoying political rights in their communities of residence. The Council had been wary of addressing this question, stressing that the granting of special rights 'posed a number of legal, political and social problems', and hence, from the point of view of the Council, special rights could only be achieved through a 'gradual approach [. . .] starting with those rights that posed the least problems'.[28] As problems existed in abundance, it had practically declared the topic of voting rights a taboo; the matter had been abandoned and had 'not been discussed by the Council' since 1979.[29]

The interrelationship between the free movement of worker-citizens and the political right to vote and stand for election represented a decisive discursive shift in EC citizenship practice, because it linked normative values to the politics of market-making. The discourse thus highlighted two different expressions of belonging in particular. The first type indicates belonging to a specific community within a bounded territory. It is defined by political citizenship rights and access to political participation. It hence defines the legal relationship between the individual and a political community. This type of discourse on belonging had been invoked by the Commission's report on the right to vote. The second type of belonging is more subtle. It builds on subjective feelings of inclusion and exclusion, which are based on the perception of participation. Hence, experience and expectation have a strong input into perceived belonging. It may, for example, be based on access to social rights (i.e. participation in the social space of a community).

The tension which arises from this sort of belonging by means of social policy or, for that matter, market involvement, is based on the partial disclosure of one type of rights (i.e. social rights) and the ongoing closure of other rights (i.e. political rights) (Brubaker 1992; Linklater 1996, 1998). The Commission's proposal on local voting rights for 'foreigners' contributed to a newly invoked discourse on democracy as one resource in the development of citizenship. Crucial for this period, and for growing political tensions later on in the process, was the decision to pursue the realization of the four freedoms

---

[27] *Bulletin of the EC*, Suppl. 7, 1986, 7.

[28] This point had been stressed by Mr. von Dohnanyi, President-in-Office of the Council, at the Florence Round Table in 1978 (European Parliament 1979).

[29] *Bulletin of the EC*, Suppl. 7, 1986, 11–12.

stipulated by the Treaty of Rome (the EEC Treaty)—that is, the free movement of goods, services, capital, and persons—outside the Community's policy framework. While this decision emerged first as a Franco-German agreement on the abolition of border controls between France and Germany in 1984, it turned into the 1985 Schengen Agreement on the Abolition of Border Controls among five signatory states.[30]

Maastricht 1991

During the preparations for Treaty revisions at the Maastricht European Council in 1991, a sudden shift occurred from what may overall be considered a balanced continuity of market-making towards the management of political turbulence. Not least among these new shifts was a sudden change in the Community's geopolitical position (Bolten 1992; Garcia 1993). Dinan notes one aspect of this change, when he writes that '[f]rom the outset, the Community had considered itself as synonymous with "Europe". With the Cold War over, could the Community foster a sense of pan-European solidarity and genuinely pan-European integration?' (Dinan 1994: 158). While 'European' identity, as then applied, meant Western Europeans (including the potential Western European citizens of new member states), the fall of the Berlin Wall now challenged the use of that term. Some Europeans had been left out all along, as non-Community nationals had been excluded from the special rights policy for years (Hoogenboom 1992). This fact became much more obvious in the border debates which dominated passport policy in the 1990s.[31]

The overall reaction of European politicians at the time was an attempt to strengthen political union.[32] For example, the Martin report, which had been adopted by the European Parliament on 27 February 1990, emphasized the urgent need to transform the EC into a federalized European union.[33] It was followed by a Belgian memorandum which suggested 'that the European Community be given a new stimulus towards political union',[34] and singled out

---

[30] After often heated debates among the politicians involved, the Schengen Agreement came to be considered as the 'out-of-Community' approach to support a step-by-step realization of the four freedoms, at a time when harmonization seemed impossible to achieve; see Gehring (1998), Weber-Panariello (1995).

[31] One possible result of the inclusion/exclusion mechanism introduced by this process was seen in a new economic divide between Eastern and Western Europe; see Saryusz-Wolski (1994: 19).

[32] Some European politicians felt they were witnessing the beginning of a new era in politics. For example, the Italian government, which was to assume the presidency of the Council from 1 July to 31 December 1990, stated that the external political changes led to the 'opening up [of] a constituent era of international relations in our Continent'; Europe Documents, No. 1611, 10 April 1990, 1.

[33] PE 137. 068/fin., 27 February 1990, 6.

[34] This Belgian memorandum was the first formal proposal on political union (Dinan 1994: 164).

two major tasks on the Community's political agenda. The first was the clarification of the 'Community's political purpose' in the light of the international political transformation; the second was dealing with the 'growing democratic deficit' which had developed along with the growth of the single market. Like the Martin report, the Belgian document stressed the need to include provisions which created a stronger link between the Community and its citizens, for example, a uniform electoral procedure and the right of Community citizens to vote in local elections.[35] Shortly afterwards, on 19 April 1990, Chancellor Kohl and President Mitterrand addressed a now famous letter[36] to the Irish President of the Council, in which they stressed that the political situation made a second conference on political union necessary.

The third stage, then, led to a shift of the normative ideal underlying EU governance towards legitimacy and democracy as challenged principles in a multilevel polity. The policy objectives attached to these ideals focused once again on political union, responding to challenges to the democratic deficit and citizens' expectations raised by talk of Union citizenship. At this time, citizenship practice had led to the establishment of formal political ties between Union citizens and the Union on the basis of Union citizenship. This dramatic change in the formal resources of the citizenship *acquis communautaire* meant two things. On the one hand, it turned third country nationals into second class citizens. On the other hand, it established a new visible link between Union citizens and the Euro-polity. Both were decisive for motivating and informing post-Maastricht citizenship mobilization.

The informal resources and the routinized practices of the citizenship *acquis* are thus driven by the double-layered framework of economy and politics. They involve policy objectives aimed at the successful realization of the internal market on the one hand, and questions of democratic participation on the other. Moving across borders to work and live in a different country has proved to be the cause of political tension. While residents in one municipality may share economic, social, and cultural activities, they may also be divided over rights to political participation. It is not surprising then, that studies of European citizenship show that the practice of citizenship in the EU is fragmented: Union citizens may sometimes vote and stand for election, pay national health insurance, collect pay cheques, and receive social benefits in a municipality of one member state, while voting and standing for regional and national elections, paying income tax in, and having the nationality of another member state. The outcome of this process was the much criticized institutionalization of 'thin' citizenship, albeit on the basis of institutionalized fragmentation of citizenship.

[35] Memorandum produced by the Permanent Representation of Belgium for the IGC, 1990; see also SI(90) 232, 26 March 1990.

[36] Indeed, the letter was described as 'a landmark in the history of [European Political Union] EPU' which 'was rightly credited with getting the negotiations going' (Dinan 1994: 165).

Amsterdam 1997

The fourth stage demonstrates a growing mobilization around, and increasing confusion over, the consequences of this fragmentation. It provides an insight into citizens' claims to the Amsterdam IGC, highlighting the peculiar contradiction between, on the one hand, citizens' expectations of the Euro-polity as a responsible governing body for their claims and, on the other, the limited mandate of the Amsterdam IGC. The European Parliament, for example, organized hearings in Brussels during which non-governmental organizations (NGOs) could forward their demands to the IGC. While NGOs were not formally entitled to participate in the IGC process, and there were no formally established democratic channels for their participation, these hearings nevertheless provided space for discursive input.[37] In the post-Maastricht period, a new debate (promoted by interest groups and the European Parliament) arose over the gap between politically included and excluded residents; that is, between those citizens who had legal ties with the Union, and so-called 'third country citizens' or individuals who did not possess legal ties with the Union but who might have developed a feeling of belonging to it.

For the emerging new dynamic in the debate over third country nationals, it is important to recall that, with the fall of the Berlin Wall, the Community faced a new challenge in the area of border politics, namely, the question of visa and asylum policy, which now involved the question of East–West migration, and how it was to be dealt with by the upcoming Schengen renegotiations. One proposed means of solving this potential political problem was the establishment of place-oriented citizenship. This demand was introduced into the debate by means of the European Parliament's Outrive and Imbeni Reports. It was enforced by advocacy groups' demands that the citizenship legislation of the treaty be changed. For example, instead of granting citizenship of the Union to '[e]very person holding the nationality of a Member State' (Article 8 (1)), the ARNE group requested citizenship for '[e]very person holding the nationality of a member State and every person residing within the territory of the European Union' (ARNE 1995).

The Amsterdam Draft Treaty of 19 June 1997, however, did not reflect these demands. Table 16.1 shows the accumulated informal resources, routinized practices, and formal resources which are now part of the embedded *acquis*. On the contrary, the nationality component of citizenship was reinforced by the altered Article F(4) TEU, which states that the national identities of the member states will be respected. The potential flexibility of the citizenship article (Article 8 TEC—Treaty of the European Community) was not used by the practitioners. While the formal institutional aspects of the citizenship *acquis* thus largely remained the same, the Amsterdam stage of citizenship practice produced more changes with regard to the

---

[37] See fn 4 above.

TABLE 16.1. The embedded *acquis communautaire* after Amsterdam

Informal resources	Routinized practices	Formal resources
Idea • EU citizenship as identity-generating	*Policy objectives* • Special rights (move, work, vote) • Passport union	• Articles 17–22 Amsterdam Treaty (8 TEU) • Municipal and European voting rights; diplomatic protection
Idea • Belonging created through day-to-day involvement in Community affairs	*Policy practice* • Step-by-step • Stage-by-stage • Area-oriented	
Value • Democracy • Solidarity	*Council decision* • Uniform passport • Residence for workers	• Directives on the Right to residence for: insured and non-welfare-dependent persons; employees and self-employed persons who have ceased their occupational activity
Shared goal • Further integration towards political union • Europe '92	*Citizenship practice* • Participation in day-to-day Community matters (elections, work, economy) • Group-by-group integration (workers, academics, young people) • Interest group mobilization	• Article 39 Amsterdam Treaty (48 EC): free movement of workers • Principle 3c Amsterdam Treaty: abolition of obstacles to free movement of goods, persons, services • Article 12 Amsterdam Treaty (5 EC): no discrimination on grounds of nationality • Article 14 Amsterdam Treaty (8a EC); area without internal frontiers. • Article 141 Amsterdam Treaty (119 EC) equal pay
Shared concerns • Democracy deficit • Transparency deficit • Legitimacy deficit	*New approach* • Communitarization of Schengen and third pillar issues	

Source: Wiener 1998: 273 (updated).

routinization of informal resources, as the Brussels-based institutions began to work with national representations, national parliaments, and NGOs to address the citizens' demands in order to fight the rising discontent which had begun to replace the 'permissive consensus' of earlier decades. Examples of such reactions are the campaigns like 'Citizens First', which were initiated by the EP and transferred by the Commission into the member states in order to bring Europe closer to the citizens. The citizens' mistrust is not only a reaction to the distance between Brussels and the citizen; it also reflects a new way of practising citizenship. The Second Report from the Commission on Citizenship of the Union sheds light on this new model of fragmented citizenship. It states that

> This diverse set of rights (entailed in Union Citizenship) is subject to different conditions. Generally speaking the rights stemming from citizenship of the Union cannot, for instance, be invoked in domestic situations which are purely internal to a Member State. Some of the entitlements such as the electoral rights can only be exercised in a Member State other than that of origin, whilst others such as access to the Ombudsman or to petition the European Parliament are extended to all natural and legal persons residing or having their registered office in a Member State.[38]

While early 'European' citizenship policy did not seek to produce this institutional setting, the events of the 1990s brought into focus an institutional fragmentation which still remains to be matched by day-to-day experiences on the ground. The EU's new decentralized institutional framework thus helps to intensify the already 'challenged confidence in the progressive and unifying force of democratic politics and value' (Saryusz-Wolski 1994). Indeed, Union citizenship contributes to the process of dissolving centred (citizenship) politics. At the same time, and 'despite certain limitations, in practice the introduction of a citizenship of the Union has raised citizens' expectations as to the rights that they expect to see conferred and protected, especially when they move to another Member State'.[39] The expectations of citizenship have now been raised, the genie is out of the bottle and the EU institutions are feeling the pressure to act. Thus, for example, the Commission's second report on citizenship states that

> [P]enalty for failure [to apply citizens' rights in practice] is that citizenship of the Union may appear to be a distant concept for citizens engendering confusion as to its means and objectives, even fuelling anti-EU feelings.[40]

In summary, the foregoing case study has depicted the developing 'European' citizenship practice as the source of the routinizing and institutionalizing of the Euro-specific terms of citizenship. This began in the early 1970s, when practitioners discussed the identity-generating capacity of citizenship. This notion was derived from the modern concept of citizenship, but subsequently lost importance in relation to other elements within the development of citizenship policy. Two decades later, the breadth of Union citizenship is like a pale reflection of a once powerful idea, now diminished to a set of minimal political rights. And yet, a shared perception identifies Union citizenship as a 'devel-

---

[38] COM(97)230 final, Brussels 27 May 1997, 6.   [39] Ibid.   [40] Ibid.

oping concept'.[41] This expression indicates an assumption shared by a considerable variety of actors, governors and governed alike, such as non-governmental organizations, interest groups, and social movements, namely that Union citizenship as stipulated by Article 8 TEU at Maastricht is not the end of the story. The demands, requests, and policy proposals put forward in the post-Maastricht period suggest two things. First, they clearly demonstrate the intention to mobilize towards a change in the existing citizenship articles, for example, towards further 'place-oriented' citizenship rights.[42] Second, these groups' demands illustrated the object of citizen's claims; they were addressed not to national parliaments, but to the IGC charged with preparing the forthcoming constitutional revision in Amsterdam. However, while citizenship practice thus enabled inclusion based on new institutions and, belatedly, new supranational practices, it also generated political tension. The normative demand for equal access to democratic participation based on the right to vote clearly brought to the fore the problem of inclusion and exclusion among member state nationals and 'other' European residents, namely the so-called 'third country nationals'.

While top-down citizenship practice (i.e. Bismarckian style policy-making) now has a history in the EU, bottom-up mobilization (i.e. the struggle of social forces) has been relatively rare.[43] It was not until after the stipulation of Union citizenship in the Maastricht Treaty of 1991 that a range of societal groups began to address the institutions of the Euro-polity, in particular the IGC, with demands for improved citizenship rights. The mobilization of hundreds of non-governmental organizations and lobby groups in the years between Maastricht and Amsterdam has introduced a shift in citizenship practice from policy to politics. The stipulation of political citizenship rights at the European level fits well with an ongoing global process of decoupling nationality and citizenship. However, this chapter has emphasized that the significance of this shift lies in the 'how' of citizenship practice as a component part of polity formation by focusing on new institutions and on changes in the way claims are made. Both have the potential to bring about substantial changes of governance.

The post-Maastricht mobilization has two potential implications: one is a rethinking of the notion of citizenship, the other is the changing structure and substance of governance beyond the nation state. This chapter has focused primarily on the latter. The argument is built on the EU's use of citizenship as a

[41] The term 'developing concept' is used by the European Commission (see European Commission, 'Report on the Operation of the Treaty on European Union', Brussels, 10 May 1995, SEC(95) final, 7), as well as by the European Parliament (see Task-Force on the Intergovernmental Conference, No. 10, 'Briefing on European Citizenship', PE 165.793, Luxembourg, 15 January 1996c, 5).

[42] Similar demands have been put forward by the Euro Citizen Action Service (ECAS) in 'Revision of Part Two of the Treaty', draft, 15 March 1996, 1. For the discussion on place-oriented citizenship in the EU, see also Wiener (1996).

[43] For the distinction between active and passive citizenship politics, see Turner (1990).

concept which, on the one hand, is intrinsically and crucially linked to the political project of state-building (Grawert 1973; Held 1991; Tilly 1975; Turner 1990) and, on the other, has been strongly contested in theory and practice. The fact that the EU is not a state pushes the conceptual contestation of citizenship even further. As this chapter has sought to demonstrate, the practitioners' application of the modern concept of citizenship as identity-generating by defining who is in and who is out, as well as the gradual emergence of a postmodern fragmented citizenship practice which includes various groups of citizens (instead of an either universally or pre-politically defined community, as the liberal and communitarian approaches contend respectively) have highlighted two substantial elements of governance. First, the case study has further contested the meaning of citizenship. Second, and more specifically, based on the concept of embedded *acquis*, the case study has identified new resources, routinized practices, and institutions. This chapter by no means sought to provide a comprehensive analysis, but has introduced a way of tackling new dimensions of governance. The thrust of the argument is intended to extend the discussion about governance in the Euro-polity by introducing constructive and historical perspectives on routinized practices and the interrelated institutionalized terms of governance.[44]

To sum up: the post-Maastricht situation seems to be the consequence of sets of practices which deviate from the familiar routines of citizenship practice under national governance. Crossing the borders of one nation state to work and settle in another—and keeping certain of the first state's citizenship rights while also acquiring politically limited new rights in the other—has created confusion. The changes have an effect on the governed and governors alike. Where to direct political claims? How to decide about rights, for whom and based on which principles? The case study in this chapter demonstrates the link between citizen mobilization over claims and changing patterns of citizenship practice. It shows that citizenship practice has entered a new cycle characterized by a change in the style, strategy, and content of citizenship practice.

Conclusion

This chapter has highlighted the link between changes in the *acquis communautaire* which were caused by the practice of policy-making, and substantive transformations of governance. I have argued that these entail information about the normative principles, shared practices and rules which contribute to 'thick' governance in the Euro-polity. The transmission belt on which this link

---

[44] This intention was specifically spurred on by Hix's (1998b) efforts to identify 'rival approaches' to governance in European integration approaches.

builds is the embedded *acquis communautaire*. In other words, while the core of the *acquis* is made up of formal resources, such as legal procedures, treaty provisions, and directives, these formal resources are not independent of previously established informal resources, such as shared values and norms on the one hand, and routinized practices and policy objectives on the other. By showing that both phenomena are linked to and constituent parts of the substance and structure of governance, this chapter has not considered governance to be simply a pattern of rule within the Euro-polity, but has instead stressed the importance of the social construction of sets of practices in creating the leading concepts and principles of governance.

Based on the threefold set of resources (informal, routinized, and formal), the case study sought to assess the apparent gap between the idea of citizenship as an identity-generating policy innovation, and the minimalist version of Union citizenship stipulated by the Maastricht Treaty. Indeed, the resources actually fill the gap. Instead of a skeleton of formal political rights, the case study on the practice of citizenship policy has shed light on the creation of a broad range of informal resources and routinized practices which provided the framework for interest group mobilization in the 1990s. In examining the policy process as it unfolded step by step, it offers an insight into the policy practices, including the discussion of ideas, the defining of policy objectives, strategies and procedures, and eventually the institutionalization of routinized new practices of governance, in the process shaping a new model of citizenship which is specific to the Euro-polity in the process. The preparatory stage of the Amsterdam IGC was particularly interesting in this process, because the conflictual discussions preceding the summit established a new political aspect of governance in the Euro-polity.

The case study suggests that, in the post-Maastricht period, the Euro-polity entered into a new stage of polity formation beyond the nation state. Citizen mobilization showed how the informal resources of the citizenship *acquis*, such as shared values and norms (equal access to political participation), were mobilized by interest groups to enforce their demands. Further, the peculiar mix of fragmented institutionalization and mobilization of the resources of the citizenship *acquis* implies that the modern concept of citizenship will lose political clout and meaning. Once viewed as a unifying concept which set the borders of order and defined who was in or out of a political community, the concept now stretches across borders. While new forms of citizenship practice contribute to a rethinking of the notion of citizenship towards what might turn out to be a post-national political theory of citizenship, for EU governance these new forms of citizenship practice mean a shift of focus with regard to political authority. This shift has sparked conflict, and it has opened up a window to import 'the political' into negotiations over the conditions of EU governance.

References

Abélès, Marc (1994), 'L'Europe en trois dimensions', *Esprit*, June: 117–28.

Abélès, Marc and Bellier, Irène (1996), 'La Commission européenne: du compromis culturel à la culture du compromis', *Revue Française de Science Politique*, **46** (3).

Abromeit, Heidrun (1998), 'How to Democratise a Multi-level, Multi-dimensional Polity', in Albert Weale and Michael Nentwich (eds.), *The Political Theory and the European Union* (London: Routledge), 112–24.

Albert, Mathias and Brock, Lothar (1995), 'Entgrenzung der Staatenwelt: Zur Analyse weltgesellschaftlicher Entwicklungsprozesse', *Zeitschrift für Internationale Beziehungen*, **2**: 259–85.

Allott, Philip (1997), Commentary presented at the University of Cambridge Centre for European Legal Studies Seminar on the Treaty of Amsterdam, 5 July. (Unpublished MS, copy on file with author.)

Altenstetter, Christa (1996), 'Regulating Healthcare Technologies and Medical Supplies in the European Economic Area', *Health Policy*, **35**: 33–52.

Anderson, Benedict (1991) (2nd edn.), *Imagined Communities: Reflections on the Origin and Spread of Nationalism* (London: Verso).

Armstrong, Harvey W. (1995), 'The Role and Evolution of European Community Regional Policy', in Barry Jones and Michael Keating (eds.), *The European Union and the Regions* (Oxford: Oxford University Press), 23–62.

Armstrong, Kenneth (1996), 'Citizenship of the Union? Lessons from *Carvel and The Guardian*', *Modern Law Review*, **59**: 582–8.

Armstrong, Kenneth (1998), 'Legal Integration: Theorizing the Legal Dimension of European Integration', *Journal of Common Market Studies*, **36**: 155–74.

Armstrong, Kenneth and Bulmer, Simon (1998), *The Governance of the Single European Market* (Manchester, UK: Manchester University Press).

ARNE (Antiracist Network for Equality in Europe) (1995), 'Modifications to the Maastricht Treaty in Sight of the 1996 Intergovernmental Conference'. (Rome: MS, 14–15 July).

Aron, Raymond (1974), 'Is Multinational Citizenship Possible?', *Social Research*, **41**: 638–56.

Attinà, Fulvio (1990), 'The Voting Behaviour of the European Parliament Members and the Problem of Europarties', *European Journal of Political Research*, **18** (3): 557–79.

Austria (1995), *Guidelines of the Austrian Government on the Subjects likely to be Dealt with at the 1996 IGC*, June 1995.

Austria (1996), *Austria's Positions of Principle on the Intergovernmental Conference*, 26 March 1996.

Avery, Graham and Cameron, Fraser (1998), *The Enlargement of the European Union* (Sheffield, UK: Sheffield Academic Press for UACES).

Bagehot, Walter (1867), *The English Constitution* (Oxford: Oxford University Press).

Bainbridge, Timothy and Teasdale, Anthony (1995), *The Penguin Companion to European Union* (London: Penguin).

Balassa, Bela (1961), *The Theory of Economic Integration* (Homewood, IL: Irwin).

Baldwin, Richard (1994), *Towards an Integrated Europe* (London: CEPR).

Barber, Benjamin R. (1984), *Strong Democracy: Participatory Politics for a New Age* (Berkeley, CA: University of California Press).

Barber, Lionel (1997), 'Socialist Victors Talk Different Languages', *Financial Times*, 7 June.

Bardi, Luciano (1996), 'Transnational Trends in European Parties and the 1994 Elections of the European Parliament', *Party Politics*, **2** (1): 99–114.

Barnard, Catherine and Hervey, Tamara (1998), 'Softening the Approach to Quotas: Positive Action after *Marschall*', *Journal of Social Welfare and Family Law*, **20**: 333–52.

Beer, Samuel H. (1969), *British Politics in the Collectivist Age* (New York: Vintage). (Original work published 1965.)

Beitz, Charles R. (1991), 'Sovereignty and Morality in International Affairs', in David Held (ed.), *Political Theory Today* (Cambridge, UK: Polity Press), 236–54.

Belgium (1995), *Government Policy Paper Addressed to the Belgian Parliament on the 1996 IGC*.

Bellamy, Richard and Castiglione, Dario (1997), 'Building the Union: The Nature of Sovereignty in the Political Architecture of Europe', *Law and Philosophy*, **16**: 421–45.

Bellier, Irène (1995), 'Une culture de la Commission européenne? De la rencontre des cultures européennes et du multilinguisme des fonctionnaires', in Yves Mény, Pierre Muller, and Jean-Louis Quermonne (eds.), *Politiques publiques en Europe* (Paris: L'Harmattan).

Bendix, Reinhard (1964), *Nation Building and Citizenship* (New York: Wiley).

Benelux (1996), *Memorandum of March 1996 of Belgium, the Netherlands and Luxembourg for the IGC*, 7 March 1996.

Benhabib, Seyla (1997), 'Fortress Europe or The United Colours of Benetton?', paper presented at the American Political Science Association meeting, Washington DC.

Bertram, Christoph (1967), 'Decision-making in the EEC: The Management Committee Procedure', *Common Market Law Review*, **5** (3): 246–64.

Bieber, Roland (1997), 'Reformen der Institutionen und Verfahren—Amsterdam kein Meisterstück', *Integration*, **20**: 236–46.

Biersteker, Th. and Weber, C. (eds.) (1996), *State Sovereignty as Social Construct* (Cambridge: Cambridge University Press).

Bolten, J. J. (1992), 'From Schengen to Dublin: The New Frontiers of Refugee Law', in J. D. M. Steenbergen (ed.), *Schengen: Internationalisation of Central Chapters of the Law on Aliens, Refugees, Privacy, Security and the Police* (Leiden: Stichting NCJM), 8–36.

Borrmann, Axel, Fischer, Bernhard, Jungnickel, Rolf, Koopman, Georg, and Scharrer, Hans-Eckart (1995), *Regionalismustendenzen im Welthandel: Erscheinungsformen, Ursachen und Bedeutung für Richtung und Struktur des internationalen Handels* (Baden-Baden: Nomos).

Bosch, Agusti and Newton, Kenneth (1995), 'Economic Calculus or Familiarity Breeds

Content?', in Oskar Niedermayer and Richard Sinnott (eds.), *Public Opinion and Internationalized Governance: Beliefs in Government*, Vol. 2 (Oxford: Oxford University Press), 73–104.

Bowler, Shaun and Farrell, David M. (1993), 'Legislator Shirking and Voter Monitoring: Impacts of European Parliament Electoral Systems upon Legislator-Voter Relationships', *Journal of Common Market Studies*, **31** (1): 45–69.

Bradley, K. St. C. (1997), 'The European Parliament and Comitology: On the Road to Nowhere?', *European Law Journal*, **3**: 230–54.

Bremner, C. and Pierce, A. (1997), 'Jobs' Summit Soured by Spanish Opt-out', *The Times*, 22 November 1997.

Brok, Elmer (1997), 'Der Amsterdamer Vertrag: Etappe auf dem Weg zur europäischen Einigung', *Integration*, **20**: 211–18.

Bromiley, Philip and Marcus, Alfred (1987), 'Deadlines, Routines and Change', *Policy Sciences*, **20** (2): 85–103.

Brubaker, W. Roger (1992), *Citizenship and Nationhood in France and Germany* (Cambridge, MA: Harvard University Press).

Brunsson, Nils (1993), 'Reform as Routine', in Nils Brunsson and Johan P. Olsen (eds.), *The Reforming Organization* (London: Routledge), 33–47.

Brzinski, Joanne Bay (1996), 'Political Group Cohesion in the European Parliament, 1989–1994', in Carolyn Rhodes and Sonia Mazey (eds.), *The State of the European Union*, Vol. 3 (London: Longman).

Bulmer, Simon (1994), 'Institutions and Policy Change in the European Community: The Case of Merger Control', *Public Administration*, **72** (3): 423–44.

Bulmer, Simon (1995), *Four Faces of European Governance: A new institutional research agenda* (Manchester, UK: University of Manchester, EPRU paper).

Bulmer, Simon (1997), *New Institutionalism, the Single Market and EU Governance* (Oslo: ARENA, Advanced Research on the Europeanisation of the Nation State), Working Paper.

Burke, Edmund (1839: 1st edn. 1774) *Works* (By and Law: London).

Burley, Anne-Marie and Mattli, Walter (1993), 'Europe Before the Court: A Political Theory of Legal Integration', *International Organization*, **47**: 41–76.

Cairns, Alan C. (1991), *Disruptions: Constitutional Struggles, from the Charter to Meech Lake*, collection of essays by Alan C. Cairns, edited by D. E. Williams (Toronto: McClelland & Stewart).

Canada, Task Force on Canadian Unity (1979), *A Future Together: Observations and Recommendations* (Ottowa: Ministry of Supply and Services).

Caporaso, James A. (1996), 'The European Union and Forms of State: Westphalian, Regulatory or Post-Modern?', *Journal of Common Market Studies*, **34**: 29–52.

Carter, Catriona (1997), 'The "European Social Model": A Framework for Analysis', paper presented in Leeds, UK, 6 November.

Chalmers, Damian (1998), 'Bureaucratic Europe: From Regulating Communities to Securitising Unions', paper presented at the Conference of Europeanists, Chicago, February.

Charbonneau, Jean Pierre (1978), *L'option* (Montreal: Editions de l'homme).

Chryssochoou, Dimitris N. (1994), 'Democracy and Symbiosis in the European Union: Towards a Confederal Consociation', *West European Politics*, **17** (1): 1–14.

Chryssochoou, Dimitris (1997), 'New Challenges to the Study of European Integration: Implications for Theory-Building', *Journal of Common Market Studies*, **35**: 521–42.

Ciavarini Azzi, Guiseppe (ed.) (1985), *The Implementation of EC Law by the Member States* (Maastricht: European Institute of Public Administration).

Cini, Michelle (1994), 'Policing the International Market: The Regulation of Competition in the European Community', Ph.D. thesis, University of Exeter, UK.

Cini, Michelle (1997), *The European Commission: Leadership, organisation and culture in the EU administration* (Manchester, UK: Manchester University Press).

Clare, Sian (1997), 'Blair's "Crusade Against Unemployment" Moves to EU', *Press Association Newsfile*, 4 June.

Cloos, J., Reinisch, G., Vignes, D., and Weyland, L. (1993), *Le Traité de Maastricht: Genèse, analyse, commentaires* (Brussels: Bruylant).

Closa, Carlos (1995), 'Citizenship of the Union and Nationality of Member States', *Common Market Law Review*, **32**: 487–518.

Cockfield, Lord Arthur (1994), *The European Union: Creating the Single Market* (New York: Wiley).

Cohen, Michael D, March, James G., and Olsen, Johan P. (1972), 'A Garbage Can Model of Organizational Choice', *Administrative Science Quarterly*, **17** (1): 1–25.

COM(1998)317 final. *Fifteenth Annual Report on Monitoring the Application of Community Law.*

COM(1998)345 final. *Legislate less to act better: the facts.* Communication from the European Commission to the European Council.

Comité des Sages (1996), *For a Europe of Civic and Social Rights*, Report by the Comité des Sages chaired by Maria de Lourdes Pintasilgo (Luxembourg: Office for Official Publications of the European Communities).

Commission of the European Communities (1985), *Completing the Internal Market*, White Paper from the Commission to the European Council (Luxembourg: Office for Official Publications of the European Communities).

Commission of the European Communities (1992a), *Agreement on the European Economic Area* (Luxembourg: Office for Official Publications of the European Communities).

Commission of the European Communities (1992b), 'Europe and the Challenge of Enlargement', *Bulletin of the EC*, Suppl. 3/92.

Commission of the European Communities (1993a), *Green Paper on Social Policy*, COM(93)551, 17 November 1993.

Commission of the European Communities (1993b), White Paper on Growth, Competitiveness, Employment: The Challenges and Ways Forward into the 21st Century, *Bulletin of the EC*, Suppl. 6/93, COM(93)700.

Commission of the European Communities (1994), *European Social Policy. A Way Forward for the Union*, COM(94)333, 27 July 1994.

Commission of the European Communities (1995a), *Report on the Operation of the Treaty on European Union* (Brussels: Office for Official Publications of the European Communities, 10 May 1995; SEC(95) final).

Commission of the European Communities (1995*b*), *Commission Communication on a Medium Term Social Action Programme (1995–97)*, COM(95)134.

Commission of the European Communities (1995*c*), *Position of 6 December 1995 on the Reflection Group Report*.

Commission of the European Communities (1995*d*), *White Paper on Preparation of the Associated Countries of Central and Eastern Europe for Integration into the Internal Market of the Union*, COM(95)163, 3 May 1995, and Annex, COM(95)163/2, 10 May 1995.

Commission of the European Communities (1996*a*), *Reinforcing Political Union and Preparing for Enlargement*, Opinion submitted to the IGC, 28 February 1996 (Luxembourg: Office for Official Publications of the European Communities).

Commission of the European Communities (1996*b*), *Work Programme for 1997*, COM(96)507.

Commission of the European Communities (1996*c*), *Eurobarometer: Top Decision Makers Survey—Summary Report* (Brussels).

Commission of the European Communities (1997*a*), 'Agenda 2000: For a Stronger and Wider Union', *Bulletin of the European Union*, Suppl. 5/97 (Luxembourg: Office for Official Publications of the European Communities).

Commission of the European Communities (1997*b*), 'Mixed Reactions to the New EU Treaty', *Women of Europe Newsletter*, **73**: 2–3.

Commission of the European Communities (1997*c*), 'Recherche sur l'exercice du droit d'initiative de la Commission en 1996', document interne au Secrétariat général.

Commission of the European Communities (1998), *1996 Intergovernmental Conference Retrospective Database*, Europa Home Page; http://europa.eu.int/en/agenda-/igc-home/index.html. (Contains texts of all the major documents, including the Treaty itself, the reports of the supranational organizations, and the negotiating positions of the member states).

Committee of the Regions (1995), *Opinion of 20 April 1995 on the revision of the Treaty on European Union*.

CONF 2500 (1996), *Draft Treaty, Irish Presidency*, 13–14 December 1996.

CONF 2500 ADD1 (1997), *Addendum to Irish Draft Treaty*, 20 March 1997.

CONF 3821 (1996), *Enhanced Co-operation—Flexibility*, 16 April 1996.

CONF 3860 (1996), *Progress Report on the Intergovernmental Conference*, 17 June 1996.

CONF 3914 (1996), *Flexibility*, 24 September 1996.

CONF 3955 (1996), *Closer co-operation with a view to increased European integration, France and Germany*, 18 October 1996.

CONF 3985 (1996), *IGC Ministerial meeting on 25 November*, 19 November 1996.

CONF 3999 (1996), *Flexibility—Draft general clause on enhanced co-operation*, Portugal, 29 November 1996.

CONF 3801 (1997), *Flexibility, Italy*, 15 January 1997.

CONF 3802 (1997), *Enhanced co-operation—Flexibility*, 16 January 1997.

CONF 3805 (1997), *Flexibility, Commission*, 23 January 1997.

CONF 3806 (1997), *Schengen and the European Union*, 4 February 1997.

CONF 3813 (1997), *Flexibility—enabling clauses approach*, 11 February 1997.

CONF 3835 (1997), *Closer Co-operation/Flexibility*, March 4 1997.

CONF 3848 (1997), *Presidency progress report on the state of play of the Conference*, 19 March 1997.

CONF 3866 (1997), *Enhanced co-operation*, Greece, 8 April 1997.

CONF 4000 (1997), *Draft Treaty of Amsterdam, Dutch Presidency*, 12 July 1997.

CONF 4002 (1997), *Draft Treaty of Amsterdam*, 20 June 1997.

CONF 4004 (1997), *Treaty of Amsterdam*, 1 July 1997.

CONF 4007 (1997), *Treaty of Amsterdam*, 2 October 1997.

Conradi, Peter (1997), 'Kohl and Chirac Bow to New Socialist Order Across Europe', *Sunday Times*, 8 June.

Corbett, Richard (1987), 'The 1985 Intergovernmental Conference and the Single European Act', in Roy Pryce (ed.), *The Dynamics of European Union* (New York: Croom Helm), 238–72.

Corbett, Richard (1994), *The Treaty of Maastricht* (Harlow, UK: Longman).

Corbett, Richard, Jacobs, Francis, and Shackleton, Michael (1995) (3rd edn.), *The European Parliament* (London: Catermill).

Council of the European Union (1993), *Treaty on European Union* (Luxembourg: Office for Official Publications of the European Communities).

Council of the European Union (1995), *Report of 6 April 1995 on the functioning of the Treaty on European Union* (5082/95).

Council of the European Union (1997), *Consolidated Version of the Treaty Establishing the European Community*, CONF 4005/97 ADD 2.

Court of Auditors (1995), *Report of May 1995 to the Reflection Group on the operation of the Treaty on European Union*.

Court of First Instance (1995), *Contribution of 17 May 1995 by the Court of First Instance on the operation of the Treaty on European Union*.

Cox, Gary W. and McCubbins, Matthew D. (1993), *Legislative Leviathan: Party Government in the House* (Berkeley, CA: University of California Press).

Cram, Laura (1993), 'Calling the Tune without Paying the Piper? Social Policy Regulation: The Role of the Commission in the European Community Social Policy', *Policy and Politics*, **21** (2): 135–43.

Cram, Laura (1994), 'The European Commission as a multi-organisation: Social Policy and IT Policy in the EU', *Journal of European Public Policy*, **1** (1): 195–218.

Curtice, John (1989), 'The 1989 Elections: Protest of Green Tide?', *Electoral Studies*, **8** (3): 217–30.

Curtin, Deirdre (1993), 'The Constitutional Structure of the Union: A Europe of Bits and Pieces', *Common Market Law Review*, **27**: 709 –39.

Curtin, Deirdre (1996), 'Betwixt and Between: Democracy and Transparency in the Governance of the European Union', in Jan Winter, Deirdre Curtin, Alfred Kellerman, and Bruno de Witte (eds.), *Reforming the Treaty on European Union: The Legal Debate* (The Hague: Kluwer), 95–121.

Cyert, Richard M. and March, James G. (1992) (2nd edn.), *A Behavioral Theory of the Firm* (Cambridge, MA: Blackwell Business).

Dahl, Robert (1956), *A Preface to Democratic Theory* (Chicago, IL: University of Chicago Press).

Dahl, Robert (1989), *Democracy and Its Critics* (New Haven, CT: Yale University Press).

Dankert, Piet (1997), 'Pressure from the European Parliament', in Geoffrey Edwards and Alfred Pijpers (eds.), *The Politics of European Treaty Reform: The 1996 Intergovernmental Conference and Beyond* (London/Washington DC: Pinter), 212–25.

Darnoux, R. (1995), 'L'étrange procédure e nomination de la Commission européenne', *Revue Politique et Parlementaire*, **978**: 17–27.

de Bresson, Henri (1997), 'Un petit mot en anglais, quelques souvenirs d'italien . . .', *Le Monde*, 9 June.

Dehousse, Renaud (ed.) (1994), *Europe after Maastricht. An Ever Closer Union?* (Munich: Law Books in Europe).

Dehousse, Renaud (1995), *Institutional Reform in the European Community: Are there Alternatives to the Majoritarian Avenue?* (Florence: European University Institute, Robert Schuman Centre: Working Paper No. 95/4).

Dehousse, Renaud (1998), *European Institutional Architecture after Amsterdam: Parliamentary System or Regulatory Structures* (Florence; European University Institute, Robert Schuman Centre), Working Paper No. 11/98; available online; http://www.iue.it-/RSC/WP-Texts/98-11.htm.

de La Serre, Françoise and Wallace, Helen (1997), *Flexibility and Enhanced Co-operation in the European Union: Placebo rather than Panacea?* (Paris: Groupement d'Études et de Recherches 'Notre Europe'), Research and Policy Papers No. 28.

Deloche, Florence and Lequesne, Christian (1996), 'Le programme PHARE: mérites et limites de la politique d'assistance de la Communauté européenne aux pays d'Europe centrale et orientale', *Politiques et Management public*, **14** (1): 143–54.

De Menil, Lois Pattison (1977), *Who Speaks for Europe? The Vision of Charles de Gaulle* (London: Weidenfeld & Nicolson).

Demers, Fanny S. and Demers, Michel (1995) (2nd edn.), *European Union: A Variable Model for Québec-Canada?* (Ottowa: University of Ottowa and Carleton University, Centre for Trade Policy and Law).

Demmke, Christoph, Eberharter, Elisabeth, Schaefer, Günther F., and Türk, Alexander (1996), 'The History of Comitology', in Robiin H. Pedler and Günther F. Schaefer (eds.), *Shaping European Law and Policy: The Role of Committees and Comitology in the Political Process* (Maastricht: European Institute of Public Administration), 61–82.

den Boer, Monica (ed.) (1997a), *The Implementation of Schengen: First the Widening, Now the Deepening* (Maastricht: European Institute of Public Administration).

den Boer, Monica (1997b), 'Justice and Home Affairs Cooperation in the Treaty on European Union: More Complexity Despite Communautarization', *Maastricht Journal of European and Comparative Law*, **4**: 310–16.

Denmark (1995a), *Dagsorden for Europa: Regeringskonference 1996*, Report of the Danish Foreign Ministry, June 1995.

Denmark (1995b), *Bases for Negotiations: An Open Europe—The 1996 IGC*, Memorandum of the Danish Government, 11 December 1995.

Derrida, Jacques (1984), *Margins of Philosophy* (Chicago, IL.: University of Chicago Press).

Deutsch, Karl W. (1957), *Political Community and the North Atlantic Area: International Organization in the Light of Historical Experience* (Princeton, NJ: Princeton University Press).

Deutsch, Karl W. (1966) (2nd edn.), *Nationalism and Social Communication: An Inquiry into the Foundation of Nationality* (Cambridge, MA: MIT Press).

Devuyst, Youri (1997), 'The Treaty of Amsterdam: An Introductory Analysis', *ECSA Review*, **X** (3): 6–14.

Dinan, Desmond (1994), *Ever Closer Union? An Introduction to the European Community* (Boulder, CO: Lynne Rienner).

Dinan, Desmond (1997), 'The Commission and the Reform Process', in Geoffrey Edwards and Alfred Pijpers (eds.), *The Politics of European Treaty Reform: The 1996 Intergovernmental Conference and Beyond* (London: Pinter), 188–211.

Dinan, Desmond (1998), 'Reflections on the IGCs', in Pierre-Henri Laurent and Marc Maresceau (eds.), *The State of the European Union. Vol. 4: Deepening and Widening* (Boulder, CO: Lynne Rienner), 23–40.

Dogan, Rhys (1997), 'Comitology: Little Procedures With Big Implications', *West European Politics*, **3**: 31–60.

Donnelly, Martin and Ritchie, Ella (1994), 'The College of Commissioners and their Cabinets', in Geoffrey Edwards and David Spence (eds.), *The European Commission* (London: Longman).

d'Oliveira, Ulrich Jessurun (1995), 'Union Citizenship: Pie in the Sky?', in Allan Rosas and Esko Antola (eds.), *A Citizens' Europe: In Search of a New Order* (London: Sage), 58–84.

Douglas, Mary (1986), *How Institutions Think* (Syracuse, NY: Syracuse University Press).

Downs, Anthony (1957), *An Economic Theory of Democracy* (New York: Harper & Row).

Duchesne, Sophie and Frognier, André-Paul (1995), 'Is There a European Identity?', in Oskar Niedermayer and Richard Sinnott (eds.), *Public Opinion and Internationalized Governance: Beliefs in Government*, Vol. 2 (Oxford: Oxford University Press), 193–226.

Dudley, Geoffrey F. and Richardson, Jeremy J. (1997), 'Competing Policy Frames in EU Policy Making: The Rise of Free Market Ideas in EU Steel Policy 1985–1996', *European Integration Online Papers*, **1**: No. 013; http://eiop.or.at/eiop/texte/1997-013a.htm.

Duff, Andrew (1997), *The Treaty of Amsterdam: Text and Commentary* (London: The Federal Trust).

Duff, Andrew, Pinder, John and Pryce, Roy (eds.) (1994), *Maastricht and Beyond: Building the European Union* (New York: Routledge).

Dumez, Hervé and Jeunemaître, Alain (1991), *La concurrence en Europe: De nouvelles règles du jeu pour les entreprises* (Paris: Le Seuil).

Dworkin, Ronald (1991), *Law's Empire* (London: Fontana).

Easton, David (1965), *A Systems Analysis of Political Life* (New York: Wiley).

Eckstein, Harry (1975), 'Case Study and Theory in Political Science', in Fred I. Greenstein and Nelson W. Polsby (eds.), *Handbook of Political Science. Vol. 1: Political Science: Scope and Theory* (Reading, MA: Addison-Wesley), 79–137.

Economic and Social Committee (1995), *Opinion of 22 November 1995 on the 1996 Intergovernmental Conference and the Role of the Economic and Social Committee.*

Edwards, Geoffrey (1998), 'The Council of Ministers and Enlargement: A Search for Efficiency, Effectiveness, and Accountability?', in J. Redmond and G. Rosenthal (eds.), *The Expanding European Union. Past, Present, Future* (Boulder, CO: Lynne Rienner), 41–64.

Edwards, Geoffrey and Philippart, Eric (1997), *Flexibility and the Treaty of Amsterdam: Europe's New Byzantium?* (Cambridge, UK: CELS, Centre for European Legal Studies), Occasional Paper No. 3.

Edwards, Geoffrey and Pijpers, Alfred (1997), 'The 1996 IGC: An Introduction', in Geoffrey Edwards and Alfred Pijpers (eds.), *The Politics of European Treaty Reform— The 1996 Intergovernmental Conference and Beyond* (London/Washington DC: Pinter), 1–14.

Ehlermann, Claus-Dieter (1997), *Differentiation, Flexibility, Closer Co-operation: The New Provisions of the Amsterdam Treaty* (Florence: European University Institute).

Eichengreen, Barry (1993), 'European Monetary Unification', *Journal of Economic Literature*, **31**: 1321–57.

Eichener, Volker (1997), *Entscheidungsprozesse in der regulativen Politik der Europäischen Union* (Ruhr-Universität Bochum: Habilitationsschrift eingereicht an der Fakultät für Sozialwissenschaft).

van der Eijk, Cees and Franklin, Mark (eds.) (1996), *Choosing Europe? The European Electorate and National Politics in the Face of Union* (Ann Arbor, MI: University of Michigan Press).

El-Agraa, A. M. (1994) (4th edn.), *The Economics of the European Community*, (New York/Toronto: Harvester Wheatsheaf).

Eleftheriadis, Pavlos (1998), 'Begging the Constitutional Question', *Journal of Common Market Studies*, **35**: 255–72.

Esaiasson, Peter and Holmberg, Søren (1996), *Representation from Above: Members of Parliaments and Representative Democracy in Sweden* (Dartmouth).

Esping-Andersen, Gøsta (1990), *The Three Worlds of Welfare Capitalism*, (Cambridge, UK: Polity Press).

Etzioni, Amitai (1996), *The New Golden Rule: Community and Morality in a Democratic Society* (New York: Basic Books).

European Council (1992), Presidency Conclusions, Edinburgh European Council, *Bulletin of the EC*, 11–12 December.

European Council (1993), Presidency Conclusions, Copenhagen European Council, *Bulletin of the EC* 21–22 June; Europe Documents. No. 1844/45, 24.06.1993.

European Council (1994a), Presidency Conclusions, Corfu European Council, *Bulletin of the EC*, 24–25 June, SN 100/94.

European Council (1994*b*), Presidency Conclusions, Essen European Council, *Bulletin of the EC*, 9–10 December.

European Council (1995), *Presidency Conclusions, Madrid European Council, Bulletin of the EC* 15–16 December; SN 400/95.

European Council (1996*a*), *Presidency Conclusions, Turin European Council, Bulletin of the EC* 29 March; SN 100/96.

European Council (1996*b*), *Presidency Conclusions, Florence European Council, Bulletin of the EC* 21–22 June; SN 300/96.

European Court of Justice (1995), *Report of May 1995 on certain aspects of the implementation of the Treaty on European Union.*

European Parliament (1979), *Proceedings of the Round Table on Special Rights and a Charter of the Rights of the Citizens of the European Community and Related Documents, Florence, 26–28 October* (Luxembourg: Office of Official Publications of the European Communities).

European Parliament (1994), *Resolution on a Multi-speed Europe*, 28 September 1994.

European Parliament (1995*a*), *Draft working document on variable integration: Principles and fields of application* (PE 211.102/rev.).

European Parliament (1995*b*), *Resolution of May 17 1995 on the operation of the Treaty on European Union with a view to the 1996 Intergovernmental Conference* (PE 190.441).

European Parliament (1995*c*), *Resolution of 14 December 1995 on the Agenda for the 1996 Intergovernmental Conference* (PE 195.289).

European Parliament (1996*a*), *Briefing on differentiated integration* (PE 165.802).

European Parliament (1996*b*), *White Paper on the 1996 Intergovernmental Conference* (Luxembourg).

European Parliament (1996*c*), *Briefing on European Citizenship* (Luxembourg: Office for Official Publications of the European Communities; PE 165.793).

European Parliament (1997*a*), *Intergovernmental Conference Briefing No. 13: European Employment and Social Policy* (Third update: 11 July 1997); http://www.europarl.eu.int/dg7/fiches/en/fiche13.htm.

European Parliament (1997*b*), *Intergovernmental Conference Briefing No. 37: Employment and the IGC* (First update: 2 April 1997); http://www.europarl.eu.int/dg7/fiches/en/fiche37.htm.

European Policy Centre (1997), *Making Sense of the Amsterdam Treaty* (Brussels: European Policy Centre).

European Social Observatory (1993), *Synoptic Analysis of the Treaties Before and After Maastricht* (Brussels: European Social Observatory—Working Paper).

European Social Observatory (1997), *Analytical Review of the Treaty of Amsterdam* (Brussels: European Social Observatory), Working Paper.

European Union (1995), *European Union: Selected Instruments Taken from the Treaties*, Book 1, Vol. I (Luxembourg: Office for Official Publications of the European Communities).

European Union (1997), *Treaty of Amsterdam: Consolidated Versions of the Treaty on*

European Union and the Treaty Establishing the European Community (Luxembourg: Office for Official Publications of the European Communities).

Europe Environment (1997), 'Amsterdam Treaty: Environment Gains Higher Billing', *Europe Environment*, No. 502, 24 June.

Evans, Peter B., Rueschemeyer, Dietrich, and Skocpol, Theda (eds.) (1985), *Bringing The State Back In* (Cambridge: Cambridge University Press).

Everson, Michelle (1995), 'The Legacy of the Market Citizen', in Jo Shaw and Gillian More (eds.), *New Legal Dynamics of European Union* (Oxford: Oxford University Press), 73–90.

Everson, Michelle (1996), 'Women and Citizenship of the European Union', in Tamara Hervey and David O'Keeffe (eds.), *Sex Equality Law in the European Union* (Chichester, UK: Wiley), 203–19.

Everson, Michelle (1998), 'Administering Europe?', *Journal of Common Market Studies*, **36** (2): 195–216.

Fafard, Patrick C. and Brown, Douglas M. (eds.) (1996), *The State of the Federation 1996* (Kingston, Ontario: Queen's University, Institute of Intergovernmental Relations).

Falke, Josef (1996), 'Comitology and other Committees: A Preliminary Empirical Assessment', in Robin H. Pedler and Günther F. Schaefer (eds.), *Shaping European Law and Policy: The Role of Committees and Comitology in the Political Process* (Maastricht: European Institute of Public Administration), 117–65.

Falkner, Gerda and Nentwich, Michael (1995), *European Union: Democratic Perspectives after 1996* (Vienna: Service Fachverlag).

Falkner, Gerda and Nentwich, Michael (1997), 'The European Parliament—Winner or Loser of the Amsterdam Treaty? A Preliminary Assessment', paper presented at the International Political Science Association seminar on 'Amsterdam and Beyond', Brussels, 9–12 July.

Featherstone, Kevin and Infantis, Kostas (1996), *Greece in a Changing Europe: Between European integration and Balkan disintegration?* (Manchester, UK: Manchester University Press).

Ferguson, Yale and Mansbach, Richard (1996), 'Political Space and Westphalian States in a World of Polities', *Global Governance*, **2**: 261–87.

Finland (1995), *Memorandum concerning Finnish points of view with regard to the 1996 Intergovernmental Conference of the European Union*, September 1995.

Finland (1996a), *Finland's points of departure and objectives in the 1996 Intergovernmental Conference*, 27 February 1996.

Finland (1996b), *The Ten Commandments of Flexible Integration*, non-paper, 30 May 1996.

Føllesdal, Andreas and Koslowski, Peter (eds.) (1997), *Democracy and the European Union* (Berlin: Springer).

France (1996), Memorandum on France's guidelines for the 1996 IGC, *Le Figaro*, 20 February 1996.

Fredman, Sandra (1997), *Women and the Law* (Oxford: Oxford University Press).

Friedrich, Carl J. (1950), *Constitutional Government and Democracy* (Boston MA: Ginn).

Friedrich, Carl J. (1963), *Man and his Government* (New York: MacGraw-Hill).

Friis, Lykke (1997), 'When Europe Negotiates. From Europe Agreements to Eastern Enlargement', Ph.D. thesis, University of Copenhagen.

Gabel, Matthew and Hix, Simon (1997), 'The Ties that Bind: The European Parliament and the Commission President Investiture Procedure'. (Unpublished mimeo.)

Garcia, Soledad (ed.) (1993), *Europe's Fragmented Identities and the Frontiers of Citizenship* (London: Chatham House, Royal Institute of International Affairs).

Gardner, David (1991), 'EC Leaders Find Social Chapter Hard to Read', *Financial Times*, 11 December.

Garrett, Geoffrey and Lange, Peter (1995), 'Internationalization, Institutions and Political Change', *International Organization*, **49**: 627–55.

Gazzo, Marina (ed.) (1986), *Towards European Union II: From the European Council in Milan to the Signing of the Single European Act* (Brussels/Luxembourg: *Agence Europe*).

Gehring, Thomas (1998), 'Die Politik des koordinierten Alleingangs', *Zeitschrift für Internationale Beziehungen*, **5**: 43–78.

George, Stephen (1996), 'The Approach of the British Government to the 1996 Intergovernmental Conference of the European Union', *Journal of European Public Policy*, **3** (1): 45–62.

Germany (1995), *Letter from Chancellor Kohl and President Chirac to the Madrid European Council of 15–16 December 1995* (Bonn/Paris, 5 December 1995).

Germany (1996a), *Common Foreign and Security Policy: Guidelines Adopted by the German and French Foreign Ministers at Freiburg*, 27 February 1996.

Germany (1996b), *Germany's Objectives for the Intergovernmental Conference*, 26 March 1996.

Gialdino, Carlo Curti (1995), 'Some Reflections on the "Acquis Communautaire"', *Common Market Law Review*, **32**: 1089–121.

Giddens, Anthony (1994), *Beyond Left and Right: The Future of Radical Politics* (Stanford, CA: Stanford University Press).

Giddens, Anthony (1996), 'There is a Radical Centre-Ground', *New Statesman*, **125**: 18–19.

Giddens, Anthony (1997), 'Centre Left at Centre Stage', *New Statesman*, **126**, May, special edition: 37–9.

Goetz, Klaus H. (1996), 'Integration Policy in a Europeanized State: Germany and the Intergovernmental Conference', *Journal of European Public Policy*, **3** (1): 23–44.

Goodin, Robert E. (1995), 'Keeping Political Time—the Rhythms of Democracy', paper presented at the Conference on Democracy and Time (Vienna: Institute for Advanced Studies).

Goodin, Robert E. (1997), *On Constitutional Design* (Oslo: ARENA, Advanced Research on the Europeanisation of the Nation State), Working Paper No. 26.

Grabbe, Heather (1999), *A Partnership for Accession? The nature, scope and implications of emerging EU conditionality for CEE applicants* (Florence: European University Institute, Robert Schuman Centre), Working Paper.

Grabbe, Heather and Hughes, Kirsty (1998), *Enlarging the EU Eastwards* (London: Pinter for the Royal Institute of International Affairs).

Grande, Edgar (1997), *Post-nationale Demokratie—Ein Ausweg aus der Globalisierungsfalle?* (Technische Universität München: Institut für Sozialwissenschaften Lehrstuhl für Politische Wissenschaft), Working Paper 2/97.

Grant, Charles (1994), *Delors: Inside the House that Jacques Built* (London: Nicholas Brealey).

Grawert, Rolf (1973), *Staat und Staatsangehörigkeit* (Berlin: Duncker & Humblot).

Gray, Paul (1993), '1993 and European Food Law: An End or a New Beginning?', *European Food Law Review*, 2: 1–16.

Greece (1995), *Conclusions of the Interministerial Committee of the Greek Government*, 7 June 1995.

Greece (1996), *For a Democratical EU with Political and Social Content: Greece's Contribution to the 1996 IGC (sic)*, 24 January 1996.

Green Cowles, Maria (1993), *The Politics of Big Business in the Single Market Program*, paper presented at the European Community Studies Association (ECSA) Third Biennial International Conference, Washington DC, 27 May.

Green Cowles, Maria (1994), 'The Politics of Big Business in the European Community: Setting the Agenda for a New Europe', Ph.D. dissertation submitted to the Faculty of the School of International Service of The American University. Washington DC.

Griller, Stefan, Droutsas, Dimitri, Falkner, Gerda, Forgó, Katrin, Klatzer, Elizabeth, Mayer, Georg Stefan, and Nentwich, Michael (1996), *Regierungskonferenz 1996: Ausgangspositionen* (Vienna: Forschungsinstitut für Europafragen), Working Paper No. 20.

Griller, Stefan, Droutsas, Dimitri, Falkner, Gerda, Forgó, Katrin, and Nentwich, Michael (1999), *The Treaty of Amsterdam: Facts, Analysis, Prospects*, Vol. 15, Series of the Research Institute for European Affairs (Vienna: Springer).

Guggenberger, Bernd G. (1986), 'Legalität und Legitimität', in Wolfgang Mickel (ed.), *Handlexikon zur Politikwissenschaft* (Bonn: Schriftenreihe der Bundeszentrale für politische Bildung), 267–72.

Guggenbuhl, Alan (1995), 'The Political Economy of Association with Eastern Europe', in Finn Laursen (ed.), *The Political Economy of European Integration* (The Hague: Kluwer), 211–82.

Guizzi, Vincenzo (1995), *Manuale di diritto e politica dell'Unione europea* (Naples/Milan: Editoriale Scientifica).

Haaland Matlary, Jane (1993), 'Beyond Intergovernmentalism: The quest for a comprehensive framework for the study of integration', *Cooperation and Conflict*, 28 (3): 181–208.

Haarscher, G. (1996), 'La crise de la représentation', *Administration Publique*, 3: 153–9.

Haas, Ernst B. (1964), 'International Integration: The European and the Universal Process', in Dale J. Hekius, Charles G. McClintock, and Arthur L. Burns (eds.), *International Security* (New York: Wiley), 229–60.

Habermas, Jürgen (1992a), 'Citizenship and National Identity: Some Reflections on the Future of Europe', *Praxis International*, 12 (1): 1–19.

Habermas, Jürgen (1992b) (4th edn., 1994), *Faktizität und Geltung* (Frankfurt: Suhrkamp).

Haggard, Stephan, Levy, Marc A., Moravcsik, Andrew, and Nicolaïdis, Kalypso (1993), 'Integrating the Two Halves of Europe: Theories of Interests, Bargaining, and Institutions', in Robert O. Keohane, Joseph S. Nye, and Stanley Hoffmann (eds.), *International Institutions and State Strategies in Europe, 1989–1991* (Cambridge, MA.: Harvard University Press), 173–95.

Hall, Peter (1989), *The Political Power of Economic Ideas* (Princeton, NJ: Princeton University Press).

Hall, Peter (1993), 'Policy Paradigms, Social Learning and the State: The Case of Economic Policymaking in Britain', *Comparative Politics*, **25** (3): 275–96.

Hanf, Kenneth and Soetendorp, Ben (eds.) (1998), *Adapting to European Integration: Small States in the EU* (London: Longman).

Hayek, Friedrich A. (1967), 'Notes on the Evolution of Systems of Rules of Conduct', *Studies in Philosophy, Politics, and Economics* (Chicago, IL: University of Chicago Press).

Hayes-Renshaw, Fiona and Wallace, Helen (1997), *The Council of Ministers of the European Union* (London: Macmillan).

Healey, Nigel M. (1995), 'From the Treaty of Rome to Maastricht: The theory and practice of European integration', in Nigel M. Healey (ed.), *The Economics of the New Europe: From Community to Union* (London/New York: Routledge), 1–41.

Heidensohn, Klaus (1995), *Europe and World Trade* (London/New York: Pinter).

Held, David (1991), 'Between State and Civil Society', in G. Andrews (ed.), *Citizenship* (London: Lawrence & Wishart), 19–25.

Held, David (1992), 'Democracy: From City-states to a Cosmopolitan Order?', *Political Studies*, **XL**: 10–39.

Helm, Toby and Jones, George (1997), 'Blair Seeks Delay over EU Laws on Workers' Rights', *Daily Telegraph*, 13 June.

Héritier, Adrienne (1994), *Die Veränderung von Staatlichkeit in Europa: Ein regulativer Wettbewerb—Deutschland, Grossbritannien, Frankreich* (Opladen: Leske & Budrich).

Herman, Didi (1994), *Rights of Passage: Struggles for lesbian and gay equality* (Toronto, Ontario: University of Toronto Press).

Herman, Didi (1996), '(Il)legitimate Minorities: The American Christian Right's Anti-Gay-Rights Discourse', *Journal of Law and Society*, **23**: 346–63.

Hitiris, Theodore (1994) (3rd edn.), *European Community Economics* (Hemel Hempstead, UK/New York: Harvester Wheatsheaf).

Hix, Simon (1994), 'The Study of the European Community: The Challenge to Comparative Politics', *West European Politics*, **17** (1): 1–30.

Hix, Simon (1998a), 'Choosing Europe: Real Democracy for the European Union', *Euro-Visions: New Dimensions of European Integration*, Demos Collection Issue 13 (London: Demos), 14–17.

Hix, Simon (1998b), 'The Study of the European Union II: The "New Governance" Agenda and its Rival', *Journal of European Public Policy*, **5**: 38–65.

Hix, Simon and Lord, Christopher (1996a), *European Political Parties* (London: St. Martin's).

Hix, Simon and Lord, Christopher (1996b), 'The Making of a President: The European Parliament and the Confirmation of Jacques Santer as the President of the Commission', *Government and Opposition*, **31** (1): 62–76.

Hix, Simon and Lord, Christopher (1997), *Political Parties in the European Union* (London: Macmillan).

Hobbes, Thomas (1914), *Leviathan* (London: Everyman's Library, Dent & Sons). (Original work published 1651.)

Hobe, Stefan (1993), 'Die Unionsbürgerschaft nach dem Vertrag von Maastricht: Auf dem Weg zum Europäischen Bundesstaat?', *Der Staat*, 245–68.

Hoebing, Joyce, Weintraub, Sidney, and Delal Baer, M. (eds.) (1996), *NAFTA and Sovereignty: Trade-offs for Canada, Mexico and the United States* (Washington DC: Center for Strategic and International Studies).

Hofrichter, Jürgen and Niedermayer, Oskar (1991), *Cross-Border Social European Integration: Trust between the Peoples of the EC Member States and its Evolution over Time*, Report prepared on behalf of DG-X of the Commission of the European Communities (Mannheim: ZEUS).

Hofstede, Geert (1996), 'The Nation State as a Source of Common Mental Programming: Similarities and Differences Across Eastern and Western Europe', in Svante Gustavsson and Leif Lewin (eds.), *The Future of the Nation State: Essays on Cultural Pluralism and Political Integration* (Stockholm: Nerenius & Santerus/Routledge), 19–48.

Holmes, Stephen H. (1988), 'Gag Rules or the Politics of Omission', in Jon Elster and Rune Slagstad (eds.), *Constitutionalism and Democracy* (Cambridge: Cambridge University Press), 19–58.

Hoogenboom, T. (1992), 'Free Movement of Non-EC Nationals: Schengen and Beyond', in J. D. M. Sternberger (ed.), *Schengen: Internationalization of Central Chapters of the Law on Aliens, Refugees, Privacy, Security and the Police* (Leiden: Stichting NJCM).

Hooghe, Liesbet and Keating, Michael (1994), 'The Politics of European Union Regional Policy', *Journal of European Public Policy*, **1** (3): 367–93.

Hooghe, Liesbet and Marks, Gary (1997), 'The Making of a Polity: The Struggle over European Integration', *European Integration Online Papers*, **1**, No. 004; http://eiop.or.at/eiop/texte/1997-004a.htm.

Hoskyns, Catherine (1996), *Integrating Gender: Women, Law and Politics in the European Union* (London: Verso).

Hosli, Madeleine (1993), 'Admission of European Free Trade Association States to the European Community Council of Ministers', *International Organization*, **47** (4): 629–43.

Howe, Paul (1995), 'A Community of Europeans: The Requisite Underpinnings', *Journal of Common Market Studies*, **33** (1): 27–46.

Hurrell, Andrew (1995), 'Explaining the Resurgence of Regionalism in World Politics', *Review of International Studies*, **21**: 331–58.

Ibanez, Alberto Gil (1992), 'Spain and European Political Union', in Finn Laursen and Sophie Vanhoonacker (eds.), *The Intergovernmental Conference on Political Union* (Maastricht: European Institute of Public Administration), 99–114.

Ionescu, Ghita (1996), 'National and European Representatives of the Will of the People: Harmony or Disharmony?', in Roger Morgan and Clare Tame (eds.), *Parliaments and Parties* (Houndmills: Macmillan), 343–64.

Ireland (1996), *White Paper on Foreign Policy: External Challenges and Opportunities*, 26 March 1996.

Italy (1995*a*), *Italian Government statement on foreign policy guidelines*, 23 February 1995.

Italy (1995*b*), *Italian Government Statement on the Intergovernmental Conference to review the Maastricht Treaty*, 23 May 1995.

Italy (1996), *Position of the Italian Government on the IGC for the Revision of the Treaties*, 18 March 1996.

Jachtenfuchs, Markus (1995), 'Theoretical Perspectives on European Governance', *European Law Journal*, **1** (2): 115–33.

Jachtenfuchs, Markus (1997), 'Democracy and Governance in the European Union', in Andreas Føllesdal and Peter Koslowski (eds.), *Democracy and the European Union* (Berlin: Springer), 37–64.

Jachtenfuchs, Markus and Kohler-Koch, Beate (1996*a*), 'Regieren im dynamischen Mehrebenensystem', in Markus Jachtenfuchs and Beate Kohler-Koch (eds.), *Europäische Integration* (Opladen: Leske & Budrich), 15–44.

Jachtenfuchs, Markus and Kohler-Koch, Beate (eds.) (1996*b*), *Regieren in der Europäischen Union* (Opladen: Beck).

Jacqué, Jean-Paul (1996), 'Compétences d'exécution et comitologie', paper contributed to the Conference on Social Regulation Through European Committees: Empirical Research, Institutional Politics, Theoretical Concepts and Legal Developments, Florence, 9–10 December.

James, B. (1997), 'Ahead of Jobs Summit, Europe is hardly United; Spain hopes Leaders will Target Flexibility', *International Herald Tribune*, 20 November 1997, 20.

Jørgensen, Knud Erik (1998), 'The Social Construction of the "Acquis Communautaire": A Cornerstone of the European Edifice', paper presented at the International Studies Association meeting, Minneapolis, 17–21 March.

Joerges, Christian and Neyer, Jürgen (1997*a*), 'From Intergovernmental Bargaining to Deliberative Political Processes: The Constitutionalisation of Comitology', *European Law Journal*, **3**: 273–99.

Joerges, Christian and Neyer, Jürgen (1997*b*), 'Transforming Strategic Interaction Into Deliberative Problem-Solving: European Comitology in the Foodstuff Sector', *Journal of European Public Policy*, **4** (4): 609–25.

Joerges, Christian and Vos, Ellen (eds.) (1999), *EU Committees: Social Regulation, Law and Politics* (Oxford: Hart).

Jovanovic, Miroslav N. (1992), *International Economic Integration* (London/New York: Routledge).

Kaase, Max and Newton, Kenneth (1995), *Beliefs in Government* (Oxford: Oxford University Press).

Katz, Richard S. (1997), 'Representational Roles', in Michael Marsh and Pippa Norris (eds.), 'Political Representation in the European Parliament', *European Journal of Political Research*, special issue, **32** (2), 211–26.

Kenen, Peter B. (1995), *Economic and Monetary Union in Europe: Moving Beyond Maastricht* (New York: Cambridge University Press).

Keohane, Robert O. (1991), 'Empathy and International Regimes', in J. Mansbridge (ed.), *Beyond Self-Interest* (Chicago IL: University of Chicago Press), 227–36.

Kim, Haknoh (1997), 'The Construction of Supranational Collective Bargaining: Why and How Did They Do It?', paper presented at the Fifth Biennial Conference of the European Community Studies Association, Seattle, Washington, 30 May–2 June.

King, Anthony (1981), 'What do Elections Decide?', in David Butler, Howard R. Penniman, and Austin Ranney (eds.), *Democracy at the Polls* (Washington DC: American Enterprise Institute).

King, Gary, Keohane, Robert O., and Verba, Sidney (1994), *Designing Social Inquiry—Scientific Inferences in Qualitative Research* (Princeton, NJ: Princeton University Press).

Kingdon, John W. (1984), *Agendas, Alternatives and Public Policy* (Boston, MA.: Little, Brown & Co.).

Klausen, Jytte and Tilly, Louise (1997), 'European Integration in a Social and Historical Perspective', in Jytte Klausen and Louise Tilly (eds.), *European Integration in a Social and Historical Perspective* (Lanham/Boulder/New York/Oxford: Rowman & Littlefield).

Klotz, Audie (1995), 'Norms Reconstituting Interests: Global Racial Equality and U.S. Sanctions against South Africa', *International Organization*, **49** (3): 451–78.

Kluth, W. (1995), *Die demokratische Legitimation der Europäischen Union* (Berlin: Duncker & Humblot).

van der Knaap, Peter (1996), 'Government by Committee: Legal Typology, Quantitative Assessment and Institutional Repercussions of Committees in the European Union', in Robin H. Pedler and Günther F. Schaefer (eds.), *Shaping European Law and Policy: The Role of Committees and Comitology in the Political Process* (Maastricht: European Institute of Public Administration), 83–116.

Knight, Jack and Sened, Itai (1995), 'Introduction', in Jack Knight and Itai Sened (eds.), *Explaining Social Institutions* (Ann Arbor, MI: University of Michigan Press), 1–13.

Kohler-Koch, Beate (1996a), 'Die Gestaltungsmacht organisierter Interessen', in Markus Jachtenfuchs and Beate Kohler-Koch (eds.), *Europäische Integration* (Opladen: Leske & Budrich), 193–222.

Kohler-Koch, Beate (1996b), 'Regionen als Handlungseinheiten in der europäischen Politik', *Welttrends*, **11**: 7–35.

Kohler-Koch, Beate (1996c), 'Regionen im Mehrebenensystem der EU', in Thomas König, Elmar Rieger and Hermann Schmitt (eds.), *Das europäische Mehrebenensystem* (Frankfurt/New York: Campus Verlag), 203–27.

Kohler-Koch, Beate (1997), 'Organized Interests in European Integration: The Evolution of a New Type of Governance', in Helen Wallace and Alasdair R. Young (eds.), *Participation and Policy-Making in the EU* (Oxford: Oxford University Press), 42–68.

Kohler-Koch, Beate (1998a), 'Europäisierung der Regionen: Institutioneller Wandel als sozialer Prozeβ', in Beate Kohler-Koch (ed.), *Interaktive Politik in Europa: Regionen im Netzwerk der Integration* (Opladen: Leske & Budrich), 13–31.

Kohler-Koch, Beate (ed.) (1998b), *Interaktive Politik in Europa: Regionen im Netzwerk der Integration* (Opladen: Leske & Budrich).

Kohler-Koch, Beate (1998c), 'Organized Interests in the EU and the European Parliament', in Paul-Henri Claeys, Corinne Gobin, Isabelle Smets, and Pascaline Winand (eds.), *Lobbyisme, pluralisme et integration européenne [Lobbying, Pluralism and European Integration]* (Bruxelles: Presse interuniversitaire européenne), 126–58.

Kohler-Koch, Beate (1998d), 'Leitbilder und Realität der Europäisierung der Regionen', in Beate Kohler-Koch (ed.), *Interaktive Politik in Europa: Regionen im Netzwerk der Integration* (Opladen: Leske & Budrich), 231–53.

Kohler-Koch, Beate (1998e), 'Europe and the Regions: The Issue of Multi-Level Governance and Sovereignty', paper prepared for the International Conference on Democracy in Europe at the University of Twente, 12–14 February.

Koslowski, Rey and Kratochwil, Friedrich (1994), 'Understanding Change in International Politics: The Soviet Empire's Demise and the International System', *International Organization*, 48: 215–47.

Koslowski, Rey and Wiener, Antje (forthcoming), 'Practising Democracy Transnationally' in Yale H. Ferguson and R. J. Barry Jones (eds.) *Political Space: the New Frontier of Global Politics*. (New York: Sunny Press).

Kostakopoulou, Dora (1996), 'Towards a Theory of Contructive Citizenship in Europe', *Journal of Political Philosophy*, 4: 337–58.

Krasner, Stephen, D. (ed.) (1983), *International Regimes* (Ithaca, NY: Cornell University Press).

Kratochwil, Friedrich (1988), 'Regimes, Interpretation and the "Science" of Politics', *Millennium*, 17: 263–84.

Kratochwil, Friedrich and Ruggie, John G. (1986), 'International Organization: A state of the art on the art of the state', *International Organization*, 40: 753–75.

Küsters, Hanns Jürgen (1987), 'The Treaties of Rome (1955–57)', in Roy Pryce (ed.), *The Dynamics of European Union* (New York: Croom Helm), 78–104.

Kux, Stefan and Sverdrup, Ulf (1997), *Balancing Effectiveness and Legitimacy in the European Integration: The Norwegian and Swiss Cases* (Oslo: ARENA, Advanced Research on the Europeanisation of the Nation State), Working Paper No. 97/31.

Kymlicka, Will and Norman, Wayne (1994), 'Return of the Citizen: A Survey of Recent Work on Citizenship Theory', *Ethics*, 104: 352–81.

Ladeur, Karl-Heinz (1997), 'Towards a Legal Theory of Supranationality: The Viability of the Network Concept', *European Law Journal*, **3**: 33–54.

Laffan, Brigid (1996), 'The Politics of Identity and Political Order in Europe', *Journal of Common Market Studies*, **34**: 81–102.

Laffan, Brigid (1997*a*), 'The IGC and Institutional Reform of the Union', in Geoffrey Edwards and Alfred Pijpers (eds.), *The Politics of European Treaty Reform: The 1996 Intergovernmental Conference and Beyond* (London: Pinter), 288–305.

Laffan, Brigid (1997*b*), 'The European Union: A Distinctive Model of Internationalisation?', *European Integration Online Papers*, **1**, No. 018; available online on http://eiop.or.at/eiop/texte/1997.

Laffan, Brigid (1997*c*), 'From Policy Entrepreneur to Policy Manager: The Challenge Facing the European Commission', *Journal of European Public Policy*, **4** (3): 422–38.

Lamy, Pascal (1991), 'Choses vues d'Europe', *Esprit*, October, 67–81.

Lange, Niels (1998), *Zwischen Regionalismus und europäischer Integration: Wirtschaftsinteressen in regionalistischen Konflikten* (Baden-Baden: Nomos).

Lange, Peter (1992), 'The Politics of the Social Dimension', in Alberta Sbragia (ed.), *Euro-Politics: Institutions and Policy-Making in the 'New' European Community* (Washington DC: Brookings Institution), 225–56.

Laredo, Armando Toledano (1992), 'The EEA Agreement: An Overall View', *Common Market Law Review*, **29**: 1199–213.

Laski, Harold (1938) (4th edn., 1925), *A Grammar of Politics* (London: George Allen & Unwin).

Laursen, Finn (1992), 'Explaining the Intergovernmental Conference on Political Union', in Finn Laursen and Sophie Vanhoonacker (eds.), *The Intergovernmental Conference on Political Union: Institutional Reforms, New Policies and International Identity of the European Community* (Maastricht: European Institute of Public Administration) 92/01, 229–65.

Laursen, Finn (1993), 'The Maastricht Treaty: Implications for the Nordic Countries', *Cooperation and Conflict*, **28** (2): 115–41.

Laursen, Finn (1997), 'The Lessons of Maastricht', in Geoffrey Edwards and Alfred Pijpers (eds.), *The Politics of European Treaty Reform* (London: Pinter), 59–73.

Laursen, Finn and Vanhoonacker, Sophie (eds.) (1992), *The Intergovernmental Conference on Political Union: Institutional Reforms, New Policies and International Identity of the European Community* (Maastricht: European Institute of Public Administration).

Laver, Michael J., Gallagher, Michael, Marsh, Michael, Singh, Robert, and Tonra, Ben (1995), *Electing the President of the European Commission* (Dublin: Trinity College), Trinity Blue Papers in Public Policy, 1.

Leibholz, Gerhard (1929), *Das Wesen der Repräsentation* (Berlin).

Lenaerts, Kuhn (1991), 'Some Reflections on the Separation of Powers in the European Community', *Common Market Law Review*, **28** (1), 11–35.

Lenihan, Donald G., Robertson, Gordon, and Tassé, Roger (1994), *Canada: Reclaiming the middle ground* (Montreal: Institute for Research on Public Policy).

Lepsius, M. Rainer (1995), 'Institutionenanalyse und Institutionenpolitik', in Birgitta

Nedelmann (ed.), *Politische Institutionen im Wandel* (Opladen: Westdeutscher Verlag), 392–403.

Lequesne, Christian (1993), *Paris-Bruxelles. Comment se fait la politique européenne de la France* (Paris: Presses de Sciences Politiques).

Lequesne, Christian (1998a), 'Comment penser l'Union européenne?', in Marie-Claude Smouts (ed.), *Les nouvelles relations internationales: Pratiques et théories* (Paris: Presses de Sciences Politiques).

Lequesne, Christian (1998b), 'Une lecture décisionnelle de la politique européenne de François Mitterrand', in Samy Cohen (ed.), *Mitterrand et la sortie de la guerre froide* (Paris: PUF), 103–34.

Lequesne, Christian and Smith, Andy (1997), 'Union européenne et science politique: où en est le débat théorique?', *Cultures et Conflits* (Paris), **28**: 7–31.

Leslie, Peter M. (1979), *Equal to Equal: Economic association and the Canadian common market* (Kingston, Ontario: Queen's University, Institute of Intergovernmental Relations).

Leslie, Peter M. (1996a), 'Asymmetry and Integration: The emergence of regional economic systems', in J. Bingen and W. Schutze (eds.), *Europe at the End of the 90s* (Oslo: Europa Programmet), 191–235.

Leslie, Peter M. (1996b), *The Maastricht Model: A Canadian perspective on the European Union* (Kingston, Canada: Institute of Intergovernmental Relations).

Lewis, Jeffrey (1998a), 'The Institutional Problem-Solving Capacities of the Council: The Committee of Permanent Representatives and the Methods of Community' (Cologne: Max-Planck-Institut für Gesellschaftsforschung), MPIfG Discussion Paper No. 98/1.

Lewis, Jeffrey (1998b), 'Is the "Hard Bargaining" Image of the Council Misleading? The Committee of Permanent Representatives and the Local Elections Directive', *Journal of Common Market Studies*, **36** (4): 479–504.

Liefferink, Duncan and Skou Andersen, Michael (1998), 'Strategies of the "Green" Member States in EU Environmental Policy-making', *Journal of European Public Policy*, **5** (2): 254–70.

Lijphart, Arend (1969), 'Consociational Democracy', *World Politics*, **21** (2): 207–25.

Lijphart, Arend (1992), *Parliamentary Versus Presidential Government* (Oxford: Oxford University Press).

Lindberg, Leon N. (1963), *The Political Dynamics of European Economic Integration* (Oxford: Oxford University Press).

Lindberg, Leon, N. (1970), 'Political Integration as a Multidimensional Phenomenon Requiring Multivariate Measurement', *International Organization*, **24** (4): 649–731.

Linklater, Andrew (1996), 'Citizenship and Sovereignty in the Post-Westphalian State', *European Journal of International Relations*, **2**: 77–103.

Linklater, Andrew (1998), *The Transformation of Political Community* (Columbia, SC: University of South Carolina Press).

Llorente, Francisco Rubio (1998), *Constitutionalism in the 'Integrated' States of Europe* (Cambridge, MA: Harvard Law School), Jean Monnet Working Paper No. 5/98.

Lodge, Juliet (1995), *The 1994 Elections to the European Parliament* (London: Pinter).

Lorenz, Detlef (1991), 'Regionalisation versus Regionalism: Problems of Change in the World Economy', *Intereconomics*, **26** (1): 3–10.

Ludlow, Peter (1991), 'The Commission', in Robert O. Keohane and Stanley Hoffman (eds.), *The New European Community: Decisionmaking and Institutional Change* (Boulder, CO: Westview), 85–132.

Luif, Paul (1995), *On the Road to Brussels: The Political Dimensions of Austria, Finland and Sweden's Accession to the European Union* (Vienna: Braumüller).

Luxembourg (1995), *Luxembourg Government Memorandum on the 1996 IGC*, 30 June 1995.

Lynch, Frances M. B. (1997), *France and the International Economy: From Vichy to the Treaty of Rome* (New York: Routledge).

Lyons, Carole (1996), 'Citizenship in the Constitution of the European Union: Rhetoric or Reality?', in Richard Bellamy (ed.), *Constitutionalism, Democracy and Sovereignty: American and European Perspectives* (Aldershot, UK: Avebury).

Lyotard, Jean-François (1985), *The Postmodern Condition: A Report on Knowledge* (Minnesota City, MN: University of Minnesota).

MacCormick, Neil (1995), 'The Maastricht-Urteil: Sovereignty Now', *European Law Journal*, **1**: 259–66.

Majone, Giandomenico (1993*a*), 'The European Community Between Social Policy and Social Regulation', *Journal of Common Market Studies*, **31** (3): 153–70.

Majone, Giandomenico (1993*b*), *The European Community: An Independent Fourth Branch of Government?'* (Florence: European University Institute), Working Paper No. 93/9.'

Majone, Giandomenico (1994*a*), 'The Rise of the Regulatory State in Europe', *West European Politics*, **17**: 77–101.

Majone, Giandomenico (1994*b*), 'The European Community: An "Independent Fourth Branch of Government"?', in Gert Brüggemeier (ed.), *Verfassungen für ein ziviles Europa* (Baden-Baden: Nomos), 23–44.

Majone, Giandomenico (1994*c*), 'L'Etat et les problèmes de la réglementation', *Pouvoirs*, **70**: 133–47.

Majone, Giandomenico (1996), *La Communauté européenne: un Etat régulateur* (Paris: Montchrestien).

Majone, Giandomenico (1997), 'From the Positive to the Regulatory State: Causes and Consequences of Changes in the Mode of Governance', *Journal of Public Policy*, **17**: 139–67.

Majone, Giandomenico (1998), 'Europe's "Democratic Deficit": The Question of Standards', *European Law Journal*, **4** (1): 5–28.

Mancini, G. Frederico (1998), 'Europe: The Case for Statehood', *European Law Journal*, **4** (1): 29–42.

March, James G. (1994), *A Primer on Decision Making* (New York: The Free Press).

March, James G. and Olsen, Johan P. (1983), 'Organizing Political Life: What Administrative Reorganization Tells Us about Government', *American Political Science Review*, **77** (2): 281–96.

March, James G. and Olsen, Johan P. (1989), *Rediscovering Institutions: The Organizational Basis of Politics* (New York: The Free Press).

March, James G. and Olsen, Johan P. (1994), *Institutional Perspectives on Political*

Institutions (Oslo: ARENA, Advanced Research on the Europeanisation of the Nation State), Working Paper No. 94/2.

March, James G. and Olsen, Johan P. (1995), *Democratic Governance* (New York: The Free Press).

Marjolin, R. (1989), *Architect of European Unity: Memoirs 1911–1986* (London: Weidenfeld and Nicolson).

Marks, Gary, Hooghe, Liesbet, and Blank, Kermit (1995), 'European Integration since the 1980s: State-Centric Versus Multi-Level Governance', paper presented at the Conference on Politics and Political Economy in Advanced Capitalist Democracies (Humboldt-University, Berlin, 26–27 May).

Marlowe, Lara (1997), 'Jospin Government Lays Down Conditions Likely to Delay EMU', *Irish Times*, 7 June.

Marsh, Michael and Norris, Pippa (eds.) (1997), 'Political Representation in the European Parliament', *European Journal of Political Research*, special issue, **32** (2): 153–289.

Marsh, Michael and Wessels, Bernhard (1997), 'Territorial Representation', in Michael Marsh and Pippa Norris (eds.), 'Political Representation in the European Parliament', *European Journal of Political Research*, special issue, **32** (2): 227–41.

Marshall, T. H. (1950), *Citizenship and Social Class* (Cambridge: Cambridge University Press).

Mayhew, Alan (1998), *Recreating Europe: The European Union's Policy towards Central and Eastern Europe* (Cambridge: Cambridge University Press).

Mayhew, David (1974), *Congress: The Electoral Connection* (New Haven, CT: Yale University Press).

Mazey, Sonia and Richardson Jeremy (1993), *Lobbying in the European Community* (Oxford: Oxford University Press).

Mazey, Sonia and Richardson, Jeremy (1996), 'Influencing the EU's Agenda: Interest Groups and the 1996 IGC', paper prepared for the 24th European Consortium of Political Research, Joint Sessions of Workshops, Oslo, 29 March–3 April).

Mazey, Sonia and Richardson, Jeremy (1997), 'Policy-Framing: Interest Groups and the Lead up to the 1996 Inter-Governmental Conference', *West European Politics*, **20** (3): 111–33.

McAleavey, Patrick (1994), 'European funded strategies for economic development in Strathclyde and northern Rhine-Westphalia', paper presented at the ECPR, Madrid.

McDonagh, Bobby (1998), *Original Sin in a Brave New World: An Account of the Negotiation of the Treaty of Amsterdam* (Dublin: Institute of European Affairs).

McNamara, Kathleen R. (1998), *The Currency of Ideas: Monetary Politics in the European Union* (Ithaca, NY: Cornell University Press).

Meehan, Elizabeth (1993), *Citizenship and the European Community* (London: Sage).

Menon, Anand (1996), 'France and the IGC of 1996', *Journal of European Public Policy*, **3** (2): 231–52.

Mény, Yves (ed.) (1985), 'Mise en oeuvre nationale des politiques communautaires: les directives de la CEE', *Revue française d'administration publique*, **34**: 177–206.

Mény, Yves (1995), 'Politiques publiques en Europe: une nouvelle division du travail', in Yves Mény, Pierre Muller, and Jean-Louis Quermonne (eds.), *Politiques publiques en Europe* (Paris: L'Harmattan).

Mény, Yves, Muller, Pierre, and Quermonne, Jean-Louis (eds.) (1995), *Politiques publiques en Europe* (Paris: L'Harmattan).

Metcalfe, Les (1994), 'Après 1992: La Commission européenne pourra-t-elle gérer l'Europe?', *Revue Française d'Administration Publique*, **63**: 401–12.

Michalski, Anna and Wallace, Helen (1992), *The European Community: The Challenge of Enlargement* (London: Chatham House, Royal Institute of International Affairs).

Middlemas, Keith (1995), *Orchestrating Europe* (London: Fontana).

Mill, John Stewart (1861) *Representative Government* (New York: The Liberal Arts Press).

Miller, David (1993), 'Deliberative Democracy and Social Choice', in David Held (ed.), *Prospects for Democracy* (Stanford, CA: Stanford University Press), 74–92.

Millon Delsol, Chantal (1993), *Le principe de subsidiarité* (Paris: PUF).

Milward, Alan S. (1992), *The European Rescue of the Nation-State* (London: Routledge).

Molle, Willem (1997) (3rd edn.), *The Economics of European Integration* (Brookfield, VT: Ashgate).

Moravcsik, Andrew (1991a), 'Negotiating the Single European Act: National Interests and Conventional Statecraft in the European Community', *International Organization*, **45** (1): 19–56.

Moravcsik, Andrew (1991b), 'Negotiating the Single European Act', in Robert O. Keohane and Stanley Hoffmann (eds.), *The New European Community* (Boulder, CO: Westview), 41–84.

Moravcsik, Andrew (1993), 'Preferences and Power in the European Community: A Liberal Intergovernmentalist Approach', *Journal of Common Market Studies*, **31** (4): 473–524.

Moravcsik, Andrew (1994), *Why the European Community Strengthens the State: Domestic Politics and International Cooperation* (New York: Center for European Studies), Working Paper Series No. 52.

Moravcsik, Andrew (1995), 'Liberal Intergovernmentalism and Integration: A Rejoinder', *Journal of Common Market Studies*, **33** (4): 611–28.

Moravcsik, Andrew (1997), 'Taking Preferences Seriously: A Liberal Theory of International Politics', *International Organization*, **51** (4): 513–53.

Moravcsik, Andrew and Nicolaïdis, Kalypso (1998), 'Federal Ideals and Constitutional Realities in the Treaty of Amsterdam', *Journal of Common Market Studies*, **36**: 13–38.

Muller, Pierre (1994), 'La mutation des politiques communautaires', *Pouvoirs*, **69**: 63–93.

Müller-Graff, Peter-Christian (ed.) (1993), *East Central European States and the European Communities: Legal Adaptation to the Market Economy* (Baden-Baden: Nomos).

Nentwich, Michael (1998), 'Opportunity Structures for Citizen Participation—The Case of the European Union', in A. Weale and Michael Nentwich (eds.), *The Political Theory and the European Union* (London: Routledge), 125–40.

Nentwich, Michael and Falkner, Gerda (1997), 'The Treaty of Amsterdam: Towards a New Institutional Balance', *European Integration On-line Papers*, **1**, No.015; http://eiop.or.at/eiop/texte/1997-015a.htm.

Netherlands (1994), *The Enlargement of the European Union: Opportunities and Obstacles*, 14 November 1994.

Netherlands (1995a), *European Foreign Policy, Security and Defence: Moving Towards a More Decisive External Action by the European Union*, 30 March 1995.

Netherlands (1995b), *European Co-operation in the Fields of Justice and Home Affairs*, 23 May 1995.

Netherlands (1995c), *Institutional Reform of the European Union*, 12 July 1995.

Netherlands (1996), *Between Madrid and Turin: Dutch priorities on the eve of the 1996 IGC*, March 1996.

Neunreither, Karlheinz (1994a), 'The Syndrome of Democratic Deficit in the European Community', in Parry Geraint (ed.), *Politics in an Interdependent World* (Aldershot, UK: Edward Elgar), 94–110.

Neunreither, Karlheinz (1994b), 'The Democratic Deficit of the European Union: Towards Closer Cooperation between the European Parliament and the National Parliaments?', *Government and Opposition*, **29** (3): 299–314.

Neunreither, Karlheinz (1995a), 'Citizens and the Exercise of Power in the European Union: Towards a New Social Contract?', in Allan Rosas and Esko Antola (eds.), *A Citizen's Europe: In Search of a New Order* (London: Sage), 1–18.

Neunreither, Karlheinz (1995b), 'The EP's Strategy in view of the Intergovernmental Conference 1996', *ECSA (US) Newsletter*, **8** (3), 16–21.

Neunreither, Karlheinz (1998a), 'Governance without Opposition: The Case of the European Union', *Government and Opposition*, **33** (4), 419–41

Neunreither, Karlheinz (1998b), 'Der Vertrag von Amsterdam als Zwischenetappe auf dem Weg zur EU-Ostweiterung', in R. Kirt (ed.), *Der Vertrag von Amsterdam—ein Vertrag für alle Bürger* (Vienna: Signum), 157–76.

Neunreither, Karlheinz (1999), 'The Evolution of the European Parliament', in Neill Nugent (ed.), *Developments in the European Union* (London: Macmillan), 62–83.

Neyer, Jürgen (1995), 'Globaler Markt und territorialer Staat: Konturen eines wachsenden Antagonismus', *Zeitschrift für Internationale Beziehungen*, **2**: 287–315.

Neyer, Jürgen (1999), 'Legitimes Recht oberhalb des demokratischen Rechtsstaates. Supranationalität als Herausforderung für die Politikwissenschaft', *Politische Vierteljahresschrift*, **3**.

Neyer, Jürgen and Wolf, Dieter (1996), 'Zusammenfügen was zusammengehört! Zur Notwendigkeit eines Brückenschlages zwischen alten und neuen Fragestellungen der Integrationsforschung', *Zeitschrift für Internationale Beziehungen*, **2**: 399–423.

Niblett, R. (1995), 'The European Community and the Central European Three, 1989–92: A Study of the Community as an International Actor', Ph.D. thesis, Oxford.

Nickel, Dietmar (1997), 'Ein Kommentar zum Amsterdamer Vertrag aus Sicht des Europäischen Parlaments', *Integration*, **20**: 219–27.

Nicolaïdis, Kalypso (1993), 'East European Trade in the Aftermath of 1989: Did International Institutions Matter?', in Robert O. Keohane, Joseph S. Nye, and Stanley

Hoffmann (eds.), *International Institutions and State Strategies in Europe, 1989–1991* (Cambridge, MA: Harvard University Press), 196–245.

Niedermayer, Oskar (1995), 'Trust and Sense of Community', in Oskar Niedermayer and Richard Sinnott (eds.), *Public Opinion and Internationalized Governance: Beliefs in Government*, Vol. 2 (Oxford: Oxford University Press), 227–46.

Niedermayer, Oskar and Sinnott, Richard (eds.) (1995), *Public Opinion and Internationalized Governance: Beliefs in Government*, Vol. 2 (Oxford: Oxford University Press).

Niedermayer, Oskar and Westle, Bettina (1995), 'A Typology of Orientations', in Oskar Niedermayer and Richard Sinnott (eds.), *Public Opinion and Internationalized Governance: Beliefs in Government*, Vol. 2 (Oxford: Oxford University Press), 33–50.

Noël, Emile (1992), 'Reflections on the Maastricht Treaty', *Government and Opposition*, **27** (2).

Non-paper (1996—5/7), 'Flexibility', Irish Presidency.

Non-paper (1996—20/12), 'Enhanced co-operation—flexibility', SN 639.

Non-paper (1997—8/1), 'Enhanced co-operation—flexibility', SN 500.

Non-paper (1997—3-4/3), 'JHA matters', Ireland.

Non-paper (1997—7/3), 'Flexibility under the first pillar', Ireland.

Non-paper (1997—18/4), 'Closer co-operation/Flexibility under the first pillar', Ireland.

Non-paper (1997—14/5), 'Compilation of texts under discussion', SN 2555.

Non-paper (1997—30/5), 'Consolidated draft treaty texts', SN 600.

Norberg, Sven (1992), 'The Agreement on a European Economic Area', *Common Market Law Review*, **29**: 1171–98.

Norris, Pippa and Franklin, Mark (1997), 'Social Representation', in Michael Marsh and Pippa Norris (eds.), 'Political Representation in the European Parliament', *European Journal of Political Research*, special issue, **32** (2): 185–210.

North, Douglass C. (1990), *Institutions, Institutional Change and Economic Performance* (New York: Cambridge University Press).

North, Douglass C. (1995), 'Five Propositions about Institutional Change', in Jack Knight and Itai Sened (eds.), *Explaining Social Institutions* (Ann Arbor, MI: University of Michigan Press), 15–26.

Nugent, Neill (1995), 'The Leadership Capacity of the European Commission', *Journal of European Public Policy*, **2** (4): 603–23.

Obradovic, Daniela (1996), 'Policy Legitimacy and the European Union', *Journal of Common Market Studies*, **34**: 191–221.

Offe, Claus (1996), 'Bewährungsproben—Über einige Beweislasten bei der Verteidigung der liberalen Demokratie', in Werner Weidenfeld (ed.), *Die Demokratie am Wendepunkt: Die demokratische Frage als Projekt des 21. Jahrhunderts* (Berlin: Siedler), 144–57.

O'Leary, Siofra (1995), 'The Relationship Between Community Citizenship and the Protection of Fundamental Rights in Community Law', *Common Market Law Review*, **32**: 519–54.

Olsen, Johan P. (1972), 'Public Policy-making and Theories of Organizational Choice', *Scandinavian Political Studies*, **7** (1): 45–62.

Olsen, Johan P. (1995a), 'Europeanisation and Nation State Dynamics', in Sverker

Gustavsson and Leif Lewin (eds.), *The Future of the Nation State* (London: Routledge), 245–85.

Olsen, Johan P. (1995*b*), *The Changing Political Organization of Europe* (Oslo: ARENA, Advanced Research on the Europeanisation of the Nation State), Working Paper No. 95/17.

Olsen, Johan P. (1997), 'Institutional Design in Democratic Contexts', *Journal of Political Philosophy*, **5** (3): 203–29.

Olson, Mancur (1965), *The Logic of Collective Action: Public Goods and the Theory of Groups* (Cambridge, MA: Harvard University Press).

Pappas, Spyros A. (ed.) (1994), *Procédures administratives nationales de préparation et de mise en oeuvre des décisions communautaires* (Maastricht: Institut Européen d'Administration Publique).

Paraskevopoulos, Christos C., Grinspun, Ricardo, and Eaton, George E. (eds.) (1996), *Economic Integration in the Americas* (Cheltenham, UK/Brookfield, VT: Edward Elgar).

van Parijs, Philippe (1997), 'Should the European Union Become More Democratic?', in Andreas Føllesdal and Peter Koslowski (eds.), *Democracy and the European Union* (Berlin: Springer), 287–301.

Patterson, William E. (1996), 'The New Germany in the New Europe', *German Politics*, **5** (2): 167–84.

Pedersen, Thomas (1994), *European Union and the EFTA Countries: Enlargement and Integration* (London: Pinter).

Pelkmans, Jacques (1980), 'Economic Theories of Integration Revisited', *Journal of Common Market Studies*, **18** (4): 333–54.

Pelkmans, Jacques (1986*a*), *Completing the Internal Market for Industrial Products* (Luxembourg: Office for Official Publications of the European Communities).

Pelkmans, Jacques (1986*b*), 'The Institutional Economics of European Integration' (Part III of 'The Federal Economy: Law and Economic Integration and the Positive State' by Thomas Heller and Jacques Pelkmans), in Mauro Cappelletti, Monica Seccombe, and Joseph H. H. Weiler (eds.), *Integration Through Law: Europe and the American Federal Experience* (Berlin/New York: de Gruyter), 318–96.

Pelkmans, Jacques (1988), 'A Grand Design by the Piece? An Appraisal of the Internal Market Strategy', in Roland Bieber, Renaud Dehousse, John Pinder, and Joseph H. H. Weiler (eds.), *1992: One European Market?* (Baden-Baden: Nomos), 359–83.

Pescatore, Pierre (1983), 'The Doctrine of "Direct Effect": An Infant Disease of Community Law', *European Law Review*, **8**: 155–77.

Peterson, John (1995), 'Decision-making in the European Union: Towards a Framework for Analysis', *Journal of European Public Policy*, **2** (1): 69–93.

Petite, Michel (1998), *The Treaty of Amsterdam* (Cambridge, MA: Harvard Law School), Jean Monnet Working Papers, Series No. 2/98;
http://www.law.harvard.edu/Programs/JeanMonnet/.

Philippart, Eric and Edwards, Geoffrey (1999), 'The Provisions on Closer Cooperation in the Treaty on European Union: Politics of a Multi-faceted System, *Journal of Common Market Studies*, **37** (1): 87–108.

Pierson, Paul (1996), 'The Path to European Integration: A Historical Institutionalist Perspective', *Comparative Political Studies*, **29** (2): 123–63.

Pierson, Paul and Leibfried, Stephan (eds.) (1995), *European Social Policy: Between Fragmentation and Integration* (Washington DC: Brookings Institution).

Pinder, John (1968), 'Positive Integration and Negative Integration: Some Problems of Economic Union in the EEC', *The World Today*, **24** (3): 88–110.

Pitkin, Hanna F. (1967), *The Concept of Representation* (Berkeley/Los Angeles, CA: University of California Press).

Planavova-Latanowicz, Jana (1998), 'Changes of the Decision-Making Process within the European Union', paper presented at the Ionian Conference 'Making Enlargement Work', Athens and Corfu, 14–17 May.

Plümper, Thomas (1997), 'Die Anpassung internationaler Wirtschaftsinstitutionen an globale ökonomische Prozesse', in Werner Fricke (ed.), *Jahrbuch für Arbeit und Technik 1997* (Bonn: Dietz), 241–55.

Pollack, Mark A. (1994), 'Creeping Competence: The Expanding Agenda of the European Community', *Journal of Public Policy*, **14** (2): 95–145.

Pollack, Mark A. (1995), 'Regional Actors in an Intergovernmental Play: The Making and Implementation of EC Structural Policy', in Sonia Mazey and Carolyn Rhodes (eds.), *The State of the European Union*, Vol. III (Boston, MA: Lynne Rienner), 361–90.

Pollack, Mark A. (1998), 'Delegation, Agency, and Agenda Setting in the European Community', *International Organization*, **51** (1): 99–134.

Pomfret, Richard W. T. (1997), *The Economics of Regional Trading Arrangements* (Oxford: Oxford University Press).

Ponzano, Paolo (1996), 'La prassi del processo decisionale nella Comunità europea: il ruolo della Commissione', *Il Diritto Dell'Unione Europea*, **1** (4).

Portugal (1996), *Portugal and the IGC for the Revision of the Treaty on European Union*, March 1996.

Preston, Christopher (1995), 'Obstacles to EU Enlargement: The Classical Community Method and the Prospects for a Wider Europe', *Journal of Common Market Studies*, **33** (3): 451–63.

Preston, Christopher (1997), *Enlargement and Integration in the European Union* (New York: Routledge).

Price, Richard and Tannenwald, Nina (1996), 'Norms and Deterrence: The Nuclear and Chemical Weapons Taboos', in Peter J. Katzenstein (ed.), *The Culture of National Security: Norms and Identity in World Politics* (New York: Columbia University Press), 114–52.

Putnam, Robert (1988), 'Diplomacy and Domestic Politics: The Logic of Two-Level Games', *International Organization* **3**: 427–60.

Quanjel, Marcel and Wolters, Menno (1993), 'Growing Cohesion in the European Parliament', paper presented at the Annual Joint Sessions of the European Consortium for Political Research, Leiden, April.

Québec, Ministère des affaires intergouvernementales (1978), *Option Europe: Analyse de la plausibilité d'une association Québec-Canada-Europe* (Québec: Editeur officiel).

Québec, Conseil exécutif (1979), *Québec-Canada: A new deal; The Québec Government proposal for a new partnership between Québec and Canada* (Québec: Editeur officiel).

Quermonne, Jean-Louis (1995), *Le système politique de l'Union européenne* (Paris: Montchrestien).

Rasmussen, Hjalte (1996), *Folkestyre, Grundlov og Høyesteret—Grundlovens §20 på prøve* (Copenhagen: Christian Ejler).

Raunio, Tapio (1996), *Party Group Behaviour in the European Parliament* (Tampere, Finland: University of Tampere).

Rawls, John (1985), 'Justice as Fairness: Political not Metaphysical', *Philosophy and Public Affairs*, **3**: 223–51.

Reflection Group (1995*a*), *Reform of the European Union (Interim Report)*, Madrid, 10 November 1995), SN 517/95 (REFLEX 18).

Reflection Group (1995*b*) *A Strategy For Europe—An Annotated Agenda; Report of the Reflection Group to the Intergovernmental Conference* (Brussels: 5 December 1995, SN 520/95 REFLEX 21.

Reif, Karlheinz (1984), 'National Election Cycles and European Elections, 1979 and 1984', *Electoral Studies*, **3** (3): 244–55.

Reif, Karlheinz and Schmitt, Hermann (1980), 'Nine Second-Order National Elections: A Conceptual Framework for the Analysis of European Election Results', *European Journal of Political Research*, **8** (1): 3–45.

Resnick, Philip (1991), *Toward a Canada-Quebec Union* (Montreal: McGill–Queen's University Press).

Reuters (1997), 'Europe Can't Be Built on Citizens' Backs', *Reuters World Service*, 6 June.

Reymond, C. (1993), 'Institutions, Decision-making Procedures and Settlement of Disputes in the European Economic Area', *Common Market Law Review*, **30**: 449–80.

Rhodes, Rod (1996), 'The New Governance: Governing Without Government', *Political Studies*, **4**: 652–67.

Richardson, Jeremy (ed.) (1996*a*), *European Union: Power and Policymaking* (London/New York: Routledge).

Richardson, Jeremy (1996*b*), 'Policy-making in the EU: Interests, Ideas and Garbage Cans of Primeval Soup', in Jeremy Richardson (ed.), *European Union: Power and Policymaking* (London/New York: Routledge).

Riker, William H. (1962), *The Theory of Political Coalitions* (New Haven, CT: Yale University Press).

Riker, William H. (1964), *Federalism: Origins, operation, significance* (Boston, MA: Little, Brown).

Risse-Kappen, Thomas (1996), 'Exploring the Nature of the Beast: International Relations Theory and Comparative Policy Analysis Meet the European Union', *Journal of Common Market Studies*, **34** (1): 53–80.

Robinson, Ian (1995), 'Trade Policy, Globalization and the Future of Canadian Federalism', in François Rocher and Miriam Smith (eds.), *New Trends in Canadian Federalism* (Peterborough, Ontario: Broadview), 234–69.

Rometsch, Dietrich and Wessels, Wolfgang (1994), 'The Commission and the Council of Ministers', in Geoffrey Edwards and David Spence (eds.), *The European Commission* (Harlow, UK: Longman).

Rometsch, Dietrich and Wessels, Wolfgang (eds.) (1996), *The European Union and Member States* (Manchester, UK: Manchester University Press).

Rosenau, J. and Czempiel (eds.) (1992), *Governance Without Government: Order and Change in World Politics* (Cambridge: Cambridge University Press).

Ross, George (1995a), *Jacques Delors and European Integration* (Cambridge, UK: Polity Press).

Ross, George (1995b), 'A Faltering French Presidency', *ECSA (US) Newsletter*, **8** (3): 13–16.

Royle, Trevor (1997), 'Blair Grabs the Wheel as Europe Goes Off Course', *Scotland on Sunday*, 8 June.

Ruggie, John G. (1993), 'Territoriality and Beyond: Problematising Modernity in International Relations', *International Organization*, **47**: 139–74.

Rugman, Alan M. (1994), *Foreign Investment and NAFTA* (Columbia, SC: University of South Carolina Press).

Russell, Peter H. (1992), *Constitutional Odyssey: Can Canadians be a sovereign people?* (Toronto, Ontario: University of Toronto Press).

De Ruyt, Jean (1986), *L'act unique européen* (Brussels: Editions de l'Université de Bruxelles).

Sack, Robert David (1986), *Human Territoriality: Its Theory and History* (Cambridge: Cambridge University Press).

Sartori, Giovanni (1987), *The Theory of Democracy Revisited* (New York: Chatham House).

Sartori, Giovanni (1994), *Comparative Constitutional Engineering* (London: Macmillan).

Saryusz-Wolski, Jacek (1994), 'The Reintegration of the "Old Continent": Avoiding the Costs of Half-Europe', in Simon Bulmer and Andrew Scott (eds.), *Economic and Political Integration in Europe: Internal Dynamics and Global Context* (Oxford: Blackwell), 19–28.

Sautter, Hermann (1983), *Regionalisierung und komparative Vorteile im internationalen Handel* (Tübingen: Mohr).

Sbragia, Alberta (1991), 'Thinking about the European Future: The Uses of Comparison', in Alberta Sbragia (ed.), *Euro-Politics: Institutions and Policymaking in the 'New' European Community* (Washington DC: Brookings Institution).

Sbragia, Alberta (1993), 'The European Community: A Balancing Act', *Publius: The Journal of Federalism*, **23** (3): 23–38.

Scharpf, Fritz (1992), 'Peut-il y avoir un équilibre fédéral stable en Europe?', *Revue Française d'Administration Publique*, **63**: 491–500.

Scharpf, Fritz (1994), 'Community and Autonomy: Multi-Level Policy-Making in the European Union', *Journal of European Public Administration*, **I**: 219–42.

Scharpf, Fritz (1997), *Games Real Actors Play: Actor-Centred Institutionalism in Policy Research* (Boulder, CO: Westview).

Scharpf, Fritz (1999), *Regieren in Europa: Effectiv und demokratisch?* (Frankfurt/New York: Campus Verlag).

Schattschneider, Elmar E. (1960), *The Semisovereign People: A Realist's View of Democracy in America* (Hinsdale, IL: The Dryden Press).

Schäuble, Wolfgang and Lamers, Karl (1994), *Reflections on European Foreign Policy*, Document of the CDU/CSU Group in the German Bundestag, 1 September 1994.

Schmidberger, Martin (1996), 'Regions and European Legitimacy: Public Attitudes Towards the EU on a Regional Level', paper presented at the Conference on Regions in an Emergent System of Governance, Mannheim, May 1996.

Schmidberger, Martin (1997), *Regionen und europäische Legitimität: Der Einfluss des regionalen Umfeldes auf Bevölkerungseinstellungen zur EU* (Frankfurt: Lang).

Schmidt, Suzanne (1998), 'Commission Activism: Subsuming Telecommunications and Electricity under European Competition Law', *Journal of European Public Policy*, 5 (1): 169–84.

Schmitter, Philippe (1996), 'Examining the Present Euro-polity with the Help of Past Theories', in Gary Marks, Fritz Scharpf, Philippe Schmitter, and Wolfgang Streeck (eds.), *Governance in the European Union* (London: Sage), 1–14.

Schmitter, Philippe (1997), 'Is it really possible to Democratize the Euro-Polity?', in Andreas Føllesdal and Peter Koslowski (eds.), *Democracy and the European Union* (Berlin: Springer), 13–35.

Schmitter, Philippe (1998), 'A Few, Very Condensed, Pages of Reflection on the Impact of the EU on Domestic Democracy', paper presented at the Europeanisation Workshop, European University Institute, Florence.

Schneider, Heinrich (1977), *Leitbilder der Europapolitik: Der Weg zur Integration* (Bonn: Europa Union Verlag).

Schneider, Heinrich (1986), *Rückblick für die Zukunft: Konzeptionelle Weichenstellungen für die Europäische Einigung* (Bonn: Europa Union Verlag).

Schneider, Volker, Dang-Nguyen, Godefroy, and Werle, Raymund (1994), 'Corporate Actor Networks in European Policymaking: Harmonizing telecommunications policy', *Journal of Common Market Studies*, 32 (4): 473–98.

Schönfelder, W. and Silberberg, R. (1997), 'Der Vertrag von Amsterdam: Entstehung und erste Bewertung', *Integration*, 20 (4): 203–10.

Schumpeter, Joseph (1942), *Capitalism, Socialism and Democracy* (London: Allen & Unwin).

Scott, Richard W. (1981), *Organizations: Rational, Natural and Open Systems* (Englewood Cliffs, NJ: Prentice-Hall).

Sedelmeier, Ulrich and Wallace, Helen (1996) (3rd edn.), 'Policies towards Central and Eastern Europe', in Helen Wallace and William Wallace (eds.), *Policy Making in the European Union* (Oxford: Oxford University Press), 353–87.

Sedelmeier, Ulrich and Wallace, Helen (2000, forthcoming) (4th edn.), 'Eastern Enlargement: Squaring a Larger and More Diverse Circle', in Helen Wallace and William Wallace (eds.), *Policy-Making in the European Union* (Oxford: Oxford University Press).

Seitz, Brian (1995), *The Trace of Political Representation* (Albany, NY: State University of New York).

Shaffer, Matthew R. (1995), 'The Applicability of Three-Level Game Analysis to EC-

Visegrad Negotiations for the Europe Agreements', paper presented at the UACES Research Conference, Birmingham, UK, September.

Shapiro, Martin (1992), 'The European Court of Justice', in Alberta M. Sbragia (ed.), *Euro-Politics: Institutions and Policymaking in the 'New' European Community* (Washington DC: Brookings Institution), 123–56.

Shaw, Jo (1997), *Citizenship of the Union: Towards Postnational Membership?* Cambridge, MA: (Harvard Law School), Jean Monnet Working Paper, Series 6/97.

Shaw, Jo (1998a), 'The Interpretation of European Union Citizenship', *Modern Law Review*, **61**: 293–317.

Shaw, Jo (1998b), 'The Treaty of Amsterdam: Challenges of Flexibility and Legitimacy', *European Law Journal*, **4**: 63–86.

Shaw, Jo (1998c), 'Flexibility and Legitimacy in the Domain of the Treaty Establishing the European Community', *European Law Journal*, **4**: 63–86.

Shepsle, Kenneth A. (1989), 'Studying Institutions: Some Lessons from Rational Choice', *Journal of Theoretical Politics*, **1** (2): 131–47.

Shrimsley, Robert (1997), '"Am I Satisfied with Europe? Frankly no"; Blair Tells EU Leaders to Follow His Example', *Daily Telegraph*, 7 June.

Shugart, Matthew A. and Carey, John M. (1992), *Presidents and Assemblies* (Cambridge: Cambridge University Press).

Siedentopf, Heinrich and Ziller, Jacques (eds.) (1988), *Making European Policies Work: The Implementation of Community Legislation in the Member States* (London: Sage), 2 volumes.

Skocpol, Theda (1992), *Protecting Soldiers and Mothers: The Political Origins of Social Policies in the United States* (Cambridge, MA: Harvard University Press).

Smart, Victor and Coman, Julian (1997), lead article (no title), *The European*, 19 June.

Smith, Alasdair, Holmes, Peter, Sedelmeier, Ulrich, Smith, Edward, Wallace, Helen, and Young, Alasdair (1996), *The European Union and Central and Eastern Europe: Pre-accession Strategies* (Sussex European Institute), Working Paper No.15.

Smith, Andy (1996), 'How European are European Elections?', in John Gaffney (ed.), *Political Parties and the European Union* (London: Routledge), 275–90.

Smith, Peter H. (ed.) (1993), *The Challenge of Integration: Europe and the Americas* (Miami, FL: North-South Center).

Soldatos, Panayotis (1979), *Souveraineté-association: l'urgence de réflechir* (Montréal: Editions France-Amérique).

Somers, Margaret (1994), 'Rights, Relationality and Membership: Rethinking the making and meaning of citizenship', *Law and Social Inquiry*, **19**: 63–112.

SOU (Statens Offentiga Utredningar) (1996: 19), *Sverige, EU och framtiden: EU 96-kommittëns bedömminger inför regeringskonferensen* (Stockholm: Utrikesdepartementet).

SOU (Statens Offentiga Utredningar) (1996: 24), *Från Maastricht til Turin: En lägesrapport från EU-96 kommittën* (Stockholm: Utrikesdepartementet).

Soysal, Yasemin N. (1994), *The Limits of Citizenship: Migrants and Postnational Membership in France* (Chicago, IL.: University of Chicago Press).

Spain (1995), *The 1996 Intergovernmental Conference: Starting Points for a Discussion*, 2 March 1995.

Spain (1996), *Elements for a Spanish Position at the 1996 Intergovernmental Conference*, 28 March 1996.

Starbuck, William (1983), 'Organizations as Action Generators', *American Sociological Review*, **48**: 91–102.

Sternberger, Dolf (1986), 'Die Wahl als bürgerliche Amtshandlung', in Max Kaase (ed.), *Politische Wissenschaft und politische Ordnung* (Opladen: Westdeutscher Verlag), 22–6.

Stone Sweet, Alec (1996), *Judicialization and the Construction of Governance*, (Florence: European University Institute, Robert Schuman Centre), Working Paper No. 96/59.

Stone Sweet, Alec (forthcoming), 'Judicialization and the Construction of Governance', *Comparative Political Studies* (London: Sage).

Stone Sweet, Alec and Brunell, Thomas (1998), 'Constructing a Supranational Constitution: Dispute Resolution and Governance in the European Community', *American Political Science Review*, **92**: 63–81.

Streeck, Wolfgang (1995), 'From Market-Making to State-Building? Reflections on the Political Economy of European Social Policy', in Stefan Leibfried and Paul Pierson (eds.), *Prospects for Social Europe: The European Community's Social Dimension in Comparative Perspective* (Washington DC: Brookings Institution).

Strom, Kaare (1990), 'A Behavioural Theory of Competitive Political Parties', *American Journal of Political Science*, **34** (2): 565–98.

Stubb, Alexander C-G. (1996), 'A Categorisation of Differentiated Integration', *Journal of Common Market Studies*, **34** (2): 283–95.

Stubb, Alexander C-G. (1997), 'The Amsterdam Treaty and Flexible Integration: A Preliminary Assessment', paper presented at the IPSA World Conference, Seoul, 17–21 August.

Stubb, Alexander C-G. (1998), 'Flexible Integration and the Amsterdam Treaty'. *ECSA Newsletter* (Pittsburg, PA).

Stubb, Alexander C-G. (1999), 'Flexible Integration and the Amsterdam Treaty: Negotiating Differentiation in the European Union', Ph.D. thesis, London School of Economics.

Stychin, Carl (1998), *A Nation by Rights. National Culture, Sexual Identity Politics, and the Discourse of Rights* (Philadelphia, PA: Temple University Press).

Sverdrup, Ulf (1996), 'Reforming the Heavy Rhythms of the Nation State', paper presented at the workshop 'The Transformation of Governance in the European Union' at the ECPR Joint Session of Workshops, Oslo, 29 March–3 April.

Swann, Dennis (1996), *European Economic Integration: The Common Market, European Union and Beyond* (Brookfield, VT: Edward Elgar).

Sweden (1995a), *Sweden's Fundamental Interests with a View to the 1996 IGC*, July 1995.

Sweden (1995b), *Svenska regeringens skrivelse: EU:s regeringskonferens 1996*, November 1995.

Taylor, Charles (1989), *Sources of the Self* (Cambridge: Cambridge University Press).

Taylor, Paul (1991), 'The European Community and the State: Assumptions, Theories and Propositions', *Review of International Studies*, **17** (1): 109–25.

The Federalist (1777), 10th article (madison), *Daily Adviser*, 22 November 1777.

Tilly, Charles (ed.) (1975), *The Formation of National States in Western Europe* (Princeton, NJ: Princeton University Press).

Tilly, Charles (1996), 'Citizenship, Identity and Social History', in Charles Tilly (ed.), 'Citizenship, Identity and Social History', *International Review of Social History*, Suppl. 3 (Cambridge: Cambridge University Press), 1–17.

Tinbergen, Jan (1954), *International Economic Integration* (Amsterdam: Elsevier).

Torreblanca, Jose I. (1998), 'Overlapping Games and Cross-Cutting Coalitions in the European Union', *West European Politics*, **21** (2): 134–53.

Trent, John E., Young, Robert, and Lachapelle, Guy (eds.) (1996), *Québec-Canada: What is the path ahead?/Nouveaux sentiers vers l'avenir* (Ottowa: University of Ottowa Press).

Trudeau, Pierre Elliott (1968), 'Quebec and the Constitutional Problem', in Pierre Elliott Trudeau (ed.), *Federalism and the French Canadians* (Toronto, Ontario: Macmillan), 3–51.

Truman, David D. (1953), *The Governmental Process* (New York: Knopf).

Türk, Alexander (1996), 'Case Law in the Area of the Implementation of EC Law: The Role of the Court in the Development of Comitology', in Robin H. Pedler and Günther F. Schaefer (eds.), *Shaping European Law and Policy: The Role of Committees and Comitology in the Political Process* (Maastricht: European Institute of Public Administration), 167–94.

Turner, Bryan S. (1990), 'Outline of a Theory of Citizenship', *Sociology*, **24**: 189–217.

United Kingdom (1995), *Memorandum on the treatment of European defence issues at the 1996 IGC*, 2 March 1995.

United Kingdom (1996), *A Partnership of Nations: The British Approach to the European Union Intergovernmental Conference 1996*.

Urwin, Derek W. (1995) (2nd edn.), *The Community of Europe: A History of European Integration Since 1945* (London: Longman).

van Schendelen, M. P .C. M. (ed.) (1998), *EU Committees as Influential Policymakers: Case Studies and Issues* (Aldershot, UK Brookfield US, Singapore, Sydney: Ashgate).

Vernet, Daniel (1997), 'La semaine ou l'Union monétaire a vacillé', *Le Monde*, 18 June.

Vibert, Frank (1995), 'Plaidoyer pour un démantèlement de la Commission', in *Quel avenir pour la Commission européenne?* (Brussels: Philip Morris Institute), 72–84.

von Sydow, Bjørn (1997), *Decision Making in a European Perspective* (svenska, del 1 and del 2), speech 14 June; http://www.sb.gov.se/databas/tal-866536338.html.

Vos, Ellen (1997), 'The Rise of Committees', *European Law Journal*, **3**: 210–29.

Vos, Ellen (1998), *Institutional Frameworks of Community Health and Safety Regulation: Committees, Agencies and Private Bodies* (Oxford: Hart).

Walker, Neil (1998), 'Sovereignty and Differentiated Integration in the European Union', paper prepared for a Workshop on Legal Theory and the European Union, Edinburgh, February.

Wallace, Helen (1990), 'Making Multilateralism Work', in William Wallace (ed.), *The Dynamics of European Integration* (London: Pinter), 213–28.

Wallace, Helen (1991), 'The Europe that Came in from the Cold', *International Affairs*, **67** (4): 647–63.

Wallace, Helen (1996a), 'The Institutions of the EU: Experience and Experiments', in Helen Wallace and William Wallace (eds.), *Policy-Making in the European Union* (Oxford: Oxford University Press), 37–67.

Wallace, Helen (1996b), 'Politics and Policy in the EU: The Challenge of Governance', in Helen Wallace and William Wallace (eds.), *Policy-Making in the European Union* (Oxford: Oxford University Press), 3–36.

Wallace, Helen (1997), 'Pan-European Integration', *Government and Opposition*, **32** (2): 215–33.

Wallace, Helen (1999), 'Whose Europe is it Anyway?', *European Journal of Political Research*, **35** (1): 1–20.

Wallace, Helen and Wallace, William (1995), *Flying Together in a Larger and More Diverse European Union* (The Hague: Netherlands Scientific Council for Government Policy).

Wallace, Helen and Wallace, William (eds.) (1996), *Policymaking in the European Union* (Oxford: Oxford University Press).

Wallace, Helen, Wallace, William, and Webb, Carole (eds.) (1983), *Policymaking in the European Community* (New York: Wiley).

Wallace, Helen, and Young, Alasdair (1996) (3rd edn.), 'The Single Market: A New Approach to Policy', in Helen Wallace and William Wallace (eds.), *Policymaking in the European Union* (Oxford: Oxford University Press), 125–55.

Wallace, William (1997), 'On the Move—Destination Unknown', *The World Today*, **53** (4): 99–102.

Walzer, Michael (1983), *Spheres of Justice: A Defense of Pluralism and Equality* (New York: Basic Books).

Walzer, Michael (1994), *Thick and Thin: Moral Argument at Home and Abroad* (Notre Dame, IN/London: University of Notre Dame Press).

Weale, A. and Nentwich, Michael (eds.) (1998), *The Political Theory and the European Union* (London: Routledge).

Weatherill, Stephen (1994), 'Beyond Preemption? Shared Competence and Constitutional Change in the European Community', in David O'Keeffe and Patrick Twomey (eds.), *Legal Issues of the Maastricht Treaty* (London: Chancery), 13–33.

Weatherill, Stephen (1995), *Law and Integration in the European Union* (Oxford: Clarendon Press).

Weber, Max (1942), 'Politics as a Vocation', in Hans H. Gerth and C. Wright Mills (eds.), *From Max Weber: Essays in Sociology* (Oxford: Oxford University Press), 77–128. (Original work published 1918).

Weber, Max (1921), *Gesammelte politische Schriften* (München: Drei Masken Verlag).

Weber-Panariello, Philippe A. (1995), *The Integration of Matters of Justice and Home Affairs into Title IV of the Treaty on European Union: A Step Towards Democracy?* (Florence: European University Institute, No. 95/32. Robert Schuman Centre), Working Paper.

Weiler, Joseph H. H. (1986), 'Supranationalism Revisited—a retrospective: The European Communities after 30 years', in Werner Maihofer (ed.), *Noi si mura. Selected Working Articles of the European University Institute* (Florence: European University Institute), 342–96.

Weiler, Joseph H. H. (1988), 'The European Parliament, European Integration, Democracy and Legitimacy', in Jean-Victor Louis and Denis F. Waelbroeck (eds.), *Le Parlement Européen* (Brussels: Études Européennes).

Weiler, Joseph H. H. (1991), 'The Transformation of Europe', *Yale Law Review*, **100** (1): 1–81.

Weiler, Joseph H. H. (1993), 'Journey to an Unknown Destination: A Retrospective and Prospective of the European Court of Justice in the Arena of Political Integration', *Journal of Common Market Studies*, **31**: 417–46.

Weiler, Joseph H. H. (1994), 'Fin-de-Siècle Europe', in Renaud Dehousse (ed.), *Europe After Maastricht: An Ever Closer Union?* (Munich: Law Books in Europe), 203–16.

Weiler, Joseph H. H. (1995a), 'Does Europe Need a Constitution? Demos, Telos and the Maastricht Decision', *European Law Journal*, **3**: 219–58.

Weiler, Joseph H. H. (1995b), *Limits to Growth? On the Law and Politics of the European Union's Jurisdictional Limits* (Oslo: Oslo University Press), IUSEF No. 15.

Weiler, Joseph H. H. (1997a), 'Legitimacy and Democracy of Union Governance', in Geoffrey Edwards and Alfred Pijpers (eds.), *The Politics of European Treaty Reform: The 1996 Intergovernmental Conference and Beyond* (London: Pinter), 249–87.

Weiler, Joseph H. H. (1997b), 'The European Union Belongs to its Citizens: Three Immodest Proposals', *European Law Review*, **22**: 150–6.

Weiler, Joseph H. H. (1997c), 'To Be A European Citizen', *Journal of European Public Policy*, **4**: 495–519.

Weiler, Joseph H. H., Haltern, Ulrich R., and Mayer, Franz C. (1995a) 'European Democracy and Its Critique', *West European Politics*, **18** (3): 4–39.

Weiler, Joseph H. H., Haltern, Ulrich R., and Mayer, Franz C. (1995b), 'European Democracy and Its Critique', in Jack Hayward (ed.), *The Crisis of Representation in Europe* (London: Frank Cass), 4–39.

Weiner, Stephen (1976), 'Participation, Deadlines and Choice', in James G. March and Johan P. Olsen (eds.), *Ambiguity and Choice in Organizations* (Oslo: Oslo University Press), 225–50.

Weintraub, Sidney (1997), *NAFTA at Three: A progress report* (Austin, TX: Center for Strategic and International Studies).

Wendon, Bryan (1998), 'The Commission as Image-Venue Entrepreneur in EU Social Policy, *Journal of European Public Policy*, **5** (2): 339–53.

Wessels, Bernhard (1995), 'Evaluations of the EC: Élite or Mass-Driven?', in Oskar Niedermayer and Richard Sinnott (eds.), *Public Opinion and Internationalized Governance: Beliefs in Government*, Vol. 2 (Oxford: Oxford University Press), 137–62.

Wessels, Wolfgang (1992), 'Staat und (westeuropäische) Integration: Die Fusionsthese', in Michael Kreile (ed.), *Die Integration Europas* (Opladen: Westdeutscher Verlag), 36–61.

Wessels, Wolfgang (1997), 'Der Amsterdamer Vertrag—Durch Stückwerksreform zu einer effizienteren, erweiterten und föderalen Union?', *Integration*, **20**: 117–35.

Wessels, Wolfgang and Rometsch, Dietrich (1996), 'Conclusion: European Union and National Institutions', in Dietrich Rometsch and Wolfgang Wessels (eds.), *The*

European Union and the Member States: Towards institutional fusion? (Manchester, UK: Manchester University Press).

Westlake, Martin (1994), *A Modern Guide to the European Parliament* (London: Pinter).

Whiteford, Elaine (1995), 'W(h)ither Social Policy?', in Jo Shaw and Gillian More (eds.), *New Legal Dynamics of European Union* (Oxford: Oxford University Press), 111–28.

Wiener, Antje (1996), 'Rethinking Citizenship: The Quest for Place-oriented Participation in the EU', *Oxford International Review*, VII: 44–51.

Wiener, Antje (1998), *'European' Citizenship Practice: Building Institutions of a Non-State* (Boulder, CO: Westview).

Wiener, Antje and Della Sala, Vincent (1997), 'Constitution-making and Citizenship Practice: Bridging the Democracy Gap in the EU?', *Journal of Common Market Studies*, **35** (4): 595–614.

Wilks, Stephen and McGowan, Lee (1995), 'Disarming the Commission: The Debate over a European Cartel Office', *Journal of Common Market Studies*, **32** (2): 259–73.

Wincott, Daniel (1995*a*), 'Institutional Interaction and European Integration: Towards an Everyday Critique of Liberal Intergovernmentalism', *Journal of Common Market Studies*, **33**: 597–609.

Wincott, Daniel (1995*b*), 'Political Theory, Law, and European Union', in Jo Shaw and Gillian More (eds.), *New Legal Dynamics of European Union* (Oxford: Oxford University Press).

Wincott, Daniel (1996), 'The Court of Justice and the European Policy Process', in Jeremy Richardson (ed.), *European Union: Power and Policymaking* (London: Routledge), 170–84.

Winkelmann, Ingo (ed.) (1994), *Das Maastricht-Urteil des Bundesverfassungsgerichts vom 12. Oktober 1993: Dokumentation des Verfahrens mit Einführung* (Berlin, Duncker & Humblot).

Wolf, Klaus Dieter (1997), 'Intergouvernementale Kooperation und staatliche Autonomie', in Thomas König, Elmar Rieger, and Herrmann Schmitt (eds.), *Europäische Institutionenpolitik* (Frankfurt: Campus Verlag), 66–78.

Wolf, Martin (1998), 'Strains of a Monetary Marriage: Union that defies modern taboos', *Financial Times*, 30 April.

Yin, Robert K. (1994) (2nd edn.), *Case Study Research: Design and Methods* (Thousand Oaks, CA: Sage).

Young, Oran (1989), *International Cooperation: Building Regimes for Natural Resources and the Environment* (Ithaca, NY: Cornell University Press).

Young, Oran (1997), *Global Governance: Drawing Insights from the Environmental Experience* (Cambridge, MA.: MIT Press).

Zürn, Michael (1995), 'The Challange of Globalization and Industrialization. A view from Europe', in Hans Henrik Holm and Georg Sorenson (eds.), *Whose World Order?: Uneven Globalization and the End of the Cold War* (Boulder, CO: Westview), 137–63.

Zürn, Michael (1996), 'Über den Staat und die Demokratie im europäischen Mehrebenensystem', *Politische Vierteljahresschrift*, **37**: 27–55.

Index